SPECTACULAR WICKEDNESS

SEX, RACE, AND MEMORY IN
STORYVILLE, NEW ORLEANS

EMILY EPSTEIN LANDAU

LOUISIANA STATE UNIVERSITY PRESS

BATON ROUGE

Published by Louisiana State University Press
Copyright © 2013 by Louisiana State University Press
All rights reserved
Manufactured in the United States of America
First printing

Designer: Barbara Neely Bourgoyne
Typeface: Calluna
Printer: McNaughton & Gunn, Inc.
Binder: Dekker Bookbinding

Library of Congress Cataloging-in-Publication Data

Landau, Emily Epstein, 1969–
Spectacular wickedness : sex, race, and memory in Storyville, New Orleans / Emily
Epstein Landau.
    p. cm.
Includes bibliographical references and index.
ISBN 978-0-8071-5014-6 (cloth : alk. paper) — ISBN 978-0-8071-5015-3 (pdf) — ISBN 978-
0-8071-5016-0 (epub) — ISBN 978-0-8071-5017-7 (mobi) 1. Red-light districts—Louisi-
ana—New Orleans—History—20th century. 2. Prostitution—Louisiana—New Orleans—
History—20th century. 3. Brothels—Louisiana—New Orleans—History—20th century.
4. Patriarchy—Louisiana—New Orleans—History—20th century. 5. Masculinity—Social
aspects—Louisiana—New Orleans—History—20th century. 6. Whites—Louisiana—New
Orleans—Attitudes—History—20th century. 7. Storyville (New Orleans, La.) —History—
20th century. 8. New Orleans (La.) —Race relations—History—20th century. 9. New
Orleans (La.) —History—20th century. I. Title.
HQ146.N6L36 2013
306.7409763—dc23

2012034237

The paper in this book meets the guidelines for permanence and
durability of the Committee on Production Guidelines for Book Longevity
of the Council on Library Resources. ∞

For Paul, Zoe, and Penelope

The contents of this book are the facts and not dreams from a "hop joint."
—STORYVILLE BLUE BOOKS

CONTENTS

CONTENTS

Illustrations follow page 108.

ACKNOWLEDGMENTS

This book began with a paper for David Brion Davis at Yale University. I wanted to explore the links between chattel slavery and free women of color practicing prostitution in the antebellum South. Professor Davis suggested that I look at a later period, and pointed me toward New Orleans. It was during the research for that project that I discovered the "Blue Books," the famous guides to Storyville. These books, three of which are at Yale's Beinecke Rare Book and Manuscript Library, early on became my own guides to researching and writing the dissertation, and then the book. A summer research fellowship at the Beinecke gave me the opportunity to read, in addition to the Blue Books, volumes of descriptive literature on New Orleans.

Numerous people helped me as I conducted my research in New Orleans over the years. I would like to thank Sarah Wheelock for introducing me to her friends in New Orleans, who put me up in their drafty house on Terpsichore Street. In several subsequent visits, Rachel Devlin let me stay at her Garden District apartment. Karen and Michael Leathem also took me in, providing me with a place to stay as well as their wonderful company, cooking, and endless knowledge about New Orleans. Karen and Michael always know exactly where to eat in New Orleans, and some of the best meals I've had in my life have been with them. I met Mike Ross at a conference in 2000, and one summer I house-sat for him, though it was he doing me the favor. At that same conference I met Rebecca Scott, who shared some fascinating information about Armand Romain with me. Her work on Cuba, Louisiana, and "creole itineraries" has influenced my thinking considerably since that first meeting. I thank her, too, for her incisive comments on a conference paper I delivered in 2012. Throughout the process of research and writing, I have been grateful to Alecia P. Long. Alecia has been exceedingly generous with me in sharing sources and insights, and her wonderful book *The Great Southern Babylon* is a model work of scholarship. Her next project promises to be the same.

I conducted the bulk of my research at the New Orleans Public Library, which houses the city archives. Irene Wainwright and Wayne Everard worked tirelessly with me, retrieving files and guiding me through their massive microfilm collections, as well as helping me figure out which sources would be particularly useful. Wayne has since retired, but he still comes in to the library to volunteer his time and voluminous knowledge. Greg Osborn also knows the city extremely well, its geography as well as its history, and he has been instrumental in helping me get to know it, too. The records at the city archives are stored folded in the basement. Before a researcher can read them, the files must be humidified overnight—so they do not break—unfolded, flattened, and placed in a properly labeled folder. Greg is often tasked with performing this service, and I am grateful. I would also like to thank Maya Lopez, Stephen Kuehling, and Charlie Brown for their help at the city archives.

I also spent many hours at the William Ransom Hogan Jazz Archive at Tulane University. Bruce Raeburn's knowledge of jazz music and its history, and of Storyville, have been indispensable to this project, up to and including selecting the images for the book. Alma Williams and Charles Chamberlain were unsparing in their aid and tireless in finding me materials. Thanks to Lynn Abbott for sending me the images for the book. At the Louisiana Collections at Tulane, I owe a special debt to Kevin Fontenot for his help, conversation, and general friendliness. Sherrie Tucker shared her work on women in New Orleans jazz, and I am grateful to her for it. Tad Jones, who tragically passed away shortly after Hurricane Katrina, shared numerous articles about Storyville with me, sending many of them to me at home in Washington. He is missed.

At the University of New Orleans, Marie Windell retrieved Supreme Court cases and copied countless pages for me. Her knowledge of the archives and of Louisiana legal history, and her wonderful demeanor and helpful hints, made working at the Earl K. Long library a special treat. Also helpful at UNO was John Kelly, especially with images. The Williams Research Center of the Historic New Orleans Collection contains the largest selection of Blue Books and other guides to Storyville. Pamela Arceneaux is an expert in the guides and was a wonderful guide for me as I navigated my way through them. Mark Cave was always on hand to help me find something I was looking for, and to point out another useful source. At the New Orleans Notarial Archives, Sally Reeves helped me immeasurably in tracing property ownership and transfers within Storyville. During my time at the Notarial Archives I often ran into Shirley Thompson, who was always engaging, and whose wonderful book, *Exiles at Home,* offers a brilliant analysis of the history of New Orleans's Creoles of color.

While in graduate school, I received a fellowship from the Social Science Research Council under their Sexuality Fellowship Research Program, funded by the Ford Foundation. The fellowship provided funds for my first year of writing and to have the collection of Blue Books at the Williams Research Center microfilmed. This made it possible for me to continue my analysis of the Blue Books in Washington without necessitating constant travel back and forth to New Orleans. Moreover, the books are quite brittle now, and the archive restricts their use. Now they will be available to researchers much more broadly.

The initial seminar for all SFRP fellows was held at the Kinsey Institute in Bloomington, Indiana. There, in the photo archives, are twelve pictures of Lulu White in various sexual postures with a dog. I am grateful to Catherine Johnson-Roehrs at the Kinsey for all her help with these photographs, and also to Alecia Long, who told me they existed. Remaining funds from that fellowship allowed me to curate an exhibit of images and archival sources at the New Orleans Public Library. Irene Wainwright and Wayne Everard helped gather the material, and Irene created a website so that the exhibit will be available online in perpetuity. Maya Lopez provided critical assistance in putting up the exhibit as well.

My graduate advisor, Jean-Christophe Agnew, gently prodded me toward clarity while I was writing my dissertation. His specific insights into my work and his breadth of knowledge continued to influence me as I revised the dissertation into this book. Glenda Gilmore, too, has been indispensable to this project. She guided me through southern history, helping me to interpret southern patriarchy, violence, gender, and race as I navigated my way through the primary sources. Her keen eye for detail (and for my mistakes and overstatements) has improved the work immeasurably. Nancy Cott's helpful comments drove me to strive for greater clarity and consistency in my writing. For their insightful comments on parts of the book and on conference papers I have given along the way, I would like to thank Peter Bardaglio, Gail Bederman, Katie Benton-Cohen, Gaines Foster, Grace Hale, Chad Heap, Mary Ting Yi Lui, Deirdre Moloney, John Rodrigue, Adam Rothman, David

Sartorius, Rebecca Scott, and LeeAnn Whites. I would also like to thank Julia Boss, Casey Christiansen, Marisa Fuentes, Katherine Hijar, Stephen Johnson, Val Marie Johnson, Jessica Pliley, Kate Unterman, and Jennifer Van Vleck for their helpful comments and intellectual engagement with this project. Martha Hodes, Lawrence Powell, Hannah Rosen, Adam Rothman, and the late David Montgomery read the whole manuscript at different stages of its completion, and I am grateful for their insightful comments. The anonymous readers for LSU Press provided invaluable criticism and clear guidance for revisions. Derik Shelor's outstanding copy editing improved the manuscript immensely. Rand Dotson, my editor at LSU, has been behind this project from the outset, and I would like to thank him for his patience, persistence, and overall good spirits throughout this process. Mary Lee Eggart was a pleasure to work with, too. She was both patient and speedy in drawing the maps.

Adam Rothman arranged a teaching gig at Georgetown for one semester, and I thank him for that as well. Mike Ross continues to be a useful sounding board and a good friend, especially since he now teaches at the University of Maryland and I need only wander down the hall to pester him in his office when I have a question. Kenny Aslakson, too, has been an intellectual fellow traveler and a good friend. Weekly runs with Mark Myers (who also read the manuscript), and the conversations that go with them, have helped maintain my sanity for going on three years. I would also like to thank Andrew Zimmerman and Johanna Bockman, terrific scholars both, and wonderful people too, for their friendship and support. Shelley Johnson Carey, a grandniece of Lulu White, found me and shared information about her notorious aunt that I never would have found on my own—and I looked! I thank her profoundly. Of course, having such incredible people help, guide, and support me along the way does not alleviate my own responsibility for the final product, and I remain accountable for mistakes and infelicities that remain.

At the University of Maryland, Whit Ridgway has consistently presented me with new teaching opportunities in the history department. I am especially grateful that he allowed me to develop a course on the history of New Orleans, which I then revised for the university's Honors College. I would like to thank Cathy Barks of the Honors College for giving me the chance to teach New Orleans history several years running, and for encouraging me to do so again in the future.

Over the last decade or so I spent countless hours in the main reading room of the Jefferson Building at the Library of Congress, working first on my dissertation and later on this book. During that time I made friends with Dave Kelly, a captive to my ramblings while stationed at the reference desk. I thank him for the conversations, the CDs, and those silly pencil sharpeners for the kids. I also wish to thank the librarians in the Music and Performing Arts, Law, and Manuscripts divisions of the library, and Mitch Yokelson and Fred Romanski at the National Archives in College Park, Maryland.

I would also like to thank my parents, Mel and Rachel Epstein. Their support, material and emotional, has been invaluable to me. My brother, Jonathan Epstein, has been a supportive commiserator—he is also a historian—and I have enjoyed sharing research and writing strategies with him over the years. My husband's parents, Sarah and Sidney Landau, and my sister-in-law, Amy, have been wonderful, always knowing when to ask (and when to stop asking) how the writing is going.

My most profound thanks go to my husband, Paul. He has lived with this project as long as we have lived together. He knows and understands it better than anybody. His thoughtful editing and loving encouragement have made me a better writer and, I believe, a better person. I could not have done it without him. Along the way we had two daughters, Zoe and Penelope. I hope to be able to share this book with them someday, when they are much, much older. Together Zoe, Penelope, and Paul have made this project a labor of love, and I dedicate the book to them.

SPECTACULAR
WICKEDNESS

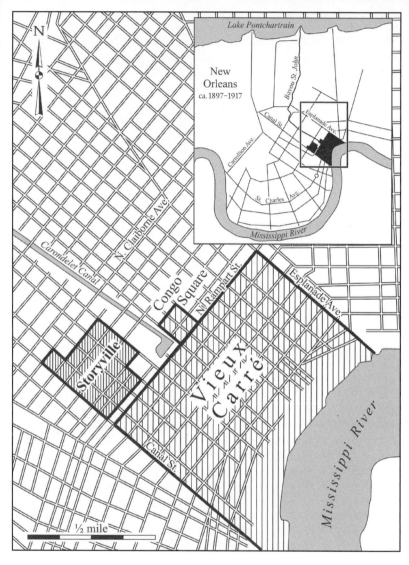

Storyville in Relation to the Vieux Carré and the Rest of New Orleans
(Map by Mary Lee Eggart)

Land of Dreams

Do you love me, baby, the way I grind you so?

—JELLY ROLL MORTON,
"Make Me a Pallet on the Floor"

This is a book about sex. Specifically, it is about sex in the most spectacular, notorious, shameful, flamboyant, and controversial commercial sex mart in American history: Storyville, the infamous New Orleans red-light district.

In 1897, the city council of New Orleans passed an ordinance establishing a red-light district. Storyville opened on January 1, 1898. Nineteen years, eleven months, and eleven days later, on November 12, 1917, Storyville closed. In the chapters that follow, Storyville's low-culture high-life comes vividly into view. In addition to prostitution, Storyville's bordellos, cribs, and honky-tonks offered jazz music, dirty dancing, gambling, liquor, and an all-around "sporting" culture. But Storyville offered much more than fraternal good times and illicit sex. I argue that Storyville offered a stage for acting out cultural fantasies of white supremacy, patriarchal power, and a renewed version of American manhood for the twentieth century.

Storyville occupied roughly nineteen square blocks just outside the French Quarter in the area of the city known as "back of town," from North Basin Street to North Robertson, and from Bienville to St. Louis.[1] The Storyville ordinance did not strictly legalize prostitution within these boundaries, but it clearly criminalized it outside them, creating a vice district where previously large areas of the city had been, in contemporary parlance, "given over" to vice. On the face of it, the creation of a red-light district at the end of the nineteenth century was nothing extraordinary. As Mark Thomas Connelly writes, "during the first two decades of the twentieth century there was at least one red-light district in virtually every American city with a population over 100,000."[2] Sex districts developed along with commerce and manufacturing, their locations determined by residential and commercial geographies.[3] Red-light districts often grew organically, as prostitutes, procurers, madams, and pimps moved into those areas most likely to give them business. Commercial sex districts, in turn, made prostitution profitable for landlords, who charged high rents, for liquor interests, who supplied the booze, and for politicians, who demanded bribes and kickbacks. So, whether cities passed ordinances limiting prostitution and its attendant activities to particular areas or simply turned a blind eye to its presence in certain precincts, prostitution became a fact of life in turn-of-the-century urban centers.[4]

Inevitably, these vice districts bled into so-called respectable areas, whose residents defined themselves *as* respectable, partly because they did not wish to tolerate prostitution. In *City of Eros,* Timothy Gilfoyle argues that the desire to create a clear moral map of New York at the end of the nineteenth century affected the way middle-class whites understood the actual sexual geography of their city. He argues that "bifurcated, polarized descriptions" reflected an ideal and not the physical reality of nineteenth-century prostitution.[5] This wishful thinking of the bourgeoisie was not simply an error, an inability to see. Rather, the desire to imagine the city as divided according to strict, dualistic, moral categories reflected a new vision, an emerging ethos that shaped the discourses of reform surrounding prostitution, and animated the bourgeoisie's efforts to impose order on society. In addition to being about sex, then, this book is concerned with the ways certain New Orleanians sought to order their city according to their own moral map, their own developing sets of binaries—licit versus illicit, respectable versus not respectable, moral versus immoral, and, crucially, white versus black. Storyville was both a product of their efforts and an affront to them.

While New Orleans's Storyville fit within national trends, it was nevertheless distinctive: *it was in New Orleans,* and this simple fact immediately sets it apart. By the late nineteenth century, New Orleans had a reputation as the wickedest city in America, long known as a city with more sexual liberty —and libertinism—than almost any other. It was notorious for promiscuous race mixing, interracial and illicit sex, and political corruption, as well as prostitution. It symbolized sexual excess, racial disorder, and extreme moral laxity. Storyville emerged as the apotheosis of New Orleans's long history of spectacular wickedness and disregard for national standards of morality. "If one wanted to be sarcastic," remarked an author in 1936, "one could say that New Orleans and prostitution are synonymous."[6] And yet, the ordinance that created Storyville was a reform measure, the attempt by a group of elite businessmen to improve the image of their city, and to draw a curtain around prostitution and its attendant vices. In 1896, after decades of entrenched Democratic Party machine rule, a reform coalition won the municipal elections. Among their chief priorities was to eliminate vice and corruption in order to better the business prospects of New Orleans, to attract investment and increase tourism. Part of the effort to develop New Orleans as a tourist attraction involved what these new leaders envisioned as a "clean up." The authors of the Storyville ordinance were not overly concerned with sexual hygiene and social purity, but they were very much attuned to the need to create clearly demarcated spaces for legitimate commerce, spaces that would not be sullied by prostitutes, illicit sexuality, and the stench of corruption, broadly defined.

In the event, Storyville did not draw a curtain around prostitution in New Orleans. On the contrary, the vice district became the nation's most notorious, securing the city's reputation for immoral indulgence, sexual licentiousness, and government corruption. Storyville shamelessly spotlighted precisely those elements of New Orleans's history that the authors of the law sought to obscure, especially prostitution and interracial sex.

The opening of Storyville coincided almost exactly with the Supreme Court's landmark *Plessy v. Ferguson* decision. The case, in fact, originated in New Orleans. *Plessy v. Ferguson* enabled legal segregation by "race," dividing the world into "black" and "white," and setting the color line in law. The Court naturalized race difference and conflated it with skin color. Louisiana's Separate Car Act, the Court explained, simply recognized the "legal distinction between the white and colored races—a distinction which is founded in the color of the two races," and stated further that that distinction "must always exist so long as white men are distinguished from the other race by color."[7] In fact, Homer Plessy served as the test case, a deliberate challenge to Louisiana's law separating train cars by race, because he was an "octoroon," and was so light-skinned that he easily passed for "white." He had to inform the train conductor of his "race" in order for the case to move forward.

The *Plessy* decision was a watershed event. Up until that point individual states had passed laws segregating the so-called races, and privately owned accommodations, such as restaurants, hotels, and entertainment venues, had drawn their own color lines as well, barring those they perceived as "negro" or "black," or reserving separate, inferior spaces for them. The Supreme Court's decision in the 1883 *Civil Rights Cases* declared such private discriminations constitutional, after which no one had yet challenged the states' rights to legislate "separate but equal."[8] In recognizing the constitutionality of the Separate Car Act, the decision in *Plessy v. Ferguson* effected a more thorough-going restructuring of American society according to the binary logic of Jim Crow. As with the municipal designation of red-light districts, segregation by race was part of the process of organizing society according to strictly defined categories and absolutes. As a racial policy, however, it was an effort to reassert a white supremacy that the Civil War and Reconstruction had severely challenged.

The segregationist sensibility of postbellum America's reorganization facilitated the unification of whites of different ethnic backgrounds in opposition to blacks as a recognizably conceived racial "other." New Orleans, however, offered a unique challenge. First, in New Orleans ethnic distinctions among so-called whites impeded conceiving of New Orleans in terms of a racial binary. The sequence of French, Spanish, and then American rule over Louisiana had exacerbated nationalist loyalties and exaggerated cultural differences within the population over the eighteenth and nineteenth centuries. Moreover, Irish, German, and Italian immigrants, among others, further diversified the "European" population of New Orleans.[9] Second, in New Orleans people of color were divided almost as dramatically among themselves as the "races" were from each other. To a degree greater than anywhere else in the nation, and certainly in the South, New Orleans's population of color was diverse. A three-tiered caste system had developed in Louisiana out of French and Spanish colonial rule, making New Orleans resemble a Caribbean enclave more than a Deep South city. What some scholars have called the process of "Americanization" began in New Orleans at the time of the Louisiana Purchase, in 1803, and continued through the nineteenth century. "Americanization" entailed, among other things, the transformation of New Orleans's social structure from a relatively dynamic three-tiered racial structure into a dualistic one, defined by the color line. The men who organized the *Plessy* case sought to reverse this process, to obliterate the color line, and to eliminate *race* as the primary organizing principle in American society. They failed, and thus in the same period in which "whiteness" became a unified racial category nationally, in New Orleans, much more than most places in the country, "blackness" did, too. In neither case was the process anything but contested, contradictory, and incomplete, but the institution of the color line, and the "one-drop rule," created a mostly black and white twentieth-century world, where previously there had been shades of gray.[10]

However, if the Court's decision in *Plessy v. Ferguson* obscured Plessy's actual ancestry and the history of free people of color in Louisiana, Storyville brought them stunningly back into view by way of its sexual specialty: the "octoroon" prostitute. For nearly twenty years, Storyville flouted the segregationist order by aggressively advertising the availability of mixed-race women for the sexual pleasure of white men. Where *Plessy v. Ferguson* mandated racial separation, Storyville promoted interracial intimacy, as the district openly offered nonwhite prostitutes for its white customers. Scarcely a year after the Supreme Court denied Plessy his octoroon status and reclassified him as "colored," his native city began showcasing "octoroons." Storyville's particular violations of racial norms grew out of New Orleans's unique history, as I will discuss in detail in chapter 2. Sex slave auctions, quadroon balls, and *plaçage* (interracial concubinage) each had distinct histories in colonial and antebellum New Orleans, and the collective memories of these practices fed into the popularity of some attractions in Storyville. Nonetheless, Storyville was neither an atavistic throwback nor an instance of cultural lag. The district was of its time; it was modern.

Storyville existed at the crossroads of the white middle class's desired binarism in race and sexuality, violating middle-class moral sensibilities *and* the dualistic imperatives of Jim Crow: this commercial sex district advertised interracial sex, with "octoroon" prostitutes as its special attraction. And yet, Storyville became a veritable laboratory for making whiteness. How can this be? That this district flourished precisely when the dominant public rhetoric of racial and sexual purity screamed that both prostitution and sex across the color line threatened the nation is the paradox that drove my research. How could Storyville openly promote "octoroon" prostitutes in the face of intensifying racial dualism? How could Storyville brazenly advertise interracial sex in an era of disenfranchisement and lynching? The answer lies in considering gender and sexuality in reevaluating the meaning of "race" in America. It is widely accepted that sexuality and race were mutually constituted through the discourses that proliferated from the end of the Civil War through the early twentieth century. Racist ideology comprised sexual proscriptions and prescribed gender norms, and sexual propriety accorded with, and perpetuated, perceived (though false) racial stereotypes. As a racial identity for American "whites" coalesced against the image of a "racial other" in the early years of the twentieth century, American sexual identities were thoroughly racialized through the constant cultural reference to sexual "others," taboos, and transgressions.

In the argument to follow, this book reveals the historical processes that informed and mutually constituted emerging racial and sexual identities. Storyville, as a space deliberately set aside *for sex,* and which promoted sex across the color line, offers us a unique opportunity to examine the processes by which the American nation created a new social order out of the chaos of Civil War and Reconstruction, the dislocations of rapid industrialization, and the racial imperatives of sectional reconciliation. That is to say, through a close look at Storyville and the people that created it, sustained it, and ultimately shut it down, the reader will witness the workings of race and sexuality in the formation of modern America.

This book, then, is also about the shifting construction of desire. Desire, though seemingly a primordial instinct, is also a product of history, created at particular times and places, in part through the dissemination of discourses about sex.[11] At the turn of the twentieth century there was a massive outpouring of such discourses, many of them concerned to prohibit particular behaviors, such as sex across the color line, sex with prostitutes, and sex outside of marriage. This public effusiveness about sex and taboo was also part of the effort by a growing middle class to impose its vision of order on American society. And yet the condemnation of certain sexual practices also nourished the desire for those same practices.[12] The effect of this ceaseless propagation of sexual discourses, whether they concerned prohibitions or propriety, was the "education" of desire, the implicit pedagogy of modern sexuality. In the turn-of-the-century South, white male desire was educated through the miscegenation taboo, the disparagement of black female sexuality, and the parody, infantalization, exaggeration, and violent repression of black male sexuality. As part of the same cultural process, these discourses also "educated" whiteness for the Jim Crow era. Storyville provided an outlet, a circumscribed space where white male desire thus educated could seek fulfillment.

Sexual discourses concerned with race preservation, and racial ideologies concerned with sexuality and sexual propriety, can only fully be understood set beside a history of practices, and this book therefore pays close attention to the social history of prostitution in Storyville. I have drawn on a wide array of sources. These include arrest and court records, tax-assessment and property records, architectural drawings, census data and city directories, maps, newspaper reports, photographs, advertisements, guidebooks, jazz lyrics, and the recorded reminiscences of musicians. These sources have allowed me to reconstruct something of the social life of Storyville. I evoke its raucous nightlife: its unsanitary streets, where prostitutes and customers fought and cursed; its "entertainment" venues, where musicians called "professors" stomped out new beats later named "jazz"; its pimps and madams, including the wealthy and ostentatious Lulu White, the "Diamond Queen of the Demi-Monde"; the anonymous women who worked in the district's barebones shacks called "cribs"; and the working-class johns, who were often robbed and cheated. I also discuss the city's corrupt police officers, politicians, and attorneys, who often had a stake in Storyville's operations, as well as the reformers who found the district reviling.

The book examines the entirety of Storyville's transgressive culture, set within the early twentieth-century's increasingly rigid Jim Crow regime and in the midst of the greatest "purity campaign" in the nation's history. Throughout the Storyville period, progressives attacked prostitution as a danger to "the race" and linked it with other perceived avenues to degeneration—indeed, prostitution became a "master symbol" during this period.[13] Reformers correctly associated prostitution with disease, and used it as an emblem of other kinds of decay. Similarly, white supremacists invoked the miscegenation taboo to support white supremacy, and made interracial sex into a metaphor for chaos and degeneration in political and civic life.[14] But in Storyville, of course, prostitution and interracial sex were not merely metaphors.

This book argues that Storyville ultimately promoted the very kind of racialized sexual morality that middle-class reformers and their followers sought to achieve. Indeed, Storyville became a site for the instantiation of white, male power in turn-of-the-century America.

The last decade of the nineteenth century and the first decade of the twentieth were years of transformation in American culture. While men and women adjusted to the "new," the anxiety produced by social flux spurred backward glances toward an idealized past, and the reinvention of elements of that past's traditions.[15] Images of a pastoral South proliferated in deliberate contrast to unruly urban spaces and restless natives, as both immigration and imperialism came to dominate the public sphere of politics and culture. Thus, leading up to and during the Storyville period, many white southerners, animated by intense nostalgia for what they perceived as a superior civilization, undertook to memorialize and, where possible, preserve the cultural values of the antebellum South.[16] Following Reconstruction, these southerners joined together to commemorate the "lost cause," to "redeem" the South, and reimagine its values in the absence of its defining institution. First among those values was white supremacy, and integral to southern white supremacy were particular gender roles. The white man was the patriarch, white women and slaves his dependents. In the South, moreover, patriarchy was organized not solely around male power, but specifically around white male *sexual* power. Among the prerogatives of mastery was the implicit right to have sex with slaves.[17] It is impossible to understand prostitution in the American South in the decades following the Civil War without an understanding of this legacy for white and black southerners.

The Civil War left southern white men feeling emasculated. White women accused them of failing in their protective roles, and at the same time they demanded the vote and greater roles in public affairs.[18] Meanwhile, former slaves and their children began to participate in the civic, political, and economic life of the country. Many white southerners found these developments intensely threatening. As the nineteenth century drew to a close, northern whites, too, looked with longing to the antebellum South as a pastoral ideal, a place apart from the racial tensions, gender uncertainty, and labor unrest prevalent in urban centers. Since part of the challenge of rebuilding the South after Reconstruction, was, for white Americans, how to reestablish the antebellum hierarchies, part of the solution was to recreate the gender and sexual hierarchies of slavery times and apply their logics to the developing social order. The ethic emerging at the close of the nineteenth century denied white women sexual agency, continued to belittle black women's sexuality, and figured all products of miscegenation as signs of white male sexual power.[19]

Of course, African American discourses of respectability responded to the dominant culture's denigration of black sexuality, and African American cultural memories of white male sexual power figured very differently in those discourses, and in the myriad strategies of racial uplift promoted and employed by the black middle and working classes.[20] Thus it is perhaps important to emphasize here that in remembering the sexual power relations of slavery days both blacks and whites recalled white domination and rape, but through dramatically different perspectives. For African Americans who labored to lift the shadow of sexualized racism and its very real effects in their everyday lives, those memories might recall and produce trauma; for white men who sought to perpetuate the power relations of the olden days, those memories might produce desire.[21]

By highlighting the recollection of white male sexual advantage over black women, Storyville fashioned the memory of the exclusive and patriarchal social order of the Old South into a New South sexual theme park. In this context, Storyville's marketing of "octoroon" prostitutes in plush surroundings imaginatively recast the plantation household as a kind of sexual funhouse, open to all white men regardless of class. Storyville effectively democratized an exclusive privilege of antebellum patriarchy, the sexual possession of women of color. When Lulu White of Mahogany Hall, for instance, promoted sex with octoroon women to her white customers, she certainly defied Jim Crow, but she also helped shape the developing culture of white supremacy. All the best bordellos, including those which featured women of color, barred black men. Thus Storyville prescribed a sexualized racial hierarchy even as it seemed to defy all social order.

Storyville also exaggerated the proscriptions and norms of the emerging racial order, making a burlesque of the ways in which the ascendant bourgeoisie defined itself; Storyville rechanneled anxiety about proper social roles by elaborating them in ridiculous or theatrical scenarios. By embracing and showcasing contradiction and ambiguity, such a burlesque helped elucidate connections that the dominant society was severing or obliterating. As Robert Allen explains, the "burlesque" was a dramatic form "grounded in the aesthetics of transgression, inversion, and the grotesque." It presented a stage on which to "'act out' cultural contradictions," and to articulate or perform the absurdities of the social hierarchy.[22] Storyville showcases entrepreneurs, black women, and white men, staging a burlesque of the nation's racializing sexual morality, the creation of the proper, white, respectable body in its different gendered iterations, while simultaneously helping to institutionalize this same morality by denying, suppressing, and erasing even the idea of black sexual respectability for men and women.

Storyville itself was unique, but through its highlighting of black women in the fulfillment of white male sexual desire, it reveals, *in extremis,* trends present in dominant society. If the hidden and unintentional messages within cultural imperatives to maintain white supremacy also contained unintentional, coded inducements to arousal and desire for interracial sex, then Storyville articulated that desire and commodified it as sex for sale. Marketing is a deliberate practice, and the district marketed miscegenation.

Storyville was dangerous to the extent that it revealed that racial and sexual taboos would always have to accommodate their own transgressions.

Here, I would like to include a few words about usage. Both "prostitution" and "interracial" are extremely charged terms, and in a book about interracial prostitution, it is necessary to provide some kind of framework for their use. I use "prostitute" rather than "sex worker," because the latter term connotes a kind of autonomous existence that many of these women did not enjoy. This is not to say that all prostitutes were, or conceived of themselves as, "victims," with no agency. Prostitutes were not a monolithic subset of women, inherently different from other women; nor were they recognizable unless they chose to be. Some were victims, some agents, some rebels, some a combination of all, or none of the above. Unlike the mid- to late nineteenth-century bourgeoisie, here we are not interested in determining a set of finite categories and fitting characters into them. There were many reasons women undertook prostitution. Poverty, perhaps, was a primary motivator. Historians of prostitution cite studies suggesting that women chose prostitution over hard manual work, as they considered it to be "easier."[23] While it is true that working-class women and girls had few opportunities in the late nineteenth century for anything resembling upward mobility, relative ease does not explain the prostitute's position in American society during the Gilded Age and the Progressive Era.

Why women engaged in prostitution is both important and fascinating, but it is not the subject of the present work. Rather than attempt to deduce the various reasons different women engaged in prostitution, I prefer to emphasize that popular sexual morality took shape in response to some of the same economic and social realities that brought women to prostitution, and led others to condemn them. These were not separate processes, easily graphed on a time line, but rather the same process, encompassing the historical construction of sexuality and the education of desire. This book analyzes the transformations in American culture that produced the conditions that led to more women becoming prostitutes, and to their "reform." Furthermore, I understand prostitution as, in Carole Pateman's term, the expression of "patriarchal sex right." In the context of prostitution, Pateman argues, "'the sex act' itself provides acknowledgment of patriarchal right. When women's bodies are on sale as commodities in the capitalist market,

. . . the law of male sex-right is publicly affirmed, and men gain public acknowledgment as women's sexual masters." ("That," she adds, "is what is wrong with prostitution.")[24]

Historians writing about race and sexuality sometimes avoid the term "interracial" on the grounds that it naturalizes race difference at the moment that that difference was being articulated through law, custom, and violence, preferring instead to use the term "sex across the color line," because of its more bounded juridical meaning. I use both. The whole book is about the construction of race, along the lines of gender, and in the context of sex, as part of the reorganization of society in the Jim Crow era, and so I trust that readers will understand my use of the term "interracial" to signify perceptions of race in and through history and not some permanent, unchanging, or transcendent biological entity. This book is concerned with the development and proliferation of hegemonic discourses and their actualization, through sex, in Storyville. For instance, if a man in Storyville went to a bordello in search of sex with an octoroon, but "really" went to bed with a white woman who considered herself to be "passing" as an octoroon, was he still having "interracial sex"? Was it still "sex across the color line"? For whom? The point, rather than attempting to answer such questions, is to explore the nature of the desire in his actions.

Chapter 1 begins by evoking life in Storyville, offering descriptions of the district gleaned from arrest records, court cases, and the recollections of musicians who made their living there. It details the experiences of men who went to the district seeking pleasure, and of the women who provided it. It describes the neighborhood that became Storyville and its history in relation to the development of the city. Chapter 1 also describes the long history of illicit sex and prostitution in New Orleans, and some sporadic (often pathetic) efforts by various authorities and reformers to control and reform the city's seeming licentiousness and immorality, which date back to its founding in 1718. From that date, and arguably before, New Orleans seemed inexorably to develop its reputation as the southern Babylon in spite of officials' efforts to stem, or redirect, the city's sexual culture. Those efforts included attempts to prevent soldiers and traders from engaging in sexual relationships with Indian women, from living in concubinage with them, and even from marrying them. The colonial officials went so far as to import French women to the city in the hopes that these "white" ladies would have a civilizing effect on the population, encouraging settlement and the development of a stable society. They miscalculated wildly, importing, among others, prostitutes into the colony. Licentiousness (and the city's reputation for it) continued more or less unabated. Storyville, in turn, later capitalized on New Orleans's longstanding reputation as the "promised land of harlotry."

Chapter 2 begins with the *Plessy v. Ferguson* case, and includes a brief history of the free people of color in the city and the different gendered trajectories within that history. I explore the foundations of Storyville's transgressive culture in the history of the slave market, quadroon balls, and the "fancy girl" auctions in New Orleans. "Fancy girls" were light-skinned female slaves, purchased as sexual servants. Quadroon balls were dances at which white men and women of color entered into contracts for concubinage, which was later termed *plaçage*. Antebellum New Orleans's sexual markets in light-skinned women, whether enslaved or free, intrigued visitors to the city, who generally assumed that all Creole of color women served as concubines to wealthy white men, and that all white men had their own personal concubines. These same markets and practices enraged abolitionists, who seized on the figure of the light-skinned, mixed-race slave girl as a symbol of the corruption and depravity of slavery. Thus, in this chapter I also look at the abolitionist literature of the "tragic octoroon" and how it anchored New Orleans in people's minds as the North American capital for interracial sex.

Of course, the myth created through the combined writings of traveling observers and abolitionist rhetoric did not accurately depict the city's history. Most particularly left out of their portrayals were the Creole of color men who lived and worked in New Orleans, and the free women of color who did not participate in any form of institutionalized sex across the color line. Together these men and women constituted the *gens de couleur libres,* or Creoles of color, a dynamic, multifaceted group that nevertheless shared a genuine identity, and who were clearly differentiated from whites and enslaved blacks. Chapter 2 therefore takes care to clearly distinguish the lives of actual men and women from the image that proliferated in antebellum times, and which Storyville later exploited.

The first two chapters of the book thus discuss the emergence of prostitution in Storyville in the context of the history of prostitution in New Orleans, and of New Orleans's unique (to North America) racial caste system. Chapter

3 analyzes the creation of Storyville the district, in conjunction with the rigidification of racial segregation and the drive to "clean up" New Orleans at the end of the century. I argue that, in fact, the same historical actors and cultural forces that desired racial segregation also brought Storyville into existence and, ironically, the octoroon prostitute to prominence within it. While white residents of New Orleans sought to clarify the borders of their own respectability and police their immediate environs, government officials and businessmen similarly desired to clear public spaces for legitimate, and profitable, endeavors. They sought to remove vice and prostitution from main thoroughfares and developing shopping districts. Storyville emerged from this latter effort. The chapter shows that for many white New Orleanians, the very notion of a "respectable" city required not only the removal of vice and disorder from public view, but also the creation of an exclusively "white" public sphere.

Attracting northern tourists and investors to New Orleans also entailed retailing a brighter image of the city, the reputation of which had suffered after the Civil War, and chapter 3 discusses the ways in which city boosters drew on the image of antebellum New Orleans, especially its commercial vitality, cosmopolitanism, and (more subtly) its reputation for luxurious debauch as part of their scheme to revive the city's fortunes for the new century. The reform administration that enacted the Storyville ordinance sought to modernize New Orleans and to integrate it into the commercial and cultural mainstream of America. Following the Civil War and Reconstruction, New Orleans was mired in economic depression. The city moreover suffered from a reputation of regional recalcitrance, and by the late 1880s this image increasingly got in the way of business. The commercial elite behind the creation of Storyville wanted to free their city of its association with sin (and secession). Storyville was part of a broader movement at the turn of the century to alter the appearance of New Orleans, to revive and repackage a "dioramic" New Orleans for the northern tourist, businessman, and investor. Promotional pamphlets advertised New Orleans as the winter capital of the United States, an Eden in the Southwest; the city boosters emphasized the romantic old city and the French Quarter, and yet also promoted New Orleans as up-to-date and ready for business. "New Orleans: The City of Opportunity, Wants Your Trade" read a typical, full-page newspaper advertisement from the city's chamber of commerce.[25] The municipal administration situated Storyville on the margins of old and new New Orleans, between the French Quarter and what was known as the

American section. This was, I suggest, a strategic move, allowing them to disavow interracial and commercial sex while still profiting from the city's longstanding reputation for both.

Chapter 4 focuses on Storyville's own advertising guidebooks and analyzes the district in the context of American popular culture, the growth of commercialized leisure, and other transformations of the social order at this time. By placing Storyville within the growing culture of commercial amusements, we see how the district resonated with the development more broadly of a modern consumer culture, its attendant gender prescriptions, and the institutionalization of the color line. Historians have analyzed the varied entertainments at the turn of the twentieth century in terms of how their sites fostered racial solidarity among "whites," often by opposing a figure of the "black other." Through exclusion, ridicule, and, in some instances, evolutionary science and ethnography, white organizers of popular culture portrayed blacks as biologically and socially inferior in the scheme of western civilization and American industry.

Twentieth-century popular culture thus developed in large part through the elaboration of racial stereotypes and the hardening of the color line. Still, that line required violent reinforcement by whites bent on asserting racial supremacy, and scholars have shown how lynching, with its gruesome rituals of dismemberment and murder, also helped to consolidate white racial consciousness in this same time period. Popular culture, lynching, and even war were linked by race, gender, and sexual discourses pitting American manhood against inferior, dark-skinned, and feminized (or emasculated) others. Without suggesting that prostitution in Storyville constituted the kind of deadly violence that lynching involved, chapter 4 explores the sexual, racial, and gender ideologies that proliferated in support of the practice, and finds that they articulate with certain aspects of the district in ways that shed light on the relationships between sex, race, gender, and violence in the formation of modern American culture.

Chapter 5 profiles Lulu White, the district's most notorious madam, analyzing her strategies of self-representation, and the city's responses to her. Known as the "Diamond Queen of the Demi-Monde," White was the proprietress of Storyville's most luxurious and infamous bordello, Mahogany Hall, also called the "Octoroon Club." Lulu White created an image of herself and marketed it profitably to sell sex with light-skinned women to white men of means. She played with contemporary notions of race, calling herself an octoroon, while claiming, too, not to have "one drop" of "black blood" in her veins. She cultivated a notion of the erotic octoroon, teasing her audience with references to the "tragic octoroon" of antebellum fiction and emphasizing the sexualization of the figure. At Mahogany Hall, White allowed her patrons to play at mastery, but on her terms, in her realm, and always with a wink. And yet, as the city's most "notorious negress," as the press persistently called her, White was a reviled and threatening figure as well. By exploring White's life on the color line, and analyzing the perceptible tension in public discourse between these two images of White, "Diamond Queen" and "notorious negress," chapter 5 offers insight into the dynamic between desire and taboo during this transitional period.

Chapter 6 documents the decline and closure of Storyville in the context of the rise of Woodrow Wilson and the triumph of progressivism. While Storyville reimagined and revived elements of the antebellum plantation, the fancy-girl auction, and "dioramic" New Orleans, the nation at large was engaged in a process of selectively remembering and forgetting slavery in a way that rendered Storyville's particular brand of spectacular wickedness extremely uncomfortable. I look at D. W. Griffith's 1915 film *The Birth of a Nation* to show how it encapsulated the cultural transformation of the octoroon from a figure of sexual desire to a symbol of sexual danger. President Woodrow Wilson viewed the film at the White House and helped legitimize its racist message.

In chapter 6, I also look at the flowering of the wartime antiprostitution campaigns, specifically for their effects on Storyville. Progressive reform and wartime propaganda undermined the district in two significant ways. First, and most obviously, reformers and government agencies renounced all red-light districts once and for all, extolling instead abstinence and a single standard of sexual morality for white men and women. Second, the national campaign for soldier morality continued the remodeling of American manhood begun in Civil War commemoration ceremonies, statues to individual (and anonymous) soldiers, and celebrations of white manhood across sectional lines. This democratization of white manhood reached a high-point in the rhetoric of the government's pamphlet *Keeping Fit to Fight.* The government's exhortations to soldier morality placed responsibility for national honor squarely on the shoulders of individual troops. That is to say, the notion of honor inhering in "blood" or lineage no longer resonated in a nation at war against European tyranny abroad. In this national ambience, the reimagining of patriarchal planter privilege as a sexual turn-on indeed became anachronistic. Insofar as Storyville itself participated in the process of remaking white manhood through the democratization of previous planter prerogative, it bore the seeds of its own demise. In a brief concluding chapter I discuss the relative success and failure of segregating vice in the era of Jim Crow, and the place of Storyville in the cultural memory of a more "authentic" New Orleans. I suggest that in remembering and memorializing Storyville as the "birthplace of jazz," the district has itself become a site of forgetting the injustices and inequalities that characterized New Orleans at the turn of the last century.

CHAPTER ONE

The Promised Land of Harlotry

Honi Soit Qui Mal y Pense.

—"Evil to him who thinks evil of it,"
the unofficial slogan of Storyville

On April 9, 1908, Newton C. Woods stopped in New Orleans on his way to Texas from his home in Alabama. From Union Station on South Rampart Street he made his way to Storyville. He went to a brothel, where he drank a few beers and had sex with one or several women. Afterward, with his pants hanging on a chair near the bed, he fell asleep. When he woke up a little later, he got dressed and walked back to the train station. There he discovered that his wallet, containing seventy dollars and his train ticket, was missing. Unable to board the train, and desirous of justice, he wandered around until the next morning, when he found a police officer and brought him to the house to arrest the three women who lived there.[1]

Two days later there was a trial. The prostitutes' defense attorney asked Woods what he was doing at the brothel. He replied, "Frolicking around." The attorney continued, "You were having fun? . . . You were frolicking around with these Negro women?" For Woods was white and the women were black. Woods replied, "Yes sir. I suppose so."[2]

Storyville enjoyed considerable notoriety by 1908. Ten years into its official existence the district was well established. It boasted some of the best real estate in the city, its more or less central location made even more so by the completion of the train station at Canal and Basin in the spring of that year —right around the time of Woods's visit.[3] Basin Street was the entryway to the district, and the district's most infamous and spectacular bordellos were there. Lulu White's Mahogany Hall was on Basin Street, between Bienville and Customhouse, Josie Arlington's was a few doors down, and Emma Johnson's House of All Nations was in the center of the block; Willie V. Piazza, also known as the Countess, lived on the next block, between Bienville and Conti. At the corner of Basin and Customhouse stood Thomas C. (Tom) Anderson's saloon, the eponymous "Mecca for Sports," according to one of the famous Blue Books, the widely available guidebooks to the district. At Anderson's saloon, bands played, men drank, and "private rooms" upstairs served for assignations.

Men flocked to Storyville to hear music, to drink, to gamble, and to have sex with prostitutes. For Woods and other unlucky fellows, the consequences of a stop in Storyville could be the loss of their money. It was a risk many men were more than willing to take. Storyville, created by ordinance in 1897 and open for business in 1898, quickly became the nation's most notorious red-light district. It was famous well beyond New Orleans for its transgressive sex, its jazz music, and its myriad other entertainments, including sex circuses and naked dances, as well as concert saloons, gambling halls, barrooms, and barrelhouses.

Basin Street Blues

"Won't you come along with me, To the Mississippi, We'll take the boat to the land of dreams, steam down the river down to New Orleans."[4] Jazz was born in the late nineteenth century, and when people say that jazz was born in a brothel they mean it was born in Storyville. Jazz did not have a single genesis, but rather a series of contemporaneous starts and a long evolution. Few dispute its origins in New Orleans. "New Orleans," writes the jazz historian Bruce Raeburn, "was a city where music was intrinsic to lifestyle." Nineteenth-century New Orleans was a cultural crossroads where European, Caribbean, and American musical forms met and melded. Jazz was forged in the crucible of the city's multicultural furnace. New Orleans also traditionally played host to multiple and diverse festivals, parties, and parades, all of which demanded music. Raeburn writes, "By the early twentieth century, this musical mélange fed a seemingly interminable calendar of festivities," from Mardi Gras balls to riverboat excursions, funerals, fish fries, and many more.[5] The "crazy quilt" pattern of residential life in New Orleans also fed the development of a new vernacular music, as white ethnics, African Americans, and Creoles of color lived in close proximity to one another throughout the nineteenth and early twentieth centuries. Whatever particular musical styles these groups brought or adapted from their places of origin (including New Orleans itself) inevitably cross-fertilized with different traditions residing in the same neighborhoods.[6]

Storyville, with its bordellos, cabarets, honky-tonks, restaurants, and bars, welcomed and nurtured jazz, provided it an ideal gestational milieu, and stamped it indelibly with prostitution and the sporting life. "Sporting life" denotes the male world of drinking, gambling, and patronizing houses of prostitution. Prostitutes were called "sporting girls" and bordellos "sporting houses." Many early jazz musicians, such as Tony Jackson, Jelly Roll Morton, and Clarence Williams, found work in the brothels and cabarets of Storyville,[7] and many of the descriptions that exist of Storyville come from the memories of the musicians who played there.

The song "Basin Street Blues" was published in the 1920s, after Storyville had been shut down by the government, and offered a kind of memorial to it. According to the lyrics, New Orleans was the "land of dreams," nothing less than "heaven on earth," and Basin Street was the very place to lose one's Basin Street Blues.[8] Much later, and in quite a different context, Williams remembered Basin Street as a "street of pleasure" with its "dance halls, honky tonks, and cabarets," and its bordellos.[9] The Basin Street bordellos, many of which resembled mansions, could be seen from the street, and aerial views of early twentieth-century New Orleans show the cupolas of Josie Arlington's and Lulu White's bordellos towering above the mansard roofs surrounding them. Indeed, Lulu White's Mahogany Hall could be seen from Canal Street all the way to Esplanade.[10] Basin Street itself was especially broad and had once housed a canal and two sets of train tracks. Only one side of the street was dedicated to bordellos, so it clearly demarcated the district and acted as a kind of entryway. One passed through Basin Street, and into a different world, a *demi-monde.* Though the district was located in a neighborhood in the back of town, the area northwest of the French Quarter, toward the lake, and behind Rampart Street, and had never been wealthy or even well-off, the houses in the district that had been built specifically for the purpose of prostitution belied the area's impoverished demographic history. Jelly Roll Morton, for instance, recalled "the mansions where everything was of the highest class. These houses were filled up with the most expensive furniture and paintings."[11] The grand bordellos on Basin Street, remembered another pioneer of jazz music, were "just like millionaires' houses."[12] Manuel Manetta, a jazz pianist, remembered Lulu White's Mahogany Hall as "plush," with two separate parlors, each with its own piano.[13]

"Those sportin' houses," remembered Morton, "had the *most* beautiful parlors, with cut glass, and draperies, and rugs, and expensive furniture." Some of them even had "mirror parlors where you couldn't find the door for the mirrors, the one at Lulu White's costing thirty thousand dollars."[14] Upstairs at White's, Clarence Williams, the musician, bandleader, and producer, said, "mirrors stood at the foot and head of all the beds." For those who were over-awed and too "scared to go in," there were smaller brothels, and even cribs—one-room shacks where prostitutes worked without the accouterments of the "high-class" bordellos. Yet, Williams recalled, "once in a while [even] a sailor" might patronize the luxurious bordellos.[15] Overall, according to a souvenir edition of the district's infamous guidebooks, "Romantic playboys and big-shot financiers alike must have found them irresistible, for the swankier houses are reputed to have paid off like gold mines to their financial backers."[16]

Musicians remembered that the "high-class" bordellos were for "rich people"—"big timers" who paid a dollar for a bottle of beer or $25 for a bottle of champagne.[17] Waiters served them in the parlor while musicians, nicknamed "professors" in Storyville, beat out proto-jazz rhythms and ragtime on pianos. Customers came to Mahogany Hall in "dress clothes" and good shoes. According to legend, a maid might even check a man's shoes, to ensure that the customers were, indeed, "well-heeled."[18] The customers at these higher-end bordellos were white without exception, according to Manetta. Even the bordellos featuring women of color were strictly Jim Crow establishments.

The prostitutes working in these lavish houses would come downstairs as the evening started "dressed in the finest of evening gowns, just like they were going to the opera." The musicians remembered that the women were "just beautiful. . . . Some of them looked Spanish, and some were Creoles, some brownskins, some chocolate-brown. But they all had to have that figure."[19] "There were always twelve to fifteen women [at Mahogany Hall]," dressed in "beautiful costumes, not naked, they wore beautiful costumes. Up to date, long evening dresses, gowns."[20] Another musician remembered the women's clothes as very expensive, evanescent and sexy, even see-through.[21] While the pianist played the "Maple Leaf Rag" or another contemporary hit on the piano, men could exchange glances over their drinks as these women, some wearing "lots of make up," slinked down the stairs into the parlor—a veritable parade of desire. The prostitutes were on display for the customers to select from, like mannequins in a department store window; they were dressed up in the finest evening clothes, and, depending on the bordello, in a rainbow of hues. Some frequent customers had their "regular girls," but others chose their "dates" from among the women working in the house that evening. The price for such a "date" ranged from $3 to $5, according to Louis Armstrong (compared to fifty to seventy-five cents in other, less glamorous areas of the city).[22]

Not all the sporting houses in Storyville were like "millionaires' houses." Within the district there was great variety. Jelly Roll Morton remembered: "They had everything in the District from the highest class to the lowest— creep joints where they'd put the feelers on a guy's clothes, cribs that rented for about five dollars a day and had just about room enough for a bed, small-time houses where the price was from fifty cents to a dollar and they put on naked dances, circuses, and jive."[23] One customer described his experience in Storyville:

> I was walking around yesterday, I started a little before two in the afternoon and I went through the red light district. I went down Customhouse to Basin and turned right. I know that I was on Customhouse street, and got four doors off from the corner, four or five doors, and there was a woman standing in the floor or on the steps—Anyway, she joined me and we walked about two doors still nearer the corner and I walked in a house with her and she sat on my lap and I stayed there a few minutes, and she began fumbling with me, and the first thing I knew we were having intercourse with each other, she across my lap. I stayed there, I guess, ten minutes or longer, but not much longer than ten minutes I am sure.[24]

During that ten minutes this man was robbed—or so he claimed:

> I then got up and walked out and walked probably fifty feet and got to the corner and just as I turned the corner the thought struck me to see if I had my money in my pocket book—I had paid her for the pleasure I had out of the odd silver money I had in change in my pocket—I opened my pocket book and saw that there were three twenty dollar bills gone, I think that there were two other bills in that side of my pocket book, but I am sure that there were three twenties gone. I immediately turned back and went to the same door and there was no one in the house, there was no one to be seen. I then saw an officer and told him the circumstances, and we walked up by this house and there was no one there. I told him just what had been done in the house,

and he told me that if I wanted to bring charges against her [and arrest her] that he would have to detain me as a material witness. I never was in jail in my life and I did not want to go to jail. I then left the officer, and did not do anything more then until between five and six o'clock in the afternoon when I consulted the sergeant and he told me to go to headquarters and make my statement, which I did, and then the gentleman in the Court room now came with me and arrested this woman.[25]

The woman arrested was not the woman Fred Smith had had intercourse with—she was rather the brothel-keeper, the "woman of the house." This he could not have been mistaken about since she was black, whereas the woman Smith had been with was white, or, as he put it, "She was as I thought a white woman." The defense attorney asked Smith, "You have anything at all to do with this woman?" Smith answered, "No sir." The attorney asked, "She steal your money?" Again, Smith replied, "No sir." Finally, when asked again, "You did not have anything to do with her at all?" Smith repeated, "No sir." The landlady was nevertheless fined $25 or, if she could not pay, sentenced to thirty days in the parish prison. The judge made his decision based on what he called "General Principles."[26]

Sometimes men were robbed without even having "the pleasure," as this man put it, of paid sex. One summer Sunday, in the wee hours of the morning, a New Orleans man named August Monlezun was walking through the district to catch a streetcar. He had been out with some friends and was headed home. When he passed the corner of Bienville and Marais streets, a woman beckoned to him to "come on in" to her crib. He kept on walking. The woman ran up to him, "snatched" his hat right off of his head, and retreated to her crib with it. When August ran after her to get it, "someone behind the door held [his] arms" down while the woman with his hat went through his pockets and took two and a half dollars from him.[27]

For sailors docked in New Orleans, the district was very often their first stop in town. Two such sailors (from a fruit steamer) lost or were robbed of their money in Storyville, one $5, the other $10. They only noticed they were missing the money after they left the brothel they had visited and had gone to get a beer. Another man, Presialiano Morina, lost significantly more money—$90—in Storyville. As he recounted his experience, "There were three women in the house, two negroes and a white woman and I went to bed with the white woman," then added, "anyway, she looked like she was white." While he was having sex with her, "the other ones went through [his] pockets." And while many instances of robbery appear to have taken place while the customer's pants hung on a chair near the bed while he slept, or even during sex, this robbery seems to have been especially bold. Morina saw them do it; he was "looking at them."[28] He was, however, in no position to make them stop.

These incidents reveal much about what went on in Storyville that was not specifically recalled by the musicians who played there: men sought sex during the day. They found it easily. The whole transaction usually lasted ten or fifteen minutes. During this brief period they were sometimes, or often, robbed. Women of color were proprietresses of brothels that included white prostitutes. The police threatened the men with imprisonment themselves if they sought to pursue their claims in court, and, finally the women were vulnerable under the "General Principles" that implied guilt by virtue of their profession. The $25 fine imposed on the landlady in the above example was a stiff penalty indeed when one considers that a single trick could be paid for with the loose change one found in his pocket. Thirty days in prison was, in addition to the unpleasantness that that certainly entailed, extremely bad for business.

Arrest records from Storyville reveal an atmosphere of violence and danger, acknowledged but winked at by the musicians' recollections, ranging from the occasional rapes and murders to the more common larceny and petty theft, pickpocketing, and street fighting.[29] Over one thousand prostitutes were arrested in Storyville every year of its operation, with the exception of one year, when the number was 922.[30] They were not arrested for prostitution, per se. For example: On January 1, 1908, Adeline Smith, an illiterate, single, black prostitute was arrested for being drunk and disturbing the peace, using obscene language, resisting arrest, and reviling police. Queen Venerable, a single, black, twenty-eight-year-old prostitute, was arrested for fighting with a white salesman the next day.[31] They were both charged with disturbing the peace and using obscene language. Bridget Ryan, a single, white, thirty-five-year-old prostitute, was arrested three times that same month for fighting and disturbing the peace, petty larceny, and being drunk.

Cribs with only enough room for a bed represent the basic business that sustained Storyville. They had none of the homosocial male camaraderie (or competition) that perhaps was found in the high-class bordellos. Beyond the fabled, glamorous district of legend was a sordid vice district. Women working in cribs could perhaps rinse off between customers; they returned to dirty beds and soiled sheets, to repeat their liaisons with a new stranger. These one-room shacks were not residences, but barebones work sites.

According to Louis Armstrong, "Lot of the prostitutes lived in different sections of the city and would come down to Storyville just like they had a job. There were different shifts for them. Sometime—two prostitutes would share the rent in the same crib together. One would work in the day, and the other would beat out that night shift." These women worked hard and constantly. "And business was so good in those days with the fleet of sailors and the crews from those big ships that come in the Mississippi River from all over the world—kept them very busy."[32] Prostitutes hung out outside of Pete Lala's, "hustling on the street," according to Kid Ory, another legendary jazz musician. "Down the block 'twas cribs, you see. They'd make a few dollars, they'd close up, you know, and say, I'm going cabareting awhile.' They'd come in, you know, pick up some guy and then go back, you see." The action was "like clockwork," according to Ory.[33] Some of the bars in the district were open all night long.[34] As Jelly Roll Morton said, "I'm telling you this Tenderloin District was like something that nobody has ever seen before or since. The doors were taken off the saloons there from one year to the next. Hundreds of men were passing through the streets day and night. The chippies in their little-girl dresses were standing in the crib doors singing the blues."[35]

Along with the "chippies" singing the blues were the pimps in their box coats and pointy shoes. Armstrong remembered the "pimps and hustlers [who] would spend most of their time at Twenty-Five [one of the clubs] until their girls would meet them and check up on their night's take."[36] His own brief attempt to pimp, or to "have a girl," as pimping was known, failed quite miserably; when Armstrong refused to go home and spend the night with her, she stabbed him. Armstrong's mother went after the woman, found her, and nearly killed her, telling her to leave Louis alone.[37] Others did not have so much trouble. Pimps were prominent in the district, even in the high-class bordellos. They were flashy and well dressed. Some of them wore diamonds the size of dimes.[38] Clarence Williams remembered how, "round about four a.m., the girls would get through work and would meet their [pimps] at the wine rooms."[39] The biggest funeral Kid Ory ever saw was that of "a boy named Kirk. He was the hottest pimp . . . in Storyville. Diamonds in his garters and all over his mouth."[40]

It is impossible to know to what extent pimps regulated the Storyville economy, but they certainly had a presence there. The Pimps Club, as it was un-self-consciously called, coerced women into prostitution and extorted money from legitimate businesses in the district. It cost a dollar a week to belong to the club. There were meetings every Saturday night, in which the fifty or so members of the Pimps Club congregated and handed over their dues. The money was used primarily for paying lawyers and fines for pimps who were arrested. "Lots of the money was used in this way." A lot of the money also went to paying off the police. "Twenty dollars [a month] for the captain, twenty dollars for the sergeant, ten dollars for the policeman." A pimp could only get out of paying his dues if his "girl was sick. The president [of the club] would say all right if your girl is sick and can't work you don't have to pay the dollar this week."[41]

This pimps' syndicate was well known in the district. Sam Felix, an immigrant from Brazil, was the president. He also ran a "white slavery" ring in New Orleans and South America, importing women from Brazil. "He always had women to come from away. He was always getting women here. The women [after] they were brought here used to talk to me about how things were," recounted Ike Schminsky, a clothing and dry goods retailer in the district who was forced to join the pimps' syndicate as their treasurer, even though he did not "have a girl." Felix ran a restaurant with rooms above it where the prostitutes were forced to take their meals. He had a constant stream of women coming to New Orleans from New York. He was, as one contemporary put it, "always sending away for new girls and getting new girls."[42]

According to one Storyville prostitute in Felix's syndicate, "there is a law here that makes all the girls have a fellow." Felix told her to ask for $2 a trick, and when she couldn't get that "to take what I could get." She paid $2.10 per night for her room in the winter, and $1.60 during the summer. She also "sometimes" paid $2.50 for her meals, which she had to take at Ike Miller's restaurant. (Miller was an associate of Felix's.) She reported that Felix told her, "if you had a pimp it is cheaper. He [Felix] said all the women who have got pimps they get their board cheaper, that if [she] did not have a pimp it would cost [her] more." The pimps beat the prostitutes as a matter of course. This upset Schminsky, who complained to the police captain that Sam Felix and Ike Miller, the vice-president of the club, would stand outside and tell the pimps to beat their girls. "[Police] Captain Coulange told Felix that he would have to stop the beating of the girls, that he ought to be glad that he let him run his restaurant." The Pimps Club responded by breaking all the windows of Schminsky's store, twice.[43]

Indeed, violence or the threat of violence was ever-present in Storyville. The piano player Frank Amacker remembered that "occasionally someone would bring a hammer to the house, which meant he wanted to break the place up. He'd break the piano and everything else, and then he'd pay the landlady for the damage done, several thousand dollars sometimes."[44] Here was an instance of contained outbursts for which Storyville provided an arena. Other forms of violence in red-light districts were neither contained nor compensated. The historian Timothy Gilfoyle shows how tensions about class and gender often exploded in violence against "public" women. Blue-collar workers targeted prostitutes out of resentment of their apparent wealth and ease of life. Sometimes men wanted only to smash the furniture or steal precious objects; other times these outbursts involved assault and battery, including rape.[45] Overt violence against prostitutes was perhaps a predictable corollary to the inherent violence entailed in prostitution in a patriarchal society.[46] An underlying misogyny (certainly based in larger cultural contexts) also guided much of the violence against prostitutes, who were often the most visible and vulnerable women around. The danger could come from pimps, madams, customers, cops, or even other prostitutes.[47] Sam Felix was known to have beaten his own wife so thoroughly that she had to be confined to a mental institution.[48] Yet, in a guide to the district from the 1910s, there is a Mrs. Sam Felix listed at 219 N. Liberty St.[49]

Storyville's streets testified to the dissipation bred of poverty and desperation. Every night ambulances carted men and women off to Charity Hospital, usually in a state of drunkenness and destitution. People were often arrested for "lying drunk" on the street. Others were arrested for "exposing their persons"—i.e., public nakedness—and causing public nuisances, as well as shouting obscenities and reviling police. Drug use was also rampant. Jelly Roll Morton remembered being "personally sent to Chinatown many times with a sealed note and a small amount of money and would bring back several cards of hop [opium]. There was no slipping and dodging. All you had to do was walk in and be served."[50] Clarence Williams also remembered the ease of buying drugs. "And do you know that you could buy all the cocaine, morphine, heroin, and hop you wanted in the section, almost right out in the open?"[51] Finally, because New Orleans still did not have an adequate sewer or drainage system, most of the beer, urine, and vomit that flowed in Storyville's streets stayed there.

Some attempted to pierce the veil of Basin Street's high camp and faux glamour by reporting what they saw beyond the façade of the big mansions. A visitor to Storyville in the 1910s described the district as "without doubt, the vilest, most brazen and most utterly degenerate spot I know of," adding, "and they all seem proud of the fact." He compared it to other contemporary red-light districts. "Neither 'Five Points' and the 'Tub of Blood' of New York's bowrey [sic] days prior to the clean up," he said, "nor Frisco's 'Barbary Coast' in its palmiest days could even qualify with New Orleans' tenderloin." An evangelist conducting revivals at the First Methodist Church described New Orleans as "the wickedest city on earth. Its red-light district is famous throughout the country as having the old-time Barbary Coast of San Francisco backed off the boards."[52] Business in Storyville boomed.

Storyville was more than a sex mart; it was a full-fledged entertainment district. Though jazz music proliferated throughout the city at a wide variety of venues, from church socials to family picnics, it is also true that Storyville featured jazz and other forms of contemporary music prominently in almost all of its wide-ranging entertainments.[53] Most of the better bordellos employed a piano player, and sometimes madams hired female entertainers to sing and dance for the male customers. The trumpeter Bunk Johnson remembered a mixed-race singer named Mamie Desdounes (or Desdunes). "She was pretty good looking, quite fair, with a *nice* head of hair." She had a following. "When Hattie Rogers or Lulu White would put it out that Mamie was going to be singing in their place, the white men would turn out in bunches and them whores would clean up."[54] Indeed, Inez "Mamie" Desdunes used to sing the popular song that was later named "Mamie's Blues," in her honor, and which Jelly Roll Morton covered in tribute to her.[55] Willie Piazza's bordello at 317 Basin Street was "the place to hear all of the latest jubilee songs." Piazza boasted "some of the latest entertainers that can be found— and she has without doubt, the most handsome and intelligent girls in the Tenderloin district . . . they are all cultivated entertainers—for singing and dancing they have no equal."[56] Piazza was one of Storyville's "octoroon" proprietresses, and entertainment in this context was charged with expectations of the "exotic" sexuality of such rare hybrid creatures. At some of the bordellos entertainment ranged from one to several prostitutes singing the latest songs to the eponymous "Naked Dance." "Of course," remembered Jelly Roll Morton, "they were naked dances all right because they absolutely was stripped. They was stripped. Of course, a naked dance was something that was supposed to be real art in New Orleans."[57] According to Morton, the pianist Tony Jackson was considered to be the "best player" of the "type of tune" that accompanied the naked dances, a fast piano number. In addition to these dances, at Lulu White's, according to one of her ads, there were "always ten entertainers, who recently arrived from the 'East,' some being well known in the 'profession,' who get paid to do nothing but sing and dance."[58] White added even more exoticism with her "oriental" entertainers.

Whether the "sport" proceeded to one of the lush bordellos on Basin Street or the less tony brothels or cribs further toward Robertson Street, he was sure to hear some new and interesting music. Indeed, he would hear it on the street as he walked toward his destination. At the swankier brothels, the musicians played and the "ladies [prostitutes] would always say, 'give the professor something.'"[59] When the pianist took a break, music continued to entertain the clientele in the form of player pianos. Spencer Williams remembered going to sleep "to the sound of the mechanical piano playing ragtime tunes, and when I woke up in the morning it would still be playing."[60] According to Clarence Williams, "it cost a silver dollar to play the mother-of-pearl inlaid white enameled pianola" at Willie Piazza's Basin Street bordello.[61] Most often the music was live. Since the piano players were "professors," it is fitting that the women singers were sometimes called "graduates."

Basin Street prostitutes themselves kept up with the music scene. When they went "shopping on Canal Street, they'd always go buy songs," Manuel Manetta recalled. Manetta could read music, and he played the songs the women brought back to Mahogany Hall while they sang, sometimes solo, sometimes in a group around the piano.[62] The high-class bordellos "hired nothing but the best, but only piano players, and sometimes a girl to sing . . . there was no loud playin' either. It was sweet, just like a hotel," recalled Clarence Williams.[63] The "sweet" playing might, however, be supplemented with less "classy" singing around the piano. For example, Marguerite Griffin was a "prime attraction" at Minnie White's house on North Basin Street. Ms. Griffin, according to Al Rose, "knew the lyrics of countless bawdy ballads."[64] Jazz songs, of course, often featured explicit lyrics about sex, liquor, cheating lovers, and even prostitution.[65]

In addition to the "ornate, perfumed brothels" where Jelly Roll Morton, Tony Jackson, Manuel Manetta, and others played piano, there were "cabarets" on Customhouse Street that featured dance orchestras. There were the large dance halls: the Tuxedo and the 101 Ranch, and at the end of Basin Street, the Globe.[66] There were also "Fewclothes' [Foucault's], Hanan's, Rice's, Huntz's, and Lala's" on Customhouse toward Claiborne. "That was the Crescent City in them days," recalled Bunk Johnson, "full of bars, honky-tonks, and barrel houses. A barrel house was just a piano in a hall," he explained. "There was always a piano player working." Johnson would go to the barrelhouses when he was a kid, and play through until morning. "We used to play nothing but the blues."[67]

In the early 1910s, "the Eagle Band was at Globe Hall, Celestin was at the Tuxedo, Perez was at Rice's, Oliver was at Huntz's, Keppard was at Hanan's, Bunk Johnson was at Lala's, and Tig Chambers was at Fewclothes."[68] Tom Anderson's saloon sometimes featured a string trio. Musicians at these dance halls were paid between $1.50 and $2.00 for a night's work, 8 p.m. to 4:00 in the morning. The musicians got "free wine [and] tips sometimes ran as high as $15.00 a piece."[69] "For a year or so the only regular orchestras in the city *not* working in the noisy, sprawling red-light district were the Robichaux Orchestra and the Silver Leaf Orchestra."[70] In a roughly nineteen-square-block area there were at least ten musical venues operating at once, not including those musicians working in the expensive bordellos or the cheap cabarets. For some, jazz was the main attraction. For example, young white boys snuck into the district to hear the music of King Oliver; they were transported by the new kind of music emanating from his cornet.[71] Jelly Roll Morton remembered one place that swung all night. "After four o'clock in the morning, all the girls that could get out of the houses they were there," in addition to the musicians, pimps, and visitors who came from "all over the country." There were times, he recalled, "that you couldn't get in," for the crowd. On the inside, Morton remembered the club having the atmosphere of "one big happy family," with everyone sitting "at different tables at any place that they felt like sitting. They all mingled together as they wished to." The music would "go on from four o'clock in the morning at a tremendous rate of speed, with plenty money, drinks of all types, till maybe twelve, one, two, three o'clock in the daytime."[72]

New Orleans was a musically inclined town, and as one historian of New Orleans jazz has noted, "one of the salient characteristics" of even poor families in New Orleans was their interest in music. "Many of the jazz greats who later made a name for themselves were reared in families possessing not only musical instruments, but a musical tradition in the person of some member or members of the family."[73] Others, like Louis Armstrong, learned to play an instrument in juvenile correctional schools. Storyville offered employment to black men, and the Jim Crow laws effectively forced musicians from all over the city into the same bars and venues. Paul Dominguez, a downtown Creole violinist, turned jazz "fiddler" in Storyville, explained that Storyville was where the jobs were, where the money was. "See, us Downtown people [. . .] we didn't think so much of this rough Uptown jazz until

St. Louis Street

Private Homes

St. Louis Cemetery No. 1

Private Homes

Private Homes

Conti Street

6

Private Homes

5/6
4
2

18 19

13

Bienville Street

8

5 14 1

3

17 11

7 9

Robertson Street
Villere Street
Marais Street
N. Liberty Street
Crozat Street
Basin Street
Southern Railroad
Apt. Houses
Rampart Street
Burgundy Street

Customhouse (later Iberville) Street

5 16 12 15

10

Tulane Med. College

Private Homes
Private Homes
Private Homes
Private Homes
Private Homes
Private Homes
Private Homes

Terminal R.R. Station

Apt. Houses

Canal Street

Rooming Houses

Rooming
Gasquet Street

Rooming Houses

Private Homes

Private Homes

Elks Place
Private Homes
Elks Square

Tulane Street

Courthouse and Parish Prison

Charity Hospital

Charity Hospital

Gravier Street

Boundary of Storyville

Saloons:

Houses of prostitution:
1. Lulu White's Mahogany Hall
2. Willie Piazza
3. Josie Arlington
4. Emma Johnson
5. Gipsy Schafer
6. Antonia Gonzales
7. Hilma Burt
• Small "houses" of prostitution

8. Lulu White's Saloon
9. Tom Anderson
10. The 25
11. The Pig Ankle
12. Fewclothes (Foucault's)
13. Toro's Saloon
14. The Tuxedo
15. The Terminal Saloon
16. Pete Lala's
17. Palm Garden Dance Hall
18. The Frenchman's Saloon
■ Other saloons

19. H. Aberdeen's Café
▼ Other cafés & restaurants
♦ Grocery stores
▲ Small businesses/shops
★ Jazz venues
† Church

Pertinent Locations in and around Storyville

(Map by Mary Lee Eggart)

we couldn't make a living otherwise."[74] Musicians from the Creole Seventh and Eighth Wards came together with others from the Ninth and other uptown "Negro" wards to play in Storyville. The resulting cross-pollination of styles and techniques fostered the development of jazz, as the technical virtuosity of the more classically trained musicians met the rhythms and musical stylings of the poor and working-class black players. In the era of Jim Crow, a gig in Storyville was often the best (or only) gig in town for black musicians, whether they were descended from the historically free Creoles of color or the African American population of the city. Basin Street was the street where the "light and dark folks meet."

Laissez les Bon Temps Rouler: Prostitution in Early New Orleans

Some of the earliest French inhabitants of Louisiana were prostitutes. France claimed the vast Louisiana Territory in 1682. As late as 1712, there were still fewer than three hundred residents in the settlements located in present-day Mobile, Biloxi Bay, and Natchez. As Herbert Asbury recounts in his colorful 1936 history of New Orleans, out of the three hundred or so residents, over a hundred were soldiers. There were a few priests as well, but most of the other men were "adventurous *voyageurs* and *coureurs de bois* who had wandered into the province from Canada and Illinois." Of the twenty-eight women in the territory, he writes, "almost without exception, [they] were deportees from the prisons and brothels of Paris."[75] A population dominated by soldiers and "loose women" troubled one priest, who wrote to the governor at the time, Lamothe Cadillac, suggesting he expel the women. Cadillac reportedly replied, "If I send away all the loose females, there will be no women left here at all, and this would not suit the views of the King or the inclinations of the people."[76]

Throughout the eighteenth century, New Orleans was known as a "veritable Babylon"—a reputation it maintained through the nineteenth century, and arguably the twentieth.[77] Reports circulated about the lax morality, the wantonness, and the utter lack of civilization in the colonial territory. In Shannon Dawdy's nice formulation, New Orleans was *la ville sauvage,* the shadow of metropolitan Paris, the City of Light.[78] Dawdy explains that following the early attempts at colonization, Louisiana was more or less abandoned by France and left to its own devices. The period of abandonment allowed for a creole culture to develop, a native culture grown from the roots up in the territory.[79] A European observer wrote in 1720, "What can one expect from a bunch of vagabonds and wrongdoers in a country where it is harder to repress licentiousness than in Europe?"[80] As early as the late 1720s New Orleans already enjoyed the distinction even within Louisiana "as a place where criminal passions ran wild."[81] Violence and licentiousness characterized perceptions of the colony and its capital city—founded in 1718—from very early on.

During the first decades of Louisiana's existence as a French colony, it was, in Caryn Cossé Bell's words, a "frontier society characterized by a high degree of social and economic fluidity."[82] Certainly the male inhabitants were not all "vagabonds and wrongdoers," but neither were they family men intent on settling down—as had been the predominant profile of Anglo-American colonials at this time and earlier. Most of the new Louisianians were from New France, or Canada, and not from across the Atlantic, and there were many more white men than women. At first, French and Canadian settlers entered into sexual relationships with Indian women. Some of these were marriages, legitimated by missionaries and other authorities, others were more or less casual, and others were slave-concubine arrangements, where Indian women were purchased as housekeepers, ostensibly to do the laundry and the cooking, but really served as sexual slaves. To be sure, these concubines most likely also did the cooking and the laundry. The degree of consent in these relationships is impossible to know.[83] All of these relationships, whatever their legitimacy, displeased the colonial authorities, who worried that they would deter the creation of a settled, farming community. They worried that the men were "going native" and losing their distinctive Europeanness. They worried that the children of such relationships were impure, and that this métissage would sully white, European bloodlines, condemning the colony to a future of barbarism rather than civilization. They worried that Catholicism would not be established in the colony. They worried that the Canadian men, reputed to be very vigorous, would never settle down if allowed to continue their backwoods liaisons. And they worried more generally about immorality and licentiousness, already (in their view) rampant in the infant possession.[84]

Religious and secular authorities alike believed that French (white) women would help settle the colony by providing wives for the male colonists. Marriage in the continental style would encourage farming and discourage the debauchery already damaging the reputation of Louisiana in Europe. Thus, very early on in the history of French Louisiana, even before the founding of New Orleans, Bienville wrote to Paris: "Send me wives for my Canadians.

They are running in the woods after Indian girls."[85] The first group of women shipped from France were girls who had been "brought up in virtue and piety." They had "no trouble finding husbands."[86] The second shipment was quite another matter. Arriving in 1713, this next group of French women was composed of undesirable women, several of whom had been seduced on the voyage across the sea. However, it was not their reputations that doomed them in the eyes of the colonists, but rather their ugliness. They were reported "as being so ugly and malformed that the habitants and especially the Canadians have no desire for them."[87] What made these women so unattractive? We have no way of knowing; we cannot but note that, questions of beauty and ugliness aside, only a few of this group married in Louisiana. In 1721, another shipment of women arrived from France. The man in charge of the whole Louisiana colony at the time was a Scottish entrepreneur named John Law. Law obtained control of the territory by Royal Grant for his Company of the West, also known as the Mississippi Company (and later known as the Compagnie des Indes).[88] He responded to Bienville's request by sending to New Orleans eighty-eight women from La Salpêtrière, a female prison in Paris. Three nuns were sent along to watch over these "correction girls."[89] Bienville wrote back: "These girls were not well selected. Whatever the vigilance exercised upon them, they could not be restrained."[90]

The needs of the colony did not mesh with the desire of French officials to rid the metropole of women of ill repute, and so prostitutes were imported to the colony specifically to prevent métissage with the Native American women on whom the colonists depended for survival. The historian Jennifer Spear makes the good point, however, that many of the women so imported probably only became prostitutes once they arrived in Louisiana, "because they had few other options." Whatever "civilizing effect" colonial officials believed French women would have on the colony, "the colony," writes Spear, "seems to have had the opposite effect on the women."[91] Clearly, this was not an appropriate solution to the problem of licentiousness in the possession, and colonial officials wrote back to ask for a better class of women to be sent to New Orleans. Thus finally came the legendary *filles à la cassette,* or "casket girls," so named for the small, neatly packed domestic trunks they brought with them. They went on view during the day and were locked up in the evening, and soon were married off. As one colonial official recounted, this "merchandise . . . was soon distributed, so great was the dearth of it in the country."[92] Spear writes that there was only one shipment of casket girls, in 1728, but others have written that renewed supplies of *filles à la cassette* arrived at intervals until mid-century. Surely this latter view, if not strictly true, has maintained its salience in part as a result of the lore that all native white New Orleanians trace their lineage to the *filles à la cassette,* and none back to the prostitutes or convicts—and certainly not to Indians or to African slaves, who were imported to the colony beginning in the early 1700s as well.[93] Indeed, it was not until Louisiana had relied on slave labor for decades that the colony became a settled plantation society. The importation of white women did not effectively end métissage, and the presence of African slaves allowed Louisiana to develop along a path more resembling the Caribbean than Canada, as black women replaced Indian women as the sex partners of white colonials.[94]

Bienville's tenure ended in 1743 and the Marquis de Vaudreuil took his place. Vaudreuil was known for his extravagant and stately parties, and his tenure in office helped initiate the stereotype of the Creole leisure class that would hold sway for a century or more. His successor, Louis Billouart, Chevalier de Kerlérec, was personally lax in morals and his administration was corrupt, a combination that would periodically characterize the city's top administrators across the decades. All the continent knew New Orleans for its extreme tolerance for "lapses from the strict moral code." During the Seven Years' War, the French troops were "so given to 'unrestrained debaucheries of liquor and women'" that Governor Kerlérec "considered his garrison more dangerous to the colony than the enemy itself."[95] These problems persisted through Spanish rule, 1763–1800, and the three years 1800–1803 when the province was technically back under French control.[96] "But curiously enough," remarks Herbert Asbury, "it was under the rule of the United States that New Orleans embarked upon its golden age of glamour and spectacular wickedness."[97]

New Orleans was a European colonial city, a "Latin American" colony, a West Indian enclave, an American frontier town, and a port city—all within the Deep South. It attracted the characters that borderlands areas typically did: speculators, sailors, riverboat men, traders, gamblers, itinerants, and vagabonds from France, Canada, Illinois, and farther west. Traders, middlemen, and their employees ferried merchandise up and down the Mississippi and Ohio rivers. The city, as mentioned, already had a reputation for libidinous license. "The boatmen," writes Michael Allen, "were anxious to go ashore."[98] These riverboat men became ambassadors of American rule over the Louisiana territory. They brought violence and vice with them, and the white Creole New Orleanians especially despised these "western rivermen," often called simply Kentuckians or "kaintocks" regardless of their precise geographic origins.[99]

When the United States took over the Louisiana Territory in 1803, the town had around eight thousand residents and, in spite of devastating fires in 1788 and 1794, boasted architecture as impressive as its commerce. The population of New Orleans quadrupled in the first four decades of the nineteenth century, and its reputation as a haven for low-lifes, gangsters, and thugs grew, too.[100] What we would consider municipal policing, as opposed to an armed military presence, did not develop in New Orleans until the 1830s, and even then it was a disorganized and lackadaisical pursuit.[101] In some areas of the city there was no law enforcement at all. Prostitutes loitered on Girod and Perdido streets, and "the low-class harlots plied their trade" even as far north as South Liberty Street. Part of this area would later become Storyville.[102] By the 1840s some elements within New Orleans were already trying to contain bad behavior, to limit it to specific districts where it could be regulated. The problem, however, was intractable. Many New Orleanians believed, with "A Resident" (in a pamphlet published in 1849), that "the extent of licentiousness and prostitution in New Orleans is doubtless without a parallel."[103] Furthermore, according to this pamphleteer, there was no sense of shame with regard to illicit sex in New Orleans. "The indulgence and practice is so general and common, that men do not seek to cover up their acts, or go in disguise; but in all these things, keeping their mistresses, or frequenting bed houses, and having women come to their rooms at night, they do it as openly, and as much before the eyes of the world, as any other act among the common civilities of the social circle."[104]

Indeed, prostitution flourished in antebellum New Orleans. It was a "major industry," of a piece with the city's old world heritage, according to Richard Tansey, but one sustained through the so-called ambassadors from the inland: the kaintocks and riverboat men. Transients and sailors lodged in brothels rather than high-priced hotels. Most of the city's prostitutes were immigrant working women and teenagers of European descent, women who had been "easy targets" for ballroom managers and brothel keepers.[105] Machine politicians, the police, and wealthy landlords received graft from brothel owners and prostitutes in return for turning a blind eye. Whole blocks of previously "respectable" homes gave way to disorderly houses and brothels. The properties so used tended to decrepitude but generated large rents, which chased out "legitimate" renters and home-owners, ruining neighborhoods. Landlords protected their lessees from the police and from eviction, and were in turn protected by powerful politicians to whom they paid graft.

Prostitution was simultaneously "the oldest profession" and an emblem of modern life. It represented a lack of progress even as it was reluctantly acknowledged as a collateral effect of greater industrialization and the growing labor force that served new industry. By the later antebellum period, some reform elements in the city had had enough of this visible vice to elect representatives who promised to root it out. Prostitution represented to these reformers "a sordid part of an antiquated economic structure which prevented New Orleans from keeping pace with her rivals in controlling the South's trade."[106] Between 1836 and 1852, New Orleans was divided into three quasi-independent municipalities. In 1851, a reform coalition of merchants and businessmen came to power over one of the city's ugliest areas, the Third Municipality.[107] This was the lowest-lying area of the city, and the most neglected by civic authorities. Comprised mostly of French-descended natives, or Creoles (both white and of color), and European immigrants, the "poor third" municipality was the section of the city below the French Quarter, northeast of Esplanade Street. The reformers blamed prostitution and its attendant vicious commerce for the municipality's inability to keep pace with growth and economic development in the much richer First and Second. They argued that the prevalence of "bawdy houses" kept would-be respectable residents and businesses out, resulting in a total absence of "banks, insurance companies, first-rate hotels, large-scale factories, wholesale firms and groceries, and dry goods stores [to serve] the needs of its almost twenty thousand residents."[108]

Another reason these reformers found to oppose prostitution in the Third Municipality was its association with the spread of disease. Aside from its obvious connection with venereal disease, prostitution was thought to contribute to the spread of yellow fever and cholera on account of the population that patronized its brothels: sailors and riverboat men who carried infectious diseases along with their cargo from far-flung ports. Legitimate business owners also joined the antiprostitution initiative, seeking both to bolster their own business and to improve the economy more generally: money spent protecting prostitution might be better spent developing railroads and maintaining levees. The reform coalition won, beating the Democratic regime, seeming to open the way for reform and improvement. Unfortunately, the ineptitude of the new administration led to the near-total nonenforcement of the antiprostitution measures they passed. The reformers also managed to demoralize the police force to the point that they refused to suppress the sex business.[109]

In 1852 the city, now reconsolidated under one central city government, effectively took administrative powers away from the individual municipalities, and short-circuited the (notably ineffective) reform efforts of the newly elected coalition. A few years later another opportunity for reform coalesced. During the disastrous business season of 1854–1855, the water levels of the Mississippi occasionally fell low enough to stop commercial ships from reaching New Orleans. The resulting economic calamity reinvigorated the business community's demand that New Orleans develop a railroad trade. This time, though, the reform drive was led by Nativists, who coupled their demand for a railway trade with attacks on mixed-race sex and prostitution.[110]

Prostitution was, and is, a powerful metaphor, and because interracial and commercial sex both fell beyond the limits of respectable sexuality, they were easily conflated.[111] Even so, as Judith Kelleher Schafer has shown, in antebellum New Orleans women of color and white women worked as prostitutes serving a spectrum of johns, sometimes in the same brothels; women of color ran brothels both independently and as the (sometimes enslaved) agents of white men. Whatever rules governed the leisure-time interactions of New Orleanians, the sex industry did not obey them.[112] The Nativists' focus on prostitution and racial taboos prevailed and their reform coalition won. Once in office, however, their economic goals overshadowed their moral ones, the railway canceling the bettering of neighborhoods in actual budgets. When residents expecting a clean-up protested, the politicians responded to their constituents' outcry with the Lorette Ordinance, which imposed high taxes on bordellos, forced madams to take out expensive licenses, and made prostitution illegal in single-story houses. White and colored prostitutes were forbidden from working side by side in the same brothels, yet white or black men could continue to patronize whomever they desired. As a concession to the more wealthy brothel owners, the ordinance also legalized prostitution in multi-story buildings throughout New Orleans.[113] Even this measure failed when property owners sued to protect their rights to rent to whomever they chose, no matter how many stories their properties had. The law was declared unconstitutional and prostitution continued to thrive everywhere.[114]

The Civil War disrupted normal relationships in the city most obviously and cataclysmically by ending slavery. However, the war did not so much disrupt prostitution as provide an army of customers, literally. General Benjamin Butler no doubt exacerbated the longstanding problem of actual prostitution in New Orleans when he preemptively labeled the city's rebellious women as prostitutes in his infamous Woman Order:

> As the officers and soldiers of the United States have been subjected to repeated insults from the women (calling themselves ladies) of New Orleans, in return for the most scrupulous noninterference and courtesy on our part, it is ordered that hereafter, when any female shall, by word, gesture, or movement, insult or show contempt for any officer or soldier of the United States, she shall be regarded and held liable to be treated as a woman of the town plying her avocation.

Butler's order was read everywhere as an insult to southern (white) womanhood, and in some quarters of New Orleans it was taken as tantamount to a threat of rape.[115] Furthermore, by ostensibly labeling all women in public as "public women," Butler highlighted what was and would continue to be New Orleans's problem with prostitution: namely, that there were no clear boundaries delineating vicious commerce from legitimate enterprise, and thus no boundaries marking the limits of respectability around individual women on New Orleans's streets.

The post-Reconstruction "Gilded Age" represented the heyday of prostitution in America, and indeed in the industrialized world. Prostitution grew everywhere in this period, from New York to Johannesburg, from Paris to Shanghai.[116] Still, New Orleans stood out, and by the 1890s, in Herbert Asbury's nice phrase, New Orleans had an "almost universal reputation as the promised land of harlotry."[117]

To reformers, prostitution posed questions about morality, disease, economics, patriarchy, sexuality, and race, and thus the problem of prostitution did not suggest a uniform response. To be sure, there were always moral reformers who sought the total eradication of vice. In the years around the turn of the twentieth century, their efforts grew into the greatest antiprostitution movement in American history.[118] Municipal authorities, perhaps more realistically, tried to contain vice and limit its spread through the creation of red-light districts in either irredeemable or marginal neighborhoods.[119] In New Orleans, at the turn of the century, the most the antivice movement could muster was to move prostitution away from the main thoroughfares. They were most concerned to mark the boundaries of legitimate commerce—and keep vicious commerce away. For instance, in

1891 the *New Orleans Daily Picayune* exposed that feature of New Orleans's burgeoning sex industry that the editors found most disturbing: young girls being enticed from New York and elsewhere to work in the men's clubs sprouting up downtown. Upon their arrival in New Orleans, these young women were shown to concert saloons, where they were expected to solicit men to purchase liquor while dressed in "scanty and immodest" clothing.[120]

The concert saloon was a "precursor of modern urban nightlife," and a center of casual or clandestine prostitution. Concert saloons therefore blurred the line between the brothel and the bar, just the sort of line that the reformers wished to clarify.[121] The law was no help, because there was no law against concert saloons, no regulation to keep them out of view, and no prohibitions to prevent minors from working in them. "Because the law permits these girls to be debauched," the *Daily Picayune* wrote of sixteen-year-old saloon workers, "does that make the evil any less flagrant?" While the newspaper called for an end to concert saloons, however, there was no sense that houses of prostitution had to be targeted, especially if they were clearly marked as such. Tidy up the margins of legitimate nightlife, the newspaper said: it was no use going after sin itself. A less respectable New Orleans newspaper, which nevertheless focused on exposing political corruption and the underworld, likewise put forth the view that prostitution itself was not the (or even a) problem. "Against houses of ill fame, the *Mascot* makes no crusade," wrote the editor, "as long as they are not located in respectable neighborhoods."[122] Respectable neighborhoods would come to be defined as those that were free from "immoral" or "disorderly" houses.

The Creation of Storyville

Thus, after almost two hundred years of nearly unchecked prostitution in the city, came the Storyville ordinance. Quite a departure from previous reforms, the ordinance prohibited prostitution outside newly demarcated areas, disallowing "from the first of October, 1897 . . . any public prostitute or woman notoriously abandoned to lewdness to occupy, inhabit, live or sleep in any house, room, or closet situated without the following limits," the delineation being the principle novelty, encompassing a specific piece of real estate: from the "South side of Customhouse street from Basin to Robertson street, east side of Robertson street from Customhouse to St. Louis street, south side of St. Louis street from Robertson to Basin Street."[123] St. Louis Street itself was to function as a border, with no prostitution allowed on either side of the street. The police notified prostitutes throughout the city that they would have to move into the new district by October 1897, when the ordinance was slated to go into effect. If they did not comply, a notice was delivered to the women, signed by the mayor, beginning the process of their eviction.

After much discussion, in July 1897 the council members wrote an addendum to the Storyville ordinance to create a separate, "uptown" vice district in a mostly black area of town already famous for its honky-tonks and gambling "hells," as betting establishments were called.[124] This second district was partly designed to forestall a large population of black prostitutes from moving into the already limited space of Storyville, itself a mixed-race neighborhood.[125] The new ordinance, No. 13,485 C.S., also extended the boundaries of Storyville to allow prostitution on St. Louis Street. This latter provision prompted a lawsuit by George L'Hote, who lived next door to this extension. His case delayed the formal passage of the ordinance for two years, by which time it had effectively been implemented anyway. The uptown district never received the kind of attention from promoters, tourists, reformers, or historians that the downtown district did, and it is this latter area—bounded by Basin, Customhouse, Robertson, and St. Louis, Storyville proper—which will interest us here.

Situated behind the dividing line of Rampart Street, in what is known as the "back of town," the neighborhood that would later become Storyville was once called the "City Commons." Early New Orleanians grazed herd animals and gathered free firewood there in the dry season, but during the rest of the year "citizens avoided the steaming inundated spaces."[126] This was the general neighborhood that later contained Congo Square, a plaza where slaves and free people socialized, danced, and sold their wares during the antebellum period. The future district also bordered on an area called the Faubourg Tremé. "Faubourg" means "suburbs" or "outskirts" in French, and Claude Tremé was a white Creole who owned a plantation on a portion of the property in the late eighteenth century and sold it in the early nineteenth.[127] His buyers were a mix of French and Spanish colonial settlers, recent immigrants, and free people of color (Creoles of color), who thenceforth formed the majority of the residents. Eighty percent of the neighborhood's lots had passed through the hands of "persons of mixed heritage" at least once since the Spanish colonial era, and free people of color still dominated the Tremé in the nineteenth century. Many jazz musicians came from the area.[128] In the 1830s the city built a parish prison in the neighborhood, on the square bounded by Orleans, St. Anne, Tremé, and Marais streets. (The prison, considered by some to have been an architectural masterpiece, was torn down in 1895.) Tremé Market, along Basin Street, opened in 1839, and streetcar tracks ran along Basin through the middle of the market. In the 1850s, German and Irish immigrants settled among the free people of color, living amid boarding houses, prostitutes, and working-class families.[129] These demographics still described the neighborhood in the 1890s, when Canal Street was developing as the city's main commercial thoroughfare, bringing the former *faubourg* (suburb) much closer to the city's business center.

We can get a sense of the character of the Storyville neighborhood at the time of the ordinance by looking at the contested views expressed in the course of the L'Hote lawsuit.[130] For instance, in response to the suit the city surveyed the neighborhood, locating twenty-seven houses of prostitution, twelve assignation houses, and one "suspicious" house within just two blocks of L'Hote's home at 520 North Liberty Street (which, again, now fell barely outside the boundaries of Storyville). At least one such house had been in use for over thirteen years. L'Hote claimed that his neighborhood was, however, a respectable working-class environment, populated by "working people of good morals," lying quite apart "from that class of people," prostitutes.[131] "Immediately in my neighborhood and upon St. Louis street between Tremé [North Liberty] and Franklin up to Rampart street, including the corner of Basin street," said L'Hote, "the people that have lived there have always been respectable, because whenever that neighborhood was invaded by people that were not respectable . . . I had them removed." To be sure, L'Hote was defending his own reputation by denying that his neighborhood, where his father lived before him, and where he now lived with his wife and eight children, was populated by prostitutes and disorderly houses. L'Hote, in fact, sat on the city council, had helped to draft the ordinance, and had surely had a say in the choice of its location. What he most objected to was the district's one-block extension, the use of St. Louis Street for houses of prostitution and not as a border between the district and respectable residences. As we will see, at issue in his representations, and present in other such cases, was a concern to firm up the disrupted (and disputed) borders around "respectability."

Yet, in fact, according to a witness, "the character [of L'Hote's neighborhood] was mixed . . . you would find in a square maybe eight or ten respectable families living in that square, and maybe one suspicious house, [and] in the next square you might find more. . . ." A police officer knew respectable people but also "kept women" who had lived there for years. He described the neighborhood as "good and bad," a sentiment that others echoed. Even more, while the issue for L'Hote was the revision allowing prostitution on St. Louis Street (his family's chief means of egress from the neighborhood), according to the superintendent of police there had been "some disorderly houses there in that vicinity on St. Louis street" for at least fifteen or twenty years. Emma Smith ran a house on St. Louis Street between Marais and Tremé (North Liberty), for instance.

Amid these disorderly houses there lived widows and respectable working families, many of them small-business owners or artisans. One resident argued that the neighborhood was "about five hundred percent" worse since the ordinance, and that the majority of the people living there had indeed been respectable folk. A Mrs. Leroy, for example, had lived in the neighborhood for fifteen years, on St. Louis between Tremé and Franklin, the same block as Emma Smith's brothel. Her husband worked for L'Hote, whose lumber business was also in the neighborhood. Their next door neighbors were an Italian family of twelve years residence. Across the street from them a widow ran a grocery store. Her neighbors, the Millers (or Muellers), were a family of husband, wife, married daughter, and grandchildren; Mr. Miller was a shoemaker. Mr. Mauberret had lived in the neighborhood for years, too, and ran a legitimate bath house. Another widow, Mrs. Doyle, had lived quietly within the "new limits" for over twenty years. A more recent addition to the neighborhood was Mr. Waters, a clerk for the second recorder's court who lived within the district's boundaries with his mother and his family. Mrs. Rockedge and her now deceased husband, a blacksmith, raised their family on Customhouse Street between Villere and Marais. There was an Italian fruit stand, run by a family man, and a venerable saddlery establishment.

Residents also included people of color, such as Mr. Dumoil of the Turf Exchange at 1522 Bienville (a betting establishment, not necessarily unrespectable), and his neighbor Joseph Page, a cook living next door. There were three more "colored" families on Bienville Street alone, and all of them were "respectable."[132] In 1897, Mrs. Mose Williams sought a waiver of the municipal permit fee for the operation of her cook shop at 322 North Liberty (Tremé), between Bienville and Conti. Her husband earned decent wages at the sugar refinery, and the city deemed her able to pay for it.[133] A different Mrs. Williams, a woman named Lilly, was not so well off, and the city granted her a permit to operate a small restaurant at 1533 St. Louis, near Villere, without a fee.[134] There were "Chinese laundries," bakeries, groceries, and (segregated) bars and concert halls, and three dance halls and a "chop house" between Customhouse and Bienville that served a "Negro" clientele. There was a "colored" Methodist Episcopal Church (which joined L'Hote's lawsuit), and a coeducational "colored" school on the corner of Robertson and Bienville streets, where the children and teachers were accustomed to taking their lunch outside. After the Storyville ordinance they ate in the building.[135]

In short, the area that became Storyville was a residential working-class neighborhood of whites and persons of color, with self-sustaining small businesses and vendors, and a significant business sector catering to drink, gambling, drugs, and prostitution.[136] It was, like much of the city, mixed in myriad ways.

Two streetcar lines ran through Storyville. There was a double track on Villere Street. Another track commenced on Basin Street and ran down Bienville Street to an old Spanish fort on the outskirts of the city, the "Spanish Fort Line." In the 1880s and 1890s the fort, with the park around it, had been an attractive destination for escaping the urban center and relaxing among trees and greenery. It became a contested site in the struggles over racial segregation in New Orleans, and Joy Jackson writes that by the end of the nineteenth century it "lost its elegance and became mostly a favorite spot for Negro picnickers." Louis Armstrong remembered taking the train there as a youth with his band from "The Waif's Home" to play for vacationers.[137] Lastly, there were the cemeteries north and south in the district. New Orleans residents tended to entomb their dead above ground for fear of flooding, so these were described as "cities of the dead," tombs of sometimes elaborate design crowding squares of land in the city proper. The two oldest and most prestigious of these "cities," St. Louis Nos. 1 and 2, fell within Storyville's boundaries, and another lay just outside them.[138]

On paper, Storyville condensed into a tiny geographic area the prostitutes of the city—and in doing so also condensed two hundred years of cultural memory, reputation, and expectation about prostitution in New Orleans. If the purpose of the Storyville ordinance was to delineate and contain prostitution, it never fully succeeded, and instead quickly lent new evidence to those who would continue to depict New Orleans as a city of sin.

"Within ten years of its founding," writes Shannon Dawdy, "New Orleans began to appear in literary descriptions as a dark, primitive, and abandoned place, governed by immoral pleasures rather than by rationality and law."[139] The city's reputation for decadence and moral deterioration as well as earthly delights added ineluctably to the city's charm, creating a sort of thrill of transgression even in those who came to the city for perfectly moral pursuits. By the time steam travel allowed relatively fast and convenient travel up and down the Mississippi River, in the 1820s, New Orleans was already "famous beyond all other American cities for its uniqueness—and its wickedness."[140] By the close of the nineteenth century, New Orleans's reputation for spectacular wickedness had been amplified. Storyville would assure its continuation into the twentieth.

CHAPTER TWO

The Quadroon Connection

The Quadroon connexions in New Orleans are all but universal,
as I was assured on the spot by ladies who cannot be mistaken.

—HARRIET MARTINEAU, *Society in America*

Rich men came there from all parts of the world to dig those
beautiful Creole prostitutes. . . . And pay big money.

—LOUIS ARMSTRONG, in *Hear Me Talkin' to Ya*

Spencer Williams's famous song "Basin Street Blues" has several sets of lyrics.[1]
While most popular versions say Basin Street is the street where the "proud and
elite" folks meet, other versions include a racial description: "Basin Street is
the street where the light and dark folks meet," or, alternatively, "where the
black and white folks meet." Blacks and whites did indeed "meet" on Basin
Street, and throughout Storyville. At this very same time, the state and municipal authorities in Louisiana sought to prevent black and white folks from
meeting in other public places, such as, most famously, passenger trains.
The *Plessy v. Ferguson* case originated in New Orleans as a challenge to racial
segregation.

Homer Plessy was a member of New Orleans's Creole of color community,
a community that rooted its prestige in ancestry and free forebears; the case
that bears his name originated in New Orleans as a challenge to racial segregation and the "color line," and marked an end of sorts to a long tradition,
dating back to the earliest days of American rule. New Orleans, in addition
to its myriad cultures of transgression, hosted a particular strain of radical
republicanism, developed from French and Haitian revolutionary principles, married to American Revolutionary ideals. This transatlantic, circum-

Caribbean union gave birth to the clearest articulation of the case for universal (i.e., nonracial) human rights in the American South, culminating with *Plessy v. Ferguson.* In that case, Plessy's personal history and community heritage were reduced to a crude racial designation: he was an "octoroon." At the end of the case, even that designation was rendered obsolete: "one drop" of "black blood" made him "colored." The only significant distinction, then, was between "white" and "black," and no longer between "light" and "dark." Yet in Storyville, in the immediate aftermath of the Supreme Court decision, women from all over were marketed as "octoroons." Lulu White, the "Diamond Queen," was the most prominent among them. "Octoroons," the feminine-gendered, publicly perceived (in white society) remnant of Homer Plessy's prior identity continued to draw business to the district for its twenty-year existence.

The *Plessy v. Ferguson* decision allowed states to set a color line in law. Storyville advertised sex across the color line. Homer Plessy was an "octoroon" from New Orleans. Octoroons were Storyville's special attraction. After the Supreme Court sanctioned racial segregation, Plessy was simply "colored." Storyville continued to put forth and profit from this octoroon status for two more decades. What are we to make of this? In considering the continuing allure of mixed-race women and sex across the color line in Storyville after *Plessy,* this chapter discusses the history of the New Orleans Creoles of color —a multifaceted community with a genuine group identity—their struggles for equality and citizenship, and the ultimate failure of their efforts. The history of the Creoles of color is juxtaposed to the popular image of mixed-race women in New Orleans, created by authors and travelers throughout the early nineteenth century, and the reprisal of that image at the close of the century in Storyville.

And so, the history of the Creoles of color highlights the crucial importance of gender in understanding cultural transformations of the meaning of "race." The same "drop" of "black blood" that relegated men like Homer Plessy to the second-class train cars elevated women like Lulu White to the first-class bordellos in Storyville.

Plessy v. Ferguson

The *Plessy v. Ferguson* case illustrates the considerable influence of the Creoles of color in New Orleans, and simultaneously dramatizes the tragic denouement of their decades-long effort to achieve legal recognition of their manhood and their equality. At the turn of the twentieth century, this population of historically free people of color, the *gens de couleur libres,* remained part of the New Orleans "imaginary," which we may view as a massive text for describing the erotic female, available for a price to wealthy white men.[2] We will see this text made flesh in Storyville. But for now it is useful to review briefly the outlines of the landmark Supreme Court case. To do so is to highlight the men who challenged segregation and saw their challenge through to its ignominious end, the enshrining of segregation and a biracial caste system.

When the separate car bill was first introduced into the Louisiana legislature in 1890, as Charles Lofgren writes, "resistance coalesced immediately."[3] The recently formed American Citizens' Equal Rights Association denounced the law, asserting that it violated the first principle of American liberty, that all men were created equal. They maintained that "citizenship is national and has no color."[4] Neither the House nor the Senate paid heed to the group's "appeal to principle," as each chamber passed the measure, the Senate doing so over the opposition votes of its eighteen black members.[5]

In the fall of 1891, two members of the American Citizens' Equal Rights Association attacked the law in the pages of *The Crusader.* Louis Martinet, the founder of the paper, and Rodolphe Desdunes, a clerk at the Customs Office, set out to test the constitutionality of the law, hoping, obviously, that the Supreme Court would find segregation by race unconstitutional. Both were influential Creoles of color. Under the instigation of Aristide Mary, another longtime crusader for equal rights, they set up the Citizens' Committee to Test the Constitutionality of the Separate Car Law. They brought in Albion Tourgée as their lead counsel. Tourgée was a northern judge who had come down South after the Civil War. He had been a radical egalitarian before the war and he had made a name for himself not only as a judge and a political writer, but as a novelist. Tourgée's most famous novel, *A Fool's Errand, by One of the Fools,* solidified his reputation as a radical advocate for equal rights.[6] In the novel, Tourgée uses the trope of the mixed-race figure to challenge the nation's racial dualism.[7] In formulating his legal strategy against Louisiana's segregation law, Tourgée's first choice of a plaintiff was a very light-skinned woman. The use of a woman was rejected and they chose instead a very light-skinned man, Daniel Desdunes, Rodolphe's son, to challenge not only the specific statute, but the very notion of legal distinctions based on "race" or "color."[8]

Daniel Desdunes boarded an interstate train. Just weeks before his trial date, however, the Louisiana Supreme Court ruled that state segregationist laws could not apply on interstate trains because of interstate commerce laws, and so Desdunes's case was decided favorably.[9] The American Citizens' Equal Rights Association needed a new test case.

Homer Plessy was a friend of the Desduneses. He was a shoemaker by trade, and a politically active member of the Creole of color community.[10] In the spring of 1892, he bought a first-class ticket and boarded a train traveling from New Orleans to Covington, completely within the state of Louisiana. When he insisted on riding in the white first-class car, he was arrested. The arrest was arranged, as Homer Plessy was an "octoroon" in whom, as his lawyers said, "'the mixture of colored blood [was] not discernible.'"[11] The case moved slowly through the local criminal district court, to the state supreme court, the appellate court, and finally, the U.S. Supreme Court. Among other arguments, Tourgée argued that because Homer Plessy was seven-eighths white, the separate car law illegally deprived him of a kind of "property" in whiteness. More specifically, Tourgée argued that the *reputation* of being a white man was the "master-key" to the "golden door of opportunity" in America, a white-dominant, racist society. Forcing Homer Plessy to sit in the "negro" section deprived him of that *reputation* and closed the door.

> How much would it be *worth* to a young man entering upon the practice of law, to be regarded as a *white* man rather than a colored one? Six-sevenths of the population are white. Nineteen-twentieths of the property of the country is owned by white people. Ninety-nine hundredths of the business opportunities are in the control of white people. These propositions are rendered even more startling by the intensity of feeling which excludes the colored man from the friendship and companionship of the white man. . . . Under these conditions, is it possible to conclude that the *reputation of being white* is not property? Indeed, is it not the most valuable sort of property, being the master-key that unlocks the golden door of opportunity?[12]

While Tourgée did not argue that the law literally enslaved Plessy, he did argue that in labeling Plessy "black" (especially since Plessy *looked* "white") in a white-dominated society the law imposed on him a badge of servitude, and thus violated the Thirteenth and Fourteenth Amendments to the Constitution.[13]

Tourgée's own racial sensibilities, his twin obsessions with racial justice and people of indeterminate race, were out of step with the Court's already well-formed opinions about the nature of race and its role in society. Even

Justice John Marshall Harlan's laudable dissent did not doubt that there were two separate—and unequal—races.[14] In the end, the Supreme Court's decision brushed aside Tourgée's arguments and disagreed that the law deprived Plessy of his property in whiteness: a person was simply white or he was colored. Indeed, Justice Henry Billings Brown averred that "distinction" in this regard did not equal discrimination.[15]

Justice Brown based his opinion on ancient, inherent, and immutable differences, that were, in truth, none of the above.[16] He concluded by stating that "legislation is powerless to eradicate racial instincts, or to abolish distinctions based upon physical differences, and the attempt to do so can only result in accentuating the difficulties of the present situation." In the case of Homer Plessy and many of his peers, the "physical difference" referred to did not accord with outward appearance.[17] Yet the Creoles of color, and Tourgée, had failed to convince the Supreme Court of the absurdity of those distinctions. Joseph Logsdon and Caryn Cossé Bell write of the decision: "Even most of the stalwarts who helped pursue the case were too discouraged or fearful to continue any further protests."[18] The citizens' committees folded up, thinking it "better to suffer in silence than to attract attention to their misfortune and weakness" (a pessimistic and forlorn Rodolphe Desdunes later wrote).[19]

Meanwhile, the defeat of the Creole leadership did nothing to lessen the "violent determination" of the white supremacists "to subordinate black Louisianians." Within a few years of the *Plessy* decision, Louisianians who, regardless of their specific heritage, were now known as "colored," "Negro," or "black," lost the franchise and their access to public education (among other gains made during Reconstruction). Even the Catholic Church, which had always allowed white and non-white Louisianians to worship together, imposed the color line.[20] The 1890s was a decade of struggle and segregation, the most racially divisive and violent decade in New Orleans's postwar history.[21] It culminated with an explosive race riot that pitted the New Orleans police force and many white citizens against Robert Charles, a migrant laborer from Mississippi. After Charles was shot and killed, white New Orleanians continued to wreak havoc, violently attacking black New Orleanians (or those they perceived as black), until, as the *Daily Picayune* reported, the "streets of the city ran with blood."[22] The leaderless mobs "moved first one way and then another. The supreme sentiment was to kill negroes."[23] New Orleans entered the twentieth century as a racially segregated city riven by racial tension, animosity, and violence, much like most other southern cities. And yet, Storyville blatantly promoted sex across the color line, advertising "octoroons" as the district's special draw. Interracial sex, especially with light-skinned, mixed-race women, had been an indelible aspect of New Orleans's unique antebellum culture; it was given new life as entrepreneurs marketed miscegenation amid the racial hatred and violence at the dawn of the Jim Crow era.

Tragic Octoroons

Tourgée's legal strategy and the logic of his argument may have owed something to the literary tradition of the "tragic octoroon." This was a significant, influential antebellum genre, and it did not die with the war, but rather became a vehicle for a national dialogue about race and the potentially tragic consequences of interracial sex. Tourgée was one of its literary practitioners. Authors on both sides of the equal rights debate employed the figure of the tragic octoroon to illustrate either the absolute necessity of racial separation, or, conversely, the tragedy (and absurdity) of racism. The mixed-race figure, often ignorant of her (or sometimes his) racial status and the origins of her birth, was a powerful symbol for American society well into the twentieth century.[24]

What might be called a national obsession with light-skinned, mixed-race women found its first mass expression in abolitionist literature. After 1831, abolitionists began to focus their attention on the sexual side of bondage.[25] They elaborated on sexual slavery, especially of women who were themselves the products of interracial sex and, thus, of sexual subordination.[26] The iconic image of the light-skinned sexual slave girl emerged in part from this new focus in abolitionist writings and popular sentimental fiction. The dominant literary genre of this type told the story of the "tragic octoroon." The novels, plays, and poems themed around the "tragic octoroon" inveighed against a slave system that corrupted the family, encouraged interracial sex and adultery, and fostered hypocrisy.[27] The evil of slavery in these tales was tied to the carelessness and greed of the masters: the planter was always indebted or overdrawn. The octoroon was always young and exceptionally beautiful, with perfect manners and an elegant demeanor. She has most often been "raised as a lady in the household of her father, who is, notwithstanding his sexual vagaries, descended from the best blood of the Old South."[28] The tragic twist most often comes with her father's death. Invariably, he "has not seen to things. His concern with attending to pleasure rather than to duties . . . betrays his daughter, who possesses only the slightest evidence of Negro blood, to the auction block."[29] A life of toil would indeed be tragic for a heroine who has grown up cosseted in aristocratic privilege, but the octoroon faced a fate worse than labor in the fields. The octoroon's beauty, her whiteness, her virtue—all the things that made her most resemble white women of the upper and upper-middle classes—made her especially attractive to the trader in "fancy girls." The "tragic octoroon" was fated to sexual slavery.

This literature contributed to the image of New Orleans in America and abroad. It relied upon and reinforced previously existing knowledge of the city, further cementing the association of New Orleans with mixed-race women, particularly as sex objects. New Orleans was already well known for its slave auctions featuring light-skinned women for sale as sexual slaves or concubines. And although New Orleans hosted a much bigger market in male slaves and dark-skinned slaves, it derived its fame from these so-called "fancy girls." Then there was the city's unique adjunct to the slave market, the quadroon balls, in which free mixed-race women (i.e., women Creoles of color) met and contracted with white men to be their mistresses. These related sex trades incensed abolitionists and gave them a hook for their antislavery argument. The tragic light-skinned slave girl encoded and embodied these related evils. Through the "tragic octoroon" literature, New Orleans was increasingly linked with interracial sex, the moral decrepitude of slave traders, and planter lust. Where else could one find so clear an example of the corrupting influence of slavery? For those who opposed slavery, the traffic in "fancy girls" showed how a system of absolute power over others promoted sexual licentiousness and adultery.[30] Furthermore, the lust provoked by slavery came dangerously close to violating the propriety in the master's own home, so nearly white were its objects.[31] Henry Wadsworth Longfellow's 1842 poem "The Quadroon Girl" exemplifies this.

> The Slaver in the broad lagoon
> Lay moored with idle sail;
> He waited for the rising moon,
> And for the evening gale.
>
> Under the shore his boat was tied,
> And all her listless crew
> Watched the gray alligator slide
> Into the still bayou.

Odors of orange-flowers, and spice,
Reached them from time to time,
Like airs that breathe from Paradise
Upon a world of crime.

The Planter, under his roof of thatch,
Smoked thoughtfully and slow;
The Slaver's thumb was on the latch,
He seemed in haste to go.

He said, "My ship at anchor rides
In yonder broad lagoon;
I only wait the evening tides,
And the rising of the moon."

Before them, with her face upraised,
In timid attitude,
Like one half curious, half amazed,
A Quadroon maiden stood.

Her eyes were large, and full of light,
Her arms and neck were bare;
No garment she wore save a kirtle bright,
And her own long, raven hair.

And on her lips there played a smile
As holy, meek, and faint,
As lights in some cathedral aisle
The features of a saint.

"The soil is barren,—the farm is old,"
The thoughtful planter said;
Then looked upon the Slaver's gold,
And then upon the maid.

His heart within him was at strife
With such acccurséd gains:
For he knew whose passions gave her life,
Whose blood ran in her veins.

But the voice of nature was too weak;
He took the glittering gold!
Then pale as death grew the maiden's cheek,
Her hands as icy cold.

> The Slaver led her from the door,
> He led her by the hand,
> To be his slave and paramour
> In a strange and distant land!

The planter, here clearly situated in Louisiana, sells his own daughter into sexual servitude. As she goes, she turns white and cold, her deathly pallor signaling not only the spiritual death brought on by her father's betrayal, but her own anticipation of the fate "worse than death" that awaited her.[32]

In *Uncle Tom's Cabin,* first published in 1852, Harriet Beecher Stowe created two mixed-race slave women to emphasize the baseness and cruelty of slavery. The reader first encounters Eliza when she enters the parlor of her master, Mr. Shelby, who is in the midst of negotiations with a slave trader. Stowe describes Eliza as the picture of feminine perfection, with her "rich, full dark eye," "long lashes," and "ripples of long silky black hair."

> The brown of her complexion gave way on the cheek to a perceptible flush, which deepened as she saw the gaze of the strange man fixed upon her in bold and undisguised admiration. Her dress was of the neatest possible fit, and set off to advantage her finely molded shape;—a delicately formed hand and a trim foot and ankle were items of appearance that did not escape the quick eye of the trader, well used to run up at a glance the points of a fine female article.[33]

Stowe counterposes Eliza's femininity with her status as a commodity; she blushes at the trader's attention, yet she is an object, an "article" of trade. The trader offers to sell her for Shelby in New Orleans, where, as he says, a man might make his fortune on a girl like her.[34] There was no doubt as to her fate in such a situation. In spite of the "brown of her complexion," Eliza was fair enough to pass for white, which she does later in the novel. "You would scarcely know the woman from a white one," remarked one of the characters on the lookout for Eliza, who was escaping to Canada.[35]

Cassy, the novel's other tragic light-skinned slave woman, first appears in the novel tending to the broken body of Uncle Tom. Viciously beaten and whipped by Simon Legree, Tom nonetheless encourages Cassy to have faith in the ultimate benevolence of God. Cassy's bitterness is apparent as she tells Tom her story, which is the generic recitation of the octoroon's story. She was raised in luxury, educated in a convent, and brought up to be a lady. "My mother was a slave woman, and my father had always meant to set me free; but he had not done it, and so I was set down on the list" to be sold after he died unexpectedly. "Nobody ever expects that a strong, healthy man is going to die. My father was a well man only four hours before he died" of cholera, which he contracted in New Orleans. The estate sold Cassy, aged fourteen years old, to a man who swore he loved her and who treated her well, even luxuriously, as his concubine. This arrangement lasted until her master was corrupted in New Orleans by gambling, lust, and betrayal—in other words, by the city itself. Traded from one white man to another, she was used as a sexual slave and lost all the children she bore through these relationships to the slave trade, including, as it turns out, Eliza.[36] Cassy's plight as a slave was compounded by the tragedy of her dismembered domesticity. The horror of losing all her children to the slave system drove her to commit the ultimate crime as a mother: she murdered her own child to save him from the evils of slavery.[37] The catalyst for the tragic turns in Cassy's life was New Orleans. Through disease, and then through debauch, New Orleans ruined the only men Cassy ever loved.

Dion Boucicault's 1859 play, *The Octoroon; or, Life in Louisiana,* tells the story of a young beauty named Zoe, the daughter of a large plantation owner. Zoe has been brought up and educated to be a lady, in accordance with her father's class, and presumably his intention has been to free her. Her father, typically, has neglected his affairs; his sudden death reveals insolvency. His wife decides to sell Zoe in order to retain the family plantation, and a Yankee slave trader covets Zoe, desiring to make her his mistress. For the fair and virtuous Zoe, the prospect of life as a slave and a concubine to the evil trader drives her to suicide.

In the early scenes of Boucicault's play, Zoe's cousin George, who had been living abroad in France, and is not aware that Zoe is an octoroon and a slave, falls deeply in love with her. The feeling is mutual, but when George asks Zoe to marry him, she becomes inconsolable. Gesturing to a "bluish tinge" in her eyes and fingernails, Zoe proclaims:

> That is the ineffaceable curse of Cain. Of the blood that feeds my heart, one drop in eight is black—bright red as the rest may be, that one drop poisons all the flood; those seven bright drops give me love like yours—hope like yours—ambition like yours—life hung with passions like dew drops on the morning flowers; but the one black drop gives me despair, for I'm an unclean thing—forbidden by the laws—I'm an Octoroon![38]

Denied her own true love, not to mention her freedom, and threatened with certain rape and sexual slavery, Zoe takes poison and dies, turning white (like Longfellow's quadroon) in the process.[39]

The whiteness of the octoroon—those "seven drops" of "white blood"—made her a powerful symbol for northern, white, middle- and upper-class women, the primary audience for the "tragic octoroon" literature. Most white women occupied precarious and dependent positions in the nineteenth century. They had little or no legal means to protect themselves, and for the most part they were, in effect, the property of their husbands.[40] In the story of the tragic octoroon they saw a situation that resonated with their own.[41] Such fiction united the worries over chattel slavery with an abiding concern for women, the home, and the family. Thus, in reading *Uncle Tom's Cabin*, for example, white women cried over the tragedies of broken-hearted motherhood, the death of a child, or forced sexual intercourse—all of which occurred in northern homes, too. While in the novels, plays, and poems, slavery lay at the root of all these tragedies, the genre appealed even to women with no memory or experience of actual slavery (either as mistress or slave). The representation of the evils of slavery through the body of a "white or nearly white" woman allowed the readers to embrace *abolition* without embracing *blacks* or reckoning with their own racist sensibilities.[42] The authors of the tragic octoroon fiction, in their focus on the white or nearly white woman, excluded from their protest the more ordinary black persons whom slave owners whipped, abused, sexually exploited, and tore from their families. The octoroon's tragedy, after all, resided in her whiteness (or her secret blackness), and it was a reversal of fortune, not unremitting servitude, that gave her story its stinging pathos. She had been the picture of privileged perfection, and then, suddenly, she was a slave. Nevertheless, it is also so, as Jules Zanger argues, that "the very existence of the octoroon convicted the slaveholder of prostituting his slaves and of selling his own children for profit."[43]

Let us return for a moment to the *Plessy* case. Tourgée's argument articulated with this long tradition of abolitionist literature, which had influenced his own writings on race in the postbellum period. Homer Plessy, a "white or nearly white" man, stood poised to reap the opportunities afforded by his education, his status, his heritage—he, too, descended from the best blood of the Old South (or France's colonial Caribbean empire). By virtue of that blood, he had reached the "golden door of opportunity." The Separate Car Act took his key to the door by labeling him a "colored" man. Plessy, like Eliza, Cassy, and Zoe, was not "colored" in the sense that slaves were or had been; they looked white, and in Plessy's case he was among the elite Afro-French-Caribbean-Creoles of color in New Orleans. The new law subjected him, and all members of that community, who had not themselves been enslaved, nor even "black" according to the historical race distinctions in New Orleans, to a tragic reversal of fortune. The special, negotiated status of the Creoles of color disintegrated as they were grouped with "negroes," freedmen, and their children. Plessy, in the logic of Tourgée's argument, was a tragic octoroon. The argument failed to resonate with the Court in the way that the literary genre resonated with the northern bourgeoisie before the war. Moreover, in Justice Brown's rejection of Tourgée's logic he said that a legal distinction between the races did not amount to discrimination—segregation was not slavery and it did not violate the equal protection clause of the Fourteenth Amendment. Thus Brown saw the new law as mere confirmation of nature, not the contravention of New Orleans history. Perhaps Tourgée would have found a more sympathetic audience if his plaintiff had been a woman, as he had originally desired.

New Orleans publicized transgressions that the rest of the South repressed. Its flamboyant sex market in slave women magnified the sexual license that underlay plantation society and which was the special subject of tragic octoroon literature.[44] Many planters used slaves for sex. This was the prerogative of planters, elaborating the privileges of patriarchy in an immediate and tangible way. But in New Orleans, as with the slave market, the institutionalization of interracial sexual subordination had a special character. The city's longstanding reputation for general licentiousness and sex across the color line, combined with its colonial heritage and subtropical climate, lent it an air of particular debauch. The abolitionist discourse of the "tragic octoroon" at once highlighted the near-universality of sexual subordination under slavery and focused special attention on the light-skinned victims of planter lust. It also fixed New Orleans as the natural milieu for these degradations, associating the city in thousands of minds with the fancy trade, octoroons, and interracial sex.[45] As we will see, Storyville would later capitalize on just this association.

The slave market was a crucial element in the impression New Orleans gave as luxuriously debauched. Specifically, the spectacular slave auctions, held in the rotundas of the grand hotels, where light-skinned enslaved women were sold among field hands and furniture, dramatized in real life the horror of the tragic octoroon. Eliza Potter, a hairdresser from the North, came upon one such auction on the steps of the St. Charles Hotel. She described it in her 1859 memoir. "On going down [the stairs], I heard a great shout below me. I stopped on the stairs and looked down in the rotunda," and there it was. Passersby could stop and watch, and Potter "stood for some time" as slaves "were put up and sold off to the highest bidder." The market made Potter, herself a free woman of color from Ohio, uncomfortable; she was anxious "to get away from this place, where I have seen people as white as white could be and as black as black could get, put up and sold in this elegant hotel," but she repeatedly found it impossible to stay away.[46]

The spectacular auctions were designed to draw people in. "In antebellum New Orleans in particular," writes literary critic and theater historian Joseph Roach, "slave auctions proved a popular and highly theatrical spectacle."[47] The St. Louis Hotel provided music "from a regular orchestra," just one of its many "inducements to spend money." The slaves were made to wear "theatrical costumes—formal wear for the male slaves and brightly-colored dresses for the women."[48] Of course, slave selling was not limited to these venues. In his 1931 history of the domestic slave trade, Frederic Bancroft wrote that New Orleans hosted "the most busy and picturesque slave emporium . . . [it was] the modern Delos of the trade for the lower Southwest."[49] In contrast to the equally visible slave markets of Charleston and Montgomery, in New Orleans slave trading "had a peculiar dash: it rejoiced in its display and prosperity; it felt unashamed, almost proud." In well-trafficked streets, "there were slave-depots, show rooms, show-windows, broad verandas and even neighborhoods where gayly dressed slaves were prominently exhibited." In New Orleans, "markets and buyers were most numerous, money was most plentiful, profits were largest."[50] *Harper's Weekly* described the scene on a New Orleans sidewalk, where slaves dressed in "their Sunday best" were "placed in a row in a quiet thoroughfare, where, without interrupting the traffic, they may command a good chance of transient custom, they stand through a great part of the day, subject to the inspection of the purchasing or non-purchasing passing crowd."[51]

The slave market constituted the "Soul of New Orleans," in the words of James Davidson, a Virginian traveling through the South in the 1830s. "He [who] does not visit it cannot [have] seen all of New Orleans."[52] It was also a tourist attraction. According to Bancroft, "to inspect some of the depots, pens, yards, booths or salesrooms and to attend a large public sale of slaves was one of the first aims of visitors from afar." The city easily accommodated the tourists' desire. In the years 1856–1860, "there were at least 25 such places within a few squares of the St. Charles Hotel." Still more markets dotted the French Quarter, "mostly on Esplanade street near the corner of Chartres or in the neighborhood of Exchange Place and St. Louis street."[53] The New Orleans slave market was thus not strictly limited by a bounded or clearly designated place. In addition to the central slave market, there were smaller marts spread through the neighborhoods; there were also slave shops and, of course, the auctions. And slavery also drove the city's other markets and deepened its position as a trading port and commercial hub.

If the slave market in New Orleans had, to repeat Bancroft's phrase, "a peculiar dash," this was particularly true of the "fancy trade," which exclusively sold light-skinned women for sex. Though present in nearly all southern slave markets, in New Orleans, "where thousands of sporting men and voluptuaries lived and other thousands came for the racing season, the Carnival and dissipation," the fancy trade market was tenfold as large. Sometimes "fancy girls" sat in shop windows to attract passersby, who would enter the shop and ask how much they cost. A visitor to antebellum New Orleans noted "a handsome quadroon girl, gaily dressed and adorned with ribbons and jewels, [who] sat in a show-window to attract attention." He observed a planter looking to buy her asking the price and, on being told, "he shook his head, leered at the slave, and said, with an oath, 'Too Expensive.'"[54]

Some "fancy girls" sold for $2,000 at a time when ordinary slaves cost well under $1,000. Traders bought pretty, light-skinned women at regional slave markets and then resold them in New Orleans at a great profit. One woman was bought in South Carolina for $600 and then sold in New Orleans for $1,500.[55] The "New Orleans Slave Sale Sample," writes Walter Johnson, "shows prices paid for women that occasionally reached three hundred percent of the median prices paid in a given year—prices above $1500 in the first decade of the century and ranging from $2000 to $5233 afterwards."[56] The fancy trade auction gave the New Orleans slave market its singular quality. As Johnson writes, "the open competition of an auction—a contest between white men played out on the body of an enslaved woman—was the essence of the transaction."[57] Joseph Roach calls the St. Louis Hotel, where such auctions took place, "a kind of homosocial pleasure dome with overlapping commercial and leisure attractions." The popular auctions and special markets in "fancy girls" were held "in an atmosphere not only charged with white privilege but with male privilege" and were, Roach writes, "pornographic."[58]

Slave masters sought light-skinned female sexual slaves for their own gratification and as symbols of their mastery. For purposes other than sex or show, however, it was in fact harder to sell lighter-skinned slaves, either male or female. Traders and planters considered them to be delicate, not capable of working as hard, and more susceptible to disease. Because most of them could pass for white, planters feared they would run away. According to Michael Tadman, slave traders generally thought that "black negroes were more desirable and freer from disease" than "yellow" slaves, and even classed "yellow women" with other "second class" slaves.[59] "Fancy girls" were the great exception to the general rule of the slave market that blacker was better.[60] The whiter a pretty young slave woman was, the more value she had in the "fancy" market. Johnson describes them as "the embodied opposites of those who were sought as field hands." In an economic system based on slave labor, these women were at best marginal to production. In a social system based on "race," these women were closer to masters than slaves. They were "visions of sexual desire and the luxury of being able to pay for its fulfillment—enslaved versions of mastery itself."[61]

"Fancy" here has several meanings. On the one hand, the women were not meant for hard labor; they were not practical, but rather emblems, decorations. On the other, they represented the "fancies" of the men who bought them—their desires for sex as well as for status.[62] Not only to the wealthy planters, but also "to gamblers, traders, saloonkeepers, turfmen and debauchees," according to Bancroft, "owning a 'fancy girl' was a luxurious ideal."[63] Slavery created its own kind of conspicuous consumption.[64] Light-skinned, attractive slave women signified the power of their owners. As Johnson writes, "The higher prices were a measure not only of desire but of dominance. No other man could afford to pay so much; no other man's desires would be so spectacularly fulfilled."[65]

The commercial enterprise of the market inculcated a kind of artifice on the part of the consumer or purchaser of goods—even here where the "goods" were people. Slave masters and potential slave masters performed independence, manhood, and honor at the slave market. In other words, they performed mastery through the purchase of slaves. Owning, buying, and selling slaves—and doing it well—thus (perhaps ironically) helped constitute the antebellum Southern republican self.[66] That is to say, all white men were putative equals at the slave market. In this context, choosing slaves wisely was of paramount importance. In a culture steeped in notions of honor and the importance of reputation, one who chose well earned a reputation for aptitude in selecting productive, obedient slaves; a man who performed poorly proved his lack of worth.[67]

The theatricality of the slave market was multivalent, and Johnson's play on words when he describes "Acts of Sale" bespeaks the performative element for all participants.[68] Slaves were forced to play the part, to display themselves as simultaneously good workers and submissive servants. They were made to act out their own commodification; the failure to comply, to act the part well, could result in severe punishments. At the same time, slaves acted out different, self-cast roles in order to direct or derail their own sales. For instance, they might become despondent when questioned by a potential buyer—or more dramatically, they might mutilate themselves.[69]

The New Orleans fancy trade and its sex slave auctions were so salient for northern whites that Henry Ward Beecher, Harriet Beecher Stowe's brother, imitated them to promote abolition at his Plymouth Church Congregation in Brooklyn, New York. In a strange twist on the competition of the slave auction, Beecher hosted a kind of emancipation competition, goading his congregants to purchase slaves in order to set them free. He also held mock auctions of light-skinned slave children, holding up their photographs for the church-goers to see, to raise money to purchase their freedom.[70]

Quadroon Balls

In addition to the shops and slave markets in "fancies," there were yet other sex markets for light-skinned women of color. At quadroon balls white men selected from an array of beautiful, cultivated, light-skinned Creoles of color. Visitors who attended quadroon balls and recorded their experiences waxed poetic about the sociology of color distinctions, reinforcing the idea of caste within the Creole of color community. The lighter-skinned "quadroons" were the more haughty, superior, and exclusive. They were, wrote Frederick Law Olmsted, "too much superior to the negroes, in general, to associate with them, and are not allowed by law, or the popular prejudice, to marry white people." Indeed, when travelers discussed the Creoles of color, they were most often discussing the women. "They are generally pretty, often handsome," wrote Olmsted, who had "rarely, if ever, met more beautiful women than the one or two whom I saw by chance, in the streets. Their beauty and attractiveness being their fortune, they cultivate and cherish with diligence every charm or accomplishment they are possessed of."[71] Among the great mélange of "races" and nations in New Orleans, the so-called quadroon women stood out. "They are better formed, and have a more graceful and elegant carriage than Americans in general, while they seem to have commonly inherited or acquired much of the taste and skill, in the selection and arrangement, and the way of wearing special ornaments, that is the especial distinction of the women of Paris."[72] Another observer wrote, "The quadroon is a very bright mulatto. They have the finest eyes and freshest skin I have ever seen."[73] Their families often sent them abroad to be educated in the arts and manners of the aristocratic classes. Yet, the law forbade marriage between free people of color and whites. A visiting noble summed up their situation in the 1820s: "Marriage between the white and coloured population is forbidden by the law of the state. And as the quadroons on their part regard the negroes and mulattoes with contempt, and will not mix with them, so nothing remains for them but to be the friends, as it is termed, of the white men."[74] Harriet Martineau, the British social reformer, elaborated on this state of affairs: "The Quadroon girls of New Orleans are brought up by their mothers to be what they have been; the mistresses of white gentlemen." They scorned men of their caste, "objecting to them, 'ils sont dégoutants!' The girls are highly educated, externally, and are, probably as beautiful and accomplished a set of women as can be found."[75]

This sort of attitude may well have characterized an elite segment of the Creoles of color. But the distortion is twofold. Creoles of color did send their children to France to be educated, the young men as well as the women, so it is not true that only the girls were educated thus. And most often the Creoles of color married one another, in contradistinction to the observations of visitors.

Olmsted described the workings of the institution of interracial concubinage, retrospectively called *plaçage,* French for "placement," which was larger than the quadroon balls.[76] "When a [white] man makes a declaration of love to a girl of this class, . . . she will usually refer the applicant to her mother." The mother then inquired as to the material circumstances of the gentleman, ascertaining whether he had the means to support a family, and "if satisfied with him, in these and other respects, requires from him security that he will support her daughter in a style suitable to the habits in which she has been bred." The mother usually insisted on a provision in the contract should the liaison come to an end for "a certain additional sum for each of the children she shall then have. . . . The wealth, thus secured, will, of course, vary . . . *with the value of the lady in the market.*"[77]

The *placée* was a liminal figure in a double sense: she existed in between white and black, as well as in a nether world between freedom and slavery. She was not a slave, but neither did she enjoy perfect liberty.[78] The quadroon mistress was thus in a way a quasi-free version of the fancy girl: she was prized for her fairness, and her occupation was clear. In reality, however, the relationships that fell within the definition of *plaçage* "ranged the gamut," in Shirley Thompson's phrase, from temporary concubinage to lifelong common law marriage.[79] Yet some observers compared *placées* to prostitutes rather than slaves or wives. Latrobe remarked that the "quadroons ... the light mulattoes of this country ... pass their life in a prostitution."[80] James Davidson wrote that he had "often heard of the beauty of the quadroons. I found them pretty. They are a very amiable looking people, and have the appearance of being virtuous; but they are generally prostitutes and kept *Mistresses*."[81]

Davidson captured the ambiguity within which these women lived their lives, within, that is, the ideologies that worked to create the kinds of images sampled here. Davidson's remark that the women appeared virtuous, but were not so, echoes Martineau's judgment, above, that the women were educated "externally." It is almost as if to say that their skin, the part of them that appeared "white" and thus virtuous, was educated, but their "blood" was not; such an education could only be superficial, deceptive, and therefore threatening (or exciting). Such a dichotomy, setting skin against blood, appearance against essence, captures an element of the racialized sexual ideology of the plantation South, embodied in the contradictory body of the mixed-race woman. In this ideology, the black woman, most often a slave, became as a "Jezebel," the diametric opposite of the white woman, who was supposed to be pure, pious, domestic, and submissive.[82] The combination of the two fictive stereotypes in an already highly sexualized environment created an amalgam of purity and wickedness, domesticity and desire. If all black women (slave or free) were "Jezebels" and all white women were pure, the combination of black and white blood, in a white-looking body, created a fantasy of (black) sexuality pushing against the restraining perimeter of white skin. The actualization of this fantasy, in the quadroon, was also the physical elaboration of this racialized sexual discourse; she was (literally) born of it.

Martineau asserted that almost all white men of a certain class had *placées*. "The Quadroon connexions in New Orleans are all but universal, as I was assured on the spot by ladies who cannot be mistaken." Martineau here repeats a myth about New Orleans to make a broad sociological claim, that all wealthy white men procured and kept mixed-race mistresses as an established rite of passage.[83] "Every young man early selects one, and establishes her in one of those pretty and peculiar houses, whole rows of which may be seen in the Remparts [*sic*]. The connexion now and then lasts for life: usually for several years."[84] James Davidson noted, too, that "young men and single men of wealth have each a quadroon for his exclusive use. They are furnished with a Chamber and sitting room and servants, and the comforts and elegancies of life. It generally costs from $1500 to $2000 a year to keep a quadroon."[85]

According to this myth, only white men of means attended quadroon balls, and quadroon balls were the only venues where such relationships formed. "At the quadroon ball, only coloured ladies are admitted, the men of that caste, be it understood, are shut out by the white gentlemen." Yet, "the quadroons [themselves] are almost entirely white: from their skin no one would detect their origin; nay many of them have as fair a complexion as many of the haughty creole females."[86] The reification and sexualization of the "one drop" of black blood in a white body had long since expanded beyond the slave market, especially in New Orleans. The physical appearance of the women at the balls was a testament to the longstanding tradition of interracial concubinage and *plaçage.* Whereas "formerly they were known by their black hair and eyes," by 1825 there were "completely fair quadroon males and females."[87] When Alexis de Tocqueville came to New Orleans in the 1830s, he took notes: "Quadroon Ball. Strange sight: all the men white, all the women colored, or at least of African blood. Single tie created by immorality between the two races. A sort of bazaar."[88] Duke Bernhard of Saxe-Weimar-Eisenach found the quadroon balls "much more decent than the [whites only] masked ball. The coloured ladies were under the eyes of their mothers, they were well and gracefully dressed, and conducted themselves with much propriety and modesty. . . . The price of admission is fixed at two dollars, so only persons of the better class can appear there."[89] James Davidson, the Virginian, attended a quadroon ball but had quite a different impression than the duke. He went "out of curiosity, and unmasked." He wrote about his experience, "Here are all sorts of characters except virtuous women." He observed the dancing and mingling, commenting that he "frequently saw a gentleman of decent appearance dancing with a Quadroon." To Davidson this was "somewhat revolting." The following morning, he went to church to do "pennance" for his previous evening's visit.[90] Perhaps the ball Davidson attended was not as exclusive or decorous as the one Bernhard had attended ten years before, because lesser balls accommodated those who paid less to participate in a kind of cut-rate patriarchy.[91]

Upper-class white women tended to blame the women of color for the institution of *plaçage,* but still reserved some animus for the men who participated. Bernhard went secretly, so that he "might not utterly destroy my standing in New Orleans . . . [and get] a cold reception from the white ladies."[92] Not only the duke spoke of the anxious and gendered hostility between white Creoles and the "nearly white" Creoles of color.[93] Thus Fanny Trollope was told that there were "two distinct sets of people, both celebrated, in their way, for their social meetings and elegant entertainments . . . [the white] Creole families, who are chiefly planters and merchants, with their wives and daughters . . . [and] the excluded but amiable Quadroons."[94] The white Creoles were "an aristocratic people" who scorned "any connection with the quadroon population," wrote Davidson.[95]

It is not surprising that white Creole women of New Orleans despised the quadroons and octoroons, women Creoles of color who, in their estimation, tempted their white husbands with a commercialized form of interracial sex.[96] Women from abroad tended more to sympathize with the elite or visible mixed-race women in spite of the hatred they inspired in southern white women. Mrs. Houstoun, for example, admired the beauty of "all" New Orleans women but particularly noted "the rich dark cheek of the quadroon." She was "far more beautiful" than either the Anglo-American or the white Creole, Houstoun thought. Her beauty itself was an index of her oppression.

> The eloquent blood in her soft cheek speaks but too plainly of her despised descent. She seems to blush at the injustice of man, who visits upon her the sins of her fathers. The passer-by arrogantly bids her to stand aside, for he is holier than she; in bitter contempt, the women of the land shrink from her contact, and the large, sleepy eye, half hid by its curled fringes, is hardly raised, as gracefully and humbly she passes them by. Poor thing! what wonder, if, feeling that she is neglected and oppressed, she should turn in the desolation of her heart to other ties. Deprived too frequently of the many consolations of kindred affection; a solitary link in the chain of human sympathies—brotherless, friendless, alone! Let those who have never known what solitude of the heart is, speak harshly of the errors of the despised Quadroon. I can but pity her.[97]

For Houstoun, the very blush on the quadroon's cheek articulated the caste system, slavery, and the sexual underside of southern life. She pitied the quadroon for her solitude, her loneliness, her lack of cultural or familial support networks. Houstoun even forgave the quadroon girl for her "errors," on account of her social isolation, and thus, through her gesture of pity and understanding, also reinscribed the quadroon's erotic agency. By placing the blame on the women of color, and their "tradition" of concubinage, even sympathetic observers lost sight of the systematic victimization of slave and free women of color within the slave regime. Their bodies became metaphors for the pain of others. Harriet Martineau, for example, found *white women* to be the utmost victims of the slave system. Their degradation came "not from their own conduct, but from that of all other parties about them." The racial and sexual double standards fomented distrust and anxiety among wives. A white woman, she wrote, "sinks to be the ornamente [*sic*] of her husband's house, the domestic manager of his establishment, instead of being his all-sufficient friend."[98] Because of the light-skinned black woman, the ambiguous octoroon, the white wife herself became "only 'the chief slave of the harem.'"[99]

Interracial sex, sexual exploitation, and rape were endemic in the slave South, quite aside from New Orleans, and travelers learned of this as well on their journeys. One planter told Frederick Law Olmsted that he knew that there was "not an old plantation in which the grandchildren of the owner are not whipped in the field by his overseer.'"[100] New Orleans was famed for its tolerance and institutionalization of "miscegenation," and Storyville, in its turn, and in the wake of the *Plessy* decision, would revive this reputation. There, brothels specializing in octoroon women repackaged and commodified the longstanding image of the light-skinned black woman not as a slave, but *literally* as a prostitute.

But, of course, and quite contrary to the discursive construction of the quadroon woman, most free women of color in New Orleans did have brothers, fathers, friends—among them the men who would in time bring suit against the state in protest of the Separate Car Act. By the 1840s, the Creoles of color (the free people of color or *gens de couleur libres*) were an endogamous group. *Plaçage* took place beyond or alongside the boundaries of family and community, not in their stead. The free men of color debated the merits of the *plaçage* arrangements, recognizing that they gave women of their group a "unique opportunity to gain social and economic status," and yet feeling that "this status came at their [the men's] expense."[101] In 1845, in a book of protest poetry called *Les Cenelles,* French-speaking free men of color, influenced by French Romanticism and by revolutionary politics, recognized in *plaçage* a potent symbol of their own cultural degradation. They viewed the practice as an acquiescence to racial injustice that belittled their manhood and brought shame on the Creole of color population.[102] The collection of poems was one product of the expression of a highly literate and politically mobilized population, whose elite members traveled back and forth between Louisiana and France, and cherished their cultural heritage and distance from slavery.[103]

Travelers' accounts of the "fancy trade," quadroon balls, and *plaçage,* as well as the literature of the "tragic octoroon," all trafficked in a common image: the light-skinned, racially mixed woman as an object of white male desire. But it cannot be overstated that the prevailing image of the quadroon woman had "little to do with the day-to-day experience of the women," as the historian Virginia Gould has written. "Most of the racially mixed daughters and granddaughters of freed slave women married men of their group."[104] Free women of color derived their identities from their families, their extended kin, and their church, that is to say, the broader Creole of color community, and not the white men some of them were connected with.[105] So, if "quadroon connexions," to repeat Harriet Martineau's phrase, proved the norm for wealthy white men—a myth, to be sure, that exaggerated the importance of the institution and its role in New Orleans history—they were certainly not the norm for free women of color, many of whom rejected the institution.[106]

The Free People of Color: A Very Brief History

The Creoles of color constituted a society within and alongside Louisiana's larger population of whites and slaves. Complete with class distinctions and gradations of "race," the Creoles of color traced their history in Louisiana almost to its first settlement. The term "creole" and its meanings have been contested culturally; its first use, from pre-seventeenth-century Portugal, meant slave. Now it means "native born," from the Spanish "criollo." Spaniards, Portuguese, and Africans born and raised in the colonies were all *criollos,* regardless of "race," color, ancestry, or social status, although the term has also been used to mean "slave" in this colonial context. In Louisiana it has also meant a person of European ancestry, as the Creoles were distinguished from Anglo-Americans, Native American Indians, Yankees, and Africans. Certainly the black and white children born on the Chesapeake were "native" as well, but that did not make them "creole." That is to say, both white Creoles and Creoles of color trace their history to the history of French colonial expansion, whether in the West Indies or in Louisiana; there were French Creoles and Creoles of color. (Though that distinction, too, is misleading, since the Creoles of color whose fathers or grandfathers were European were as much French as their "white" *frères.*) The term has since taken on a more cultural than strict racial meaning. In the postbellum period white New Orleanians contended that "Creole" was reserved for the white descendants of the French colonists. The novels of George Washington Cable, fictional accounts of Creole life in Louisiana, spurred a retrenchment of sorts among French-descended whites who claimed that the term included only whites. A person of mixed-race ancestry, born and bred in Louisiana, was considered "creole" in the same sense that a native tomato was "creole," but to be a "Creole" one had to be white.[107] In 1885, Charles Gayarré, a Louisiana historian (born in 1805) went so far as to deliver a lecture at Tulane University in response to Cable's fiction, in which he asserted that Creole meant strictly and unequivocally white. He insisted that the term signified a "title of honor" of sorts, "which could only be the birthright of a superior white race." A "Creole" was a "white human being *created*" in the French and Spanish colonies, "whose origin was known and whose superior Caucasian blood was never to be assimilated to the baser liquid that ran in the veins of the Indian or African native."[108]

The Creoles of color (and Cable), of course, contested this redefinition. White Creoles were held distinct from Americans with different heritages and immigration histories, just as Creoles of color understood themselves as different from enslaved, formerly enslaved, and even freeborn African Americans. Because the word "Creole" indicates a long family history in Louisiana, and before Louisiana, France or the French Caribbean, it also implies Catholicism, as opposed to Protestantism. In the colonial and antebellum periods, Creoles of color were also known as *gens de couleur libres,* or, in English, free people of color, which is descriptive, but which glosses over the distinction between the New Orleans Creoles of color and free people of color generally. "Colored Creole" is also found in various literatures. I have taken pains to avoid using the term "free black," another way this population has been described, because it is the transition from "Creole of color" *to* "black" that I mean to elaborate.[109] It is not a simple story, because it entails the interaction of public discourse with power (official and personal) and the everyday realities of real human beings whose lives were affected. A man might simply be a man (husband, father, brother) in his house, but be a Creole in his community, and yet become "colored" in an official record, or when confronted at the polls or on a public sidewalk, only to become "black" in a later interaction with the state, etc.

The community of free Creoles of color grew under the French, and later Spanish, attitudes around slavery, sex, and religion, and developed under the particular material circumstances of the colony, as discussed in the previous chapter.[110] White women from France were imported to help stabilize the colony; black slaves from Africa were imported to do the labor.[111]

By importing slaves in the absence of an established plantation society, the French may have exacerbated the conditions for their racial concerns. The physical conditions and political situation in early French Louisiana made collaboration and cooperation across the color line crucial for survival. The lack of large-scale plantation agriculture, and the continued dependence on Native Americans, framed the relationships between slaves and slaveowners as well as between slaves and Indians and Indians and whites. Slaveowners who were unable to feed their slaves freed them. Other owners, acceding to the *Code Noir*'s stipulation that they must not force labor on Sundays, allowed their slaves that day to cultivate their own gardens and market their produce. This practice sometimes extended to Saturdays as well.[112] Many slaves learned skills, from carpentry to surgery, in the early years after the importation of slaves. The origins of the Creoles of color lay thus in a more closely knit, mutually dependent, and less stratified slave society than was present elsewhere in the South or the Caribbean.[113] In spite of the large-scale importation of French women specifically for the purpose of marriage (and to discourage sex with Native American women), and against the *Code Noir,* the white French settlers took slave concubines.[114] According to Kimberly Hanger, "Local officials, ecclesiastics, and settlers rarely condemned these interracial unions" on the grounds of race or religion, perhaps because slavery was so clearly a white-dominated institution in Louisiana.[115]

Spain acquired the colony from France in 1762 as part of the settlement of the Seven Years' War. While under Spanish rule, slaves could purchase their own freedom.[116] The Spanish authorities in Louisiana elevated the status of free people of color and slaves in the colony in order to counter the ambitions of the elite, white, French planters, who staged an uprising in 1768.[117] And, in spite of a policy called *limpieza de sangre*—purity of blood—that stipulated harsh punishments for engaging in interracial concubinage, the practice continued and often led to freedom for the women involved as well as their children.[118] It is here important to note that even in spite of the uneven power relations in white-dominated slave societies, relationships of mutuality and even love also developed, making the term "concubinage" problematic. Some of these relationships bore a closer resemblance to marriage between people forbidden by law to wed than they did to master-slave relationships.[119]

The revolution in Saint Domingue in the 1790s intensified the racial tensions of a three-caste society for the white authorities, as streams of West Indian immigrants poured into Louisiana to escape the war. Well before the American acquisition of Louisiana, refugees from the West Indies came to New Orleans. Between 1791 and 1802, three hundred refugees (slaves, free people of color, and whites) entered and populated the city. One thousand more arrived at the time of the Louisiana Purchase. The increase in people of color frightened white American officials as they tried to negotiate the new, anomalous racial situation. They worried that free people of color devoted to (French and American) revolutionary principles and schooled in violent *coups d'état* would rally slaves to overthrow the government. William C. C. Claiborne, the first American governor of the territory, attempted to bar entry to all people of color from the West Indies, but refugees continued to stream in. Between 1803 and 1806 the population of free Creoles of color nearly doubled.[120] In 1809 the Spanish government forced the French Caribbean refugees out of Cuba, where many had fled, and a large number came to New Orleans. From 1805 to 1810, New Orleans's black or "of color" population absorbed so many refugees from the revolutionary West Indies that the percentage of people of color rose from 19 percent to 63.3 percent of the population.[121]

Governor Claiborne allowed whites, despite the ban against the international slave trade as of 1808, to enter Louisiana with their slaves, including some who had been freed by the French and Haitian revolutions.[122] As elsewhere in the South, in New Orleans the line between the free colored population and the slave population sometimes blurred, especially among the non-elite Creoles.[123] Many slaves lived among the poorer free people of color, often mingled socially, and even married them. Also, many members of the free colored community had at one time been slaves themselves, and some held their own wives and children as slaves because of antebellum prohibitions discouraging manumission.[124]

Thus New Orleans developed a unique racial profile, very unlike the rest of the biracial American South.[125] Furthermore, New Orleans was from the first a city, and it fostered a different kind of slave community than could be found in the countryside and on plantations.[126] Once New Orleans became a cosmopolitan center of culture and commerce, slaves in the city (who were not themselves on sale at the various markets) had a kind of freedom denied to plantation slaves. By then, the Creoles of color were well established in New Orleans: they constituted the urban middle class so necessary for the smooth running of a prosperous port city.[127] They had well-established niches in the economy, working "as carpenters, book-keepers, housekeepers," as well as builders and caterers. There were also stockholders, businessmen, and manufacturers. They controlled the cigar industry, for example. There were also Creoles of color who were slave-owning planters.[128] Women of color also participated in the New Orleans economy, dominating local markets, selling their own produce, cakes, and crafts. They sat in stalls or they went door to door with baskets full of fruit and other goods. Some were less well-off, but still cherished a lineage back to French colonialism, their Louisiana nativity, and a heritage of freedom in a slave society. Slaves, too, worked in the city without the direct oversight of masters, who hired them out for urban labor, collected the wages they earned, and sometimes allowed them to keep a portion themselves. Slaves worked as apprentices, learning skills which they used to make themselves more valuable. These slaves who lived more or less independently, beyond the supervision and constant surveillance of masters, might even hire themselves out, either without their master's knowledge or during time deemed their own, and keep their wages.[129] While slaves in other cities engaged in such practices as well, they were, for the most part, clearly marked as slaves because of the color of their skin. In New Orleans, the prevalence of race mixing and the various statuses within the free colored community made skin color an unreliable marker of status. These conditions gave slavery in New Orleans a different character than it had in other southern cities.[130]

New Orleans is, however, in the Deep South. When in 1804 several members of the elite among the Creoles of color planned to draft a petition to Congress demanding equal rights with whites, a white printer refused to print it and notified the governor of the plan. Claiborne met with the men to warn them not to express their desires publicly—he did not want them stirring up the territory with their potentially revolutionary ideas. Feeling the threat of possible violent reprisal, the Creoles of color recanted, apologized, and pledged their loyalty to the American regime.[131] Governor Claiborne initiated a policy of repression, tempered only by a slight hesitance to alienate this population, which had historically aligned with whites (and not slaves).[132]

When the Creoles of color pressed for their rights as free men and citizens, their efforts resulted, for the most part, in more restrictions on their movements. Distinctions of color recognized in the free colored community (Creole and otherwise) dimmed when set beside "white" in a society that prized whiteness.[133] The law required *all* free people of color who had been recently manumitted to show deference to their former masters. Whether they were recently manumitted, had purchased their own freedom, or had been born free, free men and women of color lived in danger of being enslaved. Some never regained their freedom after being kidnapped and sold into slavery.[134] The Americans even passed a law forbidding free people of color from *feeling* equal to whites. "'Never were colored persons . . .' according to the law, 'to presume themselves equal to the white.'"[135]

The municipality in antebellum New Orleans segregated public life, albeit with difficulty and never completely. Theaters, coffeehouses, bars, and brothels forbade whites and blacks from mingling.[136] The police only enforced these laws in whites-only accommodations. That is, whites were more or less free to patronize places set aside for and run by blacks.[137] Meanwhile, the tradition of interracial sex continued. White men sought mistresses among the Creoles of color, and institutions facilitating these liaisons remained intact throughout the antebellum period, although restrictions on inheritance and on manumission grew as the impending crisis of the Civil War loomed.[138] In 1828, the city "prohibited" the quadroon balls, but the balls only escalated in notoriety and popularity thereafter—interracial liaisons between white men and free women of color continued.[139]

The specter of the Haitian Revolution haunted white New Orleans, and thus authorities there were equally, if not more concerned with keeping free people of color from associating with slaves than with whites, who were presumably less likely to rise in armed rebellion against slavery. As late as 1856, the Louisiana Supreme Court affirmed that "in the eyes of Louisiana law there is . . . all the difference between a free man of color and a slave that there is between a white man and a slave," but only one year later, in 1857, the Louisiana legislature outlawed manumission, making it impossible for slaves to become free.[140] Generally speaking, American racial mores increasingly demanded that all free people of color, whether Creole or American, remain subordinate to whites, and as Caryn Cossé Bell points out, unlike the Spanish, "American slaveholders did not require an intermediate class to maintain control." To the contrary, southern politics required "the cross-class unity of all whites and the immersion of all blacks into a single and subservient racial caste."[141] In the years directly preceding the Civil War, American authorities in Louisiana acted to prevent free people of color from allying with slaves, and vigilantes terrorized free people of color outside of the city. In 1859, the Louisiana legislature passed an "Act to Permit Free Persons of African Descent to Select Their Masters and Become Slaves for Life." Many free people of color fled to France, Haiti, or Tampico, Mexico, rather than withstand this humiliation, though seventeen chose enslavement.[142]

When the Civil War came, many Creoles of color fought for the Confederacy under the aegis of their militia, the Louisiana Native Guards. Indeed, this militia had been one of Louisiana's best-established institutions for the social mobility of free people of color.[143] But when Benjamin Butler and his troops overran the city, most of them switched their allegiance to the Union, claiming that they had only served the Confederacy under duress.[144] While many Creoles of color viewed the freedmen with suspicion, resentment, and a fair measure of snobbery, there emerged from their ranks a group of men committed to republican values, equal rights, and race-blind citizenship. It was they who became the leaders of the civil rights movement in New Orleans,[145] they who engaged in a protracted battle to win their rights as citizens and as men. Truly, this battle was their inheritance, as their ancestors had fought for their rights as free men since the eighteenth century. After emancipation and the abolition of slavery, as the historical distinctiveness of the elite Creoles of color came increasingly under attack, they fought for the equal rights of all.[146]

Needless to say, they faced an uphill battle. An attempt to alter the new Louisiana State Constitution of 1864 and grant voting rights to people of color provoked a bloody riot, described by General Philip Sheridan, the military commander of Louisiana and Texas, as "an absolute massacre."[147] On July 30, 1866, as "over two hundred black marchers" proceeded toward Mechanics Hall for a new Constitutional Convention, "a white mob opened fire" on them, overcame them, and "invaded the institute."[148] They attacked "a party of two hundred negroes with firearms, clubs and knives, in a manner so unnecessary and atrocious as to compel me to say it was murder," wrote General Sheridan.[149] The New Orleans riot, and the flood of editorials praising white New Orleanians for refusing to submit to Yankee rule, "increased the perception in the North that white southerners were determined to unleash a reign of terror on the recently emancipated slaves."[150] The riot was among several events that discredited President Andrew Johnson's administration sufficiently to allow Congressional Radicals to take control over Reconstruction. The Radical plan included the provision that every former Confederate state accept universal male suffrage as a condition of reentering the Union. Louisiana accepted these terms and ratified a new constitution in 1868 that gave people of color the right to vote and hold office, a "monumental victory for the black people of Louisiana."[151] There was real hope for real change in Louisiana. "When the convention finished its work in March, 1868," writes Roger Fischer, "it had drafted a [constitution] which had, at least theoretically, outlawed racial segregation in the public schools and places of public accommodation and had made a sworn belief in racial equality a qualification for public office."[152]

The large community of people of color in Louisiana was never monolithic; even the Creoles were a diverse lot. There were indeed many "light and dark folks" well before Basin Street. Some of them identified so strongly with their white parentage that they failed to see their cause as one with the newly freed slaves in any way.[153] Other free people had themselves only been free for a short time before the war, and understood viscerally the precarious nature of freedom for all people of color in America—even in New Orleans. From within the diverse community of free people of color in New Orleans, then, a small group of mostly elite Creoles of color emerged as the voice of radical republicanism, devoted to the principle that all men indeed were created equal and that political, civic, and what they termed "public" rights must be shared by all without regard to race or skin color. Many of these men were the sons and grandsons of Frenchmen, especially refugees from the Haitian Revolution, and had a long heritage of struggle for civil rights and equality. They rejected Abraham Lincoln's suggestion that the more intelligent among them be given the franchise, and rejected also a measure, called the "quadroon bill," that would legally designate as "white" all those with less than one-fourth "black blood."[154] The point was not to be considered "*white*," but to be treated as men and as equals without regard to so-called racial distinctions at all.[155] In the quotidian realities and struggles of political negotiation and social positioning, even those Creoles of color who now aligned themselves with the former slaves, and for the rights of all people of color, regardless of their heritage,[156] encountered difficulties in dealing with the American—or non-Creole—blacks, whose life experiences and political and civic aspirations had only recently been so dramatically different from their own. Men and women who had just emerged from slavery (and their advocates), in contradistinction to men and women whose families had been free for generations, and who had enjoyed education, wealth, and customary rights, necessarily viewed emancipation and Reconstruction differently. There was, in a phrase, a culture clash.

Division within the population of color after the war ultimately weakened the power and influence of the Creoles of color.[157] Yet, internal divisions among people of color and between Creoles of color and American blacks, though real, were minimal compared to the prejudices of whites who were unwilling to allow desegregation and who were willing to take up arms and fight to prevent it. The backlash against the 1868 state constitution began immediately. One Louisiana newspaper called the new constitution "that wretched abortion of party malignity," another called it a "mongrel monstrosity," and a third referred to its creators as "social banditti, domestic bastards, catamites, scallawags, slubberdegullions, cow-thieves, and jay-hawkers." Others claimed that the constitution would "Africanize" the state of Louisiana. The *New Orleans Bee* warned its readers: "If you don't want your mothers and sisters, and wives and daughters insulted by insolent and depraved negro vagabonds. . . . If you are opposed to amalgamation and miscegenation, vote against the new constitution."[158] While men of *mixed* descent led the crusade for equality and the abolition of race, the specter of amalgamation soon became the standard justification for violence against black men.

White supremacist violence made life difficult for all people of color in the state.[159] On September 14, 1874, a paramilitary white supremacist organization called the Crescent City White League attacked agents of the Reconstruction government of Louisiana, headquartered in New Orleans, and overthrew it in the name of home rule and white supremacy.[160] The coup was short-lived, but nevertheless demonstrated the drastic lengths white New Orleanians were willing to go to to preserve white supremacy and resist Republican rule.[161]

Reconstruction ended in 1877 in Louisiana and nationally. A compromise put Rutherford B. Hayes in the White House and withdrew federal troops from the South.[162] The so-called "Redeemer" constitution of 1879 stripped away the enormous gains achieved through the 1868 state constitution. The politics of white supremacy dominated policy at the local and state levels, and the tide flowed away from equal rights for all citizens.[163]

The culmination of the struggle came in the 1890s, first with the verdict in *Plessy v. Ferguson* in 1896, and two years later with the near-total disenfranchisement of nonwhites in the state. The bloody "Robert Charles" race riots erupted in 1900.[164]

Conclusion

At the very climax of this drive to establish racial exclusivity and white supremacy, Storyville, beginning in 1897, specialized in "octoroon" prostitutes, promising even more sex across the color line. It should now be clear that the continued salience of light-skinned women available for sex cannot be read as an example of New Orleans's progressive racial sensibility, which was largely a myth, or a long history of racial tolerance, or "laissez-faire" attitudes toward sex and social transgression. By the time of the Storyville ordinance, white New Orleanians had proved themselves equally bigoted, and equally violent, as whites elsewhere in the South.

The image of the light-skinned, sexually precocious Creole of color *woman*, however, did persist throughout this entire history. A man writing in the 1890s typically remarked that there was "much to see in New Orleans," but in his opinion "the beauty of the [colored] Creole woman impresses one most of all. They are probably the handsomest women in the United States. Their figures are of matchless grace and beauty, slight and lithe, with finely-moulded limbs."[165] His description echoes Fanny Trollope's and others from sixty years earlier: "The majority of them are brunettes, with clear complexions, flowing black hair, heavy eyelids, drooping as if in pensive melancholy, and large, dark lustrous eyes, as it were bright with tears like the partially closed petals of a flower filled with pearly dew."[166]

The violence of postbellum New Orleans, and the failure of the Creoles of color to secure rights for themselves and for all people of color, in spite of the significant gains during Reconstruction, rendered the historic distinctions between light- and dark-skinned people of color, elite Creoles and former slaves, irrelevant to public life. Then the *Plessy* decision symbolically erased the Creole of color from the history of New Orleans by naturalizing an absolute racial difference, which supposedly "the law was powerless to eradicate," and approved the creation of a biracial caste system as if it had always existed, everywhere.[167] All nonwhites were relegated to a second-class status. But the male Creole of color's political erasure was met, with near simultaneity, by the spectacular showcasing of his female counterpart. Storyville's promoters exploited the longstanding association of New Orleans with beautiful quadroons and "fancy girl" slave auctions and recuperated the slave markets of antebellum New Orleans. They created an Old South emporium of exoticism and interracial sex in "New South" New Orleans.

CHAPTER THREE

Public Rights and Public Women

I am raising young ladies of daughters and feel it a
mother's duty to seek redress from your honor.
—Letter from a resident of New Orleans to Mayor Capdeville, January 23, 1900

This is simply a protest against the blending of races.
—*NEW ORLEANS DAILY STATES*, JULY 5, 1890

The historical coincidence of the *Plessy* case and the creation of Storyville
invites us to explore afresh the relationship between segregation by race and
the segregation of vice at the close of the nineteenth century and during
the first two decades of the twentieth—the duration of the life of Storyville.
These years saw a transformation in the meaning of "public," both as a metaphor for political participation and representation, and literally, in terms
of actual terrain and accommodations. The sex, race, and class of the metaphorical body politic were manifested in rhetoric and ideology about white
supremacy, manhood, and democracy, and *also* through the manipulation
and restriction of actual bodies on streets, train cars, inns, bordellos, and
voting places. The way the American subject emerged as white, predominantly male, and middle class had much to do with how public space was
ordered and how that order was enforced and violated across the country,
including in New Orleans.

At the turn of the twentieth century, New Orleanians throughout the
city petitioned the mayor and the city council to improve their neighborhoods, and, in essence, to help them police the boundaries of their own
respectability. Their efforts dovetailed with the city government's effort to
clean up the city, to render it respectable overall, and to relegate its tradi-

tional disorder to the margins. Just as George L'Hote objected to the red-light district he had helped to create when it encroached on him, men and women in neighborhoods all over New Orleans asserted their own propriety in contrast to what they saw around them. These petitions of the residents of New Orleans constitute a discourse of respectability, defining, measuring, and asserting the middle-class propriety of their signatories through complaints about neighbors who failed to meet their criteria.

Residents wrote and signed these petitions in the years surrounding the *Plessy v. Ferguson* decision and the creation of Storyville (1896 and 1897, respectively). The petitions examined here coincided with a concerted effort by New Orleans's business community to rid the government of corruption and to throw off the vestiges of Reconstruction. This effort was also racially coded. Many whites had viewed Reconstruction as an effort to "Africanize" the state through the manipulation of hapless "Negroes" by unscrupulous northern whites.[1] How to "clean up" New Orleans was the question before the (white) citizens of the city, as well as the government, and the answer increasingly appeared to involve race.

Jim Crow segregation and the creation of vice districts, then, both emerged in the late nineteenth century as ways to create order out of the increasingly disorderly urban experience.[2] As pleasure travel and tourism grew, along with new business practices and the growth of a new class of professional urbanites, red-light districts arose to serve men on the make and to employ (or entrap) women adrift. This situation was not unique to New Orleans, and indeed New Orleans was typical in this regard. So while Storyville is often conceived of as part of an entirely separate history, it was, to the contrary, an extreme example of a common trend.

Additionally, even though the city was a crucial testing ground for racial segregation, New Orleans has not tended to figure in broader studies of southern racial practices.[3] To be sure, the city was atypical. In New Orleans, the legacy of a three-tiered racial structure of whites, free people of color, and slaves endured culturally for years after the color line was sharply drawn. The population had long been distributed according to a salt-and-pepper pattern, and lines between and among groups were less than fixed. Class, culture, language, and the physical landscape of the city had as much impact as race in determining patterns of settlement and movement. The struggle to segregate the city was a struggle against centuries of habit.[4] Segregating vice was also a struggle against centuries of habit in New Orleans. Reformers had attempted both forms of segregation half-heartedly before the Civil War; now, toward the close of the nineteenth century, the job would be taken seriously. Racial segregation and the segregation of vice were two sides of the same coin in late nineteenth-century New Orleans. Both movements stemmed from the desire to clean up the city, metaphorically and literally, and to make it "modern" along the lines favored by the North among the moral reformers and urban elites. The segregation of vice was, like outright racial segregation, also infused with race and racism. Residents of the city's long-mixed neighborhoods sought to clarify the borders of their own whiteness and fulfill their middle-class aspirations, and at the same time emerging business and political classes sought to realize the New South vision in the oldest southern city. Good government, economic progress, attracting northern capital, achieving white supremacy: all these goals demanded the clear demarcation of public space as respectable, legitimate, and white.

Public Rights and Public Women

"Modernization" in New Orleans included the Americanization of racial attitudes, a process that had begun in 1803, but which did not reach its end until the war was fought, slavery was abolished, and men of color were legally disenfranchised.[5] The apotheosis of both the postbellum civil rights movement and the "Americanization" of New Orleans came with the case to test the constitutionality of the 1890 Separate Car Act, and the Supreme Court decision six years later in *Plessy v. Ferguson*.[6] Rebecca Scott describes a long road to the *Plessy* decision, one starting in the late eighteenth century, with the American, French, and Haitian revolutions. These three cataclysms and their very different outcomes spurred a subset of the free people of color to develop of a concept of "public rights," which would complement and expand the meaning of civil, political, and social rights. It was a humanistic philosophy that transcended the specific enumeration of rights in revolutionary pronouncements or legal documents.[7] Briefly, public rights encompassed all things tending toward equal, dignified treatment in all public spaces; this provision was (briefly) included in the state's constitution—only to be deleted in the 1879 post-Reconstruction version.[8] The era following the *Plessy* decision, the long Jim Crow era, was known for its demanding racial etiquette, and the potentially deadly consequences of broaching it. That is, the very opposite of "public rights," public humiliation, was enshrined into the law and maintained vigilantly and violently by custom. The Supreme

Court's decision wrought this, in part, and it also obscured the long history of political activism and hard-won customary rights of the men who brought the case in the first place. In the linguistic-legal system of race that emerged, black and white had always been the two races, separate, and, in spite of the shibboleth promoted by the decision, unequal.

This history is important to Storyville not only because *Plessy v. Ferguson* originated in New Orleans, or because Storyville invited men to cross the color line that *Plessy* helped to legitimize, but also because Storyville's creation was similarly envisioned as critical to the modernization of New Orleans. Storyville, too, may be understood as an apotheosis of sorts, the culmination of prostitution reform and the spectacular failure of that reform at the same time. Rather than simply exemplifying the long history of prostitution and interracial sex in New Orleans, Storyville was an effort to channel and curtail that history. As the *Plessy* decision (and all segregationist legislation) sought to clarify the ambiguous borders around raced bodies, the Storyville ordinance, and other similar vice legislation, sought to clarify the moral borders around sexualized bodies, to create a clear distinction between legitimate sexuality and illicit sex. The borders around raced and sexed bodies articulated and highlighted what could be considered as respectability and legitimate commerce, concepts that gained clarity as citizens and municipal officials alike sought to make order out of an inherently disorderly situation: the long aftermath of Civil War, economic depression, political upheaval, racial tensions, violence, industrialization, urban poverty, and rampant prostitution. These two projects, racial clarity and moral clarity, were intimately linked for the elite whites in business and politics in turn-of-the-century New Orleans, as well as for the striving members of the white middle and working classes who sought to define themselves against the disorder of their environs. They wished to carve out spaces reserved for bourgeois propriety in morals and commerce, a concept that was itself deeply enraced. Thus racial segregation and the segregation of vice dovetailed with the economic imperative to revive New Orleans as a commercial center, a trade hub, a traveler's destination: to revive the southern metropolis of antebellum times.

Recent scholarship has pegged either the post–World War I period or the post–World War II period as the one in which city boosters began self-consciously creating the image of the new New Orleans.[9] It was, however, earlier, at the end of the nineteenth-century, that this process began. Municipal promoters drew heavily on the image created by antebellum travelers to New Orleans, picking and choosing those most attractive and resonant elements. These men sought to retail the city's longstanding image, produced through travel accounts and other writings over the nineteenth century. As the theater historian and literary critic Joseph Roach has remarked, New Orleans "performs a simulacrum of itself, apparently frozen in time, but in fact busily devoted to the ever-changing task of recreating the illusion that it is frozen in time."[10] Segregation by race and the segregation of vice at the turn of the century may be understood as early efforts in this regard.

We can get a sense of what late nineteenth-century promoters had to draw on by sampling the same literature. "I am now in this great Southern Babylon, mighty receptacle of wealth, depravity, and misery," wrote James Davidson upon steaming into New Orleans in 1836.[11] To Americans and others, nineteenth-century New Orleans was a curiosity, a foreign city on the banks of the Mississippi River, known for "its uniqueness—and its wickedness."[12] The city's exceptional history and its picturesque heterogeneity drew many travelers, who remarked at length on the strange and exotic manners of New Orleanians. From these descriptions, recorded in private diaries and published manuscripts, a very particular picture of New Orleans emerges. It is not a full picture, but it is remarkable in its consistency over the first five decades of the nineteenth century. Part of this must be because the reputation of the city colored even visitors's firsthand impressions, directing their interests and affecting their sight; but part of it was because travel writers tended to borrow descriptions from other travel accounts, most often without acknowledgment.[13] But something deeper must also be at work. New Orleans fits Edward Said's description of the "Orient" surprisingly well. New Orleans, certainly, "is less a place than a *topos,* a set of references, a congeries of characteristics, that seems to have its origin in a quotation, or a fragment of a text."[14] The task before the Chamber of Commerce was to draw on and circulate those fragments of text that would make New Orleans attractive to investors and tourists in the post-Reconstruction era, some of which are collected below.

In 1832, Alexis de Tocqueville, upon arriving in New Orleans, jotted in his diary, "the first of January 1832, the sun rising in a brilliant tropical sky revealed to us New Orleans across the masts of a thousand ships."[15] Though James Davidson's first remarks upon steaming into the city four years later referenced Babylon, his first impression was also of masts. "The approach" to the city, he noted in his diary, "is imposing. . . . [T]he masts of the shipping appear, like a large forest of dead trees, and all at once you come around the bend, the City bursts upon your view."[16] In describing the masts of ships, both men were already repeating a trope of New Orleans travel literature, no doubt based on the visual experience of myriads of visitors. This impression of the city cut across lines of class, gender, race, and region. A runaway slave from Tennessee similarly recalled his excitement upon reaching New Orleans; the view of the harbor from the steamboat he traveled on was one of his most vivid memories as many as seventy years later. It was the "wilderness of masts" and the multicolored flags from ships representing every corner of the world.[17] It was the same for Mrs. Houstoun, the British novelist and travel writer who had set out to visit the Republic of Texas in 1843. She and her party were forced to travel to New Orleans to avoid contemporary turmoil in Mexico, and they arrived at night. When she was still fifteen miles from the city, she wrote of the city's skyline in her diary, "Its towers, and the dome of the St. Charles's Hotel, distinctly to be seen!" The countless "lights which gleamed from the houses and public buildings, and which were reflected on the river, were . . . a most welcome sight."[18] She was even more excited to see the city in the daytime, when it seemed "the busiest scene! Such forests of masts! Such flaunting colours and flags, of every hue and of every country! . . . Five tier of shipping in the harbour!"[19] Albert Pickett, who spent eight days in New Orleans in February 1847, similarly wrote of ships "from every nation, whose masts tower aloft in a dense forest for five miles" together with "steamboats, and crafts of every make and shape, from every river which empties into the Mississippi . . . mingling in the strife of commerce"; Sir Charles Lyell in 1846, and A. Oakey Hall, the self-styled "Manhattaner in New Orleans," likewise went into reveries over the flatboats, steamships, and "innumerable masts" crowded layers deep in the harbor.[20]

When Bernhard, the Duke of Saxe-Weimar-Eisenach, visited New Orleans on his extended tour of North America quite a bit earlier, in 1825–1826, he approached not from the Mississippi, but from the other direction, across Lake Pontchartrain, through what he called "a shocking marshy country." From the duke's direction, New Orleans existed over a kind of threshold of the physical landscape and of the imagination: "After we had proceeded three miles in this manner we came into a cultivated district, passed a sort of gate, and found ourselves quite in another world." The duke and his party noticed "several mansion-houses, ornamented with columns, piazzas, and covered galleries; some of these were of ancient style in building." The cultivation of land and trees bespoke a "long civilized country," which came as a relief to the duke after traveling so long in the "wilderness" of Louisiana, while "several inns and public gardens" indicated "a population that willingly seeks amusement." He, too, noted the ships in the harbor. Alongside the "white spires of the cathedral of New Orleans . . . [were] the masts of the ships lying in the Mississippi."[21]

Ships in the harbor signaled the city's bustling commerce and global significance. New Orleans lay both on the circum-Atlantic and the circum-Caribbean trade routes, as well as on the Mississippi River. In the early nineteenth century, trade had been very good. An Englishman traveling in New Orleans in 1827 hailed the city as "the great commercial capital of the Mississippi valley," describing the "immense piles" of cotton that filled the streets when the crop came in.[22] "More cotton is shipped from this port than from any other in America, or perhaps the world."[23] The levee, the elevated bank of the Mississippi River, bustled with enterprise. Pickett described it as "the master street of the world. . . . From this great thoroughfare all others diverge." While he was there he witnessed the "mart" in action. "Thirty-six thousand barrels of flour were sold in a few hours! And while this astonishing transfer was going on, thousands of other produce and commodities were changing hands. . . . The very air howls with an eternal din and noise."[24]

The flags of diverse nations in the Mississippi harbor remind us that New Orleans was indeed an international city. New Orleans struck visitors this way, and so they often compared New Orleans to ancient or mythical cities like Athens or Babylon, as well as to London and Paris: all cosmopolitan metropoles of far-reaching empires of one sort or another. "Tyre nor Carthage, Alexandria nor Genoa, those aforetime imperial metropoles of merchant princes, boasted no quay like the Levee of New Orleans."[25] New Orleans might also recall for the traveler huge, bustling cities that developed through the combined cultural and commercial influences of overlapping imperial and indigenous policies and populations. At least one traveler, for instance, called New Orleans "the Calcutta of America."[26] The city grew at a phenomenal rate in the first four decades of the nineteenth century, becoming "a beehive of activity" and producing a "glamour period."[27] In *The Standard History of New Orleans,* Norman Walker recounts Thomas Jefferson's prophecy that "the world would see in . . . New Orleans the greatest commercial entrepot of all time." Writing in 1900, Walker asserts that New

Orleans was and had been for "half a century" the nation's second port, behind New York. "There was a time," he continues, "when it promised to be first."[28] Thus, after a precarious and impoverished beginning, the Louisiana territory prospered in the early nineteenth century. The invention of the cotton gin; the advances in the technology for granulating sugar; the acquisition by the United States; and, finally, the collapse of Haiti's economy combined to make Louisiana a crucial exporter, especially of cotton and sugar. Antebellum New Orleans was a glorious commercial exchange.[29]

It was not only the commercial goods that mingled at the levee, but people, too. Human variety added to the city's "exotic" charm and cosmopolitan complexity. The layout of the city reflected its history of settlement and culture of diversity, which did not however mean harmony between groups. From 1836 until 1852 municipal authorities divided the city into three quasi-independent municipalities due to internecine conflict among the Spanish, French, and Anglo inhabitants of New Orleans.[30] Albert Pickett described the resulting urban landscape: there were "wide and beautiful streets, running perfectly straight from the river to the farthest back limits, serving not only as boundaries for municipal purposes, but absolutely separating different races." These were "the everlasting Yankees, with their shrewdness and enterprize, [who] inhabit the Second Municipality; the wealthy French and Spanish [who] fill up the First, with a large mixture of native Americans; [and] the Third Municipality [which] is entirely French and Spanish."[31] "Race" in these accounts may substitute for "nationality" or even "character" since the people described all constituted different groups that today are all considered "white"—"native American" refers to the Euro-Americans who came from elsewhere in the country after the Louisiana Purchase in 1803, in contradistinction to New Orleans (white) Creoles.

In describing the city's complex mosaic of inhabitants, travelers relied on stereotypes—creating caricatures based on the "race" or, really, the nativity of the business and social elites. Most visitors described the white Creoles as an old, noble, and aristocratic population, slightly dissipated, but still charming, while the free people of color (also Creoles, though not described as such) were scarcely visible at all in their public accounts, save for the women, who were perceived as mistresses and kept women. The Anglo-Americans were newcomers who had come to New Orleans for pecuniary reasons, or, as Bernhard said, "only by the desire of accumulating wealth."[32] W. Bullock agreed. "In respect to the manners of the people, those of the French citizens partake of their general national character. They have here their characteristic politeness and urbanity. . . . The Americans come hither from all states. Their object is to accumulate wealth, and spend it somewhere else."[33] Yet their industry could not be denied. "'Work, work, work,' is [their] unceasing cry. Every one appears in fear lest daylight should cheat him of a dollar," wrote Oakey Hall, so that "stocks, cotton, sugar, and money are the liveliest topics."[34] Mrs. Houstoun, too, was impressed by the application of merchants in looking for the best deals. Those men who appeared "in their dress [and] appearance" to be the "gentlemen of the land, are so devoted to money making" that, Houstoun noted, "I am inclined to believe, that were a mad dog at their heels, it would make but little impression upon their absorbed faculties."[35] Charles Lyell was similarly impressed with the Yankee work ethic, and was relieved to see several of them taking a holiday on Mardi Gras.[36] This was the very sort the city wished to attract in the 1890s.

In contrast to the rude and acquisitive Americans, the white Creoles appealed to visitors. Among them there were still men of leisure, charming and insouciant. Bernhard commented that the "[white] Creoles are, upon the whole, a warm-hearted generation."[37] Davidson considered the white Creoles "the fine people of the City," "the *Fashionables*," who were mainly "Merchants and Planters."[38] As Bullock put it, "of course the New Orleans people are gay, gaudy in their dress, houses, furniture, and equipage, and rather fine than in the best taste."[39] Another traveler remarked, "Among the [white] Creoles with whom I came in contact, I saw many whose manners were most polite and agreeable, and I felt . . . that I should have had more pleasure in associating with them than with a large portion of their Anglo-American rivals."[40] The charming, insouciant Creole planters were also, of course, slaveowners, as were a good many of the "Americans," even including the Yankees.[41] To an extent these early nineteenth-century visitors mistook a class division for a racial one among so-called white people. Even the Creoles were *merchants* as well as planters.[42] The importance of commerce, capitalism, and the markets, even when "othered" as gauche and (Anglo) American, was however undeniable. Historians have rescued the city from the impression that the Creoles and the Americans were locked in bitter rivalry by showing the ways they collaborated in matters of business, society, marriage, culture, and, not least, white supremacy.[43] Nonetheless, the distinction was a popular one to make, even as visitors remarked on the endless-seeming variety of nationalities represented at the city's leading markets.

The French Market offered a microcosm not only of New Orleans's varied population, but of the whole civilized (in other words, European) world, according to Pickett. "The French, English, Spanish, Dutch, Swiss and Italian languages are employed here in trading, buying, and selling, and a kind of mongrel mixture and jumble of each and all is spoken by the lower class in the market." For Pickett, "the very drums of your ears ache with the eternal jargon—with the cursing, swearing, whooping, hollowing, cavilling, laughing, crying, cheating and stealing. . . . The screams of parrots, the music of birds, the Dutch girl's organ, the French negro humming a piece of the last opera—all are going at it."[44] All of these populations, even including the "French negro," combined, to use Pickett's phrase, in a "common ground for liberty and commerce": the Kentuckian, the Yankee, the Carolinian, Georgian, and Virginian, and even "the dark and mysterious Spaniard, puffing his cigar and sending up volumes of smoke through his black imperials; the gay and frisky Frenchman; the sturdy Dutchman; the son of Erin, and the cunning Jew." He concluded, "the Levee is a world."[45]

This world was a marketplace, and for the antebellum traveler the city's markets remained its greatest attraction. New Orleans had more "good markets than any city on the continent. They may be found in all directions, affording a great abundance of the best that the whole Mississippi valley and the far western plains of Texas can produce."[46] Bullock commented on "handsome shops, filled with well-dressed people, in the European costumes, the ladies in the fashions of London and Paris,"[47] and Bernhard wrote of the "market-houses" along the Mississippi, "built of brick, modelled after the Propylea, in Athens," and of the coffee houses and oyster bars, and the "fine pineapples, oranges, bananas, peccan-nuts [sic], cocoa-nuts, and vegetables of different descriptions."[48] The market encapsulated the "exotic" tastes of the city's population, as there one found "scores of opossums, coons, crawfish, eels, minks, and frogs, brought here to satiate the fancy appetite of the French," which even made room for "five fat *puppies* about six weeks old, which the owner informed me were for French gentlemen to eat!"[49]

Less commonly found in even the more breathless accounts were the less savory elements of New Orleans; yet we know that for the better part of the nineteenth century the city "reeked of garbage and dead animals rotting in the streets."[50] The "principal promenades of the city" were "odious as well as unsanitary" due to the piles of refuse and human waste awaiting collection. Periodically, dogs dug up corpses of people who had not been given a Catholic "proper burial." "The stenches and corruption of the said filth is particularly bad in warm weather," noted a report from 1800. Subtropical New Orleans was warm for most of the year. Mosquitoes found ideal breeding places in the cisterns that served as the city's water supply as well as in the above-ground privies and the surrounding swamplands. Because the city was below sea level and lacked any kind of underground sewage or drainage system, there was "an abundance of stagnant water" lying "the whole year round in the cypress groves surrounding the city."[51] This water, too, bred mosquitoes, and the city's climate made it prey to cholera, yellow fever, malaria, and other mosquito-borne diseases. Other pestilential insects and rodents swarmed around the abattoirs of the city, whose butchers used the streets and the Mississippi River as sites to dump the barrels "filled with entrails, liver, blood, urine, dung, other refuse, portions [of which were] in an advanced stage of decomposition."[52]

Though the naturalist John James Audubon called New Orleans's French Market the "dirtiest place in all the cities of the United States," these aspects of New Orleans rarely made it into the popular travel accounts, and if they did it was mostly only as "exotic" or "sultry" atmospherics.[53] But the problems of sewage, entrails, mosquitoes, stenches, and dirt did in fact plague late nineteenth-century New Orleans still. The city boosters' attempts to fix these malodorous maladies were coupled with an effort to reimagine their contemporary city as the earlier visitors had described it.

For the antebellum traveler, the levee, the markets, the docks, and even the streets, constituted a kind of show.[54] The bustling American, the charming Creole, the singing slave hauling goods on the dock: all of these became recognizable types through the consistency of their representation. Even a bumpy ride to one's hotel could be a form of entertainment. Oakey Hall's 1851 account of his own passage through the streets by carriage encapsulates how the idea of New Orleans evolved as a simulacrum of itself. Note in the following quote the emphasis on consumption and spectacle. He wrote:

> So busy was I in fancying the surprise of my stomach, when it should once more taste the good cheer of a hotel, that I did not particularly observe, by the dim street lights, the events and scenes of a drive through some of the most singular quarters I had ever beheld, in town, village, or city. I can only recall to mind *dioramic and shifting views* of avenues of cotton bales; groups of old clo' shops, gaudily set forth with parti-colored handkerchiefs, in number and sizes enough for *a regiment of noses*; oyster stands, where *dirty mouths* and flickering tallow candles grinned ghostly satisfaction; coffee and cake stands, in a brace of deserted markets, where negresses and lazy butcher boys were engaged in *melodious quarrels* quite antiscriptural in their tone but yet suggestive of the tower of Babel; a dirty park; and streets evidently paved on

the principle of five stones to the square yard, all of which, at the end of my drive . . . sent me to my chamber in the St. Charles Hotel, with hearty thanks.[55]

In spite of his own assertion that these were "some of the most singular quarters" he had ever beheld, Oakey Hall nevertheless saw New Orleans as a representation, a kind of museum display, a "diorama," of itself.[56]

Hall's destination, the St. Charles Hotel, was itself the subject of reveries equal to those about the ships in the port. An Englishman asserted that "by far the most splendid and the most costly edifices in New Orleans are not the public buildings . . . , but the hotels," and of the St. Charles Hotel in particular, he wrote, "The St. Charles, which is sometimes called the American Exchange Hotel, is not only the largest and handsomest hotel in the United States, but, as it seemed to me, the largest and handsomest hotel in the world. At least I remember nothing equal to it in any country that I have visited."[57] Even Mrs. Houstoun and her party, who were traveling by yacht and "made it a rule, in general, not to sleep out of our own *house*," bent their rules to stay at the St. Charles because of the hotel's reputation. "Previous to our arrival," she wrote, "we had heard so much of the great Hotel of St. Charles, the immense extent of its accommodations, and the size of its apartments, that we decided upon spending a few days there, in order to see these wonders with our own eyes, and judge of them with our own understandings." She was not disappointed. "What a really magnificent building it is, with its immense *façades*, it quite strains ones [*sic*] eyes to catch a glimpse of its gigantic dome." The accommodations were as impressive as the architecture. The St. Charles, she reported, "is as good a specimen of a first-rate hotel as can be found anywhere. The establishment is conducted on a most liberal and splendid scale." The rooms were "very comfortable, well carpeted, excellent fires, luxurious furniture, and curtains of the richest blue damask." For Houstoun, she might almost have been in Paris. Even "the *cuisine* was good as possible."[58]

Lyell described the St. Charles as "the most conspicuous building in the city," and ascended to its "lofty dome" in order to take in the view of New Orleans from on high.[59] Hall compared the hotel to representative institutions in other cities. "Set the St. Charles hotel down in St. Petersburg," he wrote, "and you would think it a palace. In Boston, and ten to one you would christen it a college. In London, and it would marvelously remind you of an exchange. In New Orleans it is all three." He even compared it to a façade "builded by Barnum," as if it were a lurid prop useful for drawing in customers (and perhaps suckers, too).[60] Inside, the hotel was a palimpsest of past visitors, its halls "full of echoes, and thronged with shadows; echoes of mirth; echoes of sorrow; shadows of human life."[61]

The grand hotels in New Orleans provided the perfect stages for extravagant social displays, including, as we have seen, slave auctions. At the same St. Charles Hotel were held tremendous dances of hundreds of guests, biweekly "soirées" for unaccompanied women who might invite up to five gentlemen to attend. Such a disproportionate ratio of men to women in a huge crowd surely must have imbued the atmosphere with the frisson of competition, making courtship a game among men as much as between men and women. Participants came from all over the United States and Europe. Eliza Potter, the free woman of color who remarked about the slave auctions held in the St. Charles, also commented on these soirées. "The more gentlemen a lady knows," she wrote, "the greater belle she is."[62]

All this fun came to an end with the Civil War, and whatever charm antebellum travelers had found in the Crescent City had seriously eroded by the end of the war. Northerners saw in postwar New Orleans "a decaying, primitive, reactionary city . . . surrounded by marshy unnavigable swamps and bayous." New Orleans was to them "a rotting Gomorrah run by corrupt and ignorant officials and filled with gamblers, prostitutes, drunkards, duelists, and thugs."[63] The writer Edward King, traveling through the South in the 1870s, reported that "Louisiana is today Paradise Lost."[64] By the early 1880s, though, self-styled progressive New Orleans businessmen sought to fulfill Edward King's prophecy that Louisiana might, someday soon, be "Paradise Regained." They grasped that partisan and white supremacist violence and mob riots disturbed the pleasant images of New Orleans culled from "fragments of text," and so impeded the economic recovery of New Orleans, as in much of the South. They wanted to sanitize the neighborhoods outside a few grids marked as beyond redemption. They sought to realize in their once-fair city the New South vision articulated by Henry Grady and others in the years after the demise of Reconstruction. This vision embraced northern industry and commercial development while clearly conveying that southerners would deal with the "race question" on their own terms.[65]

Guidebooks and Advertising

Businessmen and urban reformers made concerted efforts in the 1880s to attract tourists as well as investors to the city. After the demise of Reconstruction, New Orleans city boosters sought to reclaim the very aspects of antebellum New Orleans that visitors to the city found so enchanting. They sought to reinvigorate the city by reproducing it as it had already become retrospectively known at the time of the outbreak of the Civil War. At the same time, the business community sought to show that New Orleans was not stymied or mired in the past, but was, rather, ready to soar to new heights of technological progress and market expansion. It wanted only the opportunity—and the money. How to present New Orleans as simultaneously frozen in time and rapidly developing along a progressive trajectory was the question.[66] The answer lay on the tracks. Nothing in American history represented progress more clearly than the railroad. Trains would eventually displace the Mississippi River and relegate the Port of New Orleans to a much lower station on the national and international trade routes, but this eventuality was not yet glimpsed in the 1880s. The railroad carried more than goods—it carried hope, it was the future. And during this "period of travel democratization," more people than ever before took to the rails. Train travel increased by nearly 70 percent from 1885 to 1900. By 1915, it had nearly tripled.[67]

The New Orleans Progressive Union, an association of businessmen organized to promote the city and entertain "distinguished visitors," along with the *Times-Picayune* (the city's conservative, Democratic Party newspaper), and various railroad and steamship lines all published guides to the city.[68] The guides emphasized the so-called romance of New Orleans, its unique architecture, its quaint streets, and its "colored" Creole population, qualities that were well-known through earlier visitors' accounts, but which had, in the wake of Civil War and Reconstruction, been overshadowed by images of white vigilantes and corrupt politicians. The city boosters sought to erase these latter images and to revive the dioramic New Orleans imagined and described by the antebellum traveler: "New Orleans, the Crescent City! Surnamed also, for other attributes and characteristics, 'Creole City,' 'Carnival City,' 'Paris of a New France,' 'Charming Sub-Tropic American capital!' New Orleans, the gay and worldly, scenic, and in many of its aspects foreign and bizarre!"[69] New Orleans, "mistress of the valley of the Lower River and of the region of the gulf coast," a metaphor forced by habit, was also the premier "emporium and entrepot" of the South. "The French Market is the largest mart in the South, and no one is considered to be familiar with the city until he has been there."[70] Louisiana was first among the states as a market for sugar, cotton, and rice, close to first in tropical fruits and grain, and "third in rank of American seaports!" At the same time, her main port city was also a city of "pleasant figments." But, still, New Orleans was modern and vigorous: "And from this city, the New Orleans of To-Day, what message? What tidings and what signal?" The answer was change, "Alteration, Innovation; which is, in fine, to say, IMPROVEMENT."[71]

The guides to New Orleans from the 1880s, 1890s, and early 1900s cataloged such improvements in detail, allowing tourists to take in "dioramic" New Orleans and then recuperate in comfort by taking full advantage of the modern city and its up-to-date accommodations. The proprietors of Storyville's best bordellos borrowed this strategy, too, publishing their own guidebooks, steering their customers away from scoundrels and toward a safe and pleasurable experience.

The city's guidebooks recirculated the image of New Orleans created by antebellum travelers, and placed it before every potential tourist. In doing so, these guidebooks from the 1880s through the 1920s reimagined the less savory or more frightening elements of New Orleans's past as spectacles that modern tourists could consume.[72] New Orleans promoted its own combination of characteristics or qualities: its romance, cosmopolitanism, European aesthetics (most obviously through its architecture), and also those "peculiar habits" of the inhabitants, the insouciant Creoles and its "negro" population, shopping at the French Market, hawking pralines, practicing voodoo, dancing in Congo Square. Ceremonies which threatened the antebellum American regime in their pregnant promise of alliance and rebellion now were reconceived as entertainment. The success of this marketing scheme relied not only upon the literal cleaning up of New Orleans's waste—and prostitute—infested streets, but also upon the subordination of the population of color and the suppression of their civil rights claims—the erasure, in a sense, of their centuries-long agitation for public recognition and equal citizenship. In Storyville, the octoroon, always a *woman* and literally a *prostitute,* served both these purposes at once.

One guidebook from 1882 is simply titled *"Eden,"* and it evokes an exotic and unique locale while also assuring the reader of his comfort and safety inside the modern passenger railway train.[73] New Orleans is "a city of surprises. The visitor . . . will pass through thoroughfares in no way inferior to those of Paris, Vienna, St. Petersburg, Palermo, Venice or Rome. He will find the nervous and restless business life of the Yankee in contrast with the 'dolce far niente' of the Creole; he will see many interesting pictures in the lives of the half-civilized negroes. . . ."[74] At other times any claim to bustle and industry was relinquished. The 1897 edition of *The Picayune's Guide to New Orleans* puts forth as its premise that New Orleans still lay "half asleep, blinking, as it were," on the Mississippi River, and adds that "her very name is a souvenir of gayeties; her breath is as sweet as a willow copse in June, and something about her always makes one think of the opera and the 'bal masque.' . . ."[75] New Orleans was a woman who would "unfold herself petal by petal, growing in charm each day," a feminized city waiting to be explored, especially in the older, European sections of the city. Though the sexual suggestiveness was unsubtle, nowhere was the implication that New Orleans was a *common* prostitute.

The American neighborhoods boasted industry and busy commerce, and the main thoroughfare, Canal Street, was a virile feat of engineering at 170 feet of width. The best way to see the city above Canal, that is, the "American" section, was via streetcar, and New Orleans had built 186 miles of electric street lines. Canal Street divided New Orleans into "two worlds, two civilizations," the old and the new. Thus could New Orleans become at once the city of "Old Romance and New Opportunity."[76] The visitor to New Orleans was presented with a kind of self-conscious display of characteristic traits, "its Carnival and its climate combine to furnish one of the most interesting exhibitions upon this continent of the effects of American enterprise engrafted upon French and Spanish civilizations."[77] What is more, a "ride about the city on a sunshiny winter's morning will furnish a panorama to be found nowhere else in the United States."[78] The New South tourism industry retailed the image of New Orleans as rendered conscious by nineteenth-century travelers, literature, and lore. At the same time, as we shall see, Storyville retailed the less seemly side of the city through its own set of guidebooks—which, by providing the geographical boundaries of the district, made clear that Storyville was located precisely at the juncture of the French Quarter and the "New" American section: precisely, that is, where Old Romance met New Opportunity.

Early attempts to "clean up" New Orleans met resistance and reaction. When Benjamin Butler had charge of the city he implemented measures to sanitize the water supply and regularize municipal services. He was hated, and his successes in these areas were chalked up to coincidence by the rebels.

Another effort to clean up and modernize the city was similarly rejected by the white citizens of New Orleans. During Reconstruction, the young, ambitious, carpetbagger governor, Henry Clay Warmoth, together with the biracial legislature, passed a law to regulate the slaughter of animals in New Orleans. Denounced as creating a monopoly and as a violation of the Fourteenth Amendment rights of New Orleans's traditional butchers, the new slaughterhouse law came under attack as usurpatious legislation. The battle over whether the state had the power to institute such a law went to the U.S. Supreme Court, which famously ruled that it did. A short-term victory for Warmoth and the biracial state government became a long-term defeat for the meaning of the "privileges and immunities" of American citizenship and the ability of the federal government to protect African Americans and other people of color. The slaughterhouse law might have been seen as a boon for a city population long clamoring for action against the unruly and unsanitary (not to mention exclusionary) practices of the butchers; that it was not speaks to the priorities many of them held at the time. For most white New Orleanians, racial supremacy took precedence over clean water, proper drainage, the state of the gutters, and even states' rights! After the fall of Reconstruction, when white New Orleanians were virtually assured of Democratic rule and black disenfranchisement, it seemed possible that they could have both white supremacy and clean water.

Throughout most of the postbellum period, the Democratic-Conservative party's political machine ran the council and mayor's office. This "tightly knit, well-organized hierarchy with power firmly anchored at the ward level," in Eric Arnesen's words, was known simply as "the Ring."[79] The Ring had its detractors, and groups opposed to it mounted challenges, but without much electoral success. Some progress was made with regard to civic improvements in the 1880s, but the good government crowd wanted more than regular trash collection.[80] Then, after years of defeat by the Ring, in the 1896 municipal election a group of wealthy businessmen, in the form of a "Citizens' League," campaigned against the official ineffectiveness and corruption of the city government. These progressive businessmen viewed political corruption as an atavism preventing New Orleans from moving forward. The Citizens' League proposed a "clean up." "As death destroys citizenship, dead men shall no longer be permitted to exercise the right of suffrage," they announced as one of the tenets of their reform platform. The Citizens' League's candidate for mayor was Walter C. Flower, a businessman who had, in his words, been "thrown into politics." He was a wealthy cotton merchant who had "figured creditably in the battle of September 14, 1874," the White League *coup d'état.* His racial bona fides were supplemented by a sworn commitment to democracy; Flower pledged to "know no class distinctions" as well as to return New Orleans to its former prosperity.[81]

In 1896, Flower and his cohorts won the election, in defiance of the Ring.[82] The political machine recouped the mayor's office four years later, but in 1896, for the first time, it became possible to advance and pass a red-light ordinance for the purposes of limiting and segregating prostitution and other vicious commerce. Thus (to emphasize the point for a moment) the creation of Storyville was a reform measure, undertaken by a reform administration. Flower and his backers styled themselves as progressives, desirous of ushering in a new century of civic and commercial improvement. These men favored investments other than in booze and whorehouses, while at the same time they recognized that both legitimate and "illegitimate" businesses brought revenue into the city, so there was no sense in attacking prostitution needlessly. They were realists and did not try to banish prostitution to a back street or beyond the city's proper limits, instead preferring to recognize its concentration in a much more central location where it already flourished. Prostitution, like the other disorderly yet undeniable elements that defined the city, was to be made optional, packaged for the tourist (and the local) for easy, convenient consumption. In fact, concentrating and segregating commercial sex and "sporting" culture, keeping it away from Canal Street and the growing central business district, would still permit the businessmen to have the best of both worlds. The intended client for both entrepreneurial madams and cotton merchants was a northern white man, travelling far from home.[83]

The men in Flower's administration were committed to their vision of cleaning up New Orleans and establishing borders around illicit and sexual commerce.[84] The district of Storyville was named for Sidney Story, the councilman who suggested the measure. It was to lie on the margins of both the French Quarter and the American section, at the juncture between the ancient and modern sections of the city, as if to acknowledge prostitution's special history in the city. For these business-minded reformers, chief among their concerns was the matter of creating boundaries, of demarcating and hiding the elements of urban life that detracted from the picture they wanted New Orleans to present to the world. These self-styled progressives argued for a pragmatic stance on vice, all of a piece with other efforts at reform. That is to say, their worries were not for the eternal souls of prostitutes or their patrons, nor for the innocent wives and children exposed to venereal disease through prostitution (though perhaps they cared about these issues). Their efforts, rather, focused on removing "dirt," and their language reflected an abiding concern with appearances. These concerns were not, that is, limited to prostitutes plying their trade, but rather with a whole set of unseemly aspects of New Orleans's historical development, including for them the very existence of free men of color who blurred the boundaries of whiteness. For instance, the *Daily Picayune* posed the problem of visibility (as opposed to the health of the city's residents and visitors) when it editorialized in favor of modern drainage facilities in New Orleans. At issue in New Orleans, according to the paper, was a visible surfeit of human waste. "There is no way of concealing filth in this city. . . . If we have filth here it is exposed to view in the streets and every stranger sees it."[85] Modern cities needed proper sewers for much the same reason they needed red-light districts, in this white, bourgeois, hegemonic view.

In the intellectual heritage of the proponents of Storyville, one finds the legacy of Alexandre Parent-Duchatelet, the author of the early nineteenth-century Parisian system of *reglementation*. He showed how the two concerns, prostitution and sanitation, might be dealt with in the same way. Before turning to the issue of prostitution, Parent-Duchatelet made a broad study of the Paris sewers. He saw the two as analogous, and thus the solutions to both urban epidemics were also the same: keep them out of public view. "Prostitutes are as inevitable in an agglomeration of men as sewers, cesspits, and garbage dumps," he wrote. "Civil authority should . . . survey them, to attenuate by every possible means the detriments inherent to them, and for that purpose to hide them, to relegate them to the most obscure corners, in a word, to render their presence as inconspicuous as possible."[86] In the late nineteenth century, all over America, city governments designated vice districts to protect the sensibilities of "respectable citizens."[87]

In New Orleans, reformers' efforts to tidy up the boundaries between legitimate and illicit commerce flowed from their desires to attract northern capital and to reintegrate New Orleans into the national economy. This required a revision of the image of New Orleans as "dirty" and "disorderly," an image that threatened to displace the one of glorious markets and exotic manners created by the antebellum descriptions of the city. Northerners had long played a significant role in New Orleans's economy, moving down to the city to make their fortunes in cotton, banking, and other ventures; and as always, proper New Orleanians, the Creoles white and brown, of good homes, sneered at their preoccupation with money, their lack of refinement.[88] But it was also understood that the Anglo-Americans and northern capitalists, the Yankees, had established New Orleans as the banking capital of the South before the Civil War. Indeed, when the rest of the state voted to secede, the city of New Orleans voted to remain in the Union.[89] In the midst of the postwar depression, anti-northern sentiment again disappeared in business circles, and by the mid-1880s, business in New Orleans was fully on board with the project of national reconciliation and economic progress, provided the "race question" was left to them. The effort coincided with the rapid expansion of tourism and the growth of rail travel to the South, and New Orleans, by virtue of its history and geography, was potentially an ideal New South city. Though it lacked manufacturing industries, it had a long head start as an urban center.

The aforementioned *Daily Picayune* editorial about sewers was really about commerce, the title, "The only way to get a boom here," indicating the paper's concern with bringing in capital and with the experience of the foreigner in the city. It was crucial that his experience not be dominated by excrement. The paper, echoing progressive businessmen and city boosters, sought to make New Orleans "a great winter sanitarium," but to do so they would have to rid the city of the ravages of fever and filth. The problem in New Orleans was both literal and metaphorical: how a society makes and disposes of its filth accords with its relations of power, its concrete hierarchies. As Mary Douglas famously argued, filth and pollution are felt because they are elements of a socially constructed system. Pollution emerges in society when objects and their symbols appear to be out of place, miscategorized, or more generally out of order. Thus, "ideas about separating, purifying, demarcating and punishing transgressions have as their main function to impose system on an inherently untidy experience."[90]

It is fitting that the railroad, the symbol of innovation, progress, technology, and American ascendancy, was at this time also the site and symbol of the coming system of racial hierarchy: segregation. If the railroad represented the future, then it had also to carry the projected future order of race relations. In 1890, as the Louisiana legislature proposed a bill to promote the comfort of passengers on railroad trains, they surely recognized the crucial importance of this mode of transporting people as well as goods. When the legislation introducing the Separate Car Act appeared in the newspaper, it did so inconspicuously, under "railroads," with no mention of race in "House bill No. 42, by Mr. St. Amant."[91]

At the same time that this bill was wending its way forward (the Senate did not pass it on the first go-round), the U.S. Congress and local newspapers debated a bill proposed by Massachusetts senator Henry Cabot Lodge that would have mandated federal oversight of local congressional elections. To southerners, including New Orleanians, this bill, referred to defensively as the Force Bill, represented a northern effort to continue the war and to subject them to "negro rule." "The desperate determination of the Republican leaders in Congress to place the Southern States in a condition of political subjugation, is emphasized by their efforts to enact a proscriptive and radically revolutionary law to control Congressional elections in the Southern States. When," the paper asked, "is this war of section to cease?" The paper answered its own question. Once northern commercial interests were sufficiently convinced of the money to be made down South, their avowed interest in racial justice—or, "political subjugation"—would subside.[92] Two days before this article appeared, the Separate Car Bill was approved by the House. A little over a week later the *New Orleans Daily States* ran an editorial bluntly titled, "White Supremacy." Here the editors conflate political and sexual "commingling," and reach the conclusion that resistance, armed if necessary, is the only possible response to the hated Force Bill. "White supremacy is the end towards which all Southern white people strive and will keep on striving until it is made certain beyond contingency."[93] The Force Bill represented continued political domination of the South by the North, in the form of protecting the voting rights of people of color. In New Orleans, wrote the editors, "all parties are settled in their aversion to negro suffrage. . . . They know that the white people alone constitute the sole rightful sovereign power." All were likewise agreed in the belief that during Reconstruction the "imposition of negro suffrage was a monstrous political crime," and they planned to "bear it only while under compulsion, in the meantime ignoring it and nullifying its effects in every practical way." These feelings were "simply a protest against the blending of races, a political commingly [*sic*] of two nations as distinct as it is possible to be, of two elements that cannot be and never have been assimilated. Against social equality and social blending of whites and blacks the revolt has been instantaneous, universal, and complete, nor can any power whatever prevent this social revolt from manifesting itself in a corresponding political revolt."[94]

The Force Bill did not pass. The New Orleans white dailies were elated. Rather than celebrate its defeat purely as a triumph for white supremacy, they celebrated it as evidence of the promise of future business dealings across sectional lines. The *Daily Picayune* said that the Force Bill's defeat "assured perfect peace," and a racial comity that would soon woo commercial investors. The alternative, that is if the bill had passed, was "all interests disturbed, all values unsettled, capital scared away and commercial and industrial development wholly stagnated."[95] In this view black rights, and not the violent repression of those rights, were the cause of disorder, antithetical to the development and maintenance of a good business climate.

Thus there was in New Orleans a perceived economic imperative to suppressing black rights: doing so would bring "peace" and capital, and failing would mean "all interests disturbed, all values unsettled, *capital scared away and commercial and industrial development wholly stagnated.*" Race, politics, sex, manhood, honor, and *business* were all so closely and inescapably bound together that editors and politicians apparently did not need to parse their incommensurability. People of color, along with prostitutes and human waste, were, in this view, vehicles of disease and pollution who constituted danger and disorder; they were bad for business.[96] In the context of these other efforts to carve out clear (and clean) spaces for "respectable" citizens, racial "segregation" was somehow itself legitimated and sanitized. Meanwhile, public spaces and accommodations became legible maps for discerning social hierarchies and racial ordination.[97]

Even Carnival—the epitome, it would seem, of disorder—was appropriated and reorganized by the white elite and business leaders in post-Reconstruction New Orleans as part of their efforts to control the image of their city. In the 1880s and 1890s elite Mardi Gras krewes celebrated advanced civilizations and science, subjects they considered conducive to comfortable national dialogue. The "civic-minded leaders turned a rowdy affair into an exotic and elegant public display," creating an atmosphere, in Karen Leathem's phrase, of "mannerly madness," dressing in elaborate costumes and parading through the city while bystanders passively observed.[98] This trend of distinguishing between official paraders and passive observers began in the late antebellum period with the first organized parades through the city. After the war and Reconstruction, the imperative to project order and control over the rowdier elements associated with Mardi Gras was directly tied to sectional reconciliation along the lines of business cooperation, investment, and tourism.[99] The *Daily Picayune* espoused a thoroughly orderly Mardi Gras, touting "the magnificent pageants and the entirely orderly and systematic exercises." Thus the business community billed its Mardi Gras as a celebration of the lost city of Atlantis in 1891, "calling in for its elucidation all ancient tradition and modern science. . . ." The paper's claim that "the work of the new Carnival association, the Atlanteans . . . is in itself a liberal education" worked against the idea that New Orleans itself represented a kind of topsy turvy world unsafe for northerners or their investment capital.[100] The Atlanteans were one of several Mardi Gras associations that in the last decade of the nineteenth century initiated the ritual of the Mardi Gras balls. These exclusive, class-bound events were committed to the maintenance of order and hierarchy. The association would present several tableaux representing their theme, and the audience would take them in one at a time. Dancing followed, as groups were invited to dance according to a predetermined order.[101] "As to license and vice, these hideous monsters, from which no large city is free, do not dare to show themselves in public. At no season are they *so severely repressed as in Carnival time.*"[102]

In fact, the 1890s witnessed violence and racial strife without parallel in New Orleans's postwar history, ending with the explosive race riot of 1900, in which the New Orleans police force, joined by other white citizens, chased down a black migrant laborer from Mississippi named Robert Charles. Charles had endured virulent racism in both his native Mississippi and his adopted New Orleans home and had become an advocate of the back-to-Africa movement. When three beat cops approached him on Dryades Street, he reacted defensively. One of the officers shot him and he shot back. In the end Charles shot and killed many whites, including two police officers. He was eventually shot to death himself. The riot that erupted after his demise showed how much the city had become a powder keg. White New Orleanians rampaged through black neighborhoods after Charles's death, beating up and even killing black New Orleanians, as mentioned in the last chapter.[103] And still, many white citizens viewed the riot as entirely caused by Charles, who, by the end of the carnage, was described as a barbarian and a monster.[104]

In the presentation of New Orleans to the potential tourist and the potential investor, images of riots, like the smells of sewers and calls of prostitutes, had to be suppressed. Even raucous Mardi Gras revelers had to keep quiet! In all these instances, the same kind of resolution was advanced: clarify the boundaries of respectability and sin, *and* of black and white. Modernizing the city meant establishing borders around vice, around waste, around disease, even around people of color, all of which otherwise produced "disorder." Thus we see in the project of creating a "clean," segregated (racially and morally) public sphere a projection of the bourgeois desire for order, cleanliness, and legible boundaries. The creation of Storyville, along with other efforts to "clean up" New Orleans, were part of a larger process of reordering the social hierarchy in response to perceptions of disorder, anarchy, chaos. In New Orleans, this end was self-consciously pursued by the business elite to make their city more attractive to visitors and investors. If New Orleans, the quintessential *ville sauvage,* was to become properly bourgeois, according to the whites who wanted to make it so, prostitution, sewage, interracial sex, even black men voting, and other apprehensions of "dirt" or disorder would have to be relegated to their proper places.[105] Not only the business elite, but residents of the city, too, participated in the process of reordination, claiming respectability for themselves by denouncing their neighbors' behavior and petitioning the city government to suppress disorder or to remove it from their midst.

Enforcing Storyville's Borders

In 1898, the *Daily Picayune* used an account of a rape to tout the value of the new red-light district ordinance. The crime had transpired shamefully enough in a back room at the intersection of Canal and Dauphine streets, "the very heart of what is supposed to be one of the most respectable parts of the city." Such things were to be confined to Storyville, "the Tenderloin," or in another guise, "the slums," "obscure neighborhoods, where decent people will not be constantly offended by their open and shameless flauntings."[106] The business-oriented and reform-minded communities saw great promise in the Storyville ordinance. They looked forward to its honest enforcement throughout the rest of the city. Questions of rape aside, however, prostitutes still populated the French Quarter and other areas that were being groomed for the hoped-for boom in tourism. Newspapers cited instances in which respectable citizens were harassed by "harridans" in their midst. In one article, headlined simply, "Clean 'Em Out," the *New Orleans Daily States* decried the "denizens of depravity" who "roam about the street in deshabille costumes and disgustingly display their nudity through the open windows of their bagnios." These prostitutes effectively prevented women from riding on the Burgundy street cars from Esplanade across the French Quarter (where they would shop). Two "courtesans" had, for instance, harassed a grandmother from their window as she strolled past with two of her grandchildren.[107]

The margins of the sex industry had been delineated in the years just before the Storyville ordinance. In 1893, the neighbors of Otto Schoenhausen, a major saloon proprietor, sued him, saying his business was depreciating the value of their property. Neighbors complained that Schoenhausen's club on Royal Street, the Tivoli Varieties, was in too close proximity to Canal Street and to the prominent statue of Henry Clay, and that it discouraged foot traffic on what was by then "one of the most important thoroughfares in the city."[108] In an argument reminiscent of earlier reform efforts at mid-century, the plaintiffs argued that were it not for the Tivoli Varieties, the street "would be frequented by almost all the traveling public," funneling their money into the legitimate businesses in the vicinity. By counterposing legitimate and illegitimate commerce in the courts, as Alecia Long has argued, this lawsuit paved the way for the creation of Storyville.[109] The problem was not that the nightclub promoted illicit sex (or exploited young, unsuspecting girls), but that this particular establishment interfered with the shops offering hats, shoes, and silks.

In the 1890s, gambling halls and concert saloons increasingly sprang up on Royal Street. Once more, arguments against them reflected the interests of "progressive" businessmen in hiding aspects of New Orleans's disorderly past, separating it from a cleaner, brighter, and more orderly future. In 1895 prostitutes were cleared from the upscale residential area, the Garden District, and kicked off Canal Street, which was by then the main avenue for legitimate commerce. Intermittently and quixotically to be sure, these borders were enforced.[110]

New Orleans businessmen and reformers generally agreed that the Storyville ordinance was a good law provided it was enforced. But enforcing the ordinance was never a top priority in New Orleans. The police force was notoriously corrupt and vulnerable to bribes.[111] A local dermatologist and specialist in venereal diseases, Dr. Isidore Dyer, in comments to the International Conference for the Prevention of Syphilis and Venereal Diseases, commended the Storyville ordinance as "salutary," but lamented that it was not enforced. Police inaction had allowed houses of prostitution in other areas of the city to be reoccupied by prostitutes.[112] In December 1902, the president of the New Orleans YMCA convened a group of reformers to discuss the continuing problem of prostitution outside of Storyville. They agreed unanimously that "the [Storyville] law is a good one," as it tended "toward the betterment of social conditions" and it "would remove temptation from the pain of young manhood," but that most of all it "should be enforced." The same month, the *New Orleans Item* launched a campaign against immoral and disorderly houses outside Storyville, accusing the city of ignoring the ordinance, and pointing out that bribery had permeated the poorly paid constabulary.[113] Newspapers sought to shame the city officials into action. "That the best and proudest families of the Southland should be exposed to insult and contamination by this laxity upon the part of your sworn officials is a shame, and should bring a blush to their cheeks." The *Times-Democrat* joined the *Item*'s crusade, reporting "an immoral house" in close proximity to a public school on North Rampart Street. "How long," the paper asked, "will the self-respecting public permit these insidious foes of the social order to violate with impunity the laws of this city? . . . A decent regard for the ordinary laws of morality requires that the ordinance which is intended to segregate and isolate sinful and vicious members of society be promptly and rigorously enforced."[114] Leading businessmen and property owners agreed. One headline proclaimed: "Crush out Immoral Houses Outside Storeyville [*sic*]; Cry Echoes from All Quarters." The president of Whitney National Bank said he was "heart and soul" behind this reform, as was "every right thinking man." Their outrage was not about morality *per se,* but about the maintenance of clear boundaries. The moral argument could not aim solely at "a rigid enforcement of the Story ordinance."[115]

Let us look for a moment at the essence of this appeal, with the example of Santos Oteri, a "fruit jobber, bank director and oil magnate, a leader in business circles and one of the largest realty owners in the city," according to the *New Orleans Item*.[116] The persistent presence of immorality outside of Storyville disturbed and disgusted Oteri. Sitting in his richly appointed library, moving "his hand around as if to call attention to the attractive interior of his palatial residence," according to reporters, Mr. Oteri said that in spite of the thousands of dollars he had spent on furnishings, he might be forced to move. Why? "There are immoral houses on this block, right under the very eyes of the high-toned, aristocratic residents of whom I speak. . . . Is it a square deal to allow these women to flaunt their vice in the faces of law-abiding, taxpaying citizens, and insult by their presence the innocent women and girls in a respectable neighborhood?" Prostitution was all right, he seemed to be saying, just not so close to home. Oteri felt that "there should be a place for everything and everything should be in its place. The law has made and provided a place for these women, and they should be made to stay there."

Oteri asserted that he was no "moralist" himself, but rather "a man of the world, with all of a man of the world's leniency toward indulgence." According to the city's tax assessment records, he had financial reasons for his position: Oteri owned six lots of land on Basin Street, just a few houses down from Josie Arlington's and Lulu White's famous bordellos, and several other properties inside the district to boot (a fact not mentioned in the *Item* article).[117] He offered his time and money to aid in "the enforcement of this ordinance and the protection of pure women and innocent girls from contamination," which would properly be confined to Storyville, his time and money having been liberated by the high rents he himself derived there. It should not surprise us that Oteri would prefer to erect a wall between his domestic arrangements and a source of his family's livelihood. Undoubtedly there were others like him, people who straddled all sides of the "regulation" debate. Men like Oteri sustained Storyville. (And as we shall see, Storyville's promoters deliberately appealed to their taste and self-styled "high-class" or "aristocratic" status in their advertisements for the best bordellos, spaces which bore a remarkable similarity to Oteri's own well-appointed dwelling.)

The YMCA enjoined "every good man and woman" in New Orleans to get involved in the crusade, to spot disorderly houses and file affidavits against them and to go to court if necessary to see their inhabitants removed from respectable neighborhoods; in other words, to do what George L'Hote claimed to have done in his neighborhood until his neighborhood *became* the designated vice district. Councilman Trigg Moss added his voice to the paper's crusade and enjoined residents to take action against vice in their neighborhoods. The enforcement of the Storyville ordinance would require cooperation from all members of society and would likewise redound to the benefit of all members. Temptation caused harm. "There can be no doubt," Moss proclaimed, "as to the evil effects of the non-enforcement of this good law. Temptation thrown directly in the path of young men and sin flaunted in the faces of pure young girls can not help but be dire in its consequences and disastrous to the city's standard of morality." As a member of the city council's law and order committee, Moss was "grateful" to the *Item* for launching its crusade, and encouraged the paper to keep it up "until the inmates of every immoral house in the city are moved to the confines of Storyville and [echoing Oteri word for word] made to stay there."[118] The trouble with this philosophy, however, was that there was simply too much vice in New Orleans. Even if all the "lewd and abandoned" women obeyed the order, according to one knowledgeable observer, there was "barely one-fourth enough houses to hold the women [i.e., prostitutes] in that territory."[119] From the outset, it seems, the Storyville solution was bound to fail. Still, the ordinance and the calls for its enforcement contributed to a legal-linguistic vocabulary of respectability for residents of questionable neighborhoods.

Citizens did, in the early years of Storyville, attempt to clean up their own neighborhoods, to rid them of disorder, and thus to lay claim to respectability within them. As residents attempted to police the boundaries of their neighborhoods, they objected to more than prostitution. All sorts of entertainments fell under the rubric of "disorder." The tide was turning toward residential segregation as a middle-class prerogative at the same time that residents objected to vice in their midst. We must not confuse the "cleaning up" of actual prostitution with the "cleaning up" of racial boundaries. But self-styled "reformers" did exactly that. For white petitioners there was but one discourse of respectability. Residents asked that certain businesses be denied permits, certain halls be barred from holding dances, and certain neighbors be forced to vacate their premises. For instance: "We the white residents beg of your honor not to issue any more permits to negros [sic] in the eight hundred block of Adams St. for parties or Fish Frys [sic] as they are a nuisance to the neighborhood and keep them until all hours of the morning." Another letter writer, from 1900, "respectfully call[s] your attention to the fact that there congregates at the Corner of Marais and Baguatelle [sic, now Pauger] Sts. a crowd of disreputable negroes in front of a 'bar room' located there where it is very embarrassing for ladies and children to pass, as they gamble on the sidewalk, and use the vilest language imaginable. . . ."[120] Similarly, the "undersigned commissioners of Philip Park on Clark Place who are also property holders and residents and the residents of the immediate vicinity of the corner Philip and Liberty [streets] do hereby protest against the colored hall at the above corner known as the Ladies Providence Benevolent Association Hall, insofar as the giving of Balls, Parties, Dances and the like in said hall at such unreasonable hours. The doors of said Hall are opened at about 8:30 P.M., and the music and dancing at 9:30 or 10:00 pm and last until the small hours of the morning and thereby disturbing the public peace and also causing crowds to congregate on the banquette and in the park especially after 10:00 pm." In the original petition, the word "colored" was added after the petition was drafted, inserted into the text with a caret. These commissioners asked "for relief and the public nuisance be abated and that your honor issue no more permits for entertainments etc. in this Hall."[121] A resident and property owner wrote to the city council in 1902 to complain about "concerts" in his neighborhood. "My tenants complain that the performances are continued into a late hour of the night that the negroes become drunk and boisterous and that . . . in fact, while the performance lasts pandemonium reigns supreme."[122] In another letter, a mother protested the perhaps more disorderly prospects of a bar opening in her vicinity:

> We the residents residing in the vicinity of sixth and Saratoga Streets would respectfully ask your intercession in preventing the City Council members from granting a permit to one Louisa Drell to operate a barroom at the above mentioned bar as the party that has petitioned the council does not reside there her two sons runs the place and at the present time it is a disgrace to the neighborhood. They have nightly fights there last night a young white man was almost killed by the negroes that congregate there nightly and there is a church within 260 feet from the above mentioned place they also have women dancing in the barroom and it is simply disgusting to see the carrying on as I am raising young ladies of daughters and feel it a mother's duty to seek redress from your honor. . . .[123]

One wonders if Robert Charles frequented this bar: months before the riot that would bear his name, he rented a flat only two blocks away.

Residents in the Fifth District protested against "the operation of a negro dance hall at the corner of Verret and Homer streets," and in 1907 a group of "property owners and residents on Orleans Street between Bourbon and Dauphine" decided that a house in their midst was a "nuisance," as it contained five unmarried "kept" women.[124] Another petition (signed by both "white" and "colored" residents) petitioned Mayor Martin Behrman to "have a Mrs. L. Milledon residing at 1622 Baronne Street removed from said neighborhood as she [was] conducting a house for immoral purposes at above residence." The mayor's office responded in legalistic jargon, but the message was clear: "The fact having come to the knowledge of the Mayor that house No. 823 St. Louis Street, is of the character described in Ordinance 13032, C.S., as amended by Ordinance 13485, C.S. adopted by the City Council of New Orleans, January 26 and July 6, 1897, respectively, you are hereby ordered to remove therefrom. . . ."[125]

Pressure from the community and business interests forced the police to arrest prostitutes. For example, following the *Item*'s "crusade," officers "discovered" more than fourteen immoral houses, filed notices to vacate, and arrested many "lewd and abandoned" women.[126] However, not everyone favored the Storyville ordinance's enforcement. Addresses known to have been brothels, it was strongly believed, could no longer be leased to respectable tenants. Moreover, the new boundaries could not entirely supplant demarcations that communities kept in memory. Finally, madams who were issued notices to move did not necessarily move into Storyville, where rents may have been too high and competition too great. "Women move from one respectable neighborhood to another," a newspaper complained.[127]

If designated disorderly houses had actually contained (and hidden) within their walls the illicit sex and immorality they promoted, then perhaps neighbors would not have found them so objectionable, so personally affronting. Houses of assignation or brothels, however, most often failed to do so. When the illicit and immoral activity spilled out onto the street, the whole neighborhood was affected. Consider the testimony of one resident of a supposedly "respectable" neighborhood:

> On September 12, [1909,] it was 2 o'clock, I was awakened by my wife calling to me; after going to the front window I saw a man and a woman both intoxicated and in a nude condition, the man had his privates hanging out of his under-clothes and the woman had her night gown raised up one side to her waist so that you could see her person. The woman was going in the closet, just then the man asked where in the hell she was going and the woman said can't I go take a shit without you following me. About this time she goes in the closet with a lighted candle and stands it on the seat, she said to him have you not had enough fucking, you think because you spend a few dollars you can fuck me all night, other fellows spend a damn side more than you and don't expect as much as you and the man remarked the hell with you come on inside with me and she said go inside and fuck Mrs. Sanchez [the proprietress]. After wiping herself both went inside with foul cursing passing between them.[128]

That is a vivid picture of precisely what "respectable" New Orleans sought to conceal: sex and excrement.[129] Immorality often spilled onto the sidewalks outside the witnesses's house, with raucous prostitutes soliciting passersby, talking about "screwing" and "getting a piece" at the house of "Mrs. Sanchez . . . that old bitch, that peroxide blonde."[130] Mrs. Sanchez and her customers broached the boundaries of the respectable public sphere, which was increasingly understood by white New Orleanians in terms of the civic body, and racially encoded as "white."[131] The municipal authorities, aided by outraged neighbors, stepped in to assert the boundaries of propriety and race through the courts and through eviction notices.

Yet, even if every prostitute, madam, and woman "notoriously abandoned to lewdness," from every assignation house and crib, had moved
into Storyville, the problem of visibility would have remained.[132] Storyville
made commercial and interracial sex more visible than ever before. Storyville combined racial and sexual elements of antebellum New Orleans,
which were also part and parcel of its internationalism and cosmopolitanism, and placed them in a nineteen-square-block section of the city; as it did
so, Storyville also condensed two hundred years of prostitution and became
a tourist attraction in its own right.

The men who created Storyville were self-styled progressive businessmen; they were white supremacists who believed that prostitutes, people of
color, Carnival, excrement, and illicit and interracial sex all constituted pollution, that all contaminated what they touched, literally and figuratively.
To modernize New Orleans required the erasure, or removal from public
view, of these myriad contaminants. Racial segregation and the segregation
of commercial sex were twin processes in the reformation of postbellum
New Orleans. Both processes would, it was hoped and believed, usher in a
new era of prosperity, fueled by northern capital and (old) southern charm,
mixed with New South industry. But just as certainly as black laborers, and
to an extent, consumers, were necessary to the success of New Orleans,
prostitution was a money-making proposition for businessmen in New Orleans—like Oteri, for example. The important thing was that prostitutes,
and blacks, be put in their place—and made to stay there.

Storyville quickly defied the controls of the men who created it, explod-
ing its physical boundaries to become, itself, a metonym for New Orleans.
Rather than render prostitution and its supporting culture invisible, the creation of a red-light district concentrated vice in a central location, perhaps
removing it from the daily contemplation of most New Orleanians, but in
the process focusing a spotlight on it for anyone who cared to look (and
indeed for many who could not avert their eyes). Storyville resonated with
earlier visions of the city, and its promoters recirculated popular images of
Old New Orleans, orienting them toward sex and profit. The city's commercial elite continued to promote business, the building of railroads, and the
expansion of trade. They continued, too, to build figurative bridges to the
North, encouraging tourism and investment. But the balance of power that
allowed a cohort of progressive businessmen to gain elected office in New
Orleans shifted, and the machine politicians of the Ring regained control
of the city in 1900 under Mayor Paul Capdevielle. In 1904, Martin Behrman

began his long tenure as mayor, a position he kept for sixteen years. The full extent of the involvement of these men with the operation of Storyville is not possible to gauge, but members of the Ring's social club as well as those active in city politics helped finance the construction of bordellos and also supplied attorneys for prostitutes and madams; one state legislator, Tom Anderson, was a well-known power broker inside the district.

Storyville became internationally known for its "octoroon" prostitutes: women supposedly one-eighth black who looked white. Rather than obscure the history of interracial sex in New Orleans, Storyville exploited it fully. At almost the precise moment that the U.S. Supreme Court denied the existence of, and certainly the significance of, New Orleans's people of mixed race, its *gens de couleur libres,* Storyville brought that heritage stunningly into view—but exclusively as a feminine domain, populated by prostitutes. Storyville, through its exploitation of the erotic octoroon, facilitated the marginalization of the men who had led the civil rights movement for all people of color. Storyville, perhaps more successfully than the so-called legitimate interests, reinvented antebellum New Orleans for the northerner, the tourist, the investor, even the local. In doing so, the district helped to reimagine the city's and the South's past in ways that would ultimately serve Jim Crow.

Crib Girl, by E. J. Bellocq
(Courtesy of the Hogan Jazz Archive, Tulane University)

Stockings, by E. J. Bellocq
(Courtesy of the Hogan Jazz Archive, Tulane University)

Multiple Wall, by E. J. Bellocq
(Courtesy of the Hogan Jazz Archive, Tulane University)

Bunk Johnson (*standing second from left*) and the Superior Orchestra, 1910
(Courtesy of the Hogan Jazz Archive, Tulane University)

Emile "Stalebread" Lacoume and band at a family picnic.
Lacoume is the guitarist standing on the far right.
(Courtesy of the Hogan Jazz Archive, Tulane University)

Kid Ory (*second from left*) and the Woodland Band, 1905
(Courtesy of the Hogan Jazz Archive, Tulane University)

Down the Line—view of Basin Street, New Orleans
(Courtesy of the Hogan Jazz Archive, Tulane University)

Above and right:
New Orleans Police Department "mug shots" of women of Storyville
(Louisiana Division/City Archives, New Orleans Public Library)

Up the Line—another view of Basin Street, New Orleans
(Postcard Collection, Louisiana Division/City Archives, New Orleans Public Library)

CHAPTER FOUR

Where the Light and Dark Folks Meet

What is the good of living if you can't have a good time, or, as the proverb
goes[,] Live while you have a chance. You will be dead a long time.

—STORYVILLE BLUE BOOKS

Storyville was a tourist attraction for a specific type of tourist, and in a
sense the district's promoters created in the demi-monde what the New
Orleans business community sought to create in respectable New Orleans:
a thoroughly modern economy resonant with the Old World charm of antebellum New Orleans and the spectacle of its markets in goods, slaves, and
women. Like the rotundas of the St. Louis and St. Charles hotels, Storyville
was also "a kind of homosocial pleasure dome with overlapping commercial and leisure attractions" in a "pornographic" atmosphere.[1] Nonetheless,
Storyville also, through its advertising, its architecture, and its flagrant promotion of interracial sex, mocked the legitimate enterprise of the men who
wrote its ordinance, making a world in microcosm in which social norms
were turned upside down, especially rules about race and gender. Because
Storyville occupied a clearly demarcated transgressive space, Storyville's
profiteers were released from conforming to the ascending discourse of
white supremacy and conventional marriage. At the same time, Storyville
depended on and grew out of that legitimate world and all its proscriptions.

Storyville capitalized on the fantasy of male dominance in an era of anxiety and flux. Scholarship of this period has focused on a "crisis in masculinity" in America, where the Civil War and its shattering aftermath, among
other factors, led to a loss of masculine self-assuredness.[2] Storyville was one
of many sites during this period where that crisis was reworked into new
meanings for American manhood, where whiteness and maleness were re-

figured. Storyville was a both a transitional site and a liminal space.[3] The feelings of loss and displacement, humiliation and impotence, that lingered from the defeat of the Confederacy; the anxieties about the postbellum world, a world turned upside down by the new status not only of black men but of white women in the public sphere; xenophobia and status anxiety provoked by the new immigrant populations in industrializing cities; and the blood-boiling anger from dispossession, displacement, and depression— all might be suspended in the alternative reality presented in Storyville.

Forbidden sex, including sex across the color line, was Storyville's stock-in-trade, and the district's guidebooks made it clear that so-called octoroons constituted a special class of sexual experience, much as light-skinned female slaves had been touted during slavery days. This is not to suggest that Storyville was actually an anachronism or a holdover from a previous era. On the contrary, Storyville was a modern money-making outfit with a clear marketing niche. Storyville was also what Joseph Roach calls a "stage of cultural self-invention through restored behavior."[4] The behavior here was the purchase of "fancies," as slaves and sexual servants. If the men who sought possession of a "fancy girl" during antebellum times desired "enslaved versions of mastery," men who sought possession of an "octoroon" in Storyville sought the New South corollary—acknowledgment of their status, success, and social station within the striving New South milieu.[5] Octoroons were only the most obvious throwback to the auctions of the slavery days; the whole district, with its diversity of erotic enticements, reflected the markets in goods and people that had made the antebellum city what it was. Like the legitimate tourist industry that supported the New South dreams of the city council and others interested in the modernization of New Orleans, Storyville's operatives also reimagined aspects of the antebellum past and set them within the present.

By placing Storyville in the context of larger trends in American culture, we see more clearly how Storyville promoted and profited from marketing miscegenation at a time when interracial sex was strictly forbidden and black/white distinctions were supposed to be absolute.[6] By "marketing miscegenation," I mean not only selling sex across the color line, but specifically the advertising of *octoroons*, themselves purported to be products of three or more generations of miscegenation.[7] That is to say, the district promoted, among its other pleasures, embodiments of the *history* of sexual subordination—and dominance—along with the promise to satisfy the desires of its male clientele for sex across the color line.

Spectacular Wickedness

Introduction.

How to be Wise.

A man who wants to be a thoroughbred rounder these days has to carry a certain amount of hot air and be a wise guy, no matter how painful.

Now if you are in the A.B.C. class you want to get a move on yourself and "23," and to do it proper is to read what this little booklet has to say and if you don't get to be a 2 to 1 shot it aint the authors fault.

There is more than one way to spend your coin besides going against brace games and if you pay particular attention to this guide you will never be lead astray by touts or gold brick advisers.

The contents of this book are the facts and not dreams from a "hop joint."

You will now find the boundry of the Tenderloin District, commonly known as Anderson County or Storyville: North side Customhouse st. to South side St. Louis and East side N. Basin to West side N. Robertson.

This is the boundry in which the lewd women are compelled to live according to law.

This book not mailable.[8]

Storyville produced guidebooks to the district, and newsboys waited at the city's several passenger train stations to hand them out to disembarking men.[9] One of the little books, called *The Lid,* opened with an ad for a saloon run by one of Storyville's most powerful businessmen, state senator Tom Anderson. His saloon was "The Key-Hole to the District," the ad smirked. The booklet listed the names of the "class women" of Storyville, "no matter which one you choose to ring up by phone."[10] There were other "tipster" guides as well, jocose and winking, one signed "Little Salty" that included five "Octoroon" bordellos on North Basin Street and one on Customhouse.[11]

If the traveler desired more information, many saloons, restaurants, and cafés sold the premium guidebooks to Storyville, the famous Blue Books. Each guide begins with an introduction combining innuendo and incomprehensible (from a modern standpoint) slang with the kind of useful information any tourist would desire, including a key to reading the guide. "Names in Capitals are Landladies. 'W' stands for white, 'C' for colored, and 'Oct.' for octoroon."[12] After 1910, the guides changed their rubric from their geographical orientation to an alphabetical order, with the various races of the prostitutes still accentuated: "The Directory will be found alphabetically, under the heading 'White' and 'Colored,' from alpha to omega."[13] This figurative segregation only highlighted the availability of interracial sex in the district, making seeking it more convenient.

The Blue Books imitated the conventions of the legitimate tourism industry and yet mocked the pretensions of those who lived by it, and they carried this pitch nearly perfectly. "Why New Orleans Should Have this Directory," one book explained:

> First—Because it is the only district of its kind in the States set aside for the fast women by LAW.
> Second—Because it puts the stranger on a proper grade or path as to where to go and be secure from hold-ups, brace games, and other illegal practices usually worked on the unwise in the Red Light Districts.[14]

Hence the "informative" and legalistic aspect; yet the guides maintained a tongue-in-cheek insouciance, while their legitimate counterparts in the tourism industry were earnest to a fault, even if not always honest. Note this "intruduction" [sic]: "What is the good of living if you can't have a good time, or, as the proverb goes[,] Live while you have a chance. You will be dead a long time." In other words, be prudent enough to read this guide, but reject all moral strictures in doing so. "Now," the book continued, "the only way to get next to all the good things is to pay particular attention to what this PAMPHLET has to say."[15]

The pamphlet featured "all the sporting houses in the tenderloin," delimited as "N. Basin to N. Robertson, Customhouse to St. Louis. This is Storyville." Some early editions of the Blue Book also included the customary and wider pre-Storyville parameters of the 1890s, "Anderson County (old tenderloin)," named after the aforementioned Tom Anderson, of "Customhouse to St. Peter, Dauphine to Rampart. . . ." The names in the Blue Book, according to the guide itself, constituted "the Tenderloin '400,' one of the grandest sporting societies in existence to-day." The promise of comprehensiveness made the Blue Books unique. The term "Blue Book" itself registered in several different ways: any official colonial or governmental publication is commonly called a "blue book"; French tourist guides were "Guides Bleus"; and "the blue book" was a list of the most prominent members of society, featuring young debutantes. The subtitle, "Tenderloin 400," drew out these ironic connections, highlighting the boundedness of the demimonde's elite by referring to Ward McAllister's New York social register and "The Four Hundred" guests from New York's elite circles who were invited to Mrs. William Astor's 1892 gala ball. Certainly a New Orleans bordello was not to be compared with any seriousness to Mrs. Astor's party—or was it?

The guides promised to put their readers "in the know," while their tone made a joke of the transgression they promoted. "To know a thing or two and to know it direct, go through this little book and read it carefully, and then when you go on a 'lark' you'll know 'who is who' and the best place to spend your time and money . . . [on] the 'Cream of Society.'"[16] Private advertisements by bordellos adopted the same teasing tone of the guides, brazenly claiming the absurd and the impossible. "Like the stars above, Miss Olive Russell, of Customhouse [Street] has appeared before the better class of sporting gentlemen of this community and never has her reputation been other than a highly cultivated lady." When you are "out for a good time don't over-look her house, her ladies are of a like character." Similarly, "Miss Josie Arlington, 225 N. Basin St. No pen can describe the beauty and magnificence . . . the draperies, carved furniture and oil painting or [sic: are] of foreign make and a visit will teach more than man can tell."[17] Or ever would tell. The Blue Books used the markers of class status—draperies, oil paintings, and carved furniture—to draw the customer into a disingenuous drama of upward mobility rather than a straightforward journey to sensual pleasure.[18] Photographs of the opulent parlors were included in the advertisements. For instance, Lulu White, the self-styled "handsomest octoroon" in America and proprietress of Mahogany Hall, also known as the "Octoroon Club," published photos and descriptions of all her beautiful "white-looking" girls in her own little booklet, which she called a "souvenir."[19]

Frequently customers brought home another kind of souvenir: a sexually transmitted disease. The Blue Books had an answer for this:

> When troubled with a leak use the famous Number 7 Seven, Specifics,
> A marvelous success with Gonorrhea and Gleet, Cures in 3 Days.
> When worried with with [sic] Crawlers try a bottle of
>
> ANTI-CRAB LOTION,
>   IT KILLS
>
> J.A. Legendre,
> Two Stores:
> Cor. Dauphine and Customhouse Sts.
> Corner Dauphine and Lafayette Ave.[20]

Sometimes one Blue Book featured three or four ads for cures like the above "Number 7 Seven," or Otto Hellman's No. 206 Mixture, "A sure cure in a short time. Prepared only by OTTO HELLMAN, APOTHECARY . . . Remember you won't be away from your girl long if you use No. 206." Local merchants, lawyers, pharmacies, even funeral parlors advertised in the Blue Books:

> A.E. Ravain,
> Funeral Director and Embalmer
> 302–304 N. Rampart Ave. Cor. Bienville.
> Fine Funeral Furnishings.[21]

Aside from the advertisements for houses of prostitution, the most common ads in the Blue Books were for liquor and liquor distributors. This reminds us of something important about Storyville: that the liquor industry had a keen interest in promoting prostitution and pleasure in New Orleans. "Drink Raleigh Rye, For Men of Brains." "DRINK LEMP'S BEER." "Barbarossa is the most exquisite bottled beer in the world. Moerlein's Bottled Beers are the model for purity and healthfulness." This latter ad featured a drawing of a naked woman lifting her glass, as in a toast, her naked body partially obscured by a large bottle of beer.[22]

Quite apart from the advertisements, the Blue Books listed bordellos, cribs, or "roping in" joints. In the premiere guide, from 1898, after a list of "French 69" Houses, there was a postscript (where "PS" might be read as "pssst"): "P.S.—There are also 7 or 8 roping in french resorts on Customhouse between Basin and Franklin, opposite the negro dance halls." It is hard to imagine today what "roping in french resorts" featured, but likely the term meant that requests for special sexual positions were not denied. And then, "The 'Grotto' white dance hall in 320 Marais st. Every old thing goes here—don't miss it."[23] But the ad is deceptive; "every old thing" *didn't* go if dance halls were still for "whites" or "negroes." Bordellos and cribs offered sex across the color line, but dancing, which might suggest or foster interracial fraternizing or romance, rather than paid sex, was segregated.[24]

Storyville had an answer to the exclusive, invitation-only, class-bounded Mardi Gras balls of Carnival time, too.[25]

> Fun! Fun! Fun! Don't miss the FRENCH BALLS Given by the C.C.C. Club and Two Well-Known Gentlemen. Odd Fellow's Hall, February 9th and Mardi Gras Night. Tickets for sale at Tom Anderson's Three Saloons and Lamothe's Restaurant, 716 Gravier Street.[26]

The two well-known gentlemen, one of whom was Tom Anderson, sold tickets to their own Mardi Gras ball, no invitations required. The district might have invited "slumming," like its contemporary districts in New York, Chicago, and elsewhere, but it was also a beacon to social transgressors lower down on the social ladder.[27]

It was this mix of high and low, social pretension and low humor, that characterized the Blue Books. Take, for example, an ad for the Arlington Café and Restaurant, one of Tom Anderson's three saloons. The ad featured a picture of a thoroughbred with the legend "The House of Sports."[28] Recall that "sporting" was a code word for the male world of drinking, gambling, and prostitution. Here the double entendre includes the "sport" of horse racing, which itself encoded elitism in high-priced horses and high-stakes gambling, but did not rule out the two-bit bet and the bookie. Another Anderson establishment, the Arlington Annex was a combination restaurant-saloon and assignation house:

> A Mere Dream
> is the new Arlington Annex,
> Cor. N. Basin and Customhouse Sts.
> In having this place constructed the owner, Tom Anderson,
>   has spared no money, so you can imagine its beauty.
> Connausser's [sic] say it is the finest place where sports
>   congregate in the South.
> The best service can be had here at all times. Eatables and
>   drinkables are of the very best the land affords.
> Private dining rooms up and down stairs.
> Tom Anderson, Proprietor.[29]

The "sparing of no expense" was meant to suggest a world where money flowed as freely as the wine. The ads promised a lush and exclusive environment, an atmosphere of insiders accustomed to "the best service" money could buy. Even "private dining rooms" might suggest a sense of prewar elegance if their purpose for private assignations was not also apparent. We see in this ad the mix of high and low, the assertion of *class* and its undoing in a phrase touting "Connausser's." Storyville's promoters were painting a picture of legitimacy but in an underworld milieu, where it was simultaneously preposterous. The tension behind the effort derived from the economic decline of New Orleans and the destruction of the aristocratic, slaveowning classes, along with the rise of a new category of industrial elites, parvenus, and businessmen, not to mention the middle-class middle managers and clerks who served them.

Between the end of the Civil War and the opening of Storyville, the image of the chivalrous plantation gallant developed and spread, superseding other male archetypes from the plantation imaginary. More generally, the slave plantation came to symbolize an American pastoral Eden of propriety and manners, and the polar opposite of the northern city, with its bustle of Yankee enterprise.[30] At the same time, the commercial classes in New York and other northeastern cities sought to establish their cultural bona fides by embracing higher education and high culture, and in some cases funding them, as in Carnegie Hall or the University of Chicago.[31] In a sense, through the Blue Books, Storyville retold the triumph and the tragedy of what Joseph Roach calls the "mortgage melodrama," the story of the landed aristocracy losing everything to the new commercial classes. This was a drama well-known to audiences North and South from the antebellum period, as we have seen in considering the "tragic octoroon" literary genre. Storyville borrowed the script and leading player.[32]

The Blue Books mocked New Orleans's commercial elite, the very men who created (and visited) Storyville, and their desire to reinvent the glory of antebellum New Orleans and its (ideationally distinct) "aristocratic" or Creole legacy. Yet the ads also invite these same men to join in the fun-making, to take their places in the well-appointed parlors amid the oil paintings and leather-bound volumes, to enjoy the champagne and other libations, to have sex upstairs with a woman representable as beautiful and refined. The guides envisioned a world of male bonding separate from commerce and culture, a sociality devoted to "sport" and capped by private gratifications at the end of the evening. The joking language put men at their ease, helping them toward marital infidelity and possibly sex across the color line. In the Blue Books' construction, Storyville was a milieu where men could congregate beyond the watchful eyes of wives and society's other moral arbiters, inheriting the atmosphere of the auctions in the rotundas of the city's grandest hotels.

The proprietors of Storyville's best houses aimed their ads at the new class of businessmen and professionals desired by the city fathers to redeem New Orleans, to make it once again the metropolitan capital of the South. These men laid the foundations of the New South economy, and if they adhered to the principle of the free market, well, so did Storyville's madams. In Storyville, just as in the French Market of antebellum New Orleans, could be found a true "common ground of liberty and commerce."[33] If one could pay, one got service: cash was the new class. Consider Gipsy Scheaffer's advertisement:

> To operate an establishment where everyone is treated exact is not an easy task, and Gipsy deserves great credit for the manner in which she conducts her house. Gipsie [sic] has always made it a mark in life to treat everyone alike, and to see that they enjoy themselves while in her midst.[34]

Of course "Gypsies" were reputed cheats and scoundrels, bohemian itinerants and circus performers, another iteration of the motif of self-undermining and hence self-protective humor. "There are few women who stand better with the commercial people than Gipsy," bragged her ad, appealing directly to her expected customer base. And yet, in a Blue Book from the previous year, one finds the exact text describing Grace Simpson's bordello. Did both these women make it "a mark in life to treat everyone alike," or is it the women themselves who were treated thus? In spite of their claims about the women's uniqueness and special qualities, the ads' duplication of text emphasized their lack of individuality, their ultimate interchangeability. And if Storyville's promise of total white male inclusivity was belied by such ads and the high prices in the best houses, there were always the "cribs." Modern advertising was built on its ability to create and simultaneously promise to fulfill desires, to articulate heretofore "inarticulate longings" and offer their immediate satisfaction through purchasing products. Ads tapped into communities of feeling and offered to confirm long-held values as well as give material shape to inchoate desire. Once such desire had material shape (an ironing board! lace curtains! pancake mix! toothpaste!) one need only buy it, and thus also the "bundle of attributes" associated with it. Yet desire is seldom completely fulfilled, and customers must keep coming back for more.[35]

The Blue Book ads conveyed the tasteful luxury and comfort the "high-class" bordellos afforded; and, yet, constant reference to class status and the accouterments of bourgeois living sent a mixed message. Scarcely apparent beneath these triumphal messages lay another message, about what happens when a society relies solely on money to determine worth and position—a sharp turn from the notion of bloodlines and inherent honor from the antebellum days. In New Orleans, prostitution may have seemed of a piece with its "old world heritage," or its longstanding reputation as the "Southern Babylon," but even there, reformers grasped that prostitution was also the logical (and tragic) outcome for societies that put profit over people, a consequence of industrial capitalism and laissez-faire economics.

What was the fantasy the Blue Books promised to fulfill? Storyville was, from the outset, the extreme example of the idolatry of commerce, wealth, the new riches and what could be bought with them. In Storyville the answer included not only fine wine and erotic entertainments, but people, specifically women, which was quite of a piece with the "Old World heritage" of New Orleans. Storyville distorted and amplified echoes of the slave market of Old New Orleans for new purposes. Walter Johnson writes of the slave market as a consumer's emporium, a theater and a market where people went *shopping* for slaves. He uses a modern concept, consumer culture, to describe the effect of the slave market on the antebellum South. He argues that in truly understanding the essential transaction, the point of purchase, all the relationships in the antebellum South become more clearly legible.[36] To be sure, Storyville was not *literally* a slave market,[37] but it was not simply women's labor that was for sale. These prostitutes may have been "sex workers" in one sense, but that term fails to evoke the multivalent meanings in the act of exchange on offer in Storyville, and obscures the intensely privileged and contested meanings of sex in American culture at the turn of the century.[38]

Storyville did nothing if not celebrate commerce and commercialism. Storyville was a modern market; it marketed miscegenation and prostitution by commodifying women *as sex,* but sex was never a simple matter. Combining nostalgia and taboo, Storyville served a fantasy of Old South patriarchy, mimicking the slave pens of antebellum times. Women were objects of fantasy and desire, they entertained and flirted in the parlors downstairs, but their real business was in the bedrooms upstairs. Storyville trafficked in the fantasy of the slave market, the exercise of absolute power over another human being—even if only for the evening.

Finally, Storyville offered light-skinned black women for the sexual pleasure of its customers—modern-day "fancy girls."[39] In theory at least, Storyville offered this privilege of patriarchy to all takers, provided they were white. That is, the advertisements in the Blue Books, while describing the rich appointments of the bordellos and the cultural accomplishments of the ladies inside, permitted customers from every class and region. Storyville recapitulated elements of antebellum New Orleans on a democratic, cash basis. In Storyville, therefore, we can see the transition from one kind of class structure to another, from the world of honor, breeding, privilege, aristocracy, to one of striving materialism and the ascent of the middle class, where the former is put on sale to the latter. These two "classes" had been set against each other in the antebellum travel accounts as the Old Creole versus the striving Yankee, but now, in the postbellum world, the Yankee was ascendant.

Again, like all of New Orleans's growing tourist attractions, the fine houses in Storyville were restricted to white clients: white men alone could sample the nostalgic pleasure of the octoroon, the sexual subspecialty of Storyville. If nothing else from the antebellum travel accounts persisted through the Civil War, Reconstruction, and post-Reconstruction eras, the beautiful "quadroon" or "octoroon" woman's "matchless grace and beauty" and her association with slavery and with prostitution most certainly did, and Storyville capitalized on her image. Eleven houses were simply listed under the designation "Octoroon" in the first Blue Book, in addition to advertisements from Mahogany Hall, the Crescent, and five other octoroon bordellos. These should be understood in the context of the Blue Books' other organizational schemes and rubrics, designed as they were to maximize the pleasure of the reader. This very first book listed "Speakeasy Houses," and houses designated "French 69," the latter playing both on the city's heritage and the French association with fellatio. Many subsequent guides used a labeling system:

> The letter "B" on the side of a name indicates a house where beer is sold.
> The "No. 69" is the sign of a French House.
> The Jew will be known by a "J."[40]

In the 1898 edition, the Jew is featured in the introductory code as well as later, in a section of the book devoted to the "Jew Colony," which continued until the 1906 edition.[41] There are also introductory codes including "colored" and "white" brothels, capital letters used for the madams, stars beside each "first-class house." "Octoroon" appears in the context, as a pertinent label for women as objects of desire, even after mixed-race *men,* including Homer Plessy, had become "negro."[42]

Storyville, to be sure, was a transgressive space as well as a transitional space. The district's promise to fulfill the fantasy it advertised in the form of commercial, paid-for sex clearly set it apart from more legitimate forms of mass cultural entertainment proliferating at the time. Yet in some ways it was not so dissimilar from the other places the new middle class went to on their vacations and outings. Indeed, the Blue Books, in advertising specific madams, bordellos, saloons, and cabarets, proposed similarities between the district and the nation's newfound pleasure places, referencing world's fairs, shows, and amusement parks.[43] The same drama of class aspiration and displacement may be seen in the promotion of these venues as the one playing out in Storyville at the same time. Cindy Aron describes world's fairs as attractions that substituted for the elite European Grand Tour, a comparable experience affordable to the many, and the *Visitors' Guide to the Centennial Exhibition and Philadelphia* boasted that the exhibition hall housed the "works of all the leading artists of the world." This was the same claim made by Josie Arlington, whose Blue Book advertisements highlighted the fine oil paintings to be found in her "mansion,"[44] and by Lulu White, whose Mahogany Hall possessed "some of the most costly oil paintings in the Southern country."[45] The references to world's fairs get quite specific, too. To see Lulu White at night, according to the Blue Book, was "like witnessing the electrical display on the Cascade, at the late St. Louis exposition."[46] This was on account of her diamonds. And White's souvenir booklet touted a "famous dancer" from New York:

> Many will, no doubt, recognize in this clever Creole the petite figure which caused men to go into raptures at the World's Fair, while visiting the Midway, and when we say that you must see her to properly appreciate her many charms we hope that you will take this hint.[47]

The Chicago World's Fair featured an exhibition of Egypt on its midways, with the reproduction of a street in Cairo, and the immensely popular "Little Egypt," a belly dancer who writhed in a harem-girl costume performing the "Danse du Ventre"—also known as the "hoochie coochie." She had imitators around the country in world's fairs and amusement parks.[48] Storyville had its own "Little Egypt" in the person of Bertha Golden, "The Egyptian Princess from Alexandria, Egypt":

> Miss Bertha Golden who . . . created such an excitement with her muscle dance and living pictures, and who has traveled all over the world and holds the world record, is now at 213 Basin Street. To convince yourself, give her a call and we will assure you that she can't be beat.

Whatever did Miss Golden hold the world record in?

Storyville's bordellos featured "international rooms" that resonated as much with the (European) internationalism celebrated at the world's fairs as with New Orleans's own cosmopolitan history:

> FRENCH PALLACE [sic] STUDIO: Miss Emma Johnson is the proprietor of the French Pallace Studio, No. 331 North Basin Street, and it has the name of being the only First Class house of this kind in the city and the boys who are acquainted with Emma's Palace, will say the same.[49]

An ad for Emma Johnson's in the *Sunday Sun,* the local paper dedicated to news about Storyville, claimed that the "French Studio is crowded with girls of all nations and to those who are looking for a genuine circus [this] is the place."[50] Johnson's house was also known as the "House of All Nations."

France maintained a privileged position in New Orleans and held a special place within Storyville, with its "Number 69" and "French" bordellos. Jelly Roll Morton commented that Storyville was "considered second to France, meaning the second greatest [red-light district] in the world." In addition to Emma Johnson's French Palace, however, one must also note Miss Flo Meeker's house at 211 Basin Street, "without doubt one of the most exquisitely furnished establishments in Storyville. Everything being of new make many of the articles in her domicile come from the late Paris Exposition."[51]

Finally, cafés and assignation houses also affected cosmopolitan names and displayed marquees or facsimiles of the boardwalks at amusement resorts:

WALDORF CAFE,
1515 to 1517 Customhouse St. Remember the place has lights all over the building and the name is "Waldorf."[52]

If the Waldorf name was supposed to call up the grand hotel in New York City, its tacky façade was surely more like a midway exhibit at the Chicago World's Fair, or a Luna Park ride at Coney Island. Storyville's ads may have aimed for the former, but the district more resembled the latter. The whole place radiated the atmosphere of a rollicking amusement park, with, as Jelly Roll Morton remembered, "lights of all colors . . . glittering and glaring. Music was pouring into the streets from every house." It was a carnival atmosphere, a sexual theme park, where men could go to join in the throng, gawk at the magnificent bordellos, enjoy innovative music, and hire a prostitute.

Storyville was a modern enterprise that recalled elements of the southern past as the nation around it, too, sought to reconstitute older hierarchies and fit them to new conditions, themselves rapidly changing. In order more fully to appreciate the ways in which Storyville resonated with the developing popular culture, it is helpful to review, in broad strokes, features of that culture, especially in terms of how race, class, and gender relationships articulated in the new urban spaces.

In the latter part of the nineteenth century, America underwent a massive demographic transformation. The population grew, families immigrated, and people moved from the countryside to the city, changing the make-up of America. The population almost doubled between 1870 and 1900, climbing from about 38 million people to about 76 million. Immigrants from abroad swelled the industrial work force until they made up a third of it. Together with migrants from the countryside, their presence in American cities converted America from a predominantly rural nation into what Kim Townsend calls "an urban industrial empire."[53] Advances in technology changed the way people worked, communicated, lived, and traveled. Between 1860 and 1900 all of the following inventions first appeared: the telephone, the linotype machine, the typewriter, the mimeograph, the automobile, the transcontinental railroad, the refrigerated railroad car, the silo, barbed wire, interior electric lights, and outside street lights.[54] Railroads changed people's very notions of time and space; time was standardized in this era, with time zones adopted to accommodate the rail. New business practices also altered the organization of the economy, and business corporations came to dominate the economic scene. Trusts and the captains of industry directing them amassed tremendous capital, and with it great power over the shape and operation of the American economy. Laborers organized to improve their working conditions, which often were dangerous and life-threatening, but found the federal government most often siding with the companies, who broke strikes with scab labor, private policemen, and sometimes deadly violence.[55] Likewise, farmers organized, experimenting with cooperatives and disrupting traditional political alignments.

Corporate business culture took as its model the theory of social Darwinism. John Rockefeller said, "The growth of a large business is merely the survival of the fittest, the working out of a law of nature and a law of God."[56] Social Darwinism was the perfect ideology for the cutthroat, contract-based model of industry and finance, and supported the harsh labor practices that went with it. The philosophy gave competition a "cosmic rationale."[57] Its adherents proclaimed that liberty, *inequality,* and survival of the fittest would naturally produce the most advanced civilization. Equality, on the other hand, was a shibboleth for the squeamish. Individual and class inequality was "natural" and should be let to run its course without intervention, from the state or from private charities. Yale University professor William

Graham Sumner declared that the social classes owed each other nothing; nature would ensure that the best men made it to the top.[58]

To be sure, most Americans still cherished and relied on an ideal of equality as their country's promise, whether America was their native or adopted land.[59] Yet, the very notion of evolution raised the possibility of degeneration. Cynthia Russett writes that evolutionary theory disclosed "cosmic instabilities," the potential danger of regressing, of slipping backward toward brutality. Specialists responded by prescribing strict hierarchies in society. In their efforts to stabilize relationships disrupted by Darwin, scientists inserted "lesser orders (women, savages) between themselves and the apes. . . . Women and the lesser races served to buffer Victorian gentlemen from a too-threatening intimacy with the brutes."[60] When Theodore Roosevelt warned old-stock white Americans that they risked "race suicide" in the modern era, he referred not only to the influx of immigrants, but also to white women with independent mindsets, women more likely to try and limit the number of children they bore. Women who desired professional or public lives threatened the status of middle-class men, and doctors and scientists claimed that too much intellectual activity limited women's fertility. Thus, warnings about "race suicide" not only expressed xenophobia about the swelling numbers of immigrants, but also indicted middle-class white women for failing to reproduce fast enough.

The same conflicted philosophy lay beneath commonplace worries that white men were growing effeminate, that neurasthenia was becoming endemic, and that Americans were falling into the traps of "over-civilization" and decadence.[61] The generation of American men born too late to fight in the Civil War had missed out on that manhood-making experience, and now they were foundering. Intellectuals and literati, temperance crusaders and social reformers looked for "moral equivalents of war" in many areas of life in order to bolster sagging spirits, rejuvenate American energy, and harness it for a viable, productive future.[62] For example, Harvard University developed its intercollegiate athletic program to provide "combat on the playing rather than battle fields."[63] In general, institutionalized sport expanded in the United States.[64] Culture brokers scorned the effete lifestyle of bourgeois America and celebrated a new muscularity in organized sport, in an embrace of untamed nature, and in actual war. The historian John Higham writes about the myriad activities and advertisements that sprang up to enjoin Americans to exercise, be physical, and throw off the restraints of "feminized" Victorian culture.[65]

Alan Trachtenberg has found in this same period a process he calls "the incorporation of America."[66] By this he means the coming together of disparate elements and groups in American society as well as the coalescence of an American cultural consciousness. Trachtenberg uses the metaphor of the "corporation" to describe the larger cultural process, because for him the "incorporation of America" was the creation of a society totally wrapped up in the economic marketplace. The central shift in these years was from a producerist ethos to a consumerist one.[67] That transformation relied for its success upon hiding from the consumer the methods of production and labor struggle. The character of American life became thoroughly imbricated with market relations in every aspect of personal experience, yet those market relations were mystified, invisible.[68] For every celebrated technological or economic success, there was a history of violence and exploitation that remained hidden. As Trachtenberg puts it, "the popular mode of celebration covered over all signs of trauma with expressions of confidence and fulsome praise."[69]

Meanwhile, so many middle-class men joined fraternal organizations, such as the Freemasons, the Elks, the Odd Fellows, the Knights of Pythias, the Knights of Labor, and others, that a leading publication called the last third of the nineteenth century "The Golden Age of Fraternity."[70] This quasi-mass movement was in part an antidote to the perceived problem of over-civilization and effeminacy. Men who joined these fraternal organizations, which were replete with complex and highly secret rituals, restored community in the wake of secularization, created society in anonymous cityscapes, and fostered manhood among the fictive "brothers."[71] They also created a separate sphere of action, where they were theoretically empowered but literally powerless.[72] To be sure, Storyville as well, in all its variety of entertainments, provided spaces for highly ritualized enactments of manhood, from the bars and honky-tonks, to the dance halls and saloons, to, of course, the bordellos and the cribs themselves.

Public Amusements

Beyond the secret fraternal meeting houses, there was the highly publicized world of commercial entertainment. Public amusements rose in tandem with wage labor, as workers for the first time in American history could afford them and, also for the first time, had set hours for their work.[73] Vaudeville and minstrel shows, movies, dime museums, amusement parks, and world's fairs all brought people together *en masse* in public places. Since about 1970, historians have sought to understand the role of such popular amusements as vehicles of acculturation. Kathy Peiss has shown that the new meeting places created in this urban, industrial America were "social spaces in which gender relations were 'played out,'" with deep consequences. Working-class heterosocial culture was forged largely through its members' participation in "cheap amusements," like "public halls" and "pleasure clubs."[74] Peiss's focus is on the working classes, but the white-collar workers of the urban middle class also went to museums and fairs, attended movies, and rode Ferris Wheels. In *Going Out,* David Nasaw explains that the new mode of public amusement was "more than an escape from the tedium of work, it was the gateway into a privileged sphere of everyday life." According to Nasaw, it was the shift toward this "privileged sphere" that was quintessentially modern; "the ability to take time out from work for recreation and public sociability was the dividing line between old worlds and new."[75] Paid vacations, shorter work hours, less physically demanding labor, and new modes of transportation enabled the middle and working classes to enjoy themselves in ways that had earlier been reserved for the aristocracy. Certainly, black and white workers still labored twelve hours a day, six days a week, and were generally not visible to the people enjoying the new leisure activities—even as they serviced these places.[76]

Strangers relished both the anonymity of the crowd and the shared experience the entertainments provided. John Kasson describes turn-of-the-century Coney Island's fabulous boardwalks, rides, and sideshows as removes from the workaday world. Visitors to the resort passed over a sort of liminal threshold and entered a fantasy realm that transported them from the worries of work, social struggles, and survival.[77] Not everyone could afford to participate to the same degree, but even men and women who did not have much money to spend came to walk among the throng, to see the resorts for themselves, and to escape the pressures of their daily lives.[78]

The development of a popular culture went hand in hand with the hardening of the color line and the development of a segregated public sphere; these were parts of the same process. The diverse entertainments fostered a kind of solidarity among disparate people. Recent immigrants from Europe, long-settled Irish- and German-Americans, and native-born citizens mingled together as they went from vaudeville shows to movies to world's fairs. Class and ethnic differences faded as people lined up to Shoot the Chutes or enjoy another ride. As ethnic differences faded, however, the color line was highlighted: most public amusements excluded African Americans or established separate entrances for them. Black people, thus, stood outside the community of pleasure-seekers even while the substance of the entertainment often represented them as caricatures. World's fairs, too, bloomed into mass attractions at the turn of the century, helping to consolidate "white" identity. The fairs may be seen as hegemonic institutions which mystified the progress they celebrated; they were grand celebrations of American (and Western) advancement, which in effect set the white subject apart from people of color—not only African Americans, but colonized peoples, too.[79] From stage and film actors in blackface to "African" ethnological exhibits at world's fairs, blacks figured prominently in the new commercial culture, but as workers, images, or actors. In fact, it is not too much to say that the rise of commercial, public entertainment was simultaneously the rise of a new race consciousness among "whites," set against the opposing figure of a black other put before them as entertainment. That is, the very creation of a "public" or "mass" culture at this time was its instant racialization as "white." When viewed in this context, Storyville appears as a kind of microcosm, where the white (male) subject was set against an array of racial and sexual others; Storyville thus emerges as a kind of laboratory for making national whiteness in a regional setting.[80]

Storyville resonates with other elements of these developments as well. David Nasaw highlights a significant aspect of the world's fairs in arguing for the confluence of didacticism and capitalist enterprise, not just in the grand halls, but on the side streets and midways surrounding the expositions. Fairs carried their own borderlands with them. The Philadelphia Centennial Exposition in 1876 bred an impromptu "Centennial City" just beside it, for instance. This "other" city, in clear view of the "stately exhibition halls and manicured lawns," was populated by "a small army of hustlers, showmen, saloon keepers, and performers, provid[ing] fairgoers with a taste of peanuts, beer, and sideshow 'attractions.'" Here we see shades of Storyville and the gesture that created it out of a recognition of this same kind of vulgar echo. At around the same time that business reformers pushed for a red-light district in New Orleans, fair organizers of the 1893 World's Columbian Exposition in Chicago decided to welcome, and contain, an "entertainment 'district' on the exposition site," positioned in a way "geographically distinct from the rest of the fairgrounds" (in Nasaw's description). Thereafter, each fair had two parts: the main hall, featuring exhibitions of technology and progress, and the fairway outside. At the Chicago exposition, the fairway was located on the Midway Plaisance and the name "midway" was adopted for all subsequent such adjuncts to the fairs. The midways were concessions to vulgar pleasures and needs, set apart from the displays of American enterprise and entrepreneurialism, claimed and disowned at the same time, *just like Storyville in fact.* There was a certain commercial vigor and liveliness behind the midway exhibits, and segregating them from the legitimate exhibits reinforced apparent standards of respectability in fairs while still sharing the crowd and their dollars. Storyville emerged from similar compromises in New Orleans, in which respectability and vulgar amusements were to coexist in a partnership of convenience. A souvenir guide about the midways at Buffalo's Pan-American Exposition in 1901 resonates with descriptions of Basin Street: "Here is a business street—the strangest in the world—where all business is pleasure."[81]

The midways tended more to celebrate the exoticism of "the East" and Africa, while the main fairs touted the West. Midways had exhibits of "Darkest Africa" and "ethnological villages." Anthropological and ethnological exhibits at world's fairs blended pseudo-science with entertainment, and placed black people on a lower step than whites on the evolutionary ladder. Storyville played both sides of this coin, boasting of "fine oil paintings" and advertising exotic internationalism: "There are always ten entertainers [at MahoganyHall], who recently arrived from the 'East,' some being well known in the 'profession,' who get paid to do nothing but sing and dance."[82] Many fairs showcased exhibits featuring Old South-style plantations where "darkies" might perform the "happy days of slavery" through song and dance.[83] At the southern fairs, organizers stressed the importance of southern agriculture for the nation's prosperity and black labor for the South's. The fairs emphasized "racial harmony" in southern states, but in terms of the separation and subordination of African Americans.[84] Blacks attending the fairs were treated with "consummate disdain," and Nasaw and Rydell both argue that exhibits of Africa or the Old South worked "as festivals of racist imagery and ideology."[85] African American newspapers raised serious objections to the fairs and their depictions of blacks, slavery, and Africa more generally, and encouraged blacks to boycott them.[86] At the same time, Rydell argues, such displays in effect brought huge numbers of white Americans closer together, and made them comfortable with imperialism and Jim Crow.

The fairs were, to borrow a phrase from Trachtenberg, "pedagogies of modernity," even when they relied on images of the past to frame their lessons.[87]

Immigrants who attended the fairs got their first impressions of American slavery from the midway exhibits.[88] The fairs juxtaposed stock minstrel characters, such as the shuffling slave and the mammy, with colonized civilizations, who lived in mimetic versions of their own supposedly "natural" habitations, creating dioramic representations of lost or faraway cultures.[89] While there was no reason for visitors to doubt the "reality" of these presentations, especially when it was reinforced through popular culture, advertising, academic imprimatur, and political rhetoric, the fairs offered a certain "unreality" as well, suspending for the moment the normal demands of the visitors' social worlds.[90]

Some of the popular music and songs of the period reflect the normalization of racial and gendered difference to ordinary life among middle-class whites. Song sheets caricatured blacks as sambos and simpletons, ridiculed black courtship, and mocked "passing." They parodied black sexuality and infantalized black men in a form of ritual cultural emasculation.[91] This parodic domination responded to the fears of black manhood and race despoliation with laughter rather than violence, to be sure.

The content of minstrel songs and illustrations on the sheet music show just how precariously race and sex were lived, how they constantly had to be shored up.[92] One example will suffice. "Coon Coon Coon," Lew Docksatder's "hit song of 1901," begins with a black man complaining about his lady friend, also black. She dumped him on account of his color, and now he is "feeling mighty blue." He sings, "My gal, she took a notion against the colored race. She said if I would win her I'd have to change my face." He then goes to extraordinary lengths, enameling his face and straightening his hair. On his way to meet his "babe," he walks through a park, where "two doves sat making love at night." The man mistakes their "cooing" for a racial outing: "They stopped and looked me over, I saw my finish soon, when both those birds said good and loud, 'Cooooooooooon.'" In a "special note to singers" at the bottom of the page, the songwriter advised that, "if singer prefers, the last line of 2nd verse can be sung 'Both those birds said good and loud 'Look at the Coon,' 'Look at the Coon,' 'Look at the Coon.' By speaking or singing this part, it will closely imitate pigeons cooing, and add to the comedy effect."[93]

Black can't be white—white can't be black. Popular culture reflected and reinforced Justice Brown's racial logic in *Plessy*, which itself reflected long-standing public attitudes—fantasies, really—about the immutability and meaning of race. When Albion Tourgée argued that Homer Plessy, a man seven-eighths white and one eighth black, would be deprived of his *property* without due process if the Separate Car Act was allowed to stand, he meant the potential property of any American man; but as that subjectivity had been racialized and gendered, Brown could argue that he was not entitled to such, because he was in fact a colored man. One drop of blood made him so.

The simple rule that made fine racial distinctions irrelevant in public life made them all the more significant in Storyville. In Storyville, octoroons bridged the antebellum past and the New South future: slavery and commercial prostitution. They were liminal figures in the liminal space of Storyville. Their sexualized mixed-race bodies suggested the slave auctions and the fancy trade, the quadroon balls and *plaçage*, the "Old Romance" of the Old South. Yet, again, Storyville was not an atavism; the district was of a piece with the burgeoning popular culture. Moreover, the octoroon's commercial appeal—her availability for purchase in a commercial sex district that bragged of its oil paintings and costly décor—reflected the "New Opportunity" the region offered to northern investors and sex-tourists alike.

Lynching, Race Riots, and the Spanish-American War

Violence undergirded the developing culture on both sides of the Mason-Dixon line, and what Grace Hale calls "deadly amusements" also brought whites together and created new gendered and racial solidarities.[94] Race riots, black disenfranchisement, and lynching were also constitutive elements of the larger cultural process of race- and national-identity formation. These examples invite (perhaps uncomfortable) comparisons with Storyville. This is not to say that prostitution in Storyville was tantamount to vigilante terrorism. Not at all. What we are interested in is the general context for understanding Storyville as part of what has been seen as the dominant ideological tenor of American culture at the end of the nineteenth century. Whether in the explicit violence of lynching or the more subtle, even comic, elaborations in popular entertainment, the construction of a white, American identity for the twentieth century was realized through the proliferation of rhetoric and images of sexualized racial "others" and their sometimes violent subordination.

Lynching, for instance, was not a remnant of frontier or antebellum times, but was constitutive of the *modern* South, relying on modern technologies for its cultural power.[95] The rapid proliferation of lynching images in the press helped make lynching the deadly, terroristic analogue to the minstrel show, the movie house, the midway, and to Storyville. Not only in the rhetoric promoting and defending it, but even more emphatically in its intimate destruction of human hands, faces, and genitals, lynching was a form of sexual violence. And as Jacquelyn Dowd Hall has also shown, white women in the early twentieth century understood lynching to be an exertion of social control over them as well as a punishment of black men. For white women, the rhetoric of "protection" locked them into positions of deference and dependency, recreating the nexus of antebellum patriarchal relationships.[96] Race riots in the postwar South were also "fought on the ground of gender and sexuality," according to Hannah Rosen. Race riots were so called because they were characterized by interracial violence. Most often whites instigated violence when they perceived that black men had overstepped the color line, often by asserting their citizenship and, thus, their manhood in the public sphere, through political participation, economic success, or wearing a military uniform.[97]

Scholars have examined how the Spanish-American War reflected and influenced the processes of creating a new, national identity. The Spanish-American War became a site not just for sectional reconciliation, but also for revitalizing the seemingly disabled white male body.[98] The triptych of a sexually dangerous, dark-skinned "other," a helpless virginal maiden, and a strong white hero undergirded claims to white supremacy at home and "manifest destiny" abroad. The same dynamic that animated central elements of public discourse on the Spanish-American War also generated paroxysms of violence in lynchings and riots.[99] When the United States declared war against Spain in 1898, American citizens rallied. At first a war against the Spanish Empire in the Caribbean and Pacific, the Spanish-American War soon raised the specter of America's own bid for empire, and an ideological rift opened among people who had initially supported it. Often, however, the arguments for and against expansion relied equally on a notion of American exceptionalism and white racial superiority.[100] The very question of Filipino independence, however decided, elicited clear articulations of America's superiority: in its civilization, in its "race," and in its manhood.

Manhood in this context was indisputably "white." The portrayals of the war in the press, in cartoons, and in political debate reveal how war propagandists used the coalescing of race consciousness—and all that "race" implied for gender—to argue their case.[101] Rudyard Kipling neatly encapsulated the American ambiguity about Filipinos, but not about white racial superiority, in "The White Man's Burden" by conflating the "little brown brother" with the "treacherous savage," referring to America's "new-caught sullen peoples" as "half devil and half child."[102]

It was *white men* who embodied and propagated American supremacy. Thus, at the same time that white manhood was configured at home as the protector of vulnerable (white) womanhood, the American nation as a whole was engaged in an international campaign of "protection" in Cuba and the Philippines. Along with its geo-strategic and diplomatic aims, the Spanish-American War brought North and South together, effecting sectional reconciliation through a perceived commonality of purpose involving racialized and sexualized violence. In Amy Kaplan's words, "the vitality of the male body became the symbolic medium for national restoration."[103] In Storyville, the white male body was not a metaphor.

Popular and deadly amusements relied on an ideal of white male prerogative over an array of dark-skinned, feminized or emasculated "others," and instantiated that ideal through actual or proximate, ritualized violence. Storyville instantiated it through sex. More precisely, Storyville discovered the profit in channeling the pseudo-nostalgic desires of white men for the sexual power of the past, retrospectively located in the prerogatives of the old planter aristocracy. Of course, a man might go to have sex with a Jew. In Storyville, the exotic and "dioramic" New Orleans in its entirety was brought into an ecstatic intimacy with visiting tourists. That was its particular contribution to the South's new order.

CHAPTER FIVE

Diamond Queen

> As an entertainer Miss Lulu stands foremost, having made
> a life-long study of music and literature.
>
> —*THE NEW MAHOGANY HALL,* PAMPHLET

Lulu White was Storyville's most notorious madam. She proclaimed herself, and was often called, the "Diamond Queen" of the demi-monde. And
more than any other figure, Lulu White stood for Storyville in the popular
imagination. She also embodied those very elements of New Orleans that
the businessmen who created Storyville wished most to cordon off: commercial sex, interracial sex, racial hybridity, and political corruption. In part,
the great resonance of White's persona may be explained by the fact that
she fashioned an identity for herself imaginatively from "fragments of text"
taken from the long, sensationalist history of New Orleans. She relied on
the association of New Orleans with interracial sex, slave auctions, and the
literary trope of the tragic octoroon to make her business in the flesh trade
as profitable as possible. Her tremendous success may be read as evidence
of the continued salience of those images, most particularly the trope of
the light-skinned slave girl fated to sexual servitude. White reoriented the
memory of the octoroon's tragic fate while maintaining her erotic appeal.

This chapter shows how White profited from the tradition of sexually
subordinating women of color in New Orleans. Female octoroon beauties
had been the special prerogative of upper-class southern (white) men; Lulu
White ran a brothel of them for the pleasure of Storyville's wealthier customers. Her brothel made its profits from the same men that New South
leaders hoped to draw in as investors, wealthy white businessmen. As a
woman of color and a madam, however, White was a problematic figure for

respectable New Orleans. The female octoroon was basically a subordinate figure, but Lulu White was assertive and exhibitionist. She was rich and ostentatious, with powerful connections throughout the city. She refused to identify herself in the ascendant racial categories of the day, the dualism of "negro" or "white." She instead elaborated the figure of the erotic octoroon: Storyville was her stage for its twentieth-century performance.

Lulu White embodied disorder. As a so-called octoroon and a madam, she crossed the lines that "proper," "white" society was constructing through the enforcement of the color line, and the sexual and gender arrangements that went with it.[1] She defied both the moral and the racial perimeters erected by the rising bourgeoisie and in so doing represented danger. White might thus be considered in terms of the "abject." The abject is "what disturbs identity, system, order. What does not respect borders, positions, rules. The in-between, the ambiguous, the composite." The abject is particularly disturbing in that it highlights the "fragility of the law."[2] In White's case, she represented in her actions the tenuousness of and the fallacy of Jim Crow—its racial binary and historical amnesia alike. Unlike her male contemporaries who strove for political and civic rights (public rights), White was not jettisoned through juridical maneuvers or violent disenfranchisement. Their loss in *Plessy* was her gain. That is to say, she relied on the color line not only in order to promote its transgression, but also in order that the "octoroon" appear exotic, different, atavistic, and female—all of which added to her attractiveness.

When White took her performance beyond Storyville, New Orleans's media tried hard to expose her. The press denigrated her as a black prostitute, and ridiculed her pretension to respectability as a particularly egregious instance of striving blacks overstepping the borders of their proper place. In their coverage of Lulu White the press exhibited a flippant racism couched in humorous asides. Interestingly, Lulu White represented herself and her "girls" in much the same tone of voice: a joking, in-the-know, satirical tone, which mocked and bragged at the same time. Perhaps this softened the blows of ironic detractors by adopting their irony ahead of them. There is a gap between the press's demeaning sarcasm and White's own burlesque, however—a seam that may reveal something about the fantasy so-called legitimate New Orleans wove about itself. The very nastiness of the barbs, the excessive insistence on White's "blackness," reveals the defensive insecurity of the newspapers and their readers.[3] When White was safely bounded within the red-light district, "octoroon" could be construed as solely a sexual category; when she crossed those boundaries, her racial ambiguity and sexual power threatened the project of white supremacy.

Lulu White's life on the color line allows us to see that line for what it often was: blurry, ambiguous, false, and, nonetheless, vigorously grasped and violently enforced. We may see through White's interaction with the authorities and with "respectable" New Orleans the ongoing process of racializing respectability. White's life and career highlight the dialectic of repulsion and desire animating that process, as Warwick Anderson writes of another colonial project to separate filth from public order: "At the same time as one condemns the abject, one also, paradoxically, yearns for it."[4] She was, after all, very popular within Storyville. This chapter is about Lulu White in the public record, about her talent for selling herself and the image she created for herself; it is also about her life as a businesswoman and property owner. White's life offers a unique opportunity to explore the underlying desires and unspoken urges of a portion of New Orleanians and others attracted to her bordello, as well as another chance to see how she culled "fragments of text" about New Orleans in fashioning her underworld. Because there is no corroborating evidence concerning Lulu White's own feelings and motives, and because the subject matter—race, prostitution, interracial sex—provokes controversy or silence, much in this chapter is necessarily speculative, relying on context and impersonal sources to make its case. And then, there are one or two astonishing moments when Lulu as an actual human being is suddenly encountered directly in the source material.

Birth and Adolescence

Lulu White was born in Dallas County, Alabama, near Selma. Her mother, Amanda Tipton, was about eighteen at the time, "colored," and a housekeeper, according to the 1870 census. Her father, Robert Hendley, was white. Lulu had one sister, Della, who became the mother of Spencer Williams, the jazz composer who wrote "Basin Street Blues" and other songs, and who lived in Lulu's bordello, Mahogany Hall, for a time.[5]

The 1890 census was destroyed by fire before it was preserved, and so there is no New Orleans census record on Lulu before the creation of Storyville, though there is evidence that she was already active in the underworld by that time. She first appears under the name "Lulu White" in the Louisiana census of 1900, where she is listed as having been born in Jamaica, in 1868.[6] She told the census taker that her father and mother were Jamaican, too, and that she had immigrated in 1880. White's "color" (race) was listed as "B," black. Her occupation was "boardinghouse keeper" and her five "boarders" at 235 North Basin Street (that is, Mahogany Hall) were all "seampstresses" [sic] and "black."[7] But in 1910, Lulu White told the census taker she and her parents were from Alabama, she claimed to be forty-two years old, and her race was recorded as "Mulatto."[8] Her occupation was "none." According to the census, many people in Storyville had no occupation.[9]

The next census was taken three years after the closing of Storyville. In 1920, White told the enumerator that she and her parents came from Cuba, and that she had immigrated to the United States the year before, in 1919. Her race was given as "Octoroon," and she was a "naturalized" citizen whose first language was Spanish. In this census, for White's race one thing was written and something else written over it, making the record illegible. In the Soundex index, a digest of the census compiled from the completed record, her race is "Octoroon," but in the on-line census records it is listed as "Mulatto" in the information summary. In 1930, the year before she died, she still maintained that she was Cuban, but now her "color" was recorded as "Negro." She claimed then to be only forty-nine years old, although she was sixty-two if she had been born in 1868. Also, instead of claiming to be a naturalized citizen, as she had in 1920, here she said she was an "alien."[10] She was still living on Basin Street, but on the next block, and the street had been renamed "Saratoga." She had but one lodger, Ruth Stevenson. Stevenson is an unknown, mysterious figure, though it is possible that she was the daughter White adopted as a baby at the turn of the century.

Other madams (and other citizens, to be sure) also exploited the ambiguities of race in New Orleans in listing their official identities. For instance, Willie V. Piazza was classified as "Mulatto" in 1900, "Octoroon" in 1910, "White" in 1920, and "Negro" in 1930.[11] There is much one may learn from the censuses, but little in terms of the "truth" of someone's "race."[12]

Several prosperous Storyville madams left behind large estates when they died. White, in contrast, died impoverished, awaiting her prosecution in New Orleans in a trial that had been postponed several times because of her failing health.[13] She died in August 1931, as a clerical note on the affidavit confirms: "8/21/31 Defendant dead."[14] Her death certificate indicates that she returned to her birthplace to die—Dallas County, Alabama—but the record inaccurately cites Dallas, Texas, as the place of her death.[15]

The Diamond Queen

White first listed herself in the New Orleans city directory in 1888, as a resident at 3 South Basin Street, on a block composed of "colored female boarding houses."[16] These were probably boarding houses for young women, some of whom would have engaged in prostitution. In those days Emma Johnson ran a brothel around the corner on Gasquet Street, and houses of prostitution of varying degrees of openness dominated the area. "In this city," wrote the *Mascot,* "there are many gilded palaces, which are known as immoral and can be pointed out to the young. There are also dens, where sin crouches and traps the unwary."[17] Sin "crouched" on South Basin Street when Lulu White lived there, and so, in 1890 Lulu White moved from the boarding house to 166 Customhouse Street—not exactly a "gilded palace," but certainly known to be immoral. There she opened her first bordello as proprietress and madam.[18] Alongside White on Customhouse Street were nearly fifty other madams, including Josie Arlington (then known as Josie Lobrano), Fanny Lambert, Maime Christine, Flo Meeker, Bertha Golden, and Julia Dean. All of these women later became prominent and prosperous madams in Storyville.[19] White stayed on Customhouse until 1898.[20]

White fashioned a narrative about her move to 166 Customhouse that previews her life-long manipulation of the legacy of the tragic octoroon for her own purposes and profits. Four years after her arrival there, in 1894, when her residence was certainly old news among the cognoscenti, the *Mascot* featured a story that White may have had a hand in planting. The paper reported that when Lulu was a small child, she had been "taken to New York by her father, who was a Wall street broker, and after his death she fell heiress to No. 166 Customhouse Street."[21] She was the fallen daughter of privilege in this tale, she came from money, and the Customhouse property passed to her through the legitimate mechanism of patriarchy. The "fragment of text" in play here came straight from the "tragic octoroon" narrative. The "tragic octoroon" with a wealthy white father and an unknown (or unmentionable) black mother was a familiar figure, as we have seen, maintained in the postbellum fiction of such notable New Orleanians as George Washington Cable and Grace King, who were read throughout the country.[22] Of course, White altered the story: *her* father was a northerner, his profession the apotheosis of capitalist success, the opposite of the impoverished, superannuated planter—and precisely the type New Orleans boosters hoped would invest in their city. In White's narrative, her father's legacy may have condemned her to sexual slavery and prostitution, but it also gave her property. She played different angles of the myths associated with octoroons, performing as both capitalist and commodity, proprietor and property.

White's performance was not flawless. She could not "pass" as a daughter of privilege, and there is no evidence that she truly desired to. White seems to have recognized those tropes about New Orleans that had special sexual resonance, and she exploited them in the underworld milieu. When she left that milieu, she became more like a burlesque of the type—a grotesque, exaggerated version, or perhaps even an *inversion* of it. If the octoroon's tragic fate relied upon her purity and her class (she was the planter's daughter), then White's performance as the "abject" doubly perverted the genre. But she understood the octoroon's prurient appeal.[23]

The New Orleans press relished the incidents in which White revealed inconsistencies in her claims to high-class upbringing, which were, like the ads in the Blue Books, both self-conscious and absurd. As found in the *Mascot* and the *Sunday Sun,* which followed Lulu White's slightest movement, her life was a series of comic moments. These low-brow papers mocked the reportage of society pages that announced debuts, engagements, and upper-class marriages, and they mocked White by discussing her in the same vein. For instance, in 1894 the *Mascot* reported that the "swarthy beauty, Miss Lulu White, is taking lessons in singing," in the same "Society" section in which one read that another prostitute's "dog is suffering from constipation."[24] But the paper, even in its mocking reportage, could not derail White's promotional strategies. The *Mascot* reported that prostitutes came to the race track at the opening of the winter season and the "mahogany colored ladies" were barred from the grandstand, confined to their carriages with their silks and diamonds. "Fair" Lulu White protested that "some people take her to be colored, but she says there is not a drop of negro blood in her veins. She says that she is a West Indian, and she was born in the West Indies."[25]

Was the paper mocking White's claims to whiteness? Or were they participating in her self-fashioning claims to racial ambiguity? In any event, we can read through the papers' reportage ways in which White played on current notions of race in the public construction of her persona. What did "West Indian" mean to the readers of the *Mascot*? Black Caribbeans were sometimes called "natives" rather than "negroes," despite the existence of specialized knowledge as to their hybrid and imported ancestry.[26] Even more than in Louisiana, if this were possible, explicit gradations separated whites from near-whites and so forth in the Caribbean.[27] Long before, in colonial and antebellum New Orleans and Louisiana, Creoles of color had been distinguished legally and culturally from both "negroes" and slaves, and every possible combination of mixed blood had its own special name. Plus, there were *white* French colonials in the West Indies, who fled the Revolution and settled in Louisiana (such as Homer Plessy's grandfather). Lulu White's presentation of herself as a "native" West Indian left the matter doubly obscure. Is this where her wealthy white father brought her up before bringing her to New York? Was she claiming the heritage of the *gens de couleur libres* who came to New Orleans in the wake of the Haitian Revolution? Was it the white planters she meant to associate herself with? Was she fashioning an "exotic" and colonial identity?[28]

If we look back at her census records, we can see that over the years Lulu White recapitulated the itinerary of the Caribbean-Atlantic slave trade in her various answers about her identity: Jamaica, Alabama, Louisiana, Cuba; negro, mulatto, octoroon, white, black. Most New Orleanians would have been familiar with the special circumstances setting New Orleans apart from the rest of the Deep South, and there is no reason to presume White was not also familiar with the heritage of the *gens de couleur libres* and their place in the city's exceptional history. This history served her business well. That the *Mascot* described these aforementioned women as "mahogany colored" reminds us of the name later chosen by Lulu White for her bordello on Basin Street. Mahogany, dark and tropical, grows in the "hot regions of the world"; it is an exotic wood; it was the wood of Haiti, until that country sold all its lumber to France as an indemnity to pay for its independence.[29] In contemporary race ideologies, the notion of "invisible" blackness presented a frightening specter of race despoliation to whites. As a corollary, and as a balm to those fears, it was also felt that blood "would out," and that careful observers could always tell someone with African ancestry, no matter how hidden. The marketing of miscegenation in the context of prostitution relied on the notion that blood would out through sex at the appropriate moment, fueling the special attraction toward so-called octoroons.

Photography and the Visuality of Race

When examining the life of someone like Lulu White, someone, that is, who simultaneously challenged and reinscribed racial conventions and blurred the color line, the way she looked, her physical appearance, matters.

In studying surviving photographs of Lulu White, one is taken first by her beauty, and second by the ambiguity of her "race." She does not appear "white" exactly, but neither does she appear "black." This point is worth emphasizing, since Lulu White's heyday came as that particular binary was forged in the nation's consciousness. White was not a "black" person posing as an "octoroon," nor an "octoroon" passing for "white," nor a "white" person posing as an "octoroon." The kind of dualism that channels thoughts about race into either/or dichotomies, although it developed in response to slavery, derived from the "color line" as a juridico-social problem and way of thought, firmed up for the twentieth century in the 1880s and 1890s in the aftermath of Reconstruction's failure. In a way similar to how Plessy's own "whiteness" was critical to his case, White's "whiteness" reveals cultural undercurrents about racial ideology, sexuality, and the construction of desire at the start of Jim Crow.

In the late 1880s or early 1890s, Lulu White posed for several groups of pornographic photographs. There is a literature on Victorian pornography, but it focuses on texts rather than images. The most comprehensive recent history of visual pornography, Linda Williams's *Hard Core,* on the other hand, begins with cinema and her arguments revolve around the impact of the moving image, the "frenzy of the visible," in her own phrase. Scholarship on photography, even when focused on erotic images, most often stops short of analyzing photographs produced specifically for pornographic pleasure. And, analyses of pornography often focus on the nexus of exploitation and pleasure, misogyny and desire, not necessarily on the photography itself. For instance, Deborah Willis's analysis of photographic imitations of the odalisque and "exotic" photography tells us that such pictures were pornographic, even though their producers and distributors claimed otherwise, pretending to the status of high art. Similarly, circulated images of African or other non-European women with their breasts exposed or in other stages of nakedness have received scholarly attention for their pornographic effects, but they were conceived as ethnological and therefore scientifically legitimate, emphatically not pornographic. (Or so their producers claimed.) Photographs self-consciously produced and distributed *as pornography* have received less attention.[30]

Lulu White's pornographic photographs are not come-hither pictures of a lingerie-draped lady; nor are they simply images of nudity; there is no pretense to art (or ethnography), and White does not pose as the odalisque. The pictures are hard core, meaning the sexual action is explicit and they are meant to arouse. Still, the pictures contain within them narratives that are useful in understanding White's later Storyville persona, especially insofar as they eroticize and burlesque middle-class morality while also playing with notions of racial dualism. There is no way to substantiate her precise role in the creation or circulation of the pictures, but based on White's life in Storyville and afterward, it is fair to assume she posed for the pictures of her own volition.[31] If indeed White had a hand in their design, the photographs present to us a shameless woman, in the know and, it seems, in on the joke. One group features White sexually positioned with a large dog. While the first two pictures in the series are mere teasers (in one she hugs the dog around the neck and in the next she sits on a chair with her skirt lifted, revealing her pubic hair), the photographs become more graphic, with White holding the dog's penis, then preparing to fellate the dog, and finally, being penetrated by him.[32]

This photographic drama of courtship and consummation signifies in a number of ways, not least of which is a wry commentary on current sex practices in both the underworld and respectable society. Bestiality was among the practices at bordellos and a popular subject for pornography at this time. Sex shows involving Great Danes were popular in Paris in the *maisons de tolérance,* or sometimes "with Newfoundland mongrels, which were very common in the capital."[33] New Orleans was of course the "French" city within the American South, and later on archive officials at the Kinsey Institute for Sex Research labeled White's dog photographs "French." Emma Johnson—who claimed to be the "Parisian Queen" and who later called her Storyville bordello the "French Studio"—supposedly put on sex shows at her Gasquet Street brothel that featured women copulating with animals, and Lulu White surely knew of the popularity of these "circuses."[34]

What desires do the photographs of bestiality produce and satisfy? According to Peter Gay, attending dog sex shows was itself a mode of bourgeois aspiration at the turn of the twentieth century.[35] It was widely believed that aristocratic tastes in sexual pleasure exceeded the boundaries of respectability, and sexual deviance was associated with aristocratic power. There was a sense that the decadence of the aristocracy bred perversion, and neither community nor inner morality could check it. "Blood" allowed aristocrats to transgress the norms of behavior as defined by the middle classes without paying grave social penalties, provided that perverse behavior was carried on in a private (or at least discreet) fashion. Perhaps there was also in

White's bestiality series a wink at the ritualized process of courtship, the complex social drama that had to precede intercourse for it to be considered legitimate, respectable.[36]

As Anne McClintock reminds us, the fetish is overdetermined.[37] That is to say, the sexual fetish plays host to myriad streams of desire and taboo, elaborating and creating myriad fantasies with no imperative for consistency. The only imperative is to produce pleasure. Lulu White was not limited by the narrow confines of genre; there are many mixed and contradictory messages in these photos. Bestiality inevitably involves debasement. And yet, White betrays no hint of humiliation in the pictures; she is blithely acquiescent without seeming either subordinated or particularly engaged in the action. White's expression throughout remains static; she betrays no erotic excitement. In any case, White's own racial illegibility and willing participation notwithstanding, as an anonymous image, a woman of color is sexually debased. The pictures therefore also index a desire for social and sexual power that resonates with a cultural memory of the power of the slaveholding elite of the antebellum period.

Lulu White also posed in a group of photographs with an unidentified (apparently) white man.[38] These prints flatter and eroticize contemporary bourgeois décor. The bed has an elaborate carved wood headboard, and is flanked by heavy, patterned draperies. A full-length leopard skin covers the floor. The hunting trophy was a sign of status—African safaris were elite and costly affairs, and apparently a turn-on—and wild animals and Africa were all about untamed passion.[39] Again, the fetish is overdetermined. Again, we find White at the time referencing aspects of the myth of the octoroon, highlighting the sexuality of "black blood" hidden within the externality of "whiteness," and so, perhaps, the leopard skin rug served to alert the viewer that "African blood" ran through her veins.

White is sexually assertive in the photographs, not submissive or subordinate. In one she is holding the supine man's erect penis like a shot glass, both feet firmly on the floor. If read as "black" or "octoroon," White's position as the sexual actor in these erotic fantasies of transgression reinscribed racial and sexual stereotypes by revealing White's specialized knowledge of the sexual desires of her male "partners" (none of these photographs "depicts" coercion, rape, or prostitution). The setting suggests the hidden passion of the upper middle classes for transgressive sex, including sex across the color line. Of course, if her race was read as "white" in the pictures, the transgressive acts therein merely upset dominant stereotypes about female submissiveness and purity. Whatever White meant to signify in the photos, they reveal a range of desire that the dominant ideologies of racialized sexuality sought to suppress.

Pornography, in whatever form, has the tendency to overturn the normative order of things; it exists in the specialized realm of fantasy that it also participates in creating. It is not, therefore, surprising that the social roles depicted in pornographic photographs are sometimes unconventional. What is interesting is that, because of their liminal and disordered nature, pornographic photographs reveal elements of desire and taboo fantasy that were painstakingly hidden from ordinary view—which were, in a word, "obscene."[40] They make use of the tragic octoroon genre in abolitionist literature and the continued appeal of the trope in the postbellum years, but only for perverse and prurient appeal. The tragic octoroon was always sexualized, and not just because her tragic fate was sexual slavery, but because the mix of white and black blood, the latter hidden beneath the pure sheath of white skin, enslaved her and promised a sexual awakening full of passion and lust when it mattered. Such were the ideologies of racialized sexuality generated in slavery times but retained and reinscribed as much through the mechanisms of Jim Crow as by Lulu White herself.

Another picture depicts a day at the beach. White leans over a wicker beach chair, naked down to her shoes. A white "sailor" penetrates her from behind, his bathing trunks unsnapped and hanging below his hips. He wears a sailor's hat on his head, and a sailor's shirt is slung over the chair's arm. The painted backdrop features waves lapping at their ankles, and in the far background the tall masts of ships. The sailor, "young and manly, unattached and unconstrained by conventional morality, epitomized the bachelor subculture,"[41] and White used the familiar figure to reimagine the holiday "boardwalk" as a scene of open illicit sex. Outings and excursions away from the ever-more-crowded cities had become typical working- and middle-class activities by the end of the nineteenth century, as I have discussed.[42]

At the turn of the century, the middle classes were defined by their "perpetual need . . . to redefine and defend the domain of the private, to flaunt the emblems of respectability, [and] to deserve and cope with success. . . . By the middle of the nineteenth century," writes Peter Gay, "physicians and social observers discovered that simply being a bourgeois imposed a formidable strain on that species," the dual outcome of which was "nervousness and prostitution."[43] While physicians and other "experts" attended to "nervousness," prostitution fell under the codes and regulations kept by the middle class as their special area of knowledge: what was proper, improper, perverse, lurid, and so on.[44] The fantasies elaborated by White's pornographic photographs violated the strictures of respectability espoused by the late Victorian middle classes, but were of course produced under those same conditions as well.[45] Pornography that used the bourgeois home as its backdrop suggested that even the tasteful trappings of the home could not obscure the central mechanism of its reproduction.

It seems especially pertinent to note the bourgeois elements within photographic pornography in the 1880s, as photography was then a new medium for the genre, and a much more democratic one to boot. Earlier pornography was literary, and therefore elite; it often contained references in Greek or Latin, which only the educated classes could read and understand. Thus the very act of looking at pornographic photographs in this germinal stage of their proliferation might be considered simultaneously an act of bourgeois ascendancy and a critique of aristocratic pretensions and exclusivity.[46] We can thus read both a burlesque of aristocratic perversion and a critique of bourgeois respectability in these pictures. We see the same mix of reverence, resentment, and rejection in the Blue Book advertisements, but in the service of attracting customers. It must have done the trick.

Mahogany Hall

By the time the Storyville ordinance was passed, Lulu White had already developed her identity as the underworld's "Diamond Queen." She had laid claim to being "the country's handsomest octoroon," and her self-aggrandizing mockery of the bourgeoisie was also by then apparent. But it was Storyville that provided White with her stage, and it was through Storyville that she secured her reputation. Storyville, as a space deliberately apart, acted as a kind of projection of respectable New Orleans, occupying a psychic space much larger than square feet would suggest, and making an impact incommensurate with its small geographic footprint. The same was true for Lulu White: though there were many "notorious madams" in New Orleans, she seems to have occupied a special place in the mind of the respectable community. In part this was because of her self-promoting tactics. Her reinvention of the dominant themes of antebellum New Orleans, as I have suggested, surely gave her persona greater resonance than that of prostitutes and madams who did not call up the history of interracial sex and play on the tensions animating the creation of Jim Crow.

In part, also, Lulu White's disproportionate impact on life in New Orleans was due to her magnificent bordello, Mahogany Hall. The city council wrote and passed the Storyville ordinance at the end of January 1897. By the spring, White had secured what would become some of the new district's most valuable real estate.[47] In June 1897, the Third District Building Association met and decided to sell Lulu White her piece of ground.[48] Like much of the Storyville property, this lot had previously been in the possession of a single owner, named William Goldsberry. It measured about thirty-two feet from the corner, and about thirty-two feet across, with a depth of almost ninety-seven feet. It was about thirty feet short of going through the whole block to Franklin Street. The surveyor's sketch of the lot, made in 1893, indicates it contained a structure built in the 1830s, in the style of a creole cottage. This was a small two-story frame dwelling, each story having four rooms—two parlors and two bedrooms—and a two-story-high kitchen. The dwelling had galleries in the front and the rear (probably exterior porches), hydrants, cisterns, and a paved yard.[49] When Goldsberry died in 1853, two separate purchasers acquired the property: Philip Schneider and John M. Furrell. Furrell sold his share to H. C. Fincke, who also purchased the other half from Philip Schneider four years later. Fincke built additions to the cottage, and when he sold the property in 1862 to James Durand its value had more than doubled, from $2,286 to $4,900. When Mr. Durand died, his widow sold the property and buildings to the Third District Building Association, and the property depreciated. The 1893 financial crisis might have helped lower the price of the land. Russell J. Moss bought it for $1,200 in 1894 and sold it back to the Building Association, which sold it to Lulu White, for $1,550, cash, on July 3, 1897.[50] It appears that the neighborhood had declined in the period leading up to White's purchase. White razed the structure and built the grand Mahogany Hall on the property.

Certainly others helped her buy the property and finance Mahogany Hall. Her partner in the initial purchase was Assistant City Attorney George Washington Flynn, a member of the New Orleans Democratic machine's social and political club, the Choctaw Club. He also notarized the deal.[51] Three weeks after purchasing the property, White sold it to Flynn for what she had just paid: $1,550 cash. At that point the construction of the grand bordello began. Five months later, after spending a great deal of money (the exact figure is not known), she bought the property back for $4,000 in cash, with an agreement to pay $750 a month in three-month intervals until an additional $13,500 more had been paid. It would appear that Lulu White arranged a four-and-a-half-year mortgage for some part of the expense of constructing and furnishing the new building with other connected backers.[52]

Lulu White spoke early on in her career through a souvenir booklet she released to describe her brothel. "The New Mahogany Hall," it boasted, was built "of marble and is four story; containing five parlors, all handsomely furnished, and fifteen bedrooms. Each room has a bath with hot and cold water and extension closets. The elevator, which was built for two, is of the latest style. The entire house is steam heated and is the handsomest house of its kind." Much of the South, New Orleans included, lacked indoor plumbing facilities until well after World War I, so Mahogany Hall's appointments were truly modern and luxurious.[53] The cost of the building, like everything else Lulu White said, was subject to change. Here, it was said to cost $40,000, while later she claimed to have spent $25,000 on the building and as much as $50,000 on the furnishings.[54]

Lulu White introduced herself to the reader of her brochure. "In presenting this souvenir to my multitude of friends," she began, "it is my earnest desire to, in the first place, avoid any and all egotism, and, secondly, to impress them with the fact that the cause of my successes must certainly be attributed to their hearty and generous support of my exertions in making their visits to my establishments a *moment of pleasure.*" Another section ends by calling Mahogany Hall the place "where you can get three shots for your money—the shot upstairs, the shot downstairs, and the shot in the room."[55] Note that the final chord in White's self-construction is orgasm. Such an emphasis immediately lampoons her simultaneous claims to class, reminding herself and her customer of the business she was in. Orgasm (and making money) was the purpose of all her "exertions."[56] Writing in the third person, Lulu White here identified herself as West Indian, age thirty-one. "Arriving in this country at a rather tender age, and having been fortunately gifted with a good education it did not take long for her to find out what the other sex were in search of." This was another twist on the old story of the "tragic octoroon." The claim of culture and education in the liberal arts slid quickly to the *ars erotica.* Lulu White's real knowledge was about men's desire, and how to satisfy it.

"Besides possessing an elegant form she has beautiful black hair and blue eyes. . . ." White herself was proof of the successive elevations of generations of mixed offspring toward apparent whiteness, a class ascent framed by desire. Her claim to be from the West Indies, her oft-repeated trope, simultaneously removed her from a heritage of chattel slavery in America and implicated her in the colonial history of New Orleans. Rather than descend from the "fancies" in the slave auctions, she was, in essence, claiming a heritage on par with the Creoles of color who formed the middle tier in between black and white, slave and free. At the same time, she herself embraced the identity of the octoroon as sex slave, the envied and despised object of lust, the "fancy" of the planter elite. Instead of channeling this history in order to cry over or condemn it, a move largely denied to women of color, Lulu White used it to produce further sexual desire. Lulu White was posing as a "tragic octoroon," traditionally a victim of circumstance in the South, but she eroticized the figure so completely that her "blue eyes" themselves "made" her "Queen of the Demi-Monde."[57]

Terms of race as categories of existence, to borrow from Joan Scott on the terms of gender, are both "empty and overflowing." "Empty," she writes, "because they have no ultimate, transcendent meaning. Overflowing because even when they appear to be fixed, they still contain within them alternative, denied, or suppressed definitions."[58] In the case of Lulu White, her autobiography tapped the multivalent registers of race as they were being obscured by the state and channeled into two separate categories: black and white. Her embrace and promotion of ambiguity was, to be sure, self-serving; yet it nevertheless highlights the imperatives driving the creation of a biracial caste system for white supremacists at this time. White eroticized the octoroon as complicit in her own fate, doomed by desire to repeat the carnal act. Her business boomed.

In public pronouncements Lulu White continued to claim the right to the vocabulary of respectability. In contrast to the official attempt to marginalize Storyville and separate it from the rest of New Orleans, White's booklet stressed its geographic centrality, and in turn, the central place of Mahogany Hall within it. White's bordello was faithful to the tradition of the city's famous hotels, the St. Charles and the St. Louis, which we recall had long hosted New Orleans's spectacular slave auctions.[59] Mahogany Hall even had a domed roof, a cupola. Perhaps this was a conscious act of architectural homage to the St. Charles Hotel. Calling her brothel "unquestionably the most elaborately furnished house in the city of New Orleans," and "without a doubt one of the most elegant palaces in this or any other country," White mimicked and subverted the New Orleans business community's own rhetoric, but she was not completely amiss in the implied comparison. She drew on recognizable class markers to tout herself and her brothel. "As an entertainer Miss Lulu stands foremost, having made a life-long study of music and literature. She is well-read and one that can interest anybody and make a visit to her place a continued round," she concluded, "of pleasure." Further on, it becomes apparent that White did not at all re-ject the class dimensions of race. "She has made a feature of boarding none but the fairest of girls—those gifted with nature's best charms, and would under no circumstances have any but that class in her house," she wrote.[60] Hers were the *fairest* girls: the lightest and the prettiest.

There are photographs of her prostitutes in Lulu White's booklet, and they all appear "white." Only the text, often describing them as "octoroons," and their place at Mahogany Hall suggested a "drop of African blood" in them. The actual genealogy of these women is unknown. Some of their names, Sadie Levy for example, might suggest other ethnic heritages, though of course not definitively. Lulu White's brochure and the Blue Books more generally served as a kind of menu of sexual offerings in Storyville, and in-cluded the same kind of ambiguity and self-fashioning as we find in White's New Orleans census records. In all cases, with these ads and White's souve-nir catalogue and her self-representation, there is no doubt that we are in the world of strategy and fantasy, and not fixed and unchanging "race." Still, an affiliation with Lulu White and Mahogany Hall could be used to "prove" that a person was "colored" and *not white*.[61] With these ads, moreover, we see how Lulu White and others capitalized on the transformation of "octo-roon" from a racial category into a sexual one. After all, it had been two years since *Plessy v. Ferguson* when White's brochure was published.

Notorious Negress

White could be a discomfiting figure in New Orleans when she ventured outside of Storyville. Storyville was supposed to clarify the borders between respectable New Orleans and its sordid underside, but of course it did not actually quarantine prostitutes or prostitution. When Lulu White crossed into the legitimate sphere of the ascendant bourgeois order, she brought her burlesque into full view on a bigger stage. White, as the abject, that which "disturbs identity, system, order," unmoored aspects of New Orleans's imag-ined past. She was thus herself unsettling. White represented that part of the past, and epitomized those contemporary desires, that the progressive business elite and the other representatives of "respectable" New Orleans sought to suppress. She was the "low other" in all its physicality, bursting at the seams and threatening seemly society. The media commented on her links to powerful politicians and elite businessmen, highlighting the continued corruption of New Orleans's political culture. Although White was an object of fun and scorn in respectable New Orleans, her presence there threatened to draw open the curtain on the elements of New Orleans and its past with which the municipal authorities and business community were most uncomfortable.

The New Orleans newspapers treated White with disdain, focusing on her uncouth character, her business, and her associates. These included pimps and gangsters, to be sure, but also policemen, lawyers, and politicians. The newspapers' apparent outrage on behalf of the community and business interests they represented initially targeted the inappropriateness of law enforcement and government agents' association with Lulu White and other madams. This allowed the press to attack the underworld and the government at once. As we have seen, New Orleans had a long history of municipal cooperation with vice interests. Over time, however, the complaints changed. The focus of reportage became the inappropriateness of social interaction between blacks and whites in Storyville.

White's connections in city government had helped her build Mahogany Hall. She was also connected to some of the most powerful underworld actors in the city, and was perhaps one of them herself. White was certainly a tough customer; in 1904 she fired shots at (but did not injure) her white lover, a gangster (probably a pimp) at his gambling den on lower St. Charles Street. She was arrested for the shooting under the administration of Police Inspector John Journée, but with the aid of her able lawyer, Edward Whitaker, was exonerated of any wrongdoing.[62] The following year Mayor Behrman fired Journée on the grounds that there were pimps and prostitutes in New Orleans, and hired Whitaker as police inspector in his place.[63]

Whitaker was himself a spectacularly degraded character. Certainly there are traces of his involvement in "the scarlet world" years before Storyville's designation. In 1892, for example, when Emma Johnson was arrested for violating a law that mandated she keep the blinds of her brothel closed, Whitaker, acting as a lower court judge ("Court Recorder"), imposed a trifling fine of $20 on her.[64] With Johnson's reputation for using underage girls in her Gasquet Street brothel, the further charge might have ended her business. He then advocated for Lulu White in court as a trial lawyer, and finally, was positioned by Behrman as the chief of police, the "Police Inspector." In that role he gained a reputation for abusing the prostitutes who were brought to jail, trading leniency for sexual favors. He was also accused of groping a young white girl and arrested for raping a black girl. He had a vulgar vocabulary and cursed at citizens over the telephone. His officers consorted with prostitutes, and worse, according to the city's papers, with "negroes."[65] Then, in 1908, Whitaker went a step too far, shooting a newspaper editor whose editorials offended him. Whitaker lost his job. Later, others accused him of using his influence in the city to procure young girls for sex, promising them favors and giving them nickels for the cinema. He was arrested multiple times for violating Louisiana's Act 69—crimes against nature, specifically with the mouth.[66] One of his alleged victims was only seven years old. In 1911, Whitaker was convicted for performing anilingus on a twelve-year-old girl (who was white).[67] One hardly need include his multiple indictments for embezzlement.[68] This was the man who was the chief law enforcement officer during the Storyville years.

Liquor sales and prostitution often go hand in hand, and the state did bring charges against White for nonpayment of taxes on receipts from alcohol and for selling liquor without the proper license. According to the tax collector, she owed the city thousands of dollars in taxes and fees for the beer and wine sold at Mahogany Hall. He estimated that White's profits from the years 1900 to 1905 amounted to between $10,000 and $15,000 solely from the sale of beer, wine, and hard liquor, and demanded several thousand dollars in back taxes.[69] White's two attorneys in the case were George Washington Flynn, her financial partner in the construction of Mahogany Hall, and M. D. Dimitry, who hailed from a prominent New Orleans family, one which participated in the Battle of Liberty Place, the White League *coup d'état* that briefly overturned Republican rule during Reconstruction.

Aside from demonstrating White's vulnerability, the case indicates to us something of the liquor flow in the high-priced bordellos (though White's trial mirrored an earlier trial in which the prestigious social clubs, the Boston and Pickwick Clubs, were prosecuted for selling liquor without a license)[70] and that in spite of her claim that Mahogany Hall was a "wine castle," White in fact sold a good amount of beer. According to the Blue Books, "Wine Castles" were the highest class of brothel. Countess Willie Piazza's octoroon bordello advertised its ale in a double (or triple) race-sex entendre: "The Countess wishes it to be known that while her Maison Joie is peerless in every respect, she reserves only the 'amber fluid.'"[71] To underline the contrast, Lulu White claimed at the trial that Mahogany Hall did not "cater to beer much."[72] And in fact, Louis Armstrong recalled that at Mahogany Hall "champagne would flow like water. . . . If anyone walked in and ordered a bottle of beer, why, they'd look at him twice and then—maybe—they'd serve it. And if they did, you'd be plenty sorry you didn't order champagne."[73] In her defense in 1905, Lulu White claimed that most of the beer in question went to her prostitutes, and so was not taxable as it had not been sold at a profit. She had wished to keep her "girls" out of the saloons, which debarred them by law.[74] The prosecutor, in questioning the plausibility of this story, confining his attention to one brewery, for one year, pointed out that she bought "over six thousand bottles of beer . . . from this one brewery alone. Do you mean to say that those girls drank nearly six thousand bottles of beer in the year 1904?" We have in White's answer a rare example of her recorded speech. "Let me explain. In my house I don't allow the girls to go into any saloons . . . and I give them to understand that they can have all the bottled beer they want, just at the same price I get it from the brewery, to keep them from going. . . ." She claimed they drank "sometimes six dozen bottles a day, when I have twenty or twenty-five girls in the house . . . [they would] begin at nine in the morning and stopped around four in the afternoon, when they started 'getting ready for business.'"[75] The "girls" backed up her story, stating that the "ice-box" was always open, and that they paid as they drank.[76] Many of the women who worked at Mahogany Hall apparently spent their days drinking, as the house did "most of our business at night, and none in the day."[77] As White testified, "[T]hey could drink all you would give them; but I give them, on an average, just enough to keep them from getting too much."[78]

White eventually conceded that a guest might buy a beer for fifty cents or a dollar—steep prices indeed,[79] as elsewhere in the district a bottle or glass of beer cost a nickel. District Attorney St. Clair Adams subpoenaed the records of all the breweries White dealt with and found that in 1901 White bought 4,392 quart-bottles of beer from the New Orleans Brewing Company at 12.5 cents each, $549 total, and from the American Brewing Company, $450 worth of beer between March and October of 1901.[80] White herself kept no books. Nonetheless, she was buying between six and seven hundred quarts of beer a month from those two breweries. She also dealt with the Anheuser-Busch Brewery, which did not submit any records to the court, and the local outfit Security Brewery, from which she bought 28 casks of quart bottles of beer, at six dozen bottles per cask, in 1905, the only year for which the brewery submitted records.[81] White was convicted and ordered to pay her back taxes as well as a fine, together amounting to over $1,000.

In Mahogany Hall's early years, White purchased her wine directly from the agents of the brands she desired. By 1905 most of them were "out of the business" and the source for all her alcohol had become the powerful underworld boss and state legislator Thomas C. (Tom) Anderson, whose saloon sat at the corner of Basin and Customhouse. He had bought this property from the American Brewing Company in 1899.[82] Anderson and White came to an arrangement whereby a party arriving at Mahogany Hall ordered wine or champagne, White telephoned the order to Anderson's, and a porter delivered the bottles. Anderson charged $4 each, and White $5 in her house, a truly exorbitant price at the time.[83] No wonder musicians remember patrons spending so much money on alcohol.[84]

Anderson's records, subpoenaed by the court, together with the brewery records, paint a picture of the seasonal nature of business in Storyville. In the six months between July 1, 1904, and January 1, 1905, Anderson sold Lulu White only $1,193 worth of wine. In September, the slowest month for sales, White bought only one and a half cases. In each of the months of July, August, and October, she bought three cases, but business got going in the colder months; in November White bought thirteen cases of wine, and in December she bought fifteen, at $31 per case. According to Anderson these sales were representative generally.[85]

The winter of 1905 was busy, but February, the month of Mardi Gras, was the top-grosser. White bought $382 worth of wine, mostly Mumm champagne, in pints, and White Seal, another brand of champagne from Moët and Chandon.[86] All in all, White's business thrived in the winter months and waned in the warmer ones, with a bump in early summer.[87] The same cycle is reflected in the number of women who were purported to have been living at Mahogany Hall. In the fall of 1905 there were only twelve women living at Mahogany Hall, but during the winter months White boarded as many as twenty-five prostitutes. When business slowed during the dead of summer, White left Mahogany Hall under the control of one or another of her prostitutes.[88]

A year after her liquor-tax trial, White again found herself in court. This time she was there to testify on behalf of several police officers accused of deliberately sickening the prostitutes of Willie Piazza's Basin Street bordello. The details are as follows. Two police officers went to Willie Piazza's place, ordered a round of beers for several of the prostitutes, and slipped a toxic powder into the beer glasses. According to the *New Orleans Item,* the author of the "prank" "sat in the 'Turkish Corner' of the 'mansion' and fairly split his sides with laughter while the doped victims writhed in agony. His alleged antics were of the vaudeville order."[89] The powder they put into the beer was an emetic, used to induce vomiting.

In part, class tensions animated the attack. The policemen were not paid enough to feel comfortable at the more expensive bordellos, like Willie Piazza's, and could scarcely have afforded to patronize them. The officers' trick was designed to humiliate the prostitutes physically, and indeed, scatological humor was commonplace in this world. For instance, in reporting about prostitutes at the race track, in 1894 the *Mascot* ridiculed them for retiring so frequently to the powder room: "the ladies must have known how bewitching they were, or perhaps they had taken some tropical fruit laxative before leaving home." These "fine ladies" were reduced to bodily functions unmentionable in polite company, indirectly indicating a further reduction of them to their bodily functions, something of course that went on upstairs every night.[90] In the police "prank," five of the prostitutes became seriously ill, Piazza filed a complaint against the officers, and the badly played "joke" erupted into a major police scandal.

The muckraking journalists of the city used the scandal to damn police corruption and moral laxity, and further attack Chief Whitaker. Worse than the poisoning, however, according to the *Item,* was that the police officers would socialize with "colored" women. The most senior of them "is alleged to have been carousing in one of the dens of the district occupied by low and abandoned women."[91] Perhaps, suggested the *Item,* Detective John Paderas was "showing his good fellowship and investigating the race problem, placing himself, for the time being, on a 'social equality' base with the colored female quintette."[92] The *Item* covered the grand jury trial. "The first batch of 'witnesses' to arrive and array their finery," it reported, "consisted of a half-dozen or more 'colored ladies' of the type Detective John Paderas and 'Scotty' Barry Scott, self-confessed 'beer-doper' met on terms of 'social equality' one early morning not long ago. . . . " The paper twice used the phrase "social equality" to scold the officers for consorting with the black women they poisoned at Willie Piazza's, criticizing the men for breeching racial etiquette, and calling up the old shibboleth of white supremacy that freed slaves who wanted the franchise and equal rights were really after marriage or sex with white women. Even before the end of slavery, "social equality" was code for miscegenation, for intermarriage as well as sex across the color line. Here the men were white, and their transgression was drinking with women of color, not sleeping with them. Yet perhaps the paper's larger objection was their exposure of Storyville's special attraction, octoroon prostitutes. Thus the sarcasm of the *Item* also targeted the prostitutes. "These 'ladies' were a motley-looking set. Dimond-decked [*sic*], loudly-clothed, oggle-eyed, brazen, all sense of decency gone. . . . "[93] The real offence committed by the cops was their association with such women, not their abuse of them.

Among those called to testify was Lulu White. The paper referred to White as "the lady herself," and "the notorious negro enchantress of Basin Street," setting her apart from and above the other women in the courtroom, but she was also Lulu White, "another notorious woman."[94] White came in following Detective Paderas and was shown to a seat in one of the private chambers of the courtroom. "The other 'colored ladies' were not shown so much consideration, but remained sitting in the 'outer room.'"[95] Because Whitaker had served as White's attorney before becoming police chief, the newspaper insinuated that Whitaker afforded White special consideration at the courthouse and that their relationship placed her somehow above the law. In fact, it is so that White sided with the police in this case, to the point of denying being a target herself, which she may have been, and she received special favor from Whitaker in return. The *Item*'s prose radiates a kind of discomfort with Willie Piazza, Lulu White, and Storyville: it states and restates the women's race, harping on the color of their skin and insisting on their being "negro." For instance, "The owner of the negro brothel, 'Willie' Piazza,' all her 'colored boarders,' whose facial complexion is of the octoroon tinge, and even down to the 'piano player' also a negress of several degrees blackness, swore yesterday 'Scotty' was not in Paderas' social party the night he made the rounds of Storytown 'cribs' and wound up in a negro 'joint' in Basin Street."[96]

Outside of the Storyville fantasy world, black prostitutes lost the cover of their fancy dress and hairstyles, which became a sham and a farce, and Lulu White became a "negro woman of the lowest type" (even if she was also the "queen of negro enchantresses"). The social transgression of the color line seemed to be the salient point over all others. When these transgressions came to light, the press reacted by describing the most prominent "octoroons" in the district as "negro," "pumpkin-colored," "kinky-haired," "dinge," and "dusky" in order both to degrade the women and to shame the men who consorted with them. As mentioned above, within the confines of Storyville, "octoroon" was a sexual category; once outside those boundaries, however, the ambiguity of mixed race persons forced the heated assertion of racial binaries, in accordance with Jim Crow. At the end of the trial, Whitaker averred that "he could not tolerate a white man who would drink with negroes and place himself on their level by so doing."[97] The miscreants were acquitted, but expelled from the police force.[98]

White testified for the police, and not for her fellow madam, Willie Piazza. Her defiance of Jim Crow should not be read as a progressive stance on civil rights or racial equality; nor should her power as a woman, and a "colored" woman at that, be understood to signify a commitment to women's rights in any way. She was a madam who trafficked in the ambiguous body and interracial sex; her success relied on the continued subordination of women of color and the image of the erotic octoroon. In order to maintain her position within the district, White had to make strategic compromises and unlikely alliances. When in January 1913, for instance, two of her prostitutes at Mahogany Hall got into a bloody fracas, and the responding beat cops were unhelpful, White telephoned the police superintendent directly. She had one of the women arrested, and the delinquent policemen were suspended from duty.[99]

"Lulu White's Way"

In November 1909, the *Daily Picayune* announced that "Lulu White, the negress of the Red-light District, who has had her swing for a long time, is in all the trouble she cares to have just now." She was, "Caught. Charged With Enticing Negress Below Legal Age." Did Lulu White employ minors at Mahogany Hall? Was she involved in the trafficking of young girls? The story as reported in the *Daily Picayune* was as follows: A fifteen-year-old girl named Marie Gaudette, whom the paper referred to as a "young negress," had been missing for three weeks. "[H]er people hunted about the city for her." When her grandmother learned that Marie was at Mahogany Hall, she sent a policeman to fetch her. Upon her "rescue," Marie accused her former boss, a white doctor named Koelle, of seducing her. The doctor was charged with carnal knowledge of a minor, and he was "placed under a good-sized bond." Koelle in turn was "dumbfounded to find himself a prisoner." He denied the charges and claimed that upon seeing the young girl at Mahogany Hall, which he claimed to have visited on a "professional call," he "upbraided her" and arranged for her rescue. The doctor and his friends were "surprised that he should have been accused on the word of an immoral young negress."

The newspaper described Marie's grandmother as a "typical old-time Mammy," loyal to her white employers and neighbors. Dr. Koelle made a point of saying that Marie's family was "respectable," and on good terms with many whites. The paper neither exonerated nor excoriated Dr. Koelle. White was held briefly for harboring a minor for immoral purposes, a felony that carried a three-year prison sentence. She paid a $5,000 bond and was released, and based on her presence in Storyville following the incident, apparently she did not go to prison.[100] Her listing in the city directory indicates that she remained active in the district in 1909, 1910, and 1911, and in 1912 she increased her investment in Storyville by buying the property next to Mahogany Hall, on the corner of Bienville and Basin, where she opened up a saloon.[101] Because of the use of common stereotypes in reporting the story, and because there is no further substantive information about the incident in the newspaper or court records, it is hard to uncover the actual sequence of events and White's role in them. Did Koelle seduce Marie, or did she make that up to explain why she was living at a house of prostitution? Was Marie working at Mahogany Hall, or was she staying there under the care of White? If she was a "negress," was she not light-skinned enough to "pass" as an octoroon? Or was that simply the way the papers referred to people of color, regardless of looks? Was Koelle's visit to the bordello a professional call, as he said, or was he a customer? Why did the doctor emphasize Marie's family's "respectability"? There are too many holes in the story for us to know what really happened. Still, the story forces us to ask if White regularly employed fifteen-year-old girls at Mahogany Hall.

One cannot but note that Lulu White's personal life included passion, heartbreak, and violence. In 1904, in an incident mentioned above, White stormed into a men's club at 133 St. Charles Street and fired shots at the proprietor, George Lambert, White's former lover. Lambert had left White for a white woman in the district, and had even been arrested for beating this woman, but there is no evidence that he ever physically abused Lulu White. "Lulu White seems to have no social club manners," wrote the *Daily Picayune,* "for the notorious negress broke up a poker game which was going on in George Lambert's place . . . Saturday afternoon." According to the *Daily Picayune,* White showed up at the club with a pistol, began "abusing" Lambert, "and fired two shots at him." The other men in the room quickly got up, and one took the gun from White.[102] The poker players subdued White and spirited her out of the building before the police could get there.[103] When the police did arrive, the poker players turned them away.

The police nevertheless charged Lulu White with the lesser count of carrying a concealed weapon. Again, descriptions of Lulu White carry the same automatic qualifiers: notorious, negress, infamy, etc. Again, too, the police were implicated in her actions and their consequences. "Carrying Concealed Weapons—Lulu White. This accused is a notorious negress, proprietress of a den of infamy on Basin Street." The newspaper ridiculed the police's response and expressed mock bewilderment at the diminution of the charges: "Strange to say, no report was made of the affair until Sunday night. Yesterday, instead of making the proper charges against the negress, she was simply charged with carrying concealed weapons, a charge which will hardly be proven."[104] Indeed, with Edward Whitaker as her attorney, White escaped any legal penalty.[105]

Several years later, in 1911, White again made headlines for attempting to shoot a man. "Lulu White's Way" was the headline, and the story of how White "Uses her pistol, but soon gets out of jail" was by then a familiar refrain. "This negress has a habit of taking a shot at a white man occasionally," wrote the *Daily Picayune,* "and yesterday morning she fired at George Killshaw, who is said to be a frequent visitor to the house." Killshaw, too, may have been White's lover, but apparently Lambert was not entirely out of the picture. The story continued. "George Lambert then came to the house, and he being persona non grata, was asked to leave." When he refused, White called the police. The officer "found Lambert under a bed. Lambert created a disturbance and was locked up."[106]

Other episodes in White's life offer teasing glimpses of further dimensions we know nothing about. In 1911 White was charged with attempted homicide in a stabbing. In another incident she was accused of attacking her neighbor on South Rampart Street, where White rented an apartment.[107] A later incident is more intriguing still. In 1916, two men approached a young girl who sold pictures in the district, desiring her aid in "drugging Lulu" and robbing her of the money she sent to her saloon each evening. The "drug would be effective for three weeks, and might [have been] fatal." When White learned of this plot to turn her into a zombie, and perhaps to kill her, "she became hysterical, and required her doctor's aid."[108] So, in spite of her apparent toughness, she was also vulnerable, and there was perhaps a tenderer side to White. She adopted a newborn baby girl at the turn of the century, but how and where White raised her, whose child she was, and what became of her are thus far lost to history.[109]

For the Purpose of Her Business

In 1917, the New Orleans City Council decided to make Storyville an all-white district. Interracial prostitution would be suppressed.[110] The new ordinance attempted to segregate by *race* the district ostensibly segregating *vice*. It read, "From and after the first day of March, 1917, it shall be unlawful for any prostitute or woman notoriously abandoned to lewdness, of the colored or black race, to occupy, inhabit, live or sleep in any house, room or closet situated outside of the following limits, viz.: From the upper side of Perdido Street to the lower side of Gravier Street, and from the river side of Franklin Street to the lower or wood side of Locust Street."[111]

All "colored or black" prostitutes and madams in Storyville would be compelled to move to the "uptown" red-light district, several blocks north of Canal Street. This area was not so much a vice district as a slum where vice flourished, the notorious "battlefield" of Louis Armstrong's early youth.[112] To force Lulu White, Willie Piazza, and the other prominent octoroon madams to move into what one lawyer referred to as "the narrow confines of this section of African iniquity" would deprive them of the glamour they had constructed over the years in making Storyville what it became, not to mention their *raison d'être:* selling sex across the color line. In the next chapter I will discuss the reform efforts that led to this ordinance. Here, I will focus on Lulu White's response, as she entered her third decade as the proprietress of Mahogany Hall.

On February 28, Lulu White received notice to vacate her premises at 235 North Basin Street and to leave Storyville. She refused to move, and filed a lawsuit in civil court to stop the city from evicting her.[113] The same day, Willie Piazza was served with an identical notice to vacate and also sued, along with at least twenty-five lesser-known black or "colored" prostitutes and madams.[114] Most of them used the same lawyer, M. D. Dimitry, and their petitions were virtually identical. (Dimitry had served as one of White's lawyers in the 1905 tax evasion case.) Most of the petitions were notarized by George W. Flynn, another longtime associate of White's.

Each woman's petition frankly stated her business: conducting a house of prostitution. Each petition, including Lulu White's, stated clearly that the petitioner was of the "colored or negro race," and that every aspect of the business, and sometimes the real estate, was owned entirely by the petitioner. This substantial community of black women business-owners in Storyville claimed that the law forced them to give up their property without compensation or due process, and thus discriminated against them as "colored" women, a clear violation of the Fourteenth Amendment. In its attempt "to segregate the races, the said ordinance is arbitrary, discriminatory, and unconstitutional, in that it seeks to deprive your petitioner of the equal protection of the laws."[115] Secondarily, the plaintiffs claimed that it was unlawful to separate colored prostitutes from other colored residents, in that this discriminated against residents on the basis of their employment outside the home, which was not covered in the ordinance.[116]

For Lulu White, who claimed that Mahogany Hall cost $25,000 to build and an additional $50,000 to furnish, the loss would be huge. Likewise, Willie Piazza, who had bought her 317 North Basin Street property for $12,000 and spent an additional $20,000 outfitting it, would lose her investment as well as her estimated yearly profits of more than $2,000. The other petitioners had also invested their own money in their businesses, and though the sums were smaller—from $750 to $2,000—the loss of their livelihoods would of course also have been devastating. These madams often did not own the property where they ran their brothels, but contracted with landlords who appeared on the petitions as cosigners.

The Civil District Court initially upheld the petitions, which prevented the city from evicting the women from their residences and businesses. A few months later, however, the court dissolved the petitions. Willie Piazza then filed a suspensive appeal, warding off eviction while her case went to trial. The other women who had filed suit, including Lulu White, were allowed to remain in their houses and to operate their businesses pending the outcome of Piazza's case.[117] In the events that followed, Piazza won her appeal and the law was declared unconstitutional, the city applied for a rehearing of the case, and the city council passed an amended version of the ordinance, closing the loopholes that had allowed Piazza her temporary victory. The case interests us here because it shows how Lulu White shifted identities when it suited her.[118] When the revised segregation ordinance passed, Lulu White received another notice to vacate her premises, and on August 20, 1917, in response to both the court's ruling and the city's newly worded ordinance, she filed a new petition restating her case. She now claimed that she was "*not* of the negro, colored, or black race," but that she "held herself out for the purpose of her business only as an Octoroon.'"[119] Much as she would tell the census taker in 1920, Lulu White said "her father and mother were both Spanish people of the Caucasian race; that her said parents were duly married in Havana, Cuba, where your petitioner was born of the issue of said marriage." For good measure she added, "that, however, should the Court hold that petitioner is of the negro, colored or black race that the said ordinance is null, void and of no effect as to petitioner for the reasons more fully hereinafter set forth."[120]

In this petition, White underlined both her own racial self-fashioning and the superior salability of octoroon women in Storyville as elsewhere in New Orleans. Denying having even one "drop" of "negro blood," White claimed that she passed herself off as an octoroon for the purpose of attracting customers to her brothel. (Another prominent octoroon madam, Maime Christine, who had married a white minister, prevailed in court by arguing that she was "an Indian squaw" pretending to be octoroon for business reasons.)[121] In fact, White had been claiming for over twenty years that she possessed not one drop of "black blood" while hinting otherwise, blurring the lines that were so important to Jim Crow. The history of Lulu White's racial self-fashioning must be seen as a string of strategic decisions and marketing ploys, driven by Lulu White herself (with her financial pull and political connections), caught in the end between the fantasy of Storyville and the encroaching reality of Jim Crow.

CHAPTER SIX

The Last Stronghold of the Old Regime

It is well known that New Orleans is the Sodom of the South.

—Letter to Raymond Fosdick, chairman of the Commission
on Training Camp Activities

Enforcing Boundaries within Storyville: Race and Reform

We have seen how most business leaders and councilmen wanted to confine vice to discrete (*and* discreet) locations; they desired to clear the streets for respectable persons and legitimate business concerns. As in all cities, however, some reformers continued to seek to eliminate the red-light district itself and put an end to prostitution. In New Orleans, such efforts often focused on interracial sex, race mixing, and "disorderly negroes" within the boundaries of Storyville. As early as the 1850s, Nativist politicians had linked their message of economic reform to a strong stance against illicit sex, particularly prostitution and interracial sex, in effect conflating vice, economic woe, non-white "others" (blacks and immigrants), and sex across the color line in their efforts to stem municipal corruption. In the 1890s and 1910s, reformers focused on race mixing and the perceived bad behavior of black people in Storyville to catalyze the reform of the red-light district. While they were unsuccessful, we may see in their efforts an elaboration of white supremacist ideology: they associated immorality with unruly people of color and sex across the color line—even within the red-light district—and so inscribed race in "reform."

In Storyville, at first, the dance halls received more attention even than the brothels or cribs. As in the efforts to segregate vice before the opening of Storyville, prostitution *per se* was almost never questioned as a moral problem. After legislation brought Storyville into being, prostitution was still accepted as a fact of life in New Orleans; now it was the disorderliness of establishments in Storyville, ones that did not even purport to sell sex, that drew the ire of the moral reformers. Early objections to the district focused on the clubs in the district, located in an area that one newspaper called "the Mecca of bad Negroes" toward Robertson Street, the "rear" of the district (if Basin Street was the "front"), where several dance halls catered to a black clientele. Some of these clubs predated the ordinance, contributing to the neighborhood's mixed character. Many people were afraid to go to the rear of the district, as "bloody fights in the area were commonplace." And the three barrelhouses at Franklin and Customhouse were "scenes of drunkenness, vice, and disturbance at all hours of the day and night."[1] Reformers drew attention to this corner, claiming it was the meeting place for the "lowest class of cocaine fiends, petty thieves, and the general worthless blacks who work only enough to keep alive when 'Grafts' in their particular fields cannot be worked." In fact, "the orgies and dances in these saloons were so indecent," according to the *Item,* that the chief of police was forced to denounce them publicly.

Excluding the creation of the "uptown" or "black" Storyville, Chief of Police John Journée made the first of several attempts to separate white from black vice in 1902.[2] Chief Journée "maintained that the situation warranted the removal of Negro establishments to the other side of Canal Street," asserting that such a removal would "prevent drunken 'blacks' from walking on Canal Street, either going to or coming from their orgies full of barrelhouse whiskey." Nothing was done, however, because, according to the *Item,* "the police received hush hush money from lottery vendors outside the tonks."[3] By Chief Journée's reasoning, black men in Storyville violated two sets of boundaries. First, they created disorder within the vice district. Second, they carried their disorderliness with them through the respectable neighborhoods and among the legitimate businesses on their way to and from Storyville.

We have already seen that white residents of New Orleans neighborhoods eyed with suspicion and disapproval their nonwhite neighbors as they engaged in dances, fish fries, and the like. It seems that any celebratory behavior involving people of color, especially if it involved a group, was perceived as disorderly. Storyville's white business owners even saw blacks meeting for patriotic purposes as problematic. From the 1870s onward, the Colored Veterans Benevolent Association, an organization reaching back to the War of 1812 and the Battle of New Orleans, had held their meetings at the Ramon Urbeso Hall, at 322 Marais Street, in the heart of what would become Storyville; in 1899, property owners there claimed that the veterans constituted a nuisance, and petitioned the mayor to that effect. The mayor declined to renew the Association's permit.[4] If the white property owners in Storyville no doubt wanted to make use of the Colored Veterans' prime real estate, they spoke only about black disorderliness, using terms that assured them a hearing. Black men celebrating their manhood by pursuing sexual adventures, or playing crap games, or commemorating martial valor, were a "nuisance," and dangerous to the moral order, even within Storyville.

Thus race shaped whites' concerns with respectability in marginal neighborhoods outside Storyville, and race exaggerated and deepened vice's evil within Storyville. Female sexuality, put at the service of the white male patron, was the only kind of black sexuality that was allowed. The racial order of the slave plantation was reinscribed in the early twentieth century through the sexual organization of Storyville: black men were denied the full status of manhood, while black and white women served the needs and desires of white patrons. If this racial ecology was not perfectly attained in Storyville, well, neither did it truly characterize plantation slavery. In Storyville the discursive construction of racialized sexuality—black, white, male, female, octoroon—was a recapitulation of the *fantasy* of antebellum white male supremacy. The memory gained traction culturally in part because it had never been fully realized historically.[5]

Still, some people sought to reform the culture of Storyville itself, as if rowdiness, music, and drink were themselves the causes of sin. In 1900, the Unexpected Dance Hall opened at 323 Marais Street, and it operated without incident until 1902. That year, a Reverend Cuddy established the Door of Hope Mission across the street from the dance hall and began a crusade against it. A quarrel ensued, ostensibly pitting the interests of salvation against those of sin. Cuddy enlisted on his side the help of a conglomeration of Methodist ministers and reform-minded, socially prominent women. He preached nightly sermons on the steps of his mission in an attempt to "save" Storyville's residents and visitors.[6] The Door of Hope Mission welcomed prostitutes who wished to reform, offering them beds and helping them find respectable work, according to Cuddy. Two or three women were currently taking advantage of the mission's services.

The Unexpected Dance Hall interfered with the mission, said Cuddy. While Cuddy preached outside on the mission's steps, according to the *New Orleans Item*, "within the hall across the way the dark musicians tooted and thumped for the dancers."[7] "A bullet-headed negro with a far away look in his eye" played guitar, "and a molasses-colored musician that blew the clarionet had to brace his feet against the railing of the players' stand to prevent himself from being hurled backward by the strength of his breath." The music itself, Cuddy insisted, had a ring of indecency to it.[8] "The converts hear the music and begin to waver and succumb to the temptation held out to them."[9]

From the perspective of the Unexpected Dance Hall, however, the reverend's mission interfered with its business. Here within Storyville was a boundary dispute. Which was the more legitimate business in a vice district, a religious mission or a dance hall? One evening while preaching, Cuddy was assailed by "the advertising wagon" from another dance hall, the Frolic, located at 220 North Liberty Street, also in the district. "In the midst of preaching, the [wagon] stopped in front of the Door of Hope and one of the occupants of the wagon began beating a drum."[10] The combined noise of the dance hall's orchestra and the advertising drum drowned out the preacher, even before the proprietor of the Unexpected, Tom Bryant, joined the fray, shouting curses at Reverend Cuddy. Bryant called the preacher "fakir, pickpocket and thief." According to the *Item,* which was campaigning against corrupt police at the time, the local cop on the beat advised Bryant "to cross the street and fight the minister." Bryant "yelled to the evangelist to come into the street that he might 'bust his face.'"[11]

Cuddy censured the mayor, the city council, the superintendent of police, the grand jury, the district attorney, the police captain—indeed the whole city government—for allowing the balls at the Unexpected Dance Hall to continue. But the proprietors had not violated any ordinance and had taken out all the applicable licenses; within Storyville the dance hall *was* a legitimate business. Therefore, the police captain of the Fourth Precinct, Thomas Capo, defended the dance hall: "This hall (Unexpected) has been in existence for over two years, long before the Rev. Mr. Cuddy made his appearance, and no trouble has taken place or complaint received until the one from the Rev. Mr. Cuddy." It was Cuddy, in fact, who was operating beyond the bounds of his permit, and it was he, according to Bryant, who needed to be disciplined. "[H]is permit was given him to preach the gospel and not to make a political speech denouncing the mayor and the police force," Bryant said.[12] While Captain Capo asked the chief of police to force Cuddy to adhere to his permit, the *Item* and other newspapers denounced Capo as siding with vice and "attack[ing] a minister."[13]

Cuddy and his coalition's crusade against the dance halls was having the desired effect. In the words of one proprietor, "business [was] poor, very poor." New Orleans had a "blue law," making it illegal to sell alcohol past midnight on Saturday. The Unexpected drew a curtain between the bar and the rest of the hall at that hour, but a crowd of men remained at the bar well into Sunday morning. The city only began to enforce the blue laws in earnest several years later, though the city council made several sporadic efforts to clamp down on Sabbath drinking through the years. This was difficult to enforce, and police officers were often found drinking alongside patrons, in violation of the law.[14] In the late fall of 1902, Captain Capo, in spite of his antipathy toward Cuddy and his ilk, gave his officers explicit instructions to enforce the Sunday Law, and was displeased to note that one cop "was drinking beer in the Island Queen saloon at Marais and Conti streets" at 1:00 A.M. Sunday morning, and "seemed to be in jovial spirits, for he waived [sic] his helmet a few times above his head and shouted for joy before he drained the glass." Several days later the Unexpected closed its doors, and this was hailed as a great victory for morals: "Vice Yields to Law and Order." The *Item* gave Reverend Cuddy "and the numerous ministers who cooperated with him" full credit.[15]

What happened at dance halls that made them "disreputable" within the boundaries of Storyville? Cuddy and his cohort focused on the music played by black musicians. Of course, as many scholars and popular commentators have shown, the Reverend Cuddy's point of view was echoed and expanded on by the white middle class. Whites found jazz in particular to be disreputable, an "African" influence, subversive of proper musical standards, and tending to promote passionate, lewd behavior and dangerous dancing.[16] Furthermore, even a brief review of the lyrics to some early jazz tunes shows that much of it was raunchily celebratory. That is, when not working in the "high-class" bordellos, musicians might sing about their own sexual exploits, conquests, and pleasures, in jarringly explicit terms.[17] However, within a commercial sex district devoted to pleasure and transgression, sexually explicit lyrics in an intraracial context cannot be the sole reason for Cuddy's and others' objections; perhaps the perceived danger of jazz in Storyville resonated with the pervasive fears among whites about black sexual agency and potent black masculinity more generally.

Several years after the Cuddy imbroglio, in 1907, the famous temperance crusader Carrie Nation included Storyville in her itinerary. Carrie Nation had "received an invitation signed 'Emma Johnson' inviting her to come to her house on Basin Street and see the sights." Johnson's bordello was "quickly invaded." The "landlady" summoned "all the women of the place" and they listened patiently to Mrs. Nation, "asking and answering all sorts of questions." Johnson and her employees all claimed "that it was on account of being raised in luxury but thrown on their own resources without knowing how to work" that compelled them to turn to prostitution. Johnson assured the evangelist that she was very religious and prayed regularly so that "she might go to heaven." Nation next went to Josie Arlington's "much richer and handsomer" bordello, according to the *Daily Picayune*. She prayed for the women and begged them "to repent and go back into respectable walks of life before they became utterly ruined." Josie Arlington informed Mrs. Nation that "she was worth probably $60,000 now, and was going to retire and found a home for fallen women as soon as she got a little richer." A home for "fallen women" would provide a shelter for women who had strayed from the path to domestic life. The trope of fallen women and racially tainted white heiresses naturally presented itself in such circumstances. At Storyville's cribs and smaller brothels, Nation repeated her warnings, where they were "seldom" "received with much gravity by the painted ladies." Nation capped her tour of Storyville at Tom Anderson's saloon. She "mounted a box and spoke to [the patrons], calling on them to shun the saloons and the gambling-houses and the brothels and be men." In spite of heckling by "tipsy individuals," Nation persevered in her speech until it became necessary to close the saloon. It was Saturday night, and perhaps with Nation drawing so much attention, the manager wanted to make sure not to violate the blue laws.[18]

There actually was a temperance movement in New Orleans. Protestant ministers from a wide variety of congregations led the campaign.[19] While the *Item* and the *Daily Picayune* documented the efforts of white ministers, they ignored the African American ministers, who were equally committed to temperance. Again, the white-dominated press and the white bourgeoisie associated blacks with disorderly behavior, including drinking and drunkenness, and this racism contributed to their exclusion of middle-class black reformers from their reportage.[20]

The most comprehensive temperance reform legislation came in 1908 with the passage of the Gay-Shattuck Law.[21] Not so much aimed at the consumption of alcohol itself, the law sought to regulate and control how alcohol was consumed in public, especially by women. It prohibited women and men from drinking together in public; retail liquor licenses could not be issued to women; women, girls, and minors were forbidden to "serve in any barroom, cabaret, coffee house, café, beer saloon, liquor exchange, drinking saloon, grog shop, beer house or beer garden"; it was unlawful to sell intoxicating liquors to women, girls, and minors in the above listed places, or to "set apart in such places any apartment where intoxicating liquors are sold to girls or women, or minors, or to permit girls or women, or minors, to enter or drink in any such apartment." A proviso followed that nothing in the law should interfere with the sale of liquor or wine in hotels or in connection with meals, creating a loophole big enough to foil the reformers. Bars and saloons offered peanuts or other snacks, often recycled and weeks old, and claimed they were "restaurants." They added beds to some rooms upstairs and claimed they were "hotels."[22] Nevertheless, many saloon proprietors were arrested for serving liquor to women, and police enforced the prohibition on women in many bars and saloons around the city, including some in Storyville.[23] The law also prohibited blacks and whites from drinking together in public. According to the logic of Jim Crow, morals legislation *was* race legislation.

New Orleans businessmen opposed the demands of moral reformers when they threatened their commercial interests. In January 1909, the Business Men's League of New Orleans called a meeting to discuss the commercial situation of the city. "After full consideration of the situation this meeting finds that there is a universal complaint among the merchants of the city, of every class and character, that whilst their business at this season of the year has always shown great prosperity, this year it has shown considerable depression." The reason? The "erroneous report that has gone abroad that the people of New Orleans have become ultra-puratanical [*sic*]," and that "drastic blue laws" were under consideration.[24] Drinking and prostitution might have been bad for morals, but prohibition was bad for business. Maintaining New Orleans's status as the "winter capital of the United States," as the Business Men's League and the Progressive Union desired to do, necessitated a certain moderation, provided that vice was corralled within known boundaries.

Storyville's Borders Revisited

In 1908 the city completed the building of a terminal rail station at Basin and Canal, and Storyville's margins came under new scrutiny.[25] Train tracks had lain for years across Basin Street, serving intracity trains to the Spanish Fort, and it was logical that the station should make use of the existing infrastructure. Designed by Daniel Burnham, the architect of the 1893 Chicago Columbian Exposition's "White City" and of Washington, D.C.'s Union Station, the depot was to be a monument to the commercial progress of the city and the South's integration into the national economy.[26] The New Orleans Terminal Station served multiple rail lines, and it was the last stop on the Southern Railway line, bringing passengers into the heart of New Orleans's growing commercial district.[27] As the *Times-Democrat* reported, the "depot is so near to all the leading hotels that it will not be necessary for passengers to take either cars or cabs to reach them."[28] By the same token, passengers now found themselves within easy walking distance of the city's other "grand" resorts: Mahogany Hall, the Arlington, Emma Johnson's French Palace, and Willie Piazza's octoroon bordello. That is, the New Orleans Terminal Station was only one block away from Storyville's Basin Street boundary, and the trains, filled with passengers, passed right by the ornate Basin Street bordellos. Prostitutes beckoned to them from windows and balconies.[29] Thus, in 1908 a visitor's first impression of New Orleans was not the "five tier of shipping in the harbor," which had so impressed nineteenth-century travel writers, but prostitutes in various states of undress waving and gesturing to him. Rather than simply heralding the victory of progress and prosperity, the completion of Terminal Station sent a mixed message. The borders of legitimate commerce now grated against those of illegitimate, vicious commerce. The station and the Basin Street tracks clouded the distinctions those boundaries were meant to clarify, and revived the problem of visibility that the designation of Storyville was meant to resolve.

Female moral reformers in New Orleans, concerned with the "white slavery" traffic, worried that the Terminal Station would serve as a recruiting ground for procurers looking for young girls from the countryside. New Orleans's most prominent women's reform and suffrage organization, the Era Club, convened a committee to investigate the conditions of vice in New Orleans, and, finding them reprehensible, called a mass meeting for women from New Orleans's churches and "social and educational clubs." The result was the formation of the Travelers' Aid Society of New Orleans, an organization devoted entirely to the problem of white prostitution and the respectability of white girls.[30] The Travelers' Aid Society found the location of the new train station severely disturbing. One of its first public acts was to petition the city council to move Storyville away from it. The women objected to the "long line of Basin Street frontage" which trains, "freighted with strangers and visitors," passed. The reformers said the district was a "moral cancer," and declared that if a red-light district absolutely had to exist (which they doubted), "it should be moved to the outskirts of the city."[31] Storyville, in the opinion of these women, stood as "a monument to the impotency of decent citizens to inculcate a standard of morals" by which to protect the youth of New Orleans.[32]

Seeing that their moral argument fell on deaf ears, the Travelers' Aid Society represented the fight instead as pitting legitimate commerce against vice, such that the "present centralized location of the restricted district" injured the development of commerce on Canal Street above Rampart. As part of their strategy, the women suggested that the railroad company compensate the Basin Street madams and property owners for the losses they would suffer when forced to move to a less visible locale.[33] They suggested further that the buildings, Mahogany Hall, the Arlington, Emma Johnson's French Palace, and the other spectacular bordellos, should be redeployed to house the working men and women of the city.[34]

Clearly, the district no longer functioned, if indeed it ever had, to "cleanse" the city. In 1910, Philip Werlein, the president of the New Orleans Progressive Union, teamed up with the Era Club to fight "evil conditions" in New Orleans. The New Orleans Progressive Union investigated the area around the Terminal Station, and they, like the club women before them, were horrified. They repeated the Travelers' Aid Society's efforts to remove the Basin Street bordellos, to alter the boundaries of Storyville, and to create a greater buffer between the illegitimate business of prostitution and the legitimate business of capitalism. Though they in fact still favored the red-light district, they objected to its proximity; Werlein denounced "the glaring immorality and lack of common decency which is so apparent to everyone who uses the terminal station."[35]

In March of that year Werlein, acting in his capacity as the chairman of the Progressive Union's Committee of Municipal Affairs, drafted a resolution asking Mayor Behrman to shut down the Basin Street bordellos. "Your Committee finds the situation in the restricted district on Basin Street, facing the Terminal Station, to be disgraceful and a serious detriment to the best interests of the City, morally and commercially." The mayor should remove "such houses of prostitution facing Basin Street and fronting the

Terminal Station, as well as those houses of prostitution on Iberville and Bienville Streets between Basin and Franklin Streets." The proposal called upon the mayor to act in accordance with the Storyville ordinance, which gave him the power to remove houses if they became morally repugnant. While the Progressive Union board approved the proposal unanimously, Mayor Behrman was not persuaded.[36] Removing the Basin Street houses would have deprived Storyville of the most prominent and well-appointed bordellos in the district.

Although Storyville's borders were to remain where they were, the state did initiate further reforms to clarify and police the borders between black and white inside Storyville, and throughout the city. The 1908 Gay-Shattuck Law, mentioned above, criminalized interracial fraternizing in bars, saloons, and restaurants, and entrepreneurs applying for permits to operate barrooms had to specify which "race" they would serve. The many instances in which saloon-keepers were arrested for "selling to whites and negroes" tell us that there was in fact plenty of mixed-race socializing within New Orleans's still mixed-race neighborhoods. (Some of the cases were dropped before going to trial, others resulted in fines.)[37] Storyville severely irked the reformers who still wanted to "clean up their city," because it harbored twin evils: prostitution and miscegenation. The district's heightened visibility and national notoriety exacerbated the problem. Plus, white segregationist imperatives demanded a stricter adherence to the hardening color line as time went on, and customs that had been part of New Orleans's distinct history came under attack.

To wit: the state legislature outlawed interracial concubinage in Act 87 of 1908. The law stated that "concubinage between a person of the Caucasian or white race and a person of the negro or black race is hereby made a felony." Lawmakers apparently intended to put an end to the centuries-long practice of all forms of interracial concubinage in New Orleans. Marriage across the color line had become a felony in Louisiana in 1894, but interracial concubinage had been left alone; now, however, New Orleans had been assimilated into the racial and sexual culture of the rest of the nation such that the visibility of interracial sex became increasingly unacceptable. Yet the precise meaning of "interracial," and how to regulate such relations, was still not settled fourteen years after *Plessy v. Ferguson.* In 1910 the Louisiana Supreme Court heard a case regarding the 1908 law.[38] Octave Treadaway was arrested for violating the act, but he claimed he was innocent because, while he was white, his lover was not a negro, but an octoroon. According to Treadaway and his lawyers, the law's prohibition against white-negro concubinage did not include octoroons.

Thus the Treadaway case functioned like a sexualized version of *Plessy v. Ferguson.* Where the former case addressed gender only in terms of "nurses" attending children of a different race—the "mammy clause"—Treadaway forced the Court to acknowledge the gendered history of racial inequality and its sexual side effects. The judges wrestled with legal and popular definitions of "negro" before finally concluding that an octoroon was a person of color, or "colored person," but not a "negro." The Court defined the term "griff," a lesser known racial designation, "indicating the issue of a negro and a mulatto," and then quadroon, who was "distinctly whiter than the mulatto." The Court breezily concluded that "between these different shades, we do not believe there is much, if any, difficulty in distinguishing." Why were these distinctions not moot in 1908 Louisiana? The Louisiana Supreme Court revived, for the purpose of outlawing sex, the racial logic that Justice Brown had rejected in his ruling in the *Plessy* case in 1896. In this instance, Louisiana's special history demanded a refinement of the "one-drop rule."

The state argued that the present law was supposed to "prevent the mixing of bloods, and that that object would not be accomplished if only the blacks and not also the mulattoes and quadroons and octoroons and others of lesser mixture" were covered. In fact, "the concubinage of the whites with the blacks is practically unknown." The Court was moved to speak truthfully, stating that from "the birth of the state up to the last session of the Legislature, concubinage with even the pure-blooded negro was not forbidden."[39] The Court thus doubted that the state lawmakers had "*all of a sudden . . . awakened to the necessity of making*" all interracial concubinage a felony. "If the intention was thus to go at one clean sweep from one extreme to the other, terms expressive of that intention should have been used."[40]

When the state, in defending its law, suggested that "the Legislature would hardly permit whites and octoroons to live in concubinage when forbidding them to ride together in railroad coaches and street cars," the Court rejoined that "the Legislature has as a matter of fact done that very thing." Yet, there was a definite logic to the course of legislation: "without separate car statutes the whites would be brought into contact with the colored no matter how objectionable the proximity might be to them," while concubinage or "illicit commerce" with them "could only be voluntary." Whereas the segregation statutes were designed to protect the *individual,* the Court said that "now the time has ripened for *the protection of the race.*"[41] The present law, however, was inadequate because it was ineptly written. Treadaway was acquitted, because an octoroon woman was still not a negro. The legislature then amended the statute to prohibit all concubinage between whites and persons of color, including octoroons.

The Treadaway case shows that women could not be corralled into the two categories of "black" or "white" in the same way men were. Homer Plessy was an octoroon, but *he was a man.* In the anti-concubinage law and the Treadaway case, we see the prohibition of racial hybridity and interracial sex extending to those women who were traditionally the sexual objects of white male desire. Certainly this lag owes much to the fact that women, regardless of race, color, ethnicity, or "previous condition of servitude," did not have the right to vote and were not potential participants in the public sphere in the same way that men were. Yet the case indicates a change in the sexual politics of racial patriarchy as well. In discussing race classification in Louisiana, Virginia Dominguez notes that "the use of statutory law to prevent interracial concubinage signified a changing ideological climate that stressed blood purity to a much greater degree than ever before."[42] The case also signals a change in tone, indicating greater moral opprobrium toward white men who crossed the color line for sex.

Philip Werlein, in his attempts to remove the Basin Street bordellos, drew strength for his argument from the new legislation, and extended its logic to prostitution. He targeted Storyville in code when he complained in 1910 that "conditions" in New Orleans "offer[ed] a notorious attraction." He then specified. He argued against the open hypocrisy in that "the association between white men and negro women, which is forbidden by the concubinage law under moral conditions, is openly permitted on Basin Street under immoral conditions." If interracial marriage and concubinage were to be prohibited by the law, certainly interracial prostitution should also be prohibited. "The one thing that all southerners agree upon is the necessity of preserving our racial purity," Werlein said. "The open association of white men and negro women on Basin Street, which is now permitted by our authorities, should fill us with shame as it fills the visitor from the North with amazement. . . . We should take immediate steps to remove the evil or we should stop condemning miscegenation."[43]

The evil was not prostitution as such—certainly no northerner would have been amazed to find prostitution in New Orleans—but, rather, the "open association of white men and negro women." For Werlein, interracial prostitution and sex across the color line, even in cases where the *men* were white, constituted an evil that had to be immediately stopped. Werlein added that the "filthy hovels in which the negro and French women live are distasteful to the women who conduct their houses in better style."[44] The black prostitutes especially must be "stamped out of the district."[45] According to him it was "a shame and a disgrace that Negro dives like those of Emma Johnson, Willie Piazza, and Lulu White, whose infamy is linked abroad with the fair name of New Orleans, should be allowed to exist and boldly stare respectable people in the face. These resorts should be exterminated and the Negresses who run them driven from the city."[46] The "real cancer of the district," Werlein underlined, "is the congregation of the whites and negroes under practically the same conditions."[47] Increasingly, the boundaries of respectability and legitimate commerce, even in the case of *prostitution,* were becoming the boundaries of "whiteness."

Birth of a Nation

At the same time, as North-South reconciliation proceeded on a racial basis through celebrations of Civil War veterans, reunion ceremonies, and the erection of monuments to individual (white) soldiers, the memories of planter patriarchy and its sexual prerogatives faded as a collective cultural fantasy.[48] Moreover, as Glenda Gilmore writes, in the face of evolutionary science and increasing racism at the turn of the century, white men's liaisons with black women signified in a new way. "No longer was a white man who slept with a black woman demonstrating his strength; instead, he was proving his weakness."[49] By the time it became necessary to make the world safe for democracy, the kind of total power and aristocratic privileges that slave masters symbolized had lost much of their resonance. Thus, the octoroon, once the potent emblem of that absolute power, now came to represent a threat to white domesticity and nationhood. In a country obsessively committed to erasing racial ambiguity, female "octoroons" presented an especial danger. They decreasingly embodied white male prerogative and privilege, yet they remained as specters of interracial sexuality and impurity of blood; increasingly, they suggested white racial vulnerability.

We have seen in the Treadaway case how Louisiana wrestled with this emergent ideological shift. The same shift can be seen in the national blockbuster film *The Birth of a Nation.* D. W. Griffith's 1915 film was based on Thomas Dixon's Reconstruction trilogy, *The Leopard's Spots: A Romance of* the White Man's Burden (1903), *The Clansman* (1905), and *The Traitor: A Story of the Rise and Fall of the Invisible Empire* (1907). Dixon aimed to present the southern white point of view regarding the Civil War and its aftermath, especially of the evils of Radical Reconstruction. The film portrays a postwar South overrun by sexually predatory, ambitious, ignorant blacks and their complicit and manipulative white sponsors from the North. To combat these rapists and "carpet-baggers," a secret society of avenging angels is formed, the Ku Klux Klan. The Klan is the ostensible "nation" of the film's title, but its formation also represents the birth of the modern American nation: a *re*birth of white supremacy, the salvation of the South, and the regeneration of America, united on a racial as well as a national basis.

Griffith's film has inspired a large body of historical writing and film criticism on its significance in American history.[50] Its relevance to the history of Storyville, which concerns us here, lies first in its representation of two mixed-race characters, and second, and relatedly, in what the film's release and reception tells us about a New South fraternity entering the corridors of national power.

The mixed-race characters in the film are both intimately connected with August Stoneman, a northern congressman in Reconstruction-era South Carolina. The first is Silas Lynch, Stoneman's protégé. Hungry for political power and overwhelmed with lust for white women, the figure of Lynch stands to show that "black blood" prevented men from being refined by education and the trappings of respectability, even when mixed with a generous proportion of "white blood." Lynch's lust is the more dangerous precisely because he is not ignorant, and because he has the power and authority to enact laws enforcing "social equality." His name signals the potential fate of blacks transgressing the color line in the New South. The film thus shows the acceptance of conflating black political aspiration with a lascivious desire for interracial sex, and it associates that desire with northern weakness, not southern strength.[51]

Even more relevant to us is the other mixed-race character, Lydia, Stoneman's housekeeper and presumed lover. Dixon and Griffith modeled Stoneman's character after the Radical Republican Reconstruction-era congressman from Pennsylvania, Thaddeus Stevens, Dixon's historical political "bête noir." Stevens had in fact employed a housekeeper named Lydia Smith, and Dixon, in essence, accused him of keeping her as a concubine.[52] In *The Birth of a Nation,* August Stoneman preaches social equality while he is secretly dominated by Lydia. For her part, Lydia is rabid with desire, rolling her eyes and ripping at her clothes in uncontained frenzies of lust. When it looks as if she might become queen to Stoneman's king of Carolina, she falls into paroxysms of passion. Stoneman's relationship with Lydia was characterized by an intertitle as, "The great leader's weakness that is to blight a nation."[53]

Even before the movie reached a national audience, groups protested its treatment of history and its racism. Dixon surmounted these objections by calling on "an old acquaintance, a friend from his college days at Johns Hopkins": President Woodrow Wilson.[54] Dixon appealed to the president as a scholar and a friend; in making the film, Griffith and Dixon had relied on Wilson's *History of the American People,* and had even borrowed lines from that book for the intertitles.[55] Wilson agreed to watch the film, and invited Dixon to show *The Birth of a Nation* at the White House.[56] There the president, along with members of his staff and cabinet, watched the movie. He was instantly swayed. Wilson's response became famous: "It's like writing history with Lightning. And my only regret is that it is all so terribly true."[57]

Next, Dixon turned to his old friend from the early "North Carolina days," Josephus Daniels. Daniels had risen in the national Democratic Party ranks by helping to orchestrate the disenfranchisement of people of color in North Carolina; he also played a key role in directing the Democratic nomination toward Wilson in 1912.[58] Now Daniels was Wilson's secretary of the navy. Dixon asked him to arrange a meeting with the chief justice of the U.S. Supreme Court, Edward D. White, who hailed from Louisiana. At first Justice White was reluctant to take the time to view a movie, but when Dixon explained the nature of the film, White changed his mind. "'You tell the true story of the Klan?' he inquired. [Dixon replied,] 'Yes—for the first time.'" According to Dixon, the justice leaned in close and said, "I was a member of the Klan, sir. Through many a dark night I walked a sentinel's beat through the ugliest streets of New Orleans with a rifle on my shoulder. You've told the true story of that uprising of outraged manhood?" Dixon made arrangements for Justice White, several of his colleagues on the bench, and even some members of Congress to see the film.[59] These men's endorsement, and particularly Wilson's enthusiasm, bolstered the film's legitimacy in the face of protests.[60]

The film opened in New Orleans in March 1916, only a few blocks from Mahogany Hall and Basin Street. Audiences flocked in such numbers to see it that the Tulane Theater held it over for two additional weeks.[61] As the *New Orleans Item* wrote, "A second extension of the engagement of 'The Birth of a Nation' has been arranged . . . and the Griffith spectacle will be presented twice daily all next week . . . in the same massiveness and splendor that they have enthralled nearly 50,000 New Orleans playgoers to date." The manager of the Tulane Theater encouraged people to buy their tickets long in advance. Innovative, breathtaking, and sealed with the approval of the country's leader, the movie "swept Southern Louisiana like a tidal wave."[62] The paper described the movie as "the Wagnerian idea outdone and fitted to a massive screen drama in which 18,000 people and 3,000 horses are seen in a reproduction of the principle stormy periods of American history."[63] The old abolitionist trope of the tragic octoroon was played out, and out-played, by the spectacle of *The Birth of a Nation.* And thereby, the Storyville "octoroon" madams, who yet owned valuable property in the city, and commanded influence with the city's politicians, began to appear more like the domineering Lydia than Boucicault's tragic Zoe.

War, the Rise of the South, and the Fall of Storyville

Woodrow Wilson was the first southern Democrat to occupy the White House since Andrew Johnson. His own political ascendancy can best be understood as part of the same culture of reunion represented by *The Birth of a Nation,* and the emergence of a hegemonic interpretation of the Civil War, its causes, and its outcome. Dixon, Daniels, and Wilson together represented a New South fraternity on the national stage, an enlarged ruling stratum united by race and region more than wealth or family, and tied together by a mutual commitment to progressive reform and white supremacy. This cohort's newfound power and influence demonstrated the renaissance of southern influence in politics, the law, literature, and film.

Critical to the ascendancy of this New South and Democratic Party ethos was the Spanish-American War. The Spanish-American War provided the geographic and ideological landscape on which to enact key elements of the reunion of North and South. Northerners looked to the South, in C. Vann Woodward's formulation, "for guidance in the new problems of imperialism resulting from the Spanish war." For white supremacists, America's international expansion demonstrated the "divine right of the Caucasian to govern the inferior races," and the southern policy of black disenfranchisement was "amply vindicated" through the imperial policies of the nation.[64] The United States' expansion overseas internationalized and reinforced the racial view of American society at home. Pro- and anti-imperialists argued about racial inferiority and assimilability in making their cases about acquiring the Philippine Islands.[65] Northern whites were relieved to allow the South to deal with its "race problem" in its own way, even when that way meant lynchings and riots; after all, they were forced to deal with waves of "inassimilable" immigrants at home and overseas populations in the new colonies who were equally unsuited, in their minds, to democracy and citizenship as southern blacks. Southerners breathed a sigh of relief (and a whisper of "I told you so") as the North seemed finally to understand the special problem slavery's aftermath posed for whites in the South. Even those who deplored the openness of America's immigration policies and the influx of "ethnics" still set "white" immigrants against American "blacks."[66]

The "whitening" of American citizenship and the reconstructing of American nationalism involved processes of sectional reunion, revisions of Civil War memory, and black disenfranchisement. Popular culture nationalized the Democratic shibboleth of "white supremacy" familiar to southern politics, and presidential hopefuls Theodore Roosevelt, William Howard Taft, and Woodrow Wilson each promised to keep his party—whether Republican, Democratic, or Progressive—a "white man's" party.[67] In 1912, for the first time in fifty years, the South "played a conspicuous and perhaps even decisive role" in the presidential election, in a "most heated contest."[68] After Wilson's election to the presidency, one contemporary magazine remarked, "All the way from styles in head-gear to opinions on the tariff, the flavor and color of things in Washington are Southern."[69] That color was white. When Wilson segregated the offices of the federal government, forcing black government workers to do their jobs behind curtains and to use separate facilities, there came barely a peep of protest from northern whites.[70]

Wilson was a Democrat and a "progressive." The progressive movement in America brought the values of the ascendant middle class to the forefront of public rhetoric; during the Progressive Era the rise of cities, corporations, and bureaucracies transformed the middle class. The small-town bourgeoisie of the nineteenth century gave way to an urban, professional class by the start of the twentieth. This expanding class sought out experts with specialized knowledge and turned to municipal governments and national solutions for social problems.[71] Reform movements were driven and undergirded by a kind of urgent bourgeois propriety and the demand for its inculcation among the laboring and immigrant classes. The federal government also became more involved in matters of home, family, and individual morality than it had historically been.[72] President Wilson embodied the prim moralism of this group, and his presidency signaled the success of southern progressivism and the deep-seated racism within it.[73]

White Blackbirds

Self-styled "progressive" businessmen in New Orleans had in fact been responsible for the creation of the Storyville red-light district at its beginning. Twenty-odd years later, progressive moral reformers, including the likes of Dixon, Daniels, and President Wilson, ensured its demise. As we have seen, the efforts by reformers to encourage city officials to segregate Storyville by race at times gained traction but ultimately failed. The 1917 attempt to segregate Storyville racially, however, most certainly responded to the revivified clean-up campaign sweeping New Orleans (and the nation) in 1917, as many groups increased their pressure on Mayor Behrman to close Storyville. The tireless antivice crusader Jean Gordon held Storyville responsible for the moral decay of New Orleans.[74] "The Good women of New Orleans have been asking for years the question, 'What is the matter with our homes and our husbands?'" The answer was "Storeyville [sic]."[75] The city's attitude toward this "vile and shameless marketplace of fallen humanity" was, according to Gordon, to protect the district at the expense of the good, moral, citizens of New Orleans.[76]

Up to 1917, Gordon's long campaign against Storyville amounted to little: prostitutes were forbidden to solicit on the street, a rule that was seldom enforced; some "cribs" had been shuttered and the "women were driven into the streets." Gordon regretted that hardly anything was done for them, and called the action of the police inhuman, as raids were "made during the cold wave which was the most severe that the South has suffered in many years."[77] Now, however, it appeared that the city was finally beginning to take action against Storyville. Commissioner of Public Safety Harold Newman "quickly zeroed in on what local reformers deemed the most dangerous, disgusting and disorderly aspect of the district"—interracial sex.[78] The city then passed Ordinance 4118, C.C.S., mandating the racial segregation of Storyville. This was the ordinance that prompted Lulu White, Willie Piazza, and at least twenty-five other nonwhite madams in Storyville to sue the city, as discussed in chapter 5. Like the anti-concubinage law of 1908, this segregating ordinance would seem on its face to have been straightforward and unambiguous in its intent. Nonwhite prostitutes were to leave Storyville at once and take up residence uptown, in the three square blocks above Canal Street outlined in the Storyville ordinance's first amendment. The ordinance made it "unlawful for any prostitute or woman notoriously abandoned to lewdness, of the colored or black race, to occupy, inhabit, live or sleep in any house, room or closet" within the boundaries of Storyville. Before the Louisiana Supreme Court, Piazza argued that prohibiting colored prostitutes from *living* in Storyville was not equivalent to prohibiting them from *working* in Storyville.

It had long been decided that the regulation of prostitution fell within the police powers of the city, but the question of enforced *residential* segregation was another matter entirely. The law would force black prostitutes who lived in Storyville—but did not necessarily *work* there—to leave their residences without compensation, which amounted to the seizure of property without due process of the law. At roughly the same time as the Louisiana Supreme Court was hearing the arguments about Storyville, the U.S. Supreme Court, under Chief Justice Edward White, declared a law comparable to the one Piazza challenged, segregating residents by race, unconstitutional.[79] The Louisiana Supreme Court therefore wished to make sure the New Orleans City Council expressed itself clearly, and in July of 1917 it found the Storyville segregation ordinance unconstitutional "on the ground that the city could not prohibit a person's living anywhere he or she wants to live."[80]

"The Court erred," according to the city's attorneys, "in holding that 'A reading of the ordinance [would] restrict colored prostitutes from selecting homes outside of their houses of prostitution.'" The city said that the Court was presupposing cases, "hitherto as rare as white blackbirds," of "mere bawds, not even keepers of bawdy houses . . . still 'plying their vocation,' and yet acquiring homes apart from [their brothels] in such numbers as to provoke the intervention of the public authorities."[81] In making their case, the city's attorneys used the phrase "as rare as white blackbirds" to describe the situation Piazza's attorneys posited—prostitutes with homes in the red-light district that were distinct from their work sites. But the image conjures up a contradiction that, according to the prevailing racial ideology, applied especially to octoroons. While the ordinance aimed to separate all nonwhite prostitutes from all white prostitutes—based on the racial distinction set in law twenty-one years previously in the *Plessy* case—the octoroons in Storyville remained problematic. These "white blackbirds" flew in the face of Jim Crow. They had to be caged. Whereas their implicit claim to the legacy of the antebellum "fancy girls," slave auctions, and tragic octo-roons made them the queens of the demi-monde in Storyville, by the end of the 1910s they were increasingly subsumed under the category of "colored," even within the district's own guidebooks. In a red-light district reserved for "colored" prostitutes, they would lose their caché entirely; they would no longer serve white men. In its bid to effect actual segregation by race in Storyville, the city cited *Plessy v. Ferguson* and quoted Justice Brown's spe-cious reasoning: "Legislation is powerless to eradicate racial instincts or to abolish distinctions based upon physical differences, and the attempt to do so can only result in accentuating the difficulties of the present situation."[82] The problem with the "present situation" in this case was not antipathy between whites and nonwhites as was presumed in *Plessy,* but the opposite: a "notorious attraction."

In its intentions, the city sought to erase the ambiguity of the misce-genous body even among women and to end, once and for all, sex across the color line. The city demanded that the racially ambiguous women of Storyville declare for one race or the other: white or colored (black). Lulu White declared that she was white in spite of having "held herself out" as an octoroon. Willie Piazza declared herself "colored" in order to fight the seg-regation law and retain her property.[83] The Storyville octoroon thus ceased legally to exist.

Piazza won her case, and the city applied for a rehearing. The coun-cil introduced an amendment to the segregation ordinance, clarifying the language of the original, making it illegal for "blacks to conduct immoral houses in the district for whites." According to the *Item,* the city believed this amendment would "stand the test of the courts and at the same time bring about [racial] segregation" in Storyville.[84] Pressing matters on the na-tional stage would prevent that eventuality and lead, in fact, to the closing of the district.

Fit to Fight

Throughout the country, as American troops prepared for the possibility of mobilizing for a world war overseas, men and women at home were mobi-lizing against prostitution, warning of women who looked chaste enough but who carried diseases that could then spread, undetected, to spouses and unborn children. Here was another invisible empire, an internal domestic enemy, that the good (white) people of America had to fight in order to survive—culturally, racially, and politically.[85] According to race ideology, there were always signs, visible to the well-trained eye, that would reveal the true race of any given individual. Similarly, immorality was supposed to be written on the body itself,[86] but physical signs of degeneracy likewise appeared only to the observant. The national campaign to protect soldiers and citizens from disease and moral decay warned that immoral women could hide their own depravity until it was too late.

Though red-light districts ostensibly marked prostitutes by containing them within known boundaries, they had never really done so, and had instead simply provided easy access to commercial sex for men.[87] That men went to prostitutes had long been winked at as a regrettable but acceptable outlet for men's sexual energies—energies that could not be properly ex-pended elsewhere. In the first decade of the twentieth century this ceased to be the case. New research into the causes and effects of venereal dis-eases played a part in changing this attitude, as did new understandings of the role of sex in heterosexual coupledom.[88] At around the same time the "absolute interdiction of sex before marriage" eased somewhat. Women's reputations were still fragile enough to be ruined for "going all the way," especially with more than one partner, but, as Nancy Cott writes, "sexual experimentation before marriage by couples in love moved out of the shad-ows; some premarital heterosexual activity was granted to be normal."[89]

Within marriage, sex was elevated to the sacred. The Victorian ideal of "passionlessness" for women gave way to a fuller appreciation of wom-en's sexuality as something to be nurtured, within matrimonial, domes-tic bounds.[90] Women's greater public role in politics, the labor force, and society generally, through volunteer organizations, charity work, and the suffrage movement, accompanied their elevated status within marriage. Still, white women committed to middle-class values and a single standard of sexual morality for men and women employed a rhetoric of proper do-mesticity even as they sought greater representation in the public sphere. Prostitutes and red-light districts underlined the intersection of sex and commerce and ran counter to bourgeois discourses of domesticity *and* capi-talism.[91] The tide was turning decisively against the very idea of red-light districts.

Woodrow Wilson asked Congress for a declaration of war against Ger-many in April 1917. As propaganda for the war escalated, another moral im-perative emerged. The nation had to keep its young men "fit to fight." This meant eradicating venereal disease and ensuring the physical (and moral) health of young soldiers. As with earlier struggles against venereal diseases, this was figured as much more than a medical necessity. Young men who contracted a sexually transmitted disease endangered themselves and their fellow troops and therefore the war effort. They endangered their homes, the citadels of respectable middle-class life they were fighting for. The only way to safeguard the American nation while also protecting Europe from tyranny was to prevent American troops from consorting with prostitutes or other "loose" women. "Making men moral," as historian Nancy Bristow put it, became an adjunct to the war effort in the same way as did other programs of the Progressive Era.[92]

To protect the soldiers from prostitutes, as well as alcohol and other vices, and to provide positive amusements in the camps, the government created the Commission on Training Camp Activities. This commission was a coordinating body, working with the YMCA and other organizations to keep the soldiers wholesomely entertained.[93] Secretary of War Newton Baker mandated the CTCA to provide the soldiers with "an invisible armor" —a moral sense that would shield them from the less valorous injuries of war: syphilis and gonorrhea. Propaganda posters circulated idealized images of the American family with captions such as, "Don't let a she-hooker ruin your family reunion."[94] The families depicted in these posters were all white.

The CTCA also distributed pamphlets prepared by the American Social Hygiene Association outlining the dangers of patronizing prostitutes for the soldiers, and through them the nation. *Keeping Fit to Fight* was the most prominent of these pamphlets.[95] It was a bold departure in that it contained graphic information about illicit sex and the disease that would follow. The intense focus on the white male body might perhaps be read as an echo of the countrywide memorialization of Civil War soldiers in the decades before World War I. In that period, the statues of solitary standing soldiers proliferated, challenging the earlier iconicity of the mounted general, celebrating instead the manliness of individual troops. These statues and their accompanying memorial rituals forged bonds across sectional lines based on mutual respect for valor in war.[96] *Keeping Fit to Fight* similarly reoriented "manhood," laying the responsibility for preserving it on the soldier himself. His individual, private choices and *actions* would determine his manhood and his honor.

The authors of *Keeping Fit to Fight* and the lecturers on the circuit went to great lengths to dispel the common notion that sexual intercourse outside of marriage was "manly." On the contrary, they insisted, abstinence made the man. The pamphlet assured young soldiers that they were no less manly for refusing to go with prostitutes or loose women. "This is a man-to-man talk," it began, "straight from the shoulder without gloves. It calls a spade a spade without camouflage. Read it because you are a soldier of the United States. Read it because you are loyal to the flag and because you want the respect and love of your comrades and those you have left at home." The pamphlet emphasized soldiers' "health" as the *sine qua non* of battle and triumph: "Your health is even more important than guns. Without health, guns cannot be effectively manned. Your health is even more important than bravery. Bravery in bed does not win battles."[97] The authors surely meant by "bravery in bed" that soldiers in the infirmary were useless to a fighting army, but the double entendre implied that men should save their courage for battle and not jeopardize their manhood through illicit sexual relations. The "greatest menace to the vitality and fighting vigor of any army is venereal diseases (clap and syphilis) . . . [and] the escape from this danger is up to the patriotism and good sense of soldiers like yourself."[98] Resisting temptation was more manly than giving in. "Will-power and courage go together. A venereal disease contracted after deliberate exposure through intercourse with a prostitute, is as much of a disgrace as showing the white feather." The "white feather" was the sign of cowardice, dereliction of duty, and effeminacy.

Pragmatists, on the other hand, doubted the effectiveness of such moralizing and were unconvinced of the "abstinence makes the man" argument's worth. Samuel Gompers thought the whole enterprise foolish, commenting that "real men will be men." But these voices were drowned out by the din of progressive reform. As Josephus Daniels himself put it, "Men must live straight if they would shoot straight."[99] For the new generation of American men, the army would provide the fraternal camaraderie that their fathers' generation had sought in bordellos and red-light districts.

The imminence of war helped to consolidate reform agendas, creating a consensus among reformers and adding urgency to the situation. The need to protect soldiers overrode that of protecting young girls, and with this new national, moral imperative came a renewed antipathy toward prostitutes, and a renewed zeal in separating them from the dominant population. As John D'Emilio and Estelle Freedman put it, "military mobilization bent Progressivism to its own ends, emphasizing efficiency over uplift, and social order over benevolence."[100] Segregation of vice was an outmoded method of dealing with prostitution—but so, it seems, were reform and reintegration. Whereas the brunt of purity crusaders' zealousness in the past fell on the evils of prostitution as the worst evidence of corruption elsewhere, the antiprostitution rhetoric now focused on the prostitute herself as an agent of immorality, pollution, disease, and decay. Prostitutes, in this rhetoric, became dangerous subversives, agents of the enemy, and inherently inassimilable. Female camp followers were scarcely any better. Civilians referred to them as "the diseased vultures that hover around the outskirts" and in letters to the War Department requested that they be "discovered, arrested, and put in detaining camps until the close of the war or for life." Others thought detention too lenient: "Shoot the lewd women as you would the worst German spy."[101] Though the government did not shoot prostitutes or promiscuous women, the military arrested large groups of women and held over "fifteen thousand in detention centers for periods averaging ten weeks."[102] Where they would go or what they would do once they were released, or once prostitution was entirely suppressed, was not the military's concern. Meanwhile, "no men were arrested for patronizing prostitutes."[103]

It followed that prostitution was not merely an occupation, as the Louisiana Supreme Court had decided the year before the pamphlet was distributed. Prostitutes were an extreme example of so-called "loose" women generally, and they were dangerous whether "sitting for company" or not. Moreover, going with a prostitute might inadvertently lead to aiding the enemy. *Keeping Fit to Fight* emphasized this by putting its warning in bold capital letters: "WOMEN WHO SOLICIT SOLDIERS FOR IMMORAL PURPOSES ARE USUALLY DISEASE SPREADERS AND FRIENDS OF THE ENEMY."[104] Local groups, like the New Orleans Travelers' Aid Society, continued their attempts to rescue young women, often from soldiers; but the *national* discourse shifted to embrace the idea that soldiers deserved more attention.[105] The morality campaign explicitly divided women into two groups: "the 'pure' women to whom the war was dedicated—the mothers, sisters, and sweethearts patiently waiting for their heroes to return home[, and] those who would subvert the war effort by seducing American fighting men,"[106] the age-old opposition between the madonna and the whore.

The Sodom of the South

In this context, Secretary of the Navy Josephus Daniels identified personal morality and community responsibility as the two joint forces that would protect the soldiers. Both he and Secretary of War Newton Baker agreed that it was "incumbent upon the federal government to make the training camps healthy environments, free of sexual temptation and venereal disease." In true progressive fashion, Daniels said, "Negative work is not enough. We must create competitive interests to replace the evils we are trying to eliminate."[107] The Commission on Training Camp Activities therefore provided activities and chaperoned meeting rooms for family and sweethearts.[108] As part of the positive environment the government wished to create, they also sought to cleanse the cities in which soldiers were encamped. After decades of rhetoric of "protection" for white women—from "black beast rapists" and "white slavers"—the government now called on communities to help protect the white men who were responsible for protecting women, democracy, and the "American race." Little concern was shown for the domestic affairs of blacks, except insofar as they threatened white domesticity. The armed forces were segregated. The training camps were segregated. And the activities set up to occupy soldiers and sailors while they trained and awaited deployment were segregated. Black soldiers did not reap the benefits of the CTCA's programs; they *did not* have "separate but equal" facilities in which to play cards, write letters, or visit with their mothers, girlfriends, or wives; the "protection" afforded the American soldier was offered in Jim Crow style.

Most cities cooperated with the CTCA. Governors and mayors rushed to ingratiate themselves with the federal officials in order to secure troop encampments. Red-light districts were closed, their bordellos shuttered and their prostitutes scattered. Despite such efforts, however, wartime soldiers were not reformed. According to one observer, "the soldier is very much more unmoral than when he entered the army."[109] Certainly the soldier encamped in New Orleans had every opportunity to practice "unmorality."

Indeed, the arrival of troops in New Orleans in the late 1910s gave Storyville a much-needed economic boost. According to one informal history of the district, in the early 1910s Storyville had "hit the skids," its last years being "vicious and bloody ones. . . . Anyone who entered now was lucky if he got away with as much as his shirt and carfare home!"[110] To be sure, this was a colorful exaggeration, but Storyville's heyday had passed. A double murder in the district in 1913 spurred the city authorities to crack down on its nightlife. The last edition of the Blue Book appeared in 1915. The "thin veneer of faked respectability, once proudly boasted of," was all but gone gone by 1917.[111] World War I soldiers brought Storyville back to life. The district's resuscitation was quite at odds with the agenda of New Orleans's moral reformers, who were by then desperate to close Storyville and clamp down on vice beyond its borders, too.

The New Orleans government refused to enforce that agenda and paid little heed to the CTCA's demands for a "clean-up." In June, a reporter from the *New Orleans Item*'s "Women's Division," Ethel Huston, wrote to James Foster of the American Social Hygiene Association of the troops in New Orleans, including sailors: "So far as I know, nothing has been done to safeguard these young men from either prostitution or venereal disease. . . . The police have been requested not to allow saloonkeepers to *sell liquor* to men in uniform, but I do not hear that any request has been made to prevent men in uniform from frequenting houses of ill-fame." She added that the restricted district, "which is in the heart of the city," was "doing a banner business."[112]

Mayor Behrman said publicly that he would be happy to close the district, but behind the scenes he fought to keep Storyville open, insisting that the segregation of vice was still the best policy for safeguarding the morals of the troops and, indeed, the city.[113] As Ethel Huston put it, "that's an obsolete view, but Commissioner [of Public Safety] Harold W. Newman and Mayor Martin Behrman have not yet been converted to a modern standpoint."[114] Thus the "progressive" strategy to modernize New Orleans in 1897 with a discrete red-light district was, by 1917, "obsolete." Foster forwarded Huston's letter to CTCA chairman Raymond Fosdick, and the next month sent him the following telegram: "Situation here not substantially improved/ Recent regulations largely disregarded/ District frequented by men in uniform in spite of police orders to keep them out/ More sailors observed than National Guard/ Vice not confined to district."[115]

In August 1917, the reformer and founder of a new Citizens' League, Jean Gordon, wrote to Secretary of War Newton Baker, urging him to send his own inspectors to gauge the situation. In the letter she implicated the police and politicians in actions much worse than tolerating vice. "I am writing to ask you to make an investigation, WITH YOUR OWN MEN, of THE MORAL CONDITIONS surrounding the life of the soldiers at Camp Nicholls." She made a strong case. Her letter continued, "The city administration is *on record* for the non-enforcement of the liquor laws. The 'Restricted District' in New Orleans [Storyville] is by statement of everyone who has ever investigated it, the most shameless, the most debasing of any such place in the Union." Nothing had been done to remedy the situation because, according to Gordon, "some of the most prominent politicians in the city have large interests in this neighborhood." Those who attempted to cooperate with the moral reformers, for the benefit of the city or the soldiers, tended to be thwarted. "The Commissioner of Police," she wrote, "was forced to resign because he was trying to co-operate with us." More alarming still, she wrote, "Two weeks ago the Chief of Police was murdered in his office in a manner which causes many of us to feel it was an assination [sic] due to his efforts to enforce the laws relative to the open saloons and the conduct in the 'District.'" She repeated her request that Baker send his own team to investigate, because "to ask for reports from the city administration or the police force is simply wasting you [sic] time."[116]

Meanwhile, the president of the Citizens' League, William Railey, made himself a thorn in Fosdick's side, constantly agitating for greater attention to the problem of vice in New Orleans and haranguing him with tales of municipal lassitude and corruption. The members of the Citizens' League took it upon themselves to investigate the vice situation in the restricted district and its environs.

The inspectors worked two nights a week, Saturdays and Sundays, and found sixty-seven instances of soldiers patronizing saloons and immoral houses between September 1, 1917, and October 27, 1917. In most of these instances there were "several" soldiers involved, and most of the Sundays in question were early morning holdovers from the previous Saturday. For example, on September 2, at around 2:30 A.M., the investigator found "two soldiers" outside of Tom Anderson's place at Iberville (Customhouse) and North Basin. They were "very drunk. They said they were broke and asked for a loan, which [the] investigator advanced. They went to the above place [Anderson's] and bought drinks. These soldiers said they could also buy beer on Sunday at #1529 Canal Street." At another of Anderson's establishments the inspector found "several soldiers and sailors drinking" the following week. Later that night the investigator found "five sailors and two soldiers" at an "immoral house" on Iberville Street, "drinking beer with several girls." It is not clear from the report how many inspectors were working these nights, and therefore how much ground they were able to cover. But the range of soldiers and sailors caught in and around Storyville during this time was probably somewhere between 200 and 470.

Sunday Laws were still on the books, though they were honored by "unobtrusive non-observance," and drinks could "be obtained in hotels, clubs, and at the back doors of saloons any Sunday."[117] Beginning in 1917, the Commissioner of Public Safety, Harold Newman, had attempted to enforce the

Sunday Laws, and he had waged an aggressive campaign against violations not only of blue laws, but also of racial etiquette in Storyville and its uptown corollary. But the police and municipal authorities were generally not interested in cooperating with him and his allies in the reform community, and, as mentioned above, he resigned his position.[118]

President Railey was undeterred. He sent the Citizens' League findings to Fosdick. "Since the 1st of September," he wrote, "the police have been keeping soldiers and sailors out of the district, but there are now so many houses on the opposite side of Rampart St. between Iberville [formerly Customhouse] and Orleans, Chartres and Rampart . . . that you will see that there is no reliance whatever to be placed on the police."[119] Saloons and cabarets had begun proliferating into this area, known as the "Tango Belt," around 1913.[120] Mayor Behrman's view may indeed have been "obsolete," but few could any longer claim that Storyville segregated vice. Railey wrote to Fosdick that Behrman was still "firmly committed to the belief which he has often expressed, that segregation is the proper way to deal with vice," but that "as it is your aim to protect soldiers and sailors against the vices of prostitution and drinking, your task will not end with the closing of the district, whether real or nominal." In fact, Railey listed thirty-seven houses of prostitution operating outside the bounds of Storyville.[121]

Citizens and soldiers also wrote to Fosdick and his associates with their fears. A minister from nearby Shreveport, Louisiana, wrote to Fosdick: "Fifteen boys from my church have volunteered for service in defense of our national honor. . . . It is well known that New Orleans is the sodom of the South and if our boys cannot be protected there, I earnestly request your consideration in moving them."[122] A member of the Louisiana branch of the Woman's Christian Temperance Union complained to the organization's national superintendent in July 1917. "Why is it," she asked, "that the Government makes an exception of New Orleans? They have made other places clean up, or failing in that, have moved the boys, must the La. boys be sacraficed [sic] to the brewers of the state while the mothers who have borne these sons, and reared them to young manhood beg and implore the Government to protect them?" She could not stand to "have it so," as she put it. "The mothers have a right to go on a strike, and say they will furnish no more soldiers to a Government that puts brewers above boys." This woman was "heart sick and disgusted." She felt "the spirit of Carrie Nation coming upon me, and I want to 'Rise and smash 'em.'" Conditions in New Orleans were "indescribable, and if the Government does not do something to close those saloons and brothels, many of the boys will be rendered unfit for service, and we will be punished for our part in their destruction."[123] As in the Civil War, a generation of American men would be lost, rendered "unfit." But now, in contrast to that earlier conflagration, prostitution and venereal disease rather than internecine warfare itself threatened to destroy American manhood.[124]

For the most part, these communications only confirmed what Fosdick and his commission already knew. The CTCA had many investigators working in New Orleans. Fosdick himself wrote to Daniels, describing Storyville as "one of the most vicious red-light districts" he had ever seen. He said "sailors in uniform make it a Mecca." In Fosdick's opinion, purging Storyville would set a good example for the nation; it would highlight the effectiveness and purpose of the commission. "If the New Orleans district is closed it will have a far reaching effect on the whole problem in the South." It would end definitively the era of red-light districts. Storyville, he wrote, was the "last stronghold of the old regime."[125]

Mayor Behrman remained adamant. Ignoring the fact that prostitution then existed beyond the confines of Storyville (and always had), he continued to advocate the segregation of vice. He claimed that strict rules forbade saloons from selling liquor to men in uniform and prostitutes from taking soldiers or sailors as clients. Behrman insisted that police officers patrolled Storyville to prevent soldiers and sailors from patronizing its establishments. Of course these rules were more honored in the breach than the observance, and soldiers and sailors patronized the district's brothels and saloons as well as those in the neighboring areas. CTCA inspectors always found soldiers in the district during their investigations. The soldiers paid hobos to buy them alcohol and drank it on corners. They sneaked into "cribs" and had sex in dark alleys. In saloons, the soldiers ordered soft drinks while their "dates" ordered liquor and beer. When they sat down together the men and women switched drinks.[126] Perhaps the most ingenious scheme was the renting of civilian clothing to soldiers. Vice inspectors found "two captains from Hattiesburg wearing civilian's clothes" in an immoral house at 223 North Basin Street. "They were both intoxicated." The inspectors reported that civilians' clothes were being furnished to soldiers by a number of area taxi and limousine companies. "The Chaufeurs [sic] bring the clothes to the hotels, where the officers make the necessary changes, and the chauffeurs then take them down into the district."[127] The in-the-know drivers also provided them with up-to-date tips about locations in the district.

The New Orleans police force had never been interested in preventing prostitution. As we have seen, the police department, and the whole municipal apparatus, was deeply imbricated in the operations of Storyville. One inspector reported to Fosdick that a whole row of "cribs" was owned by a police officer. Another reported that a prostitute "belonged" to a "higher up" on the force. The police and the prostitutes developed a warning system whereby the cops signaled to prostitutes in the cribs or on the street by making loud noises with their billy clubs, letting them know an inspector was approaching.

In early September 1917, Behrman went to Washington to meet with Secretary of War Newton Baker, a former mayor of Cleveland. Behrman reiterated his view that the segregation of vice was the most efficient, and indeed the only possible, way to control vice in his city. The police force was not adequate to handle "scattered" prostitution, and Behrman was certain that the Storyville women would disperse throughout the city if the district were closed. Behrman reported to the secretary that the National Guard was stationed about two and a half miles from the district, and that there were in addition about six hundred soldiers about three-quarters of a mile from it. The National Guard was scheduled to "move out" that very week, and therefore did not pose much of a problem. The mayor "was very anxious not to have the situation violently disturbed." Baker disagreed vehemently based on his own experience as "a municipal executive," but temporized, avoiding decisive action. He told Behrman that he "would not require anything to be done about his district unless [he] was told that soldiers were admitted to it, in which case it would have to be closed." Otherwise, the secretary of war had "a feeling that we ought not to use this power to interfere with local police regulations which are satisfactory to the people of the community."[128]

But the people of the community were not satisfied. William Railey of the Citizens' League had been complaining to Fosdick for months. Now he was eager to learn what Behrman was up to in D.C. He wired Fosdick: "Mayor has surrounded his visit to Washington with mystery and has done nothing since his return/ He would like public to understand it was about business of naval station/ We are very anxious to know what answer Secretary Baker gave him/ Won't you please enlighten us."[129] Fosdick enjoined Railey to avoid publicizing Behrman's trip: "Unwise to give Mayor Behrman's trip any publicity. No information can be given at present time."[130] Fosdick wanted the local reformer, Railey, to keep quiet so that the national organization, the CTCA, could take care of the situation. Railey did not keep quiet, even after being apprised of Secretary Baker's response. In a letter following up the telegram exchange, he thanked Fosdick for his time and attention and pointed out that the mayor had already volunteered to close the district if Baker requested it. In a postscript he added: "P.S. The Naval Station at Algiers [a close suburb of New Orleans] is the darling of the Mayor's heart. He lives in Algiers himself. He is constantly boasting before the public about what he does for the Naval Station. A threat to close that station would simply kill him."[131] And so that is what would come to pass.

In September 1917, Secretary of the Navy Josephus Daniels took matters into his own hands. Daniels sent a copy of a brief report of New Orleans vice to the governor of Louisiana, Ruffin G. Pleasant. He wrote, "I am sure you will agree with me that we should see to it that the young men who have enlisted in the military and naval service of the country should be shielded from those temptations to immoral conduct which, in some instances, have done more to undermine the fighting strength of an army than the bullets of the enemy." Covering the dates August 23 to September 2, 1917, the report listed twenty instances of soldiers or sailors being served alcohol or drinking with prostitutes in brothels. Daniels sent a copy of the letter and the report to Behrman, so "that he may know of my intense desire that immediate action be taken."[132] That was enough for Behrman. On October 9, 1917, he introduced the ordinance closing Storyville, effective midnight November 12, 1917, and he reiterated the illegality of prostitution in New Orleans more generally. Gertrude Dix, a prominent white madam (and wife of Tom Anderson), filed an injunction against the city to prevent the closing of the district, but it was rejected.[133]

It is no surprise that even after the district was officially "closed," Storyville continued to operate as an active red-light district. CTCA investigators witnessed many soldiers patronizing prostitutes. Interracial sex remained a top attraction, but the terminology shifted, so that, interestingly, "Creole" replaced "octoroon." Places like "The Arlington" and its "Annex" now supplied "Creole inmates dressed in fancy gowns," even though they were run by the white madam Gertrude Dix. Lulu White, who was called a "Colored madam" in the CTCA report, had five "Creole" inmates at 235 North Basin Street. The price for sex was $5, and "Liquor [was] sold."[134] Octoroon, a hybridity born of slavery, disappeared in favor of another still ambiguous but colonial term, more specific still to New Orleans's own history.

As the United States solidified its role as an international, imperial power abroad, sex with exotic "Creole" or "native" women was apropos, and more familiar to a national soldiery born and raised during Jim Crow's ascendance. New Orleans's international origins reemerged as the American vision of sexualized hybridity receded. In addition to the cribs and bordellos, plenty of women still walked the street. "These prostitutes strongly favor the uniformed men. Thirty two sailors and soldiers were seen to go with women," one report said. "One woman was seen to fairly run up to an officer and throw her abdomen against the officer's."[135] Soldiers were also reported going into alleys with "Negro fairies." "These creatures constitute a grave menace to the soldiers and sailors. . . . Two were seen in the company of sailors on N. Basin and Franklin Streets. Both 'couples' were seen to enter an alley immediately south 1519 Iberville Street. All came out within ten minutes."[136] The report concluded that "Mayor Behrman seems to have but scraped the surface." If nothing further was done, prostitution would fully revive, as "the underworld is getting its nerve again."[137] Prostitution never went away in New Orleans, but Storyville, as such, disappeared.

The Tragic Octoroon

Meanwhile, the abolition of Storyville had the unintended effect of permitting Lulu White to remain on Basin Street in contravention of the 1917 segregation-of-prostitutes ordinance. That law became moot when prostitution was no longer accepted as permissible anywhere in New Orleans. Prostitution did not cease, however, and White continued to live in Mahogany Hall and to run her business. At the same time, she lost her clout—and she suffered repeated raids by local police and federal agents. In 1918, agents of the U.S. Department of Justice arrested White on eleven violations of different elements of the ordinance that abolished Storyville. White disputed the charges, claiming that she was running a legitimate business. She had put a hotel sign in front of Mahogany Hall and had opened a restaurant at her corner saloon. She took out this ad in a racing paper:

ANNOUNCEMENT

The proprietress of this restaurant has embarked in a legitimate business, and hereby respectfully solicits the patronage of all her former friends, as well as the public at large. Patrons will be served by waitresses who are REAL SOUTHERN BEAUTIES.

Our specialty is Southern fried chicken and hot biscuits.

LULU WHITE'S HOTEL
235 N. Basin Street.

Adjoining this restaurant is Lulu White's Hotel, equipped with modern
conveniences for making patrons comfortable.[138]

Her boarders were men, she insisted to her prosecutors, not prostitutes,
and White denied practicing prostitution herself over the previous "ten or
fifteen years." She had, she claimed, thirty days before the ordinance went
into effect, evicted all eighteen of the prostitutes living at Mahogany Hall,
and "sent a letter to that effect to the Superintendent of Police." She then
"went to the City Hall and State office, and got a license to keep a restaurant and hotel."[139] She took on four male boarders, renting to the "transient
trade." A maid stayed with her through the nights, because she was "afraid
to stay alone," and her "legally adopted daughter" was staying with her at
Mahogany Hall, having moved to New Orleans from her home in West Virginia after her husband had "gone to war." In spite of this the police harassed her four or five times a night, so that "I could not do anything wrong
if I wanted to," she said.[140] She described the harassment:

> The police would come in and wake up the boarders and ask them their
> names and where they came from; Capt. Johnson gave his men instructions
> to go into my house every five minutes, and if the door was not opened right
> away, to break open the door. . . . [the boarders] would leave because they [the
> police] would wake them up every night five and six times and sometimes
> more often and when Capt. Johnson would come he would call me for every-
> thing he knew in the way of curse words. . . . Capt. Johnson even called me
> a Cock-sucker in front of the other officers, something which I have never
> done in my life.[141]

White's power in the city seems to have eroded very quickly once the district
closed, and the police who perhaps had resented her earlier success no longer
protected her.

There can be little doubt that White continued to run a brothel at Mahogany Hall, in spite of her claims to legitimacy and respectability. She may
have been lying, but she was no longer winking. A Special Agent testified
that he entered Mahogany Hall "on or about ten o'clock" with a partner. The
maid let them in and led them to White's famous mirror parlor, a "sitting

room where there were two pianos, [and] the walls and ceiling were in look-ing glasses." While the officers waited, three girls entered. "Some beer was ordered and paid for and some music by placing money in the music box, and dancing by one of the girls," who did the "Hoochy Macoochy" in the center of the room. The officer spoke to another one of the girls, "a thin slim girl [who] wanted me to go to bed with her and I put her off." The women were wearing loose "chemises" or "kimonos," one with "her bust hanging out."[142] Two johns were busy upstairs, one of whom subsequently tried to hide himself behind an armoire.[143]

From the officers' descriptions it appears that Lulu White's fortunes had already declined. "Beer was ordered" and the girls were scantily clad—a far cry from the champagne bottles and the women dressed to the nines, as described by the musicians. Found guilty, she was sentenced to pay a small fine, but more terribly, she was to "be imprisoned in the Parish Prison" for thirty days. Her lawyer filed an appeal. The appeal was rejected and the lower court's ruling affirmed. She applied for a rehearing on May 3, 1918. But before this case came up, White was arrested again—this time on fed-eral charges for operating a brothel within five miles of a military installa-tion, Camp Nicholls.[144] On November 6, 1918, Lulu White and two of her boarders (or prostitutes) were indicted again for "unlawfully receiv[ing] and permit[ting] to be received for immoral purposes" two men into Mahogany Hall.[145] On November 29, they were tried and convicted, and "Lulu White, probably the most notorious operator of an immoral house in the old New Orleans district, was sentenced by Judge Foster to serve a year and a day in the Federal penitentiary. . . . This is the severest penalty ever imposed here for such an offense."[146]

The sentence *was* particularly harsh. Most women convicted of the same crime spent only one or two months in the penitentiary—as did the women with whom White was convicted. Foster offered leniency to White as well, but only if she sold her house and all her furnishings. (As the *New Orleans States* put it: "'Lulu' must sell out or serve term in Pen.")[147] The judge claimed that this method of eradicating prostitution had proven effective, and he of-fered White this way out. White agreed, but did not follow through, and so got the long sentence. In fact, she was arrested on the same charges *again* while awaiting indictment, and was charged by the U.S. District Court for violating the Draft Act by receiving for the "purposes of lewdness, assignation, and prostitution" Paul Cucullu, another john. Perhaps because of the charges already pending against her, this case was dismissed.[148] At any rate, in March of 1919 two federal marshals arrived in New Orleans to escort Lulu White to Oklahoma. "Heavy Men Take Lulu to Prison," read the headline. "Two of the biggest and heaviest men in the Federal and State service . . . will leave New Orleans Friday night for McAlester, Okla., with Lulu White, the former 'diamond queen' of New Orleans red-light district. Because of the actions of the woman when sentenced Judge Foster asked that she have an especial bodyguard."[149] Apparently he was afraid she would not go quietly. According to her federal prison record, Lulu White, alias Lula White and Lula Hendley, who supposedly had no previous criminal record, was "Spanish" in her coloration and ethnicity.[150]

Prison was not kind to this hard-living woman who was already in poor health. With the help of the prison doctor, White applied for a reduction in her sentence.[151] According to the physician she had hemorrhoids, fistula, and several tumors in her abdomen. He said that "according to her statements, she has been a heavy drinker, and drunk the greater portion of the time for 30 years. She is a nervous physical wreck, and has about all the ailments a human could possibly have."[152] Her lawyer, the same M. D. Dimitry who had represented prostitutes and madams in the 1917 segregation case, wrote to the attorney general in April 1919 pleading her case. There was no answer. Then on June 6, 1919, White wrote a letter in her own hand to the attorney general requesting executive clemency:

A. Palmer Mitchell [sic]
Attorney General, Washington D.C.

Dear Sir:—

My lawyer told me over a month ago that he had sent you my papers for my release, that the Judge and prosecuting attorney had signed these and I would be out in a few weeks. I am suffering dearly every day I am full of fistroyer [sic: fistula], rheumatism, and the doctor says I have two or three tumors in my abdomen—and can hardly walk and it is a matter of a short time I believe I will die, for God Sake do not let me die in this place! I am sixty years old and always tried to live within the law, I never served a jail term. This was a put up job on me by a man I thought was my friend.

At the time I was running a restaurant and hotel, I am a tax payer and property owner for twenty five years in New Orleans, and, please be considerate and let me know my fate as I am suffering terrible pains—obliged, Lula White

P.S. I have been here 3 mo. 6 da.[153]

Lulu White's application included appeals not only from her lawyer and the prison doctor, but even from the sentencing judge, Rufus Foster, who now believed that the example had been adequately supplied, that three months in prison was sufficient, and that White should be released in the interest of mercy.[154] White hit the notes that resonated with the respectable, bourgeois society that she had mocked during her Storyville career: she was a law-abiding, tax-paying, property-owning, respectable citizen running a legitimate business. Yet now all jocularity was gone. Foster's letter and White's own pathetic appeal, along with the letter from the prison doctor bearing out her claims of ill health, convinced Attorney General Palmer to help White apply to the president of the United States for executive clemency. In his letter to President Woodrow Wilson, Palmer wrote that he did "not at all agree with the view expressed by the judge that the sentence was severe. The woman received precisely the sentence she should have received and if the law had permitted it should have been made longer." The issue, however, was "the state of the woman's health." Palmer wrote in his letter to the president that White had "now served nearly five months on her sentence which, with the allowance for good conduct, is equivalent to a sentence of six months" (in fact, she had served three and a half months), and Palmer advised that the sentence "be commuted to expire at once."[155] President Wilson commuted Lulu White's sentence by cable from Paris on June 16, 1919, and she was released from prison. And thus Woodrow Wilson, the progressive and segregationist product of three generations of the Presbyterian ministry, effectively pardoned Lulu White, the "diamond queen" of the demi-monde, the most "notorious negress" in New Orleans, for breaking a federal law designed to protect American soldiers from illicit and interracial sex.[156] Twelve days later he signed the Treaty of Versailles.

White returned to New Orleans. In December, she leased Mahogany Hall to an agent named George Danziger, for a period of ten years.[157] White moved into 1200 Bienville Street, her saloon on the corner, and occupied the second-floor residence. From this location she ran what she called a soft drink company, but in fact she continued to operate a brothel.[158] To the U.S. Public Health Service, a division of the Treasury Department, White constituted a menace, and her "pardon" was incredible. An official wrote to Palmer, requesting documentation that would confirm Wilson's role.[159] Palmer was quick to note that a commutation was not the same thing as a pardon, but he did forward the information.[160] Others were similarly disbelieving about Wilson's intervention, a reporter from the *Times-Picayune* suspecting a backroom connection: "Find out from the Department of Justice without fail Friday who signed and interceded for a presidential pardon obtained from [sic] Lulu White prostitute sentenced from New Orleans during the war."[161]

In November 1920, White was again arrested for running a brothel, with one Clyde Robinson, who was probably white, as the affidavit gives White's race as "col" for "colored" without noting Robinson's. By that year, the two of them ran a brothel at 239 North Basin Street, not Mahogany Hall.[162] White and Robinson were convicted again in 1922 for possessing and selling "intoxicating liquors," including gin and Canadian Club Whiskey, during Prohibition.[163] Robinson was fined $25 and White $100 (indicating her greater role in the business). The next year, White and the bartender for her corner saloon, Corrolanus Hopkins, were arrested and charged again with violating Prohibition. The jury found White "not guilty," but Hopkins was convicted and sent to the house of detention for three months.[164] All three partners, White, Robinson, and Hopkins, were arrested in 1924, again for selling liquor at their "soft-drink stand" on Bienville. Judge Rufus Foster, who had previously sentenced her and then pleaded her clemency, signed the arrest warrants and White paid the steepest fine, $200.[165]

Despite these details, Lulu White's declining years are nearly invisible to us. According to the records, White was not arrested again until 1929. In addition to the usual charges of possessing and selling alcohol, this arrest also included the charge of maintaining "a nuisance" at 1200 Bienville Street, "operated as a cabaret and speakeasy" in New Orleans. Defending her in this case was St. Clair Adams Jr., the son of the venerable district attorney who had successfully prosecuted White in 1905, when she was convicted of selling liquor without a license and of tax evasion. This time White was found not guilty.[166] In another Prohibition case from 1929, the clerk who tried to deliver a subpoena to White claimed that she had moved to California. No further information about a trip west exists, and she lived in New Orleans in 1930. She was listed in the city directory in 1930 at 241 Saratoga Street (in contrast to the census, which had her living at 309–311 North Saratoga, a brothel run by a series of apparently Jewish madams).[167] Basin Street's name had been changed in the years after Storyville's closure, and 241 Saratoga Street was the new address of White's corner saloon; White lived in the upstairs residence there from 1919. In a 1929 Prohibition case, where White acted as surety for an associate, John Constantine, her address was still 1200 Bienville Street, but she claimed to own a two-story brick building at 241 North Basin Street, "valued at $35,000.00 with a mortgage of $6,000.00." (Given the street number, this probably was the Basin Street Saloon.) Constantine defaulted and White had to pay a bond of $1,000. This was in March. In April she broke her ten-year lease with George Danziger for Mahogany Hall and sold it to Leon Heymann, the New Orleans department store mogul, for $10,000 cash. In July he also bought the corner saloon business for $12,300.[168]

White was last arrested in February 1931, when she was living at 322 North Franklin Street, still in the old district's boundaries, but not in either of her previous properties.[169] She was charged with violating Act 199 of 1912 —a state law that empowered the authorities to define disorderly houses and to arrest their proprietors. Her health was very poor and she was apparently obese. She died before the case, several times delayed, came to trial.[170] "8/21/31 Defendant dead," is the spare notation on the affidavit. No memorial or institution marked the occasion.[171]

That the "notorious Basin Street enchantress" died in obscurity, poor and alone, accords with the version of her infirmity given by Eleanor Early, who wrote a popular history of New Orleans in the 1940s.[172] In an interview Early recorded with a social worker, Lulu White was recalled as having descended to panhandling in the street.[173] In the 1930 census, her dwelling was listed as a rental worth only $50.[174] By comparison, Willie Piazza's, which was listed as her own property, was worth $8,000. Piazza still owned the bordello she bought in 1912, 317 North Basin (then Saratoga) Street, and owned real estate in a suburb of New Orleans as well as a yacht when she died.[175] Lulu White appears not to have left any such estate. Indeed, there was no recorded will for her, and no accounting of her property at her death, despite the existence of an heir, her mysterious adopted daughter. What happened to the money from her 1929 sale of Mahogany Hall and the corner saloon, or whether the sale of those buildings was needed to pay off outstanding debts, is unknown.

Lulu White is, and was, like Storyville itself, as much a myth as a reality. The "Diamond Queen of the Demi-Monde," the country's most famous octoroon and New Orleans's most "notorious negress," was an image that Lulu White herself crafted, drawing on diverse social wellsprings with artistic virtuosity. Once the district lost its protected status, and the publicity and advertising ceased, the image was impossible to perpetuate. With the demise of Storyville and a federal law prohibiting prostitution, and another prohibiting the sale of alcohol, prostitution went underground, removed from the celebrity and commercial prestige it had enjoyed. The "spectacular wickedness" of Storyville went into hiding. Prostitution itself changed, too, so that private services supplanted the public culture of male fraternizing and camaraderie.[176] No longer able to defy identity, order, or system, Lulu White herself proved less powerful than the racial binary of black and white. Jim Crow was not, by 1931, so fragile anymore. In the end, there was no place for Lulu White. Without Storyville, Lulu White ceased to belong anywhere and died a relic of a different time, perhaps now truly a "tragic octoroon."

Farewell to Storyville

All you old-time Queens, from New Orleans, who lived in Storyville
You sang the blues, try to amuse, here's how they pay the bill
The law stepped in and call it a sin to have a little fun
The police car made a stop and Storyville is done.

— SPENCER WILLIAMS, "Farewell to Storyville"

Storyville was the segregation of vice in New Orleans: for the brief moment
that a reform administration controlled the municipality, the idea was to
better police the "legitimate" commercial and residential areas of New Orleans, to keep them "respectable." The law drew a clear boundary around
the district, separating prostitution from the rest of the city. The hope was
that the creation of Storyville would also draw a *cordon sanitaire* around
New Orleans's past and its reputation for wickedness, clearing a path for a
more respectable future. The authors of the Storyville ordinance believed
that if the city's streets and neighborhoods were clear of vice, streetwalkers,
and gamblers, northerners would be more likely to invest in New Orleans
and the city would regain its former glory as the southern metropolis and
southwestern center for transcontinental and international trade. After
the Democratic machine reclaimed New Orleans's city government, its operatives still saw Storyville as a good solution to the city's entrenched vice
problem, especially if illicit practices generated a profit. Both the reform-
minded business community and the machine politicians believed they
would benefit from the red-light district. The former envisioned a new image of municipal control and civic cleanliness, while the latter anticipated
bribes from madams, property owners, and the liquor interests of Storyville.

Both groups understood that they would gain from tourism to the district and the high rents and property taxes the houses there generated.

As this book has shown, the flip side of the Storyville ordinance was the concentration not only of vice, but of memory. Storyville was a place of memory, a recollection of New Orleans's past and all the spectacular wickedness it symbolized. Storyville celebrated past and present transgressions in an ideationally bounded, liminal space—a site where fantasies of the past and desires for the future were acted out. As such, Storyville was part of the transition from slavery's racial patriarchy to the New South's fraternal white supremacy, from slavery, that is, to segregation.

Part of the challenge of rebuilding the South after Reconstruction for whites was how to reestablish the antebellum hierarchies in the absence of slavery. The solution lay in part in reimagining the gender and sexual hierarchies of slavery times and applying their logics to the developing social order. Jim Crow, after all, was not only a system of racial segregation; it was also a sexual order whose success required the remaking of whiteness along strict gender lines, and of conceiving sexuality in terms of race. This involved necessarily a reimagination of the plantation South and how white nonplanters fit into that hierarchical society. The Old South became, through the generation of collective, cultural memory, the pastoral South, the noble South, the honorable—and not the dishonored and defeated—South. There, many white Americans came to believe, race relations were clearly delineated to everyone's mutual benefit, white women knew and cherished their special place, and white men clearly held power and authority. The reimagination of the patriarchal, honor-bound South into a Herrenvolk democracy also entailed a reorientation of the class parameters of respectability. No longer tied exclusively to wealth and status, nor strictly adhering to particular sets of behaviors, "honor" or "respectability" became, in the Jim Crow era, not only part of white privilege but the general realm of whites. "Respectability" was encoded with racial ideology; reformers, suffragists, businessmen, muckraking newspapers, citizens, and residents of New Orleans battled over the delimitation of respectability in local and national forums. These battles were part of the war for white supremacy and thus of control over the memory of slavery.

The city's Jim Crow order was itself backed up by a discourse about respectability, reform, and race. To be sure, there were disrespectable or dishonorable white people who were recognized as such, but a discursive, linguistic shift made respectability a notion bounded by race. White people, according to this logic, might lose status, but black people could not attain it.[1] This was despite the efforts of African American men and women, uplift ideology, strict community policing, and an upwardly mobile black middle class who claimed respectability as their own while also worrying about "low-class" blacks who made vulnerable those claims.[2]

Thus, at the turn of the century, in the Deep South, part of the task of creating a respectable city was the renunciation and erasure of the abuses of slavery—the revision of that chapter in the nation's history into something more easily read within a modern American lexicon. While people of color labored against the stereotypes developed to justify antebellum sexual abuse, and white moral reformers called up the memory of slavery to redraw the lines of respectability for white women and girls, Storyville exploited the same memory of sexual slavery explicitly for profit. Thus the nominal *cordon sanitaire* around Storyville echoed the repackaging in literature and public political discourse of the legacy of slavery and slave marketing in New Orleans. Storyville celebrated the sexual slavery of white-skinned "black" women in its prominent octoroon bordellos, recapitulating the antebellum slave auction and the trade in "fancy girls." The (white) city around Storyville rejected that past, banished its memory, and sought racial clarity in a biracial caste system, in which blacks were not "respectable" and whites were.

As we have seen, Storyville's marketing of miscegenation transgressed the social and cultural norms of a nascent Jim Crow order; but by advertising the miscegenation taboo and offering its transgressions exclusively to white men, Storyville also served white supremacy. Out of the foggy, revisionist memories of the Civil War and Reconstruction, white citizens of New Orleans organized municipal economic renewal and their city's national integration into a bourgeois social order, one in which the white male head of household became (again) the definitive subject of American democracy.[3] Storyville participated in this process by reimagining the antebellum past—the commercial glory of New Orleans as well as its spectacular slave auctions and quadroon balls—and by inviting white men to indulge in the fantasy of mastery. Storyville recapitulated the old order in a modern, contained setting, channeling nostalgia for a romanticized past into contemporary desire and the promise of its satisfaction.

The enchanting, erotic octoroon was the central symbolic figure in this drama of cultural renewal; the erotic—even exotic—octoroon woman, in New Orleans made literally into a prostitute, came to embody the mixed-race heritage of the New Orleans *gens de couleur libres* for a white, commercial, male public, even as people of color continued to press for civil and political equality. Their legacy was thus emasculed, feminized, and sexualized through the combination of violent repression, legal disfranchisement, and discursive displacement. We may see signs of this legacy in play when historians assert that "for centuries the term *quadroon* has been nearly synonymous with 'seductress.'"[4] The tragic octoroon, the placée, the fancy girl, all familiar tropes of antebellum New Orleans, were recirculated in the 1890s and 1900s in service to "visions of sexual desire and the luxury of being able to pay for its fulfillment." Lulu White and other entrepreneurs created, in Walter Johnson's words, "enslaved versions of mastery" for a new generation of striving "masters."[5]

The renunciation of slavery nationally involved the selective remembering and forgetting of the institution, its abuses, and its legacy. White Americans remembered and celebrated the valor of white Civil War soldiers on both sides of the Mason-Dixon Line, commemorating the Civil War in ceremonies, statues, and speeches throughout the nation. Willfully forgotten and ignored (or resented) were the slaves freed by the Civil War. This forgetting, too, was part of the war for white supremacy after Reconstruction. Historians have analyzed how Americans after the war constructed memories in order to create new founding myths for the postbellum era. The creation of cultural memory was simultaneously the creation of new racial norms and gender roles. To be sure, these, too, grew out of an earlier era and had roots in the antebellum period; how else could they have entered the dominant culture as "memory"? However, racial and sexual ideologies that had served the slaveholding regime were reoriented and reinscribed in the postslavery nation to serve the Jim Crow regime. That is to say, the forging of cultural memory and national myth also racialized and sexualized bodies anew, and Storyville became part of this process. The nostalgia the district tapped, and the fantasies it projected, resonated with a nation in the throes of change, where whiteness lacked the certainty it had during slavery, or was believed to have had.

The Storyville fantasy was a fantasy about white male power, instantiated through sex with subordinated women, many of them nonwhite. There were other cultural sites wherein fantasies of white power were acted out through the subordinated bodies of black people: world's fairs, minstrel shows, amusement parks, and, most violently, lynching. Even the Spanish-American War might be considered part of this renewal of national whiteness over the bodies of racial (and sexual) "others." I have argued that the racial discourses that produced the binary undergirding Jim Crow were also, inherently, discourses of sexuality. The strategic remembering and forgetting of slavery that took place in Storyville figured white men as the only possible subjects with sexual agency, thus democratizing sexual privilege as access to black, white, and even octoroon, women's bodies. I have argued that Storyville recapitulated the sexual organization of the slave plantation. Here was a kind of remembering that supported the New South order because white men were the social and sexual agents over the bodies of subordinated women. Still, this recuperation of the antebellum plantation and slave market called up precisely what another Progressive Era discourse on prostitution, "white slavery," obscured: the sexual abuse of *black* women. That is, moral reformers in New Orleans and nationally also evoked memories of sexual slavery; however, unlike the profiteers in the sex district who oriented that memory toward the sexual fantasies of white men, these crusaders reimagined slavery exclusively as a threat to contemporary white women. So, in this way, Storyville carried the seeds of its own demise; as slavery and prostitution were successfully conflated and refigured as *white*, interracial prostitution as a reenactment of antebellum planter privilege began to lose its erotic salience.

In New Orleans, female moral reformers decried "white slavery" while denouncing the visibility of "negro" prostitutes on Basin Street. For them, the dangers of the city and the vulnerability of girls unmoored from family and community appeared as threats to white respectability, as did the extravagant bordellos on Basin Street. The completion of the Terminal Station in 1908, and the routing of trains past Basin Street, eroded the boundaries set up by the city council when they chose the neighborhood that became Storyville. This was especially problematic because the visibility of places like Mahogany Hall and Willie Piazza's bordello mocked both sets of boundaries set up and maintained by Jim Crow, those between black and white as separate races, and those between "whites" and "blacks" as actual human beings.

Throughout Storyville's brief history, many sought to reform the district, to abolish it, to segregate it, or all three. Once it became clear that Storyville's businesses brazenly and successfully advertised precisely those things that the city boosters desired to repress, businessmen and moral reformers alike looked for ways to change the appearance of Storyville, too. Changes in the dominant culture, including changes the district was helping to bring about, affected Storyville's ability to promote interracial sex, to market miscegenation. As Jim Crow's talons spread wider and plunged deeper into modern American culture, and race became the dominant organizing principle of American life, the female octoroon came to seem less like an erotic enchantress and more like a category violation, a vehicle of pollution and danger.[6]

In one sense, it was certainly World War I that ended America's red-light era in the early twentieth century. The rise of the progressive sensibility, with all its moral strictures, prohibitions, and rules, culminated in Woodrow Wilson's presidency. After decades of developing along the discursive lines of medicine, hygiene, and morality, this progressive consciousness coalesced in response to the imperatives brought by the war; even so, the power of the federal government was still necessary to close the red-light districts. But by that time, the desire Storyville elaborated and fulfilled had already ceased to animate public discourse and private yearnings both. Sex across the color line was still transgressive, to be sure, but once Jim Crow was fixed in law and culture, marketing miscegenation no longer resonated with nostalgia for the antebellum past.

So, while the war provided the incentive, urgency, and organization that ultimately closed Storyville, the national consolidation of race (and the middle-class sensibility that went along with it) had already gone a long way toward making it obsolete. The now deaccessioned district of Storyville continued to furnish myriad examples of immorality for progressives to condemn: again and again it was "discovered" that sailors and soldiers went to prostitutes in New Orleans. But aside from a few interested parties, like Behrman, White, and Dix, nobody argued that segregated vice provided any kind of solution. By 1917 the segregation of the races had been nearly completed in public conveyances, spaces, and institutions, such as education and marriage, and the segregation of vice had run its course. The "modern" viewpoint held that red-light districts were ineffective. The better men, the defenders and representatives of the emerging twentieth-century white middle class, abstained from illicit sex in order to safeguard their families and maintain their national resolve, just as they did when they rode in segregated street cars, sent their children to all-white schools, and drank at their racially designated drinking fountains.

Storyville no longer exists in any physical reality. The Housing Authority of New Orleans began buying and destroying the Storyville buildings in the late 1930s in order to replace them with a low-income housing project for whites. Today the area is an urban ghetto. On most printed maps of the city, the entire space that Storyville occupied is blank. The district has been erased and it is as if the residents who now live in the area do not really exist; they certainly do not in representations of New Orleans produced on tourist maps. There is even doubt as to whether they will be able to continue to live there since Hurricane Katrina's deadly blow to the city in 2005.[7]

Storyville still lives on as part of our collective memory of turn-of-the-century New Orleans—only now the memories of Storyville, like those of slavery, have been sanitized. The very essence of Storyville, prostitution, has been jettisoned in popular cultural recollections of the district to accommodate a narrative about jazz. As the "birthplace of jazz," Storyville has been romanticized; the district has become a symbol of a rosier past, and, ironically, a more authentic New Orleans. Part of this supposed authenticity includes the notion that race relations in New Orleans were not characterized by the ideology of white supremacy and its attendant suppression of nonwhites, in terms of political equality, public rights, and social aspiration, and, most basically, the imposition of a hard-and-fast color line based on a strict racial dualism. The "octoroon" prostitutes in Storyville, not less than the "Creole" jazz musicians, have come to symbolize tolerance and a laissez-faire attitude toward race, commensurate with the *laissez les bons temps roulez* attitude that continues to characterize the marketing of the city to myriads of tourists around the world. That octoroon prostitutes served white supremacy, and that most Creole musicians could not have worked outside of the district even if they wanted to, do not figure in the popular history of Storyville, nor of the "birth" of jazz that has so colored its place in collective memory.

Storyville is remembered to add an element of danger, the *frisson* of transgression, to jazz music—to make it sexy. During "the first two decades of the twentieth [century], jazz matured in Storyville clubs and brothels," writes J. Mark Souther. "Attracting jazz musicians as well as gamblers and prostitutes," he continues, "Storyville solidified in the tourist mind the ribald image of New Orleans."[8] As part of this "ribald image," the prostitutes themselves have become almost background figures in the history of the development of jazz music. More than this, the celebration of jazz as an African American art form—and the *only authentically American art form*—has helped to rewrite a history of oppression and survival into a triumphalist narrative of overcoming—and with *swing*. This is doubly ironic, since jazz music and its association with black culture increased the sense of danger that Storyville itself represented to white supremacy and bourgeois morality, at least for white reformers, including those who sought to segregate the district.

And so, the development of the idea of jazz as a form of high art has also been a process of selective remembering and forgetting. Early jazz was raunchy and raw, and its music and lyrics celebrated the low, the physical, and the forbidden: sex, violence, prostitution, and infidelity. What's more, much of it was blatantly and unabashedly misogynistic. This is not to say that the music did not contain and showcase genius; nor is it to say that all practitioners were pimps and misogynists, though some clearly were. There were also women jazz artists, and their songs of sex, desire, and betrayal (of their husbands as well as of themselves) are also worth recollecting along with the women who worked as prostitutes in the district.[9]

Still, in the story of jazz that posits Storyville as its "birthplace," largely for marketing purposes, we have an instance of the legitimizing art form erasing the actual practitioners of prostitution—the women—in favor of the men who were oftentimes their pimps. There are jazz bands and jazz clubs that have adopted the name Storyville; it is a record label and the name of a prominent journal devoted to jazz; a t-shirt store on Magazine Street in New Orleans calls itself Storyville. This is not even to mention the now-defunct lingerie shop called, "Lulu White's," which was located in New Orleans's Louis Armstrong International Airport. The popular celebration of the district as part of New Orleans's storied past serves to mystify that very past, to obscure the trauma of poverty, racism, and gender inequality, over-shadowing the material reality of prostitution and Jim Crow in turn-of-the-century New Orleans, as if that "more authentic" New Orleans existed outside of history. On the contrary, however, prostitution in New Orleans at the turn of the century was not only *not* separate from the emergence of Jim Crow, but in fact, Storyville served the Jim Crow order through a selective recuperation of New Orleans's past. By deliberately marketing the memories of sexual slavery and interracial concubinage, Storyville exploited the "notorious attraction" the city had long been famous for. The cycle continues. As developers in post-Katrina New Orleans claimed a desire to "honor" the city's past through their plans to memorialize Storyville with the creation of a "jazz district," I, for one, was struck by a fatalistic *déjà vu*, and left with the words of Abigail Adams echoing in my head: "remember the ladies."[10]

NOTES

1. For Rampart Street as a dividing line between "front-of-town" and "back-of-town," see Richard Campanella, *Geographies of New Orleans: Urban Fabrics Before the Storm* (Lafayette: Center for Louisiana Studies, University of Louisiana, Lafayette, 2006), 297–311. The reason it is hard to count the exact number of blocks in Storyville is that Customhouse Street (later Iberville) only housed bordellos on one side, and thus those blocks are not "square," and there were no bordellos, of course, in the cemeteries on Storyville's lakeside boundary.

2. Mark Thomas Connelly, *The Response to Prostitution in the Progressive Era* (Chapel Hill: Univ. of North Carolina Press, 1980), 3.

3. Timothy J. Gilfoyle, *City of Eros: New York City, Prostitution, and the Commercialization of Sex, 1790–1920* (New York: Norton, 1992), 199 and, more generally, chapter 10, "Sex Districts Revisited," 197–223.

4. Neil Larry Shumsky, "Tacit Acceptance: Respectable Americans and Segregated Prostitution, 1870–1910," *Journal of Social History* 19, no. 4 (Summer 1986): 665–679.

5. Gilfoyle, *City of Eros*, 223. See also Mary Ting Yi Lui, *The Chinatown Trunk Mystery: Murder, Miscegenation, and Other Dangerous Encounters in Turn-of-the-Century New York City* (Princeton, N.J.: Princeton Univ. Press, 2005), especially chapters 1 and 2, pages 17–80, on the social geography of racial and sexual boundaries.

6. Semper Idem (pseud.), *The "Blue Book," a Bibliographical Attempt to Describe the Guidebooks to the Houses of Ill-Fame as They Were Published There. Together with some pertinent and illuminating remarks pertaining to the establishments and courtesans as well as to harlotry in general in New Orleans,* Heartman's Historical Series, no. 50 ([New Orleans?]: Privately printed, 1936), Sterling Memorial Library, Yale University, New Haven, Connecticut.

7. *Plessy v. Ferguson* 163 U.S. 537 (1896), Docket No. 210, 3.

8. It was found, however, that states could not legislate segregation on trains traveling across state lines. I discuss this in more detail in chapter 2. See Barbara Young Welke, *Recasting American Liberty: Gender, Race, Law, and the Railroad Revolution, 1865–1920* (Cambridge, Eng.: Cambridge Univ. Press, 2001), for a thorough history of race legislation and the railroad.

9. Campanella, *Geographies of New Orleans,* 193 and passim.

10. See, for example, Arnold R. Hirsch, "Simply a Matter of Black and White: The Transformation of Race and Politics in Twentieth-Century New Orleans," in *Creole New Orleans: Race and Americanization,* ed. Arnold Hirsch and Joseph Logsdon (Baton Rouge: Louisiana State Univ. Press, 1992), 262–320.

11. Michel Foucault, *The History of Sexuality,* vol. 1, *An Introduction,* trans. Robert Hurley (New York: Vintage Books, 1990), 35.

12. Ann Laura Stoler, *Race and the Education of Desire: Foucault's* History of Sexuality *and the Colonial Order of Things* (Durham, N.C.: Duke Univ. Press, 1995), 165.

13. Allan M. Brandt, *No Magic Bullet: A Social History of Venereal Disease in the United States Since 1880* (New York: Oxford Univ. Press, 1987), introduction and chapter 1, 2–51 and passim. "Master symbol" is from Connelly, *Response to Prostitution in the Progressive Era,* 6.

14. Peggy Pascoe, *What Comes Naturally: Miscegenation Law and the Making of Race in America* (New York: Oxford Univ. Press, 2009), especially the introduction and parts 1 and 2, to page 159.

15. Terence Ranger and Eric Hobsbawm, *The Invention of Tradition* (London: Verso, 1985).

16. Marjorie Spruill Wheeler, *New Women of the New South: The Leaders of the Woman Suffrage Movement in the Southern States* (New York: Oxford Univ. Press, 1993), 4.

17. Peter W. Bardaglio, "Rape and the Law in the Old South: 'Calculated to excite Indignation in every heart,'" *Journal of Southern History* 60, no. 4 (November 1994): 749–772; Saidiya Hartman, *Scenes of Subjection: Terror, Slavery, and Self-Making in Nineteenth-Century America* (New York: Oxford Univ. Press, 1997), chapter 3, 79–112.

18. Cf. Glenda Gilmore, *Gender and Jim Crow: Women and the Politics of White Supremacy in North Carolina, 1896–1920* (Chapel Hill: Univ. of North Carolina Press, 1996), and LeeAnn Whites, "Rebecca Latimer Felton and the Problem of 'Protection' in the New South," in *Visible Women: New Essays on American Activism,* ed. Nancy A. Hewitt and Suzanne Lebsock (Urbana: Univ. of Illinois Press, 1993), 41–61. Not all advocates of woman suffrage were against patriarchal privilege. See Drew Gilpin Faust, *Mothers of Invention: Women of the Slaveholding South in the American Civil War* (New York: Vintage Books, 1997), and Wheeler, *New Women of the New South.*

19. See Martha Hodes, *White Women, Black Men: Illicit Sex in the 19th-Century South* (New Haven, Conn.: Yale Univ. Press, 1997), and Diane Somerville, "The Rape Myth in the Old South Reconsidered," *Journal of Southern History* 61, no. 3 (August 1995): 481–518; Peter W. Bardaglio, *Reconstructing the Household: Families, Sex and the Law in the Nineteenth-Century South* (Chapel Hill: Univ. of North Carolina Press, 1995).

20. Cynthia M. Blair, *I've Got to Make My Livin': Black Women's Sex Work in Turn-of-the-Century Chicago* (Chicago: Univ. of Chicago Press, 2010); Georgina Hickey, *Hope and Danger in the New South City: Working-Class Women and Urban Development in Atlanta, 1890–1940* (Athens, Univ. of Georgia Press, 2003); Victoria Widgeon Wolcott, *Remaking Respectability: African American Women in Interwar Detroit* (Chapel Hill: Univ. of North Carolina Press, 2001).

21. Genevieve Fabre and Robert O'Meally, eds., *History and Memory in African-American Culture* (New York: Oxford Univ. Press, 1994).

22. Robert C. Allen, *Horrible Prettiness: Burlesque and American Culture* (Chapel Hill: Univ. of North Carolina Press, 1991), 26.

23. Ruth Rosen, *The Lost Sisterhood: Prostitution in America, 1900–1918* (Baltimore: Johns Hopkins Univ. Press, 1982).

24. Carole Pateman, *The Sexual Contract* (Stanford, Calif.: Stanford Univ. Press, 1988), 208.

25. *New Orleans Item,* August 30, 1908.

I. THE PROMISED LAND OF HARLOTRY

1. *City v. Freddie Crockett, et al.* (1908), Criminal District Court, Docket No. 18,051 [18,061], City Archives, Louisiana Division, New Orleans Public Library. He would have walked about thirteen blocks to get to Basin Street. The Southern Terminal Station, which was much closer to Storyville, was not quite complete by April. See below.

2. Ibid.

3. *New Orleans Daily Picayune,* May 31, 1908, p. 13, c. 3.

4. Spencer Williams, "Basin Street Blues" (Edwin H. Morris and Co., 1926). The lyrics were written by Glenn Miller and Jack Teagarden, though their names never appear on the song. They have since been changed by various artists and performers. See Jack Teagarden in *Hear Me Talkin' to Ya: The Story of Jazz by the Men Who Made it,* comp. Nat Shapiro and Nat Hentoff (1955; New York: Dover Publications, 1966), 280–281.

5. Bruce Boyd Raeburn, *New Orleans Style and the Writing of American Jazz History* (Ann Arbor: Univ. of Michigan Press, 2009), 7–8. See also Charles Hersch, *Subversive Sounds: Race and the Birth of Jazz in New Orleans* (Chicago: Univ. of Chicago Press, 2007), 29.

6. Raeburn, *New Orleans Style,* 8.

7. Ibid., 66.

8. Williams, "Basin Street Blues."

9. Spencer Williams, in Shapiro and Hentoff, comps., *Hear Me Talkin',* 6–7.

10. *L'Hote vs. City of New Orleans, et al.,* Division B, Docket No. 54,533 (1897), 47.

11. Jelly Roll Morton, in Shapiro and Hentoff, comps., *Hear Me Talkin',* 6–7; and Alan Lomax, *Mister Jelly Roll: The Fortunes of Jelly Roll Morton* (1950; New York: Grove Press, 1956).

12. Clarence Williams, in Shapiro and Hentoff, comps., *Hear Me Talkin',* 11–12.

13. Interview with Manuel Manetta, Oral History Collection, William Ransom Hogan Jazz Archive, Tulane University, New Orleans, Louisiana.

14. Jelly Roll Morton, in Shapiro and Hentoff, comps., *Hear Me Talkin',* 6–7.

15. Clarence Williams, in Shapiro and Hentoff, comps., *Hear Me Talkin',* 11–13; Alan Trachtenberg, *The Incorporation of America: Culture and Society in the Gilded Age* (New York: Hill and Wang, 1982), chapter 4, "Mysteries of the Great City," especially 130–135, and "pedagogy of modernity" on p. 131.

16. Thurman W. Reeves, *From the Scarlet Past of Fabulous New Orleans: Souvenir Edition of the World Famous Tenderloin Directory "The Blue Book" with a Brief Story of Storyville* (New Orleans: T. W. Reeves, 1951, n.p.), PAM HQ 146 .N4 .R4 1951, Williams Research Center, The Historic New Orleans Collection.

17. Clarence Williams, in Shapiro and Hentoff, comps., *Hear Me Talkin'*, 11–13, on the price of beer and rich people, and Manetta, Oral History Collection, Hogan Jazz Archive, Tulane University, on champagne and "big timers." Elsewhere in the district, beer sold for a nickel.

18. Repeated to author by Shelley Johnson Carey, a relative of one of the proprietors.

19. Clarence Williams, in Shapiro and Hentoff, comps., *Hear Me Talkin'*, 11–12.

20. Manetta, Oral History Collection, Hogan Jazz Archive, Tulane University.

21. Kid Ory, Oral History Collection, Hogan Jazz Archive, Tulane University.

22. Louis Armstrong, in Shapiro and Hentoff, comps., *Hear Me Talkin'*, 7–8, 65.

23. Lomax, *Mister Jelly Roll*, 50, and Morton, in Shapiro and Hentoff, comps., *Hear Me Talkin'*, 6–7.

24. *City v. Freddie Crockett, Appeal,* Criminal District Court, Docket No. 33,603, City Archives, Louisiana Division, New Orleans Public Library.

25. Ibid.

26. Ibid.

27. *State v. Freddie Crockett,* Criminal District Court, Docket No. 42,032, City Archives, Louisiana Division, New Orleans Public Library (October 16, 1913).

28. *City of New Orleans v. Freddie Crockett,* Criminal District Court, Docket No. 33,816, City Archives, Louisiana Division, New Orleans Public Library (September 24, 1904).

29. For a brilliant example of the tone with which everyday violence in turn-of-the-century New Orleans may be described, see Louis Armstrong, *Satchmo: My Life in New Orleans* (1954; New York: Da Capo Press, 1968).

30. New Orleans Board of Police Commissioners, *Annual Report of Board of Police Commissioners and the Superintendent of Police of the City of New Orleans, 1889–1915,* reports from 1889–1915, City Archives, Louisiana Division, New Orleans Public Library.

31. Arrest Books (microfilm), City Archives, Louisiana Division, New Orleans Public Library. Venerable was one of Lulu White's "boarders" in the 1910 census. U.S. Bureau of the Census, *Thirteenth Census of the United States (Louisiana), Schedule 1—Population,* Enumeration District 58, page 6. In the 1920s, Queenie Venerable was arrested for operating her own disorderly house. Docket Books, Louisiana Division, New Orleans Public Library.

32. Louis Armstrong, in Shapiro and Hentoff, comps., *Hear Me Talkin'*, 4–5.

33. Kid Ory, Oral History Collection, Hogan Jazz Archive, Tulane University. The mechanical "clockwork" quality to this work calls to mind the mechanization of almost all forms of manual labor in this general period.

34. Records of the Police Inspector, box 3, folder "January 1899," City Archives, Louisiana Division, New Orleans Public Library.

35. Jelly Roll Morton, in Shapiro and Hentoff, comps., *Hear Me Talkin'*, 6–7.

36. Louis Armstrong, in Shapiro and Hentoff, comps., *Hear Me Talkin'*, 4–5.

37. Armstrong, *Satchmo,* 87–88.

38. Kid Ory, Oral History Collection, Hogan Jazz Archive, Tulane University.

39. Clarence Williams, in Shapiro and Hentoff, comps., *Hear Me Talkin'*, 11–13.

40. Kid Ory, Oral History Collection, Hogan Jazz Archive, Tulane University. Funerals in New Orleans can be elaborate affairs; musicians accompany the casket to the cemetery

playing jazz dirges, and once they deposit the body, they return with a more lively parade, loud music, and a general party. The "second line" in jazz music is a funeral tradition. To have an elaborate and large funeral in New Orleans is a mark of status.

41. Testimony from *State of Louisiana ex rel John Journee vs. Board of Commissioners of the Police Department of the City of New Orleans,* Supreme Court of Louisiana, Docket No. 16,506 (1907), Louisiana Supreme Court Collection, Louisiana and Special Collections, Earl K. Long Library, University of New Orleans.

42. Ibid.

43. Ibid.

44. Frank Amacker, Oral History Collection, Hogan Jazz Archive, Tulane University.

45. Timothy J. Gilfoyle, *City of Eros: New York City, Prostitution, and the Commercialization of Sex, 1790–1820* (New York: Norton, 1992), chapter 4, "Brothel Riots." Cf. Charles Van Onselen, *The Fox and the Flies: The Secret Life of a Grotesque Master Criminal* (New York: Walker, 2007).

46. Carole Pateman, *The Sexual Contract* (Stanford, Calif.: Stanford Univ. Press, 1988). See especially chapter 7, "What's Wrong with Prostitution?"

47. Cf. Judith Kelleher Schafer, *Brothels, Depravity, and Abandoned Women: Illegal Sex in Antebellum New Orleans* (Baton Rouge: Louisiana State Univ. Press, 2009).

48. *State of Louisiana ex rel John Journee vs. Board of Commissioners,* op cit.

49. Blue Book, Acc. No. 1969.19.11, Williams Research Center, The Historic New Orleans Collection, New Orleans, Louisiana.

50. Lomax, *Mister Jelly Roll,* 22.

51. Clarence Williams, in Shapiro and Hentoff, comps., *Hear Me Talkin',* 11–13.

52. Quotes from *New Orleans Item,* July 22, 1916. Quoted in Russell Levy, "Of Bards and Bawds: New Orleans Sporting Life Before and During the Storyville Era, 1897–1917" (Master's thesis, Tulane University, 1967), 38–39.

53. Sherrie Tucker, "A Feminist Perspective on New Orleans Jazz Women" (New Orleans Jazz National Historic Park, National Park Service, New Orleans, Louisiana, 2004), 236–244. Cf. Armstrong, *Satchmo*; Samuel B. Charters, *A Trumpet around the Corner: The Story of New Orleans Jazz* (Jackson: Univ. Press of Mississippi, 2008); Hersch, *Subversive Sounds*; Raeburn, *New Orleans Style*; Shapiro and Hentoff, comps., *Hear Me Talkin'.*

54. Bunk Johnson, in Shapiro and Hentoff, comps., *Hear Me Talkin',* 6.

55. See Tucker, "A Feminist Perspective on New Orleans Jazz Women," 236–244. Thanks to Sherrie Tucker for sharing this report, and also to Bruce Raeburn for this information and for putting me in contact with Professor Tucker.

56. *Blue Book,* Acc. No. 1969.19.3, Williams Research Center, Historic New Orleans Collection.

57. Jelly Roll Morton, *Jelly Roll Morton: The Complete Library of Congress Recordings by Alan Lomax* (Rounder Records, 2005), disc 1, track 11 (transcript page 18)

58. *Blue Book,* Acc. No. 1969.19.6, Williams Research Center, Historic New Orleans Collection.

59. Manetta, Oral History Collection, Hogan Jazz Archive, Tulane University.

60. Spencer Williams, in Shapiro and Hentoff, comps., *Hear Me Talkin',* 7.

61. Clarence Williams, in Shapiro and Hentoff, comps., *Hear Me Talkin'*, 11–13.

62. Manetta, Oral History Collection, Hogan Jazz Archive, Tulane University.

63. Clarence Williams, in Shapiro and Hentoff, comps., *Hear Me Talkin'*, 11–13.

64. Al Rose, *Storyville, New Orleans: Being an Authentic, Illustrated Account of the Notorious Red-Light District* (Tuscaloosa: Univ. of Alabama Press, 1974), 78.

65. See chapter 6 and the conclusion, below.

66. Samuel Barclay Charters, *Jazz: New Orleans, 1865–1963, An Index to the Negro Musicians of New Orleans*, rev. ed. (New York: Oak Publications, 1963), 18.

67. Bunk Johnson, in Shapiro and Hentoff, comps., *Hear Me Talkin'*, 6.

68. *Jazz: New Orleans*, 18.

69. Roy Carew, "The New Orleans Legend," *Jazz Music: The International Jazz Magazine* 5, no. 6 (July–August 1954): 3–10, 23–24.

70. *Jazz: New Orleans*, 18–19.

71. Joe "King" Oliver was the cornetist who allowed Louis Armstrong to play in his band, giving Armstrong his start and acting as a mentor to the much younger musician. Edmund Souchon, "King Oliver: A Very Personal Memoir," *Jazz Review* 3, no. 4 (May 1960): 6–11. Souchon was white, and he refers to New Orleans as "The citadel of white caste privileges." His black babysitter introduced him to jazz and thus began a life-long love of jazz. See also Armstrong, *Satchmo.*

72. Morton, *Interviews with Alan Lomax*, disc 1, track 8, transcript page 13.

73. Paul Eduard Miller, ed., *Esquire's 1945 Jazz Book* (New York: A. S. Barnes and Company, 1945), 3.

74. Quoted in Lomax, *Mr. Jelly Roll*, 84.

75. Herbert Asbury, *The French Quarter: An Informal History of the New Orleans Underworld* (New York: Garden City Publishing, 1936), 4. See also Hodding Carter et al., eds., *The Past as Prelude: New Orleans, 1718–1968* (New Orleans: Tulane University, 1968); Eleanor Early, *New Orleans Holiday* (New York: Rinehart, 1947); Thomas Harnett Kane, *Queen New Orleans, City by the River* (New York: W. Morrow, 1949); Lura Robinson, *It's an Old New Orleans Custom* (New York: Vanguard Press, 1948); Charles Etienne Gayarré, *History of Louisiana*, 4 vols. (New Orleans: Armand Hawkins, 1885); Grace King, *New Orleans: The Place and the People* (New York: Macmillian, 1904). On the construction of "mythic" New Orleans, see Violet Harrington Bryan, *The Myth of New Orleans in Literature: Dialogues of Race and Gender* (Knoxville: Univ. of Tennessee Press, 1993), as well as Joseph Roach, *Cities of the Dead: Circum-Atlantic Performance* (New York: Columbia Univ. Press, 1996), and Shirley Elizabeth Thompson, "The Passing of a People: Creoles of Color in Mid-Nineteenth Century New Orleans" (Ph.D. diss., Harvard University, 2001). For a nuanced vision of early New Orleans, see Emily Clark, "'By All the Conduct of Their Lives': A Laywoman's Confraternity in New Orleans, 1730–1744," *William and Mary Quarterly*, 3rd ser., vol. 54, no. 4 (October 1997): 769–794, and Jennifer M. Spear, "'They Need Wives': Métissage and the Regulation of Sexuality in French Louisiana, 1699–1730," in *Sex, Love, Race: Crossing Boundaries in North American History*, ed. Martha Hodes (New York: New York Univ. Press, 1999), 35–59.

76. Asbury, *The French Quarter*, 4.

77. Shannon Lee Dawdy, *Building the Devil's Empire: French Colonial New Orleans* (Chicago: Univ. of Chicago Press, 2008), 25–61.

78. Ibid., 26.

79. Ibid., 1–23, and cf. Mathé Allain, *Not Worth a Straw: French Colonial Policy and the Early Years of Louisiana* (Lafayette: Center for Louisiana Studies, University of Southwestern Louisiana, 1988). For a thorough history of the development of New Orleans, from the beginnings of French exploration of the Mississippi River through the early nineteenth century, see Lawrence N. Powell, *The Accidental City: Improvising New Orleans* (Cambridge, Mass.: Harvard Univ. Press, 2012).

80. Quoted in Dawdy, *Building the Devil's Empire*, 26.

81. Dawdy, *Building the Devil's Empire*, 210–211.

82. Caryn Cossé Bell, *Revolution, Romanticism, and the Afro-Creole Protest Tradition in Louisiana, 1718–1868* (Baton Rouge: Louisiana State Univ. Press, 1997), 11. See also Daniel H. Usner Jr., *Indians, Settlers, and Slaves in a Frontier Exchange Economy: The Lower Mississippi Valley Before 1783* (Chapel Hill: Univ. of North Carolina Press, 1992).

83. Spear, "'They Need Wives,'" 35–59; Spear, *Race, Sex, and Social Order in Early New Orleans* (Baltimore: Johns Hopkins Univ. Press, 2008).

84. Jennifer Spear, "'They Need Wives.'"

85. Quoted in Asbury, *The French Quarter*, 11.

86. First quote: Pontchartrain to Bienville, January 30, 1704, *Mississippi Provincial Archives French Division*, 3:15–16; second quote: Bienville to Pontchartrain, September 6, 1704, *MPAFD*, 3:24. Both quotes can be found in Jennifer Spear, *Race, Sex, and Social Order*, 47.

87. Duclos to minister, July 15, 1713, Archives des Colonies, Archives nationals de France series C, C13a, 3:139–40, in Spear, *Race, Sex, and Social Order*, 47.

88. His grant succeeded the one given Antoine Crozat several years earlier. Jerah Johnson, "Colonial New Orleans," in *Creole New Orleans: Race and Americanization*, ed. Arnold Hirsch and Joseph Logsdon (Baton Rouge: Louisiana State Univ. Press, 1992), 36.

89. Asbury, *The French Quarter*, 12.

90. Quoted in Asbury, *The French Quarter*, 12; see Kane, *Queen New Orleans*, 55.

91. Spear, *Race, Sex, and Social Order*, 49.

92. Quoted in, Spear, "'They Need Wives,'" 49.

93. Asbury, *The French Quarter*, 11–12; see also Kane, *Queen New Orleans*, 55; Gayarré, *History of Louisiana*, 890, John Smith Kendall, *History of New Orleans*, 3 vols. (Chicago: Lewis Publishing Company, 1922), 1:9.

94. Spear, *Race, Sex, and Social Order*, 51. The next chapter covers this development and its meanings for Storyville.

95. Ned Sublette, *The World That Made New Orleans: From Spanish Silver to Congo Square* (Chicago: Lawrence Hill Books, 2008), 80, 84.

96. For questions regarding the veracity of this image and its relationship to the Enlightenment, see Dawdy, *Building the Devil's Empire*, especially chapter 1, "A Veritable Babylon: Enlightenment and Disorder," 25–61.

97. Asbury, *The French Quarter*, 3.

98. Michael Allen, *Western Rivermen, 1763–1861: Ohio and Mississippi Boatmen and the Myth of the Alligator Horse* (Baton Rouge: Louisiana State Univ. Press, 1990), 53, 56.

99. Allen, *Western Rivermen*, and cf. John Churchill Chase, *Frenchmen, Desire, Good Children, and Other Streets of New Orleans: A Delightful History of America's Most Romantic City*, 3rd ed. (1949; New York: Simon and Schuster, 1997), chapters 6 and 7.

100. Asbury, *The French Quarter*, 98–99.

101. Dennis Charles Rousey, *Policing the Southern City: New Orleans, 1805–1889* (Baton Rouge: Louisiana State Univ. Press, 1996), 6 and passim.

102. Asbury, *The French Quarter*, 98–99; Gilfoyle, *City of Eros*; Levy, "Of Bards and Bawds," 10; Chase, *Frenchmen, Desire, Good Children*, 72. The area known as "the Swamp" included sections of what would become Storyville as well as the uptown red-light district. It was the former "city commons," and literally a swamp.

103. A Resident, "New Orleans As It Is: Its Manners and Customs—Morals—Fashionable Life—Profanation of the Sabbath—Prostitution—Licentiousness—Slave Markets and Slavery, &c. &c" (Utica, N.Y.: Dewitt C. Grove, Printer, 1849), 36, Williams Research Center, The Historic New Orleans Collection, New Orleans, Louisiana.

104. A Resident, "New Orleans as It Is," 36.

105. Richard Tansey, "Prostitution and Politics in Antebellum New Orleans," *Southern Studies* 19, no. 4 (winter 1980): 449–479, especially 449, 451. For the pattern of prostitution elsewhere in the United States, see Ruth Rosen, *The Lost Sisterhood: Prostitution in America, 1900–1918* (Baltimore: Johns Hopkins Univ. Press, 1982), introduction.

106. Tansey, "Prostitution and Politics," 449, citing the merchants who felt this way.

107. In 1836, New Orleans had been divided into three municipalities: the first constituted the French Quarter, the second the American Sector, and the third simply the Third Municipality.

108. Tansey, "Prostitution and Politics," 449.

109. Ibid., 469–470.

110. Ibid., 473.

111. Judith Kelleher Schafer, *Becoming Free, Remaining Free: Manumission and Enslavement in New Orleans, 1846–1862* (Baton Rouge: Louisiana State Univ. Press, 2003), 106. See also Martha Hodes, *White Women, Black Men: Illicit Sex in the 19th-Century South* (New Haven, Conn.: Yale Univ. Press, 1997); Joshua D. Rothman, *Notorious in the Neighborhood: Sex and Families across the Color Line in Virginia, 1787–1861* (Chapel Hill: Univ. of North Carolina Press, 2003); Victoria Bynum, *Unruly Women: The Politics of Social and Sexual Control in the Old South* (Chapel Hill: Univ. of North Carolina Press, 1992). Though sex across the color line was not as uncommon, and not as violently repressed, as has been generally understood, it is nonetheless important to recall that interracial relationships were taboo. Black men in such relationships might face greater danger than social ostracism, but it was not until the postbellum period that lynching became the popular way to punish black men for sexually transgressing the color line.

112. Cf. Schafer, *Brothels, Depravity, and Abandoned Women.*

113. Tansey, "Prostitution and Politics," 475, and New Orleans City Ordinance No. 3267, O.S. (March 10, 1857), known as "the Lorette Ordinance"; see also Alecia P. Long, *The Great*

Southern Babylon: Sex, Race, and Respectability in New Orleans, 1865–1920 (Baton Rouge: Louisiana State Univ. Press, 2004), 3.

114. Tansey, "Prostitution and Politics," 477; Long, *Great Southern Babylon,* 3; Schafer, *Brothels, Depravity, and Abandoned Women,* passim.

115. General Order No. 28, May 15, 1862, cited in Chester G. Hearn, *When the Devil Came Down to Dixie: Ben Butler in New Orleans* (Baton Rouge: Louisiana State Univ. Press, 1997), 102, 103; and see Mary P. Ryan, *Women in Public: Between Banners and Ballots, 1825–1880* (Baltimore: Johns Hopkins Univ. Press, 1990), 144. See Alecia P. Long, "(Mis)Remembering General Order No. 28: Benjamin Butler, The Woman Order, and Historical Memory," paper presented at the Southern Historical Association conference, October 2008, in the possession of the author, and in *Occupied Women: Gender, Military Occupation, and the American Civil War,* ed. LeeAnn Whites and Alecia P. Long (Baton Rouge: Louisiana State Univ. Press, 2009), 17–32. See also Catherine Clinton, "'Public Women' and Sexual Politics during the American Civil War," in *Battle Scars: Gender and Sexuality in the American Civil War,* ed. Catherine Clinton and Nina Silber (New York: Oxford Univ. Press, 2006), 61–77.

116. For some examples of the spread of prostitution in the Gilded Age, see Alain Corbin, *Women for Hire: Prostitution and Sexuality in France after 1850,* trans. Alan Sheridan (Cambridge, Mass.: Harvard Univ. Press, 1990); Gilfoyle, *City of Eros;* Gail Hershatter, *Dangerous Pleasures: Prostitution and Modernity in Twentieth-Century Shanghai* (Berkeley: Univ. of California Press, 1997); Barbara Meil Hobson, *Uneasy Virtue: The Politics of Prostitution and the American Reform Tradition* (Chicago: Univ. of Chicago Press, 1987); Joanne J. Meyerowitz, *Women Adrift: Independent Wage Earners in Chicago, 1880–1930* (Chicago: Univ. of Chicago Press, 1988); Peggy Pascoe, *Relations of Rescue: The Search for Female Moral Authority in the American West, 1874–1939* (New York: Oxford Univ. Press, 1990); Rosen, *The Lost Sisterhood;* Charles Van Onselen, *Studies in the Social and Economic History of the Witwatersrand, 1886–1914,* vol. 1, *New Babylon,* and vol. 2, *New Nineveh* (Johannesburg, South Africa: Ravan Press, 1982); Van Onselen, *The Fox and the Flies;* Judith R. Walkowitz, *City of Dreadful Delight: Narratives of Sexual Danger in Late-Victorian London* (Chicago: Univ. of Chicago Press, 1992); Judith R. Walkowitz, *Prostitution and Victorian Society: Women, Class, and the State* (Cambridge, Eng.: Cambridge Univ. Press, 1982).

117. Asbury, *The French Quarter,* 424.

118. Paul Boyer, *Urban Masses and Moral Order in America, 1820–1920* (Cambridge, Mass.: Harvard Univ. Press, 1978); Mark Thomas Connelly, *The Response to Prostitution in the Progressive Era* (Chapel Hill: Univ. of North Carolina Press, 1980); John D'Emilio and Estelle B. Freedman, *Intimate Matters: A History of Sexuality in America* (New York: Harper and Row, 1998); David J. Pivar, *The Purity Crusade: Sexual Morality and Social Control, 1860–1900* (Westport, Conn.: Greenwood Press, 1973); Gaines Foster, *Moral Reconstruction: Christian Lobbyists and the Federal Legislation of Morality, 1865–1920* (Chapel Hill: Univ. of North Carolina Press, 2002).

119. Allan M. Brandt, *No Magic Bullet: A Social History of Venereal Disease in the United States Since 1880,* expanded ed. (New York: Oxford Univ. Press, 1987); Neil Larry Shumsky, "Tacit Acceptance: Respectable Americans and Segregated Prostitution, 1870–1910," *Journal of Social History* 19, no. 4 (Summer 1986): 665–679.

120. *New Orleans Daily Picayune,* February 16, 1891.

121. Ibid., January 1, 1891; Gilfoyle, *City of Eros,* 224–225 and passim. See also Allen, *Horrible Prettiness,* 76.

122. *Mascot* (1892), quoted in Ruth Rosen, *The Lost Sisterhood,* 5.

123. New Orleans City Ordinance No. 13,032, C.S. (1897).

124. For life in this section, see Armstrong, *Satchmo,* and William Ivy Hair, *Carnival of Fury: Robert Charles and the New Orleans Race Riot of 1900* (Baton Rouge: Louisiana State Univ. Press, 1976).

125. New Orleans City Ordinance No. 13,485 C.S. (1897) and Council Meeting Minutes, July 1897, City Archives, Louisiana Division, New Orleans Public Library.

126. Friends of the Cabildo, *New Orleans Architecture,* vol. 6, *Faubourg Tremé and the Bayou Road* (Gretna, La.: Pelican, 1971), 56. See also Richard Campanella, *Geographies of New Orleans: Urban Fabrics before the Storm* (Lafayette: Center for Louisiana Studies, University of Louisiana, Lafayette, 2006).

127. The figurative meaning of the plural, faubourgs, is "working classes." Nineteenth-century red-light districts tended to concentrate near central business districts. See Shumsky, "Tacit Acceptance."

128. Friends of the Cabildo, *New Orleans Architecture,* 6:85, 13–17, 63.

129. Ibid., 6:71.

130. L'Hote won the initial lawsuit: *George L'Hote v. City of New Orleans et al.* (1897), Docket No. 54,533, Civil District Court for the Parish of New Orleans, Division B, City Archives, Louisiana Division, New Orleans Public Library. The city appealed to the Louisiana Supreme Court, and won (*L'Hote v. City of New Orleans et al.* (1898), Supreme Court of Louisiana, Docket No. 12,753, Supreme Court of Louisiana Collection, Acc. No. 106, Department of Archives and Manuscripts, Earl K. Long Library, University of New Orleans, and digested in 51 *Louisiana Annual,* 94). L'Hote then brought the case to the U.S. Supreme Court, which affirmed the Louisiana Supreme Court's ruling, in favor of the city and the constitutionality of the ordinance. The U.S. Supreme Court Case is *L'Hote v. City of New Orleans,* 177 U.S. 587 (1900). Both the lower court's records and the U.S. Supreme Court's final ruling are contained in the Louisiana Supreme Court records; page numbers refer to the numbers on the top right corner of the page, and the case is hereafter cited as *L'Hote.*

131. *L'Hote,* 29, 44–45.

132. Examples taken from *L'Hote,* 30–31, 49, 88, 50–51, 123, 139, 148, 161.

133. Police Inspector Records, City Archives, Louisiana Division, NOPL.

134. Police Inspector Records, City Archives, Louisiana Division, NOPL.

135. *L'Hote,* 95–96.

136. For the "salt and pepper" residential pattern, see Pierce F. Lewis, *New Orleans: The Making of an Urban Landscape,* 2nd ed. (1976; Santa Fe, N. Mex.: Center for American Places, 2003), 50, and Campanella, *Geographies of New Orleans,* 297–298 and passim.

137. Joy Jackson, *New Orleans in the Gilded Age: Politics and Urban Progress, 1880–1896* (Baton Rouge: Louisiana State Univ. Press, 1969), 24; Armstrong, *Satchmo,* 47.

138. See Roach, *Cities of the Dead.* Homer Plessy lies buried in St. Louis No. 1.

139. Dawdy, *Building the Devil's Empire,* 26.

140. Florence Roos Brink, "Literary Travellers in New Orleans between 1803 and 1860," *Louisiana Historical Quarterly* 31, no. 2 (April 1948): 398.

2. THE QUADROON CONNECTION

1. Jack Teagarden, in *Hear Me Talkin' to Ya: The Story of Jazz as Told by the Men Who Made It*, comp. Nat Shapiro and Nat Hentoff (1955; New York: Dover Publications, 1966), 280-281.

2. Edward Said, *Orientalism* (New York: Vintage Books, 1979).

3. Charles A. Lofgren, *The Plessy Case: A Legal-Historical Interpretation* (New York: Oxford Univ. Press, 1987), 28.

4. Ibid.

5. Ibid., 29. See also *New Orleans Daily Picayune,* June 25, 1890, 6; July 10, 1890, 8; July 11, 1890, 8. The bill did not pass right away, and this paper's editors expressed surprise and dismay, but were certain the bill would pass the next time around, which it did after winning "reconsideration."

6. See Mark Elliott, *Color-Blind Justice: Albion Tourgée and the Quest for Racial Equality from the Civil War to* Plessy v. Ferguson (New York: Oxford Univ. Press, 2006).

7. Albion Tourgée, *A Fool's Errand, by One of the Fools* (New York: Fords, Howard, and Hulbert, 1880).

8. And most likely the half-brother of Mamie Inez Desdounes, the singer who headlined in Storyville. See the previous chapter.

9. Lofgren, *The Plessy Case,* 32-40. See also Barbara Young Welke, *Recasting American Liberty: Gender, Race, Law, and the Railroad Revolution, 1865-1920* (Cambridge, Eng.: Cambridge Univ. Press, 2001), 338-351.

10. Rebecca J. Scott, *Degrees of Freedom: Louisiana and Cuba after Slavery* (Cambridge, Mass.: Harvard Univ. Press, 2008), 77. For Plessy's biography, see Keith Weldon Medley, *We as Freemen:* Plessy v. Ferguson (Gretna, La: Pelican, 2003), 13-35.

11. Lofgren, *The Plessy Case,* 41.

12. Tourgée, "Brief of Plaintiff in Error," *Plessy v. Ferguson* 163 U.S. 537 (1896); see also Mark Elliot, "Race, Color Blindness, and the Democratic Public: Albion Tourgée's Radical Principles in *Plessy v. Ferguson,*" *Journal of Southern History* 67, no. 2 (May 2001): 287-330.

13. *Plessy v. Ferguson* 163 U.S. 537; *Ex parte Plessy* 45 La. Ann. 80; Mark Elliott, "Race, Color Blindness, and the Democratic Public."

14. *Plessy v. Ferguson,* Justice Harlan's dissent.

15. *Plessy v. Ferguson*; Lofgren, *Plessy Case,* 176.

16. Brown's racial theory rested on an understanding of natural, biological, and immutable differences between the so-called races. He was not open to the kind of radical arbitrariness embraced and elaborated by Tourgée. See Brook Thomas, *Plessy v. Ferguson: A Brief History with Documents* (Boston: Bedford Books, 1997), and Elliott, *Color-Blind Justice.*

17. *Plessy v. Ferguson* 163 U.S. 537.

18. Caryn Cossé Bell and Joseph Logsdon, "The Americanization of Black New Orleans," in *Creole New Orleans,* ed. Arnold R. Hirsch and Joseph Logsdon (Baton Rouge: Louisiana

State Univ. Press, 1992), 258. It is interesting to note that the legal press at the time barely remarked upon the decision.

19. Bell and Logsdon, "The Americanization of Black New Orleans," 259. For an analysis of Desdunes's response to the case, see Shirley Elizabeth Thompson, "'Ah, Toucoutou, Ye Conin Vous': History and Memory in Creole New Orleans," *American Quarterly* 53, no. 2 (June 2001): 232–266.

20. James B. Bennett, *Religion and the Rise of Jim Crow in New Orleans* (Princeton, N.J.: Princeton Univ. Press, 2005).

21. Eric Arnesen, *Waterfront Workers of New Orleans: Race, Class, and Politics, 1863–1923* (Urbana: Univ. of Illinois Press, 1994), chapters 4 and 5; see also Dale Somers, "Black and White in New Orleans: A Study in Urban Race Relations, 1865–1900," *Journal of Southern History* 40, no. 1 (February 1974): 19–42.

22. Arnesen, *Waterfront Workers,* 148–49. For the Robert Charles riot in New Orleans, see William Ivy Hair, *Carnival of Fury: Robert Charles and the New Orleans Race Riot of 1900* (Baton Rouge: Louisiana State Univ. Press, 1976).

23. *New Orleans Daily Picayune,* July 26, 1900, quoted in Somers, "Black and White in New Orleans," 42.

24. William Faulkner is perhaps the most famous twentieth-century example of an author who uses the mixed-race figure to explore these themes.

25. Ronald G. Walters, "The Erotic South: Civilization and Sexuality in American Abolitionism," *American Quarterly* 25, no. 2 (May, 1973): 177–201, 178, and passim.

26. Jean Fagin Yellin, *Women and Sisters: The Antislavery Feminists in American Culture* (New Haven, Conn.: Yale Univ. Press, 1989); Walters, "Erotic South," passim.

27. Some authors used "quadroon," others "octoroon," and still others "mulatto" to describe their tragic heroines.

28. Anna Elfenbein, *Women on the Color Line: Evolving Stereotypes and the Writings of George Washington Cable, Grace King, Kate Chopin* (Charlottesville: Univ. Press of Virginia, 1989), 3.

29. Ibid., 3. See also Glenn Cannon Arbery, "Victims of Likeness: Quadroons and Octoroons in Southern Fiction," *Southern Review* 25, no. 1 (winter 1989): 52–71; Judith Berzon, *Neither White Nor Black: The Mulatto Character in American Fiction* (New York: New York Univ. Press, 1978); Margaret Kellow, "The Fair Circassian: The Concubine in Feminist Antislavery Discourse," unpublished paper in the possession of the author; Margaret Kellow, "The Oriental Imaginary: Constructions of Female Bondage in Women's Antislavery Discourse," unpublished paper in the possession of the author; Susan Gillman, "The Mulatto, Tragic or Triumphant? The Nineteenth-Century American Race Melodrama," in, *The Culture of Sentiment: Race, Gender and Sentimentality in Nineteenth-Century America,* ed. Shirley Samuels (New York: Oxford Univ. Press, 1992), 221–243; James Kinney, *Amalgamation! Race, Sex, and Rhetoric in the Nineteenth-Century American Novel* (Westport, Conn.: Greenwood Press, 1985); Werner Sollors, *Neither Black nor White yet Both: Thematic Explorations in Interracial Literature* (Cambridge, Mass.: Harvard Univ. Press, 1997); Helen Taylor, *Gender, Race, and Region in the Writings of Grace King, Ruth McEnery Stuart, and Kate Chopin* (Baton Rouge: Louisiana State Univ. Press, 1989). Other sources in the genre are cited as necessary below.

30. Walters, "The Erotic South."

31. Cf. Drew Gilpin Faust, *James Henry Hammond and the Old South: A Design for Mastery* (Baton Rouge: Louisiana State Univ. Press, 1982).

32. Henry Wadsworth Longfellow, "The Quadroon Girl," *Leed's Antislavery Series*, no. 50 (1842), Beinecke Rare Book and Manuscript Library, Yale University.

33. Harriet Beecher Stowe, *Uncle Tom's Cabin, or, Life among the Lowly,* in Harriet Beecher Stowe, Three Novels (1852; New York: Library of America, 1982), 14.

34. Ibid.

35. Ibid., 451.

36. Ibid., 423.

37. Ibid., 427.

38. Dion Boucicault, *The Octoroon; or, Life in Louisiana* (1859; Miami, Fla.: Mnemosyne Publishing, 1969), 16–17.

39. Eva Saks, "Representing Miscegenation Law," *Raritan* 8, no. 2 (Fall 1988): 39. Zoe's death outraged British audiences, and Boucicault rewrote the ending of the play for the 1861 London production, "to reflect popular prejudice (and keep Zoe alive)" (Saks, "Representing Miscegenation Law," 69).

40. Nancy F. Cott, *The Bonds of Womanhood: "Woman's Sphere" in New England, 1780–1835,* 2nd ed. (1977; New Haven, Conn.: Yale Univ. Press, 1997); Nancy F. Cott, *Public Vows: A History of Marriage and the Nation* (Cambridge, Mass.: Harvard Univ. Press, 2000); Pamela Haag, *Consent: Sexual Rights and the Transformation of American Liberalism* (Ithaca: Cornell Univ. Press, 1999); Amy Dru Stanley, *From Bondage to Contract: Wage Labor, Marriage, and the Market in the Age of Slave Emancipation* (Cambridge, Eng.: Cambridge Univ. Press, 1998).

41. Elfenbein, *Women on the Color Line,* 5.

42. Karen Sánchez-Eppler, *Touching Liberty: Abolition, Feminism, and the Politics of the Body* (Berkeley: Univ. of California Press, 1997), 41. See also George M. Fredrickson, *The Black Image in the White Mind: The Debate on Afro-American Character and Destiny, 1817–1914* (Middletown, Conn.: Wesleyan Univ. Press, 1971), especially, chapter 4, "Uncle Tom and the Anglo-Saxons: Romantic Racialism in the North," 97–129. And see Mary Niall Mitchell, "'Rosebloom and Pure White,' or So It Seemed," *American Quarterly* 54, no. 3 (September 2002): 369–410.

43. Jules Zanger, "The 'Tragic Octoroon' in Pre-Civil War Fiction," *American Quarterly* 18, no. 1 (Spring 1966): 63–70, 66.

44. There is now a large body of scholarship documenting the sexual abuses and excesses of the southern slave system. For example, see Peter W. Bardaglio, *Reconstructing the Household: Families, Sex, and the Law in the Nineteenth-Century South* (Chapel Hill: Univ. of North Carolina Press, 1995); Peter W. Bardaglio, "'Shameful Matches': The Regulation of Interracial Sex and Marriage in the South before 1900," in *Sex, Love, Race: Crossing Boundaries in North American History,* ed. Martha Hodes (New York: New York Univ. Press, 1999), 112–138; Catherine Clinton, "'Southern Dishonor': Flesh, Blood, Race, and Bondage," in *In Joy and in Sorrow: Women, the Family, and Marriage in the Victorian South,* ed. Carol Bleser (New York: Oxford Univ. Press, 1991), 52–68; Harriet A. Jacobs, *Incidents in the Life of a Slave Girl, Written by Herself,* ed. Jean Fagan Yellin, enlarged ed. (Cambridge, Mass.: Harvard Univ.

Press, 2000); Melton A. McLaurin, *Celia, a Slave: A True Story* (New York: Avon Books, 1991); Nell Irvin Painter, "Soul Murder and Slavery: Toward a Fully Loaded Cost Accounting," in *U.S. History as Women's History: New Feminist Essays,* ed. Linda K. Kerber, Alice Kessler Harris, and Kathryn Kish Sklar (Chapel Hill: Univ. of North Carolina Press, 1995), 125–146; Deborah Gray White, *Ar'n't I a Woman? Female Slaves in the Plantation South,* rev. ed. (New York: Norton, 1999). For the repression/elaboration complex, see Michel Foucault, *The History of Sexuality,* vol. 1, *An Introduction;* trans. Robert Hurley (New York: Vintage Books, 1990); Michel Foucault, *Discipline and Punish: The Birth of the Prison,* trans. Alan Sheridan (New York: Vintage Books, 1979). See also Ann Laura Stoler, *Race and the Education of Desire: Foucault's* History of Sexuality *and the Colonial Order of Things* (Durham, N.C.: Duke Univ. Press, 1995).

45. On the iconicity of the "Mulatress" in colonial Cuba, see Vera M. Kutzinski, *Sugar's Secrets: Race and the Erotics of Cuban Nationalism* (Charlottesville: Univ. Press of Virginia, 1993).

46. Eliza Potter, *A Hairdresser's Experience in High Life* (1859; New York: Oxford Univ. Press, 1991), 171, 172, 174.

47. Joseph Roach, "Slave Spectacles and Tragic Octoroons: A Cultural Genealogy of Antebellum Performance," *Theatre Survey* 33, no. 2 (November 1992): 167–187, 171–172, and passim.

48. Ibid., 171.

49. Frederic Bancroft, *Slave Trading in the Old South* (1931; Columbia: Univ. of South Carolina Press, 1996), 312. Delos, the mythical birthplace of Apollo and Artemis, was a large commercial center in the Aegean where goods, including slaves, were sold. Rome made the island a center of free trade and put it under Athenian control in 166 BC.

50. Bancroft, *Slave Trading in the Old South,* 312.

51. Quoted in Roach, "Slave Spectacles," 171.

52. Herbert A. Kellar, ed., "A Journey through the South in 1836: Diary of James D. Davidson," *Journal of Southern History* 1, no. 3 (August 1935): 345–377, 358.

53. Bancroft, *Slave Trading in the Old South,* 319–320.

54. Quoted ibid., 328–330.

55. Ibid., 330.

56. Walter Johnson, *Soul by Soul: Life inside the Antebellum Slave Market* (Cambridge, Mass.: Harvard Univ. Press, 1999), 113.

57. Ibid., 112.

58. Roach, "Slave Spectacles," 173–174.

59. Michael Tadman, *Speculators and Slaves: Masters, Traders, and Slaves in the Old South* (1989; Madison: Univ. of Wisconsin Press, 1996), 125–126.

60. Ibid., 125.

61. Quote in Walter Johnson, "Masters and Slaves at the Market: Slavery and the New Orleans Trade, 1804–1864" (Ph.D. diss., Princeton University, 1995), 130. See also Walter Johnson, "The Slave Trader, the White Slave, and the Politics of Racial Determination in the 1850s," *Journal of American History* 87, no. 1 (June 2000): 18, and Mary Niall Mitchell, "'Rosebloom and Pure White,' or So It Seemed."

62. Special thanks to Julia Boss, who helped clarify this with the distinction of "fancy" versus "plain" stitching work. Johnson, "The Slave Trader, the White Slave, and the Politics of Racial Determination in the 1850s," 18.

63. Bancroft, *Slave Trading in the Old South,* 329.

64. Thorstein Veblen, *The Theory of the Leisure Class* (1899; New York: Modern Library, 2001). Veblen coined the term "conspicuous consumption." Walter Johnson's *Soul by Soul* shows brilliantly how the study of consumer culture may indeed be applied to the slave market and the chattel principle. See Jean-Christophe Agnew, "Capitalism, Culture and Catastrophe: Lawrence Levine and the Opening of Cultural History," *Journal of American History* (December 2006): 772–791.

65. Johnson, *Soul by Soul,* 113. Also cf. Stoler, *Race and the Education of Desire.*

66. Cf. Stephanie McCurry, *Masters of Small Worlds: Yeoman Households, Gender Relations, and the Political Culture of the Antebellum South Carolina Low Country* (New York: Oxford Univ. Press, 1997), and Stephanie McCurry, "The Two Faces of Republicanism: Gender and Proslavery Politics in Antebellum South Carolina," *Journal of American History* 78, no. 4 (March 1992): 1245–1264.

67. Kenneth Greenberg, *Honor and Slavery* (Princeton, N.J.: Princeton Univ. Press, 1996); Bertram Wyatt-Brown, *Southern Honor: Ethics and Behavior in the Old South* (New York: Oxford Univ. Press, 1982).

68. Johnson, *Soul by Soul,* chapter 6. See also Saidiya Hartman, *Scenes of Subjection: Terror, Slavery, and Self-Making in Nineteenth-Century America* (New York: Oxford Univ. Press, 1997).

69. And many refused to play any part at all. Johnson, *Soul by Soul*; cf. James C. Scott, *Domination and the Arts of Resistance: Hidden Transcripts* (New Haven, Conn.: Yale Univ. Press, 1992.)

70. Debby Applegate, *The Most Famous Man in America: The Biography of Henry Ward Beecher* (New York: Doubleday, 2006), 226–230, 316–317.

71. Frederick Law Olmsted, *The Cotton Kingdom: A Traveller's Observations on Cotton and Slavery in the American Slave States, 1853–1861,* ed. Arthur M. Schlesinger (1953; New York: Da Capo Press, 1996), 235–236.

72. Ibid.

73. Kellar, ed., "Journey through the South," 358.

74. Karl Bernhard, Duke of Saxe-Weimar-Eisenach, *Travels through North America, during the Years 1825 and 1826,* 2 vols. (Philadelphia: Carey, Lea and Carey, 1828), 2:61, Beinecke Rare Book and Manuscript Library, Yale University, New Haven, Connecticut.

75. Martineau, *Society in America,* 326. *Ils sont dégoutants* means "they are disgusting."

76. Thomas Ingersoll has argued that because the term *plaçage* was not used in the antebellum period, the institution did not exist; see, Thomas Ingersoll, *Mammon and Manon in Early New Orleans: The First Slave Society in the Deep South, 1718–1819* (Knoxville: Univ. of Tennessee Press, 1999). For clear evidence that it did, and on how the term was used, see Kenneth Aslakson, "The 'Quadroon-*Plaçage*' Myth of Antebellum New Orleans: Anglo-American (Mis)interpretations of a French-Caribbean Phenomenon," *Journal of Social History* 45, no. 3 (Spring 2012): 709–734.

77. Olmsted, *Cotton Kingdom,* 236. My emphasis.

78. Virginia Gould has argued that free women of color during the Spanish colonial period had more freedom than white women because they were not held to the same standards of purity and honor that constrained white women of a certain class to dependent

positions within the patriarchal household. See Virginia Gould, "A Chaos of Discord and Iniquity," in *The Devil's Lane: Sex and Race in the Early South,* ed. Catherine Clinton and Michele Gillespie (New York: Oxford Univ. Press, 1999), 232–246.

79. Thompson, "Ah, Toucoutou," 242.

80. Latrobe quoted in Joan M. Martin, "*Plaçage* and the Louisiana *Gens de Couleur Libre*: How Race and Sex Defined the Lifestyles of Free Women of Color," in *Creole: The History and Legacy of Louisiana's Free People of Color,* ed. Sybil Kein (Baton Rouge: Louisiana State Univ. Press, 2000), 57–70, 65.

81. Kellar, ed., "Journey through the South," 358; see also Lois Virginia Meacham Gould, "In Full Enjoyment of Their Liberty: The Free Women of Color of the Gulf Ports of New Orleans, Mobile, and Pensacola, 1769–1860" (Ph.D. diss., Emory University, 1991), 230–231.

82. Barbara Welter, "The Cult of True Womanhood," in *The Dimity Convictions: The American Woman in the Nineteenth Century* (Athens: Ohio Univ. Press, 1976); White, *Ar'n't I a Woman?*; Victoria Bynum, *Unruly Women: The Politics of Social and Sexual Control in the Old South* (Chapel Hill: Univ. of North Carolina Press, 1992).

83. For a refutation of the myth, see Aslakson, "The 'Quadroon-*Plaçage*' Myth." Aslakson does not deny the existence of these relationships, but rather their exclusive formation at quadroon balls and their class boundedness. Interracial concubinage was common across the spectrum of class in New Orleans, both before and following the Civil War. See Alecia P. Long, "Because You Are a Colored Woman," in *The Great Southern Babylon: Sex, Race, and Respectability in New Orleans, 1865–1920* (Baton Rouge: Louisiana State Univ. Press, 2004), 10–59.

84. Martineau, *Society in America,* 326.

85. Kellar, ed., "Journey through the South," 358; see also Gould, "In Full Enjoyment," 230–231.

86. Bernhard, *Travels,* 61–62.

87. Ibid., 61.

88. G. W. Pierson, "Alexis de Tocqueville in New Orleans, January 1–3, 1832," *Franco-American Review* 1, no. 1 (June 1936): 36.

89. Bernhard, *Travels,* 62. See Samuel B. Charters, *The Trumpet around the Corner: The Story of New Orleans Jazz* (Jackson: Univ. Press of Mississippi, 2008), for good descriptions of the more rowdy and raunchy quadroon ball-type gatherings. They were, according to many, interracial orgies rather than the stately affairs described by some antebellum travelers.

90. Kellar, ed., "Journey through the South," 361–362.

91. Monique Guillory, "Some Enchanted Evening on the Auction Block" (Ph.D. diss., New York University, 1999). See also Monique Guillory, "Under One Roof: The Sins and Sanctity of the New Orleans Quadroon Balls," chapter five in *Race Consciousness: African-American Studies for the New Century,* ed. Judith Jackson Fossett and Jeffrey Tucker (New York: New York Univ. Press, 1997).

92. Bernhard, *Travels,* 62, 63n.

93. For the disputes over racial "purity" and reputation, see Joseph Logsdon, "The Great Pandely Case: Race, Politics, and Family in Antebellum New Orleans," unpublished paper in the possession of the author. Shirley Elizabeth Thompson also treats the "Pandelly Affair"

in her dissertation, "The Passing of a People: Creoles of Color in Mid-Nineteenth Century New Orleans" (Ph.D. diss., Harvard University, 2001), 149–188, and in her book, *Exiles at Home: The Struggle to Become American in Creole New Orleans* (Cambridge, Mass.: Harvard Univ. Press, 2009). Thompson uses the different spelling, explaining that the records and documents of the affair were inconsistent.

94. Frances Milton (Fanny) Trollope, *Domestic Manners of the Americans,* ed. Pamela Neville-Sington (1832; London: Penguin, 1997), 16.

95. Kellar, ed., "Journey through the South," 358.

96. Cf. Elizabeth Fox-Genovese, *Within the Plantation Household: Black and White Women of the Old South* (Chapel Hill: Univ. of North Carolina Press, 1988), as well as McCurry, *Masters of Small Worlds,* and McCurry, "The Two Faces of Republicanism." For examples of white wives, sisters, and daughters disputing inheritances left to women of color, see Judith Kelleher Schafer, "Open and Notorious Concubinage: The Emancipation of Slave Mistresses by Will and the Supreme Court in Antebellum Louisiana," *Louisiana History* 28, no. 2 (Spring 1987): 165–182, and Judith Kelleher Schafer, *Slavery, the Civil Law, and the Supreme Court of Louisiana* (Baton Rouge: Louisiana State Univ. Press, 1997), especially chapter 7, "Open and Notorious Concubinage," 180–200.

97. Matilda Charlotte (Jesse) Fraser Houstoun, *Texas and the Gulf of Mexico; or, Yachting in the New World* (1844; Austin, Tex.: W. Thomas Taylor, 1991), 55.

98. Martineau, *Society in America,* 338.

99. Ibid., 327–328, according to a woman with whom Martineau spoke.

100. Olmsted, *Cotton Kingdom,* 240.

101. Thompson, "Ah, Toucoutou," 242.

102. Floyd D. Cheung, "*Les Cenelles* and Quadroon Balls: 'Hidden Transcripts' of Resistance and Domination in New Orleans, 1803–1845," *Southern Literary Journal* 29, no. 2 (Spring 1997): 5–16. See also Caryn Cossé Bell, *Revolution, Romanticism, and the Afro-Creole Protest Tradition in Louisiana, 1718–1868* (Baton Rouge: Louisiana State Univ. Press, 1997); Thompson, *Exiles at Home*; and Thompson, "The Passing of a People."

103. Bell, *Revolution,* passim; Gould, "In Full Enjoyment," passim; Thompson, *Exiles at Home*; and Thompson, "The Passing of a People," passim.

104. Gould, "In Full Enjoyment," 9.

105. Ibid., 14, and chapters 5 and 6.

106. Kenneth Aslakson, "The 'Quadroon-*Plaçage*' Myth." See, for instance, Emily Clark and Virginia Meacham Gould, "The Feminine Face of Afro-Catholicism in New Orleans, 1727–1852," *William and Mary Quarterly* 59, no. 2 (April 2002): 409–445. See also Emily Clark, *Masterless Mistresses: New Orleans Ursulines and the Development of a New World Society, 1727–1834* (Chapel Hill: Univ. of North Carolina Press, 2007).

107. Edward Larocque Tinker was prolific on this score. See, for instance, "Cable and the Creoles," *American Literature* 5, no. 4 (January 1934): 313–326.

108. Charles Etienne Gayarré, "The Creoles of History and the Creoles of Romance: A Lecture Delivered in the Hall of the Tulane University, New Orleans, by the Hon. Charles Gayarré, on the 25th of April, 1885" (New Orleans, 1885), at the Rare Book Division, Library of Congress, Washington, D.C.

109. See Arnold R. Hirsch, "Simply a Matter of Black and White: The Transformation of Race and Politics in Twentieth-Century New Orleans," in *Creole New Orleans: Race and Americanization,* ed. Arnold Hirsch and Joseph Logsdon (Baton Rouge: Louisiana State Univ. Press, 1992), 262–320.

110. See Bell, *Revolution,* 11. See also Daniel H. Usner Jr., *Indians, Settlers, and Slaves in a Frontier Exchange Economy: The Lower Mississippi Valley Before 1783* (Chapel Hill: Univ. of North Carolina Press, 1992).

111. Elizabeth Fussell, "Constructing New Orleans, Constructing Race: A Population History of New Orleans," *Journal of American History* 94, no. 3 (December 2007): 846–855.

112. Jerah Johnson, "Colonial New Orleans: A Fragment of the Eighteenth-Century French Ethos," in *Creole New Orleans: Race and Americanization,* ed. Arnold Hirsch and Joseph Logsdon (Baton Rouge: Louisiana State Univ. Press, 1992), 12–57.

113. Gwendolyn Midlo Hall, "The Formation of Afro-Creole Culture," in *Creole New Orleans: Race and Americanization,* ed. Arnold Hirsch and Joseph Logsdon (Baton Rouge: Louisiana State Univ. Press, 1992), 58–87.

114. Jennifer M. Spear, "'They Need Wives': Métissage and the Regulation of Sexuality in French Louisiana, 1699–1730," in *Sex, Love, Race: Crossing Boundaries in North American History,* ed. Martha Hodes (New York: New York Univ. Press, 1999), 35–59, and Jennifer M. Spear, "Colonial Intimacies: Legislating Sex in French Louisiana," *William and Mary Quarterly* 60, no. 1 (January 2003): 75–98; Joseph G. Tregle Jr., "Creoles and Americans," in *Creole New Orleans: Race and Americanization,* ed. Arnold R. Hirsch and Joseph Logsdon (Baton Rouge: Louisiana State Univ. Press, 1992), 131–185.

115. Kimberly S. Hanger, *Bounded Lives, Bounded Places: Free Black Society in Colonial New Orleans, 1769–1803* (Durham, N.C.: Duke Univ. Press, 1997), 11.

116. See Ira Berlin, *Slaves without Masters: The Free Negro in the Antebellum South* (New York: Pantheon, 1974), 109; Gould, "In Full Enjoyment," chapter 2. See also Bell, *Revolution,* 18; Hanger, *Bounded Lives, Bounded Places.* Hanger argues convincingly that the community of free Creoles of color coalesced under Spanish rule. On *coartacion,* see pages 25–26 and passim.

117. Bell, *Revolution,* 18; Shannon Lee Dawdy, *Building the Devil's Empire: French Colonial New Orleans* (Chicago: Univ. of Chicago Press, 2008).

118. Gould, "A Chaos of Iniquity and Discord"; Hanger, *Bounded Lives, Bounded Places.*

119. See, for example, Rebecca J. Scott and Jean M. Hébrard, *Freedom Papers: An Atlantic Odyssey in the Age of Emancipation* (Cambridge, Mass.: Harvard Univ. Press, 2012). Also see Gould, "A Chaos of Iniquity and Discord," and Schafer, "Open and Notorious Concubinage."

120. Berlin, *Slaves without Masters,* 114–115. See also Donald E. Everett, "Emigrés and Militiamen: Free Persons of Color in New Orleans," *Journal of Negro History* 38, no. 4 (October 1953): 377–402; Donald E. Everett, "Free Persons of Color in Colonial Louisiana," *Louisiana History* 7, no. 1 (winter 1966): 21–50; Thomas Fiehrer, "Saint Domingue/Haiti: Louisiana's Caribbean Connection," *Louisiana History* 30, no. 4 (Autumn 1989): 419–437; Paul F. Lachance, "The 1809 Immigration of Saint-Domingue Refugees to New Orleans: Reception, Integration, and Impact," *Louisiana History* 29, no. 2 (Spring 1988): 109–141.

121. Bell, *Revolution*, 38; Dennis Charles Rousey, *Policing the Southern City: New Orleans, 1805–1889* (Baton Rouge: Louisiana State Univ. Press, 1996), 11. The actual numbers are as follows, from Bell's calculations, pages 37–38: in 1788 New Orleans had a population of 2,370 whites, 823 free people of color, and 2,126 slaves. In 1805 those numbers were 3,804 whites, 1,566 free people of color, and 3,105 slaves. In 1810, the population reached 17,242, of whom 6,331 were white, 4,950 were free people of color, and 5,961 were slaves.

122. Fiehrer, "Saint Domingue/Haiti"; Lachance, "The 1809 Immigration"; and Rebecca J. Scott, "Reinventing Slavery, Securing Freedom: From Saint-Domingue to Santiago to New Orleans, 1803–1809," paper given at the Southern Historical Association, New Orleans, October 2008, and Rebecca J. Scott, "'She . . . Refuses to Deliver Herself Up as the Slave of Your Petitioner': Émigrés, Enslavement, and the 1808 Louisiana Digest of the Civil Laws," *Tulane European and Civil Law Forum* 24 (2009): 116–136; Rebecca J. Scott, "Public Rights and Private Commerce: A Nineteenth-Century Atlantic Creole Itinerary," *Current Anthropology* 48, no. 2 (April 2007): 237–256.

123. Rodolphe Desdunes, *Our People and Our History* (Baton Rouge: Louisiana State Univ. Press, 1973).

124. Judith Kelleher Schafer, *Becoming Free, Remaining Free: Manumission and Enslavement in New Orleans, 1846–1862* (Baton Rouge: Louisiana State Univ. Press, 2003); Schafer, "Open and Notorious Concubinage," 165–182.

125. Jerah Johnson, "Colonial New Orleans." David Rankin makes the important distinction between how the ruling powers treated slaves in a slave society and how society more generally dealt with emancipation, manumission, and formerly enslaved people. It is this distinction, he argues, that the Tannenbaum thesis is lacking, and which is crucial for understanding colonial, and then antebellum, Louisiana and its difference from the emerging order of the United States. David Rankin, "The Tannenbaum Thesis Reconsidered: Slavery and Race Relations in Antebellum Louisiana," *Southern Studies* 18, no. 1 (1979): 5–31. See also Donald Gray Eder, "Time under the Southern Cross: The Tannenbaum Thesis Reappraised," *Agricultural History* 50, no. 4 (October 1976): 600–614.

126. Richard C. Wade, *Slavery in the Cities: The South, 1820–1860* (New York: Oxford Univ. Press, 1964), ix.

127. Jerah Johnson, "Colonial New Orleans." See also Medley, *We as Freemen.*

128. Laura Foner, "The Free People of Color in Louisiana and St. Domingue: A Comparative Portrait of Two Three-Caste Societies," *Journal of Social History* 3, no. 4 (Summer 1970): 425; Mary Gehman, "Visible Means of Support: Businesses, Professions, and Trades of Free People of Color," in *Creole: The History and Legacy of Louisiana's Free People of Color,* ed. Sybil Kein (Baton Rouge: Louisiana State Univ. Press, 2000), 208–222.

129. Berlin, *Slaves without Masters;* John Blassingame, *Black New Orleans, 1860–1880* (Chicago: Univ. of Chicago Press, 1973); Wade, *Slavery in the Cities,* passim.

130. Arnold Hirsch and Joseph Logsdon note historians' too-facile comparison of New Orleans to Charleston, for example, explaining that the Creole communities in the two cities were really very different. (Introduction to Part III, in *Creole New Orleans: Race and Americanization* [Baton Rouge: Louisiana State Univ. Press, 1992], 189–200.)

131. Berlin, *Slaves without Masters*, 119; Donald Edward Everett, "Free Persons of Color in New Orleans, 1803–1865" (Ph.D. diss.: Tulane University, 1952), 57–58.

132. For their role in the military, for example, see Mary Frances Berry, "Negro Troops in Blue and Gray: The Louisiana Native Guards, 1861–1863," *Louisiana History* 8, no. 2 (Spring 1967): 165–190, 166–167.

133. See Virginia R. Dominguez, *White by Definition: Social Classification in Creole Louisiana* (1986; New Brunswick, N.J.: Rutgers Univ. Press, 1997); F. James Davis, *Who Is Black: One Nation's Definition* (University Park, Pa.: Pennsylvania State Univ. Press, 1991).

134. Schafer, *Becoming Free, Remaining Free*.

135. Gould, "In Full Enjoyment," 157.

136. Roger A. Fischer, "Racial Segregation in Antebellum New Orleans," *American Historical Review* 74, no. 3 (February 1969), 931; Richard Tansey, "Prostitution and Politics in Antebellum New Orleans," *Southern Studies* 19, no. 4 (winter 1980): 449–479.

137. Fischer, "Racial Segregation," 931.

138. Schafer, "Open and Notorious Concubinage"; Schafer, *Slavery, the Civil Law, and the Supreme Court of Louisiana,* especially chapter 7, "Open and Notorious Concubinage," 180–200.

139. Fischer, "Racial Segregation," 935.

140. Quoted in Foner, "Free People of Color," 417.

141. Bell, *Revolution,* 40.

142. Gould, "In Full Enjoyment," and Schafer, *Becoming Free, Remaining Free,* chapter 9, 145–162. For the seventeen who chose enslavement, see Schafer, *Becoming Free, Remaining Free,* 152.

143. Hanger, *Bounded Lives, Bounded Places,* esp. 109–135. See also Mary Frances Berry, "Negro Troops in Blue and Gray."

144. Ted Tunnell, *Crucible of Reconstruction: War, Radicalism, and Race in Louisiana, 1862–1877* (Baton Rouge: Louisiana State Univ. Press, 1984), 70.

145. See Bell and Logsdon, "The Americanization of Black New Orleans," passim; Thompson, "The Passing of a People"; Thompson, *Exiles at Home.*

146. Rebecca J. Scott, "The Atlantic World and the Road to *Plessy v. Ferguson,*" *Journal of American History* 94, no. 3 (December 2007): 726–733. The language of manhood is equally prevalent here as it is in other instances where black men sought political rights. See Martha Hodes, "The Sexualization of Reconstruction Politics: White Women and Black Men in the South after the Civil War," *Journal of the History of Sexuality* 3 (January 1993): 402–417.

147. P. H. Sheridan to U. S. Grant, August 2, 1866, quoted in James G. Hollandsworth, Jr., *An Absolute Massacre: The New Orleans Race Riot of July 30, 1866* (Baton Rouge: Louisiana State Univ. Press, 2001), epigraph.

148. Bell, *Revolution,* 261.

149. Quoted ibid., 262.

150. Hollandsworth, *An Absolute Massacre,* 148. See also Donald E. Reynolds, "The New Orleans Riot of 1866, Reconsidered," *Louisiana History* 5 (1964): 5–27.

151. Roger A. Fischer, *The Segregation Struggle in Louisiana, 1862–77* (Urbana: Univ. of Illinois Press, 1974), 55.

152. Ibid., 55.

153. For a poignant and fascinating example, see Michael A. Ross, "Creole Icarus," unpublished paper delivered at the meeting of the Historical Society, Washington, D.C., Spring 2010, in the possession of the author.

154. Bell and Logsdon, "The Americanization of Black New Orleans," 230.

155. Scott, *Degrees of Freedom.*

156. Bell and Logsdon, "The Americanization of Black New Orleans," esp. 221-228.

157. Bell and Logsdon, "The Americanization of Black New Orleans."

158. All quoted in Fischer, *Segregation Struggle,* 58-59.

159. Joel Williamson, *A Rage for Order: Black/White Race Relations in the American South since Emancipation* (New York: Oxford Univ. Press, 1986), 78 and passim.

160. For more White League activity in and around New Orleans, see Tunnell, *Crucible of Reconstruction,* esp. 2, 6, 7, and chapter 9.

161. Lawrence N. Powell, "The Battle of Canal Street: An Upper-Class Dream of Power and Preferment," unpublished paper in the possession of the author, 15. *The Slaughter-House Cases* 83 U.S. 36 (1873) and *United States v. Cruikshank* 92 U.S. 542 (1876) emerged out of other efforts to resist Republican authority and assert white supremacy.

162. For a brief recounting of the end of Reconstruction and a description of the Compromise of 1877, see Eric Foner, *A Short History of Reconstruction* (New York: Harper and Row, 1990), 238-253, and C. Vann Woodward, *Origins of the New South, 1877-1913* (1951; Baton Rouge: Louisiana State Univ. Press, 1997), 24-45. For details of the end of Reconstruction in Louisiana, see Joe Gray Taylor, *Louisiana Reconstructed, 1863-1877* (Baton Rouge: Louisiana State Univ. Press, 1974), and Tunnell, *Crucible of Reconstruction.*

163. William Ivy Hair, *Bourbonism and Agrarian Protest: Louisiana Politics, 1877-1900* (Baton Rouge: Louisiana State Univ. Press, 1969); Tunnel, *Crucible of Reconstruction*; Taylor, *Louisiana Reconstructed.*

164. See Somers, "Black and White in New Orleans," 19-42; Germaine A. Reed, "Race Legislation in Louisiana, 1864-1920," *Louisiana History* 6 (Fall 1965): 379-392.

165. B. Kroupa. *An Artist's Tour: Gleanings and Impressions of Travels in North and Central America and the Sandwich Islands* (London: Ward and Downey, 1890), Louisiana Collection, Descriptions file, Vertical Files, Howard-Tilton Library, Tulane University.

166. Trollope, *Domestic Manners of the Americans.*

167. See Arnold Hirsch on the politics of accommodation in New Orleans: "Strictly a Matter of Black and White," in *Creole New Orleans: Race and Americanization,* ed. Arnold R. Hirsch and Joseph Logsdon (Baton Rouge: Louisiana State Univ. Press, 1992), 262-321.

3. PUBLIC RIGHTS AND PUBLIC WOMEN

1. John Rodrigue, introduction to Henry Clay Warmoth, *War, Politics, and Reconstruction: Stormy Days in Louisiana,* ed. Rodrigue (Columbia: Univ. of South Carolina Press, 2006); Michael A. Ross, *Justice of Shattered Dreams: Samuel Freeman Miller and the Supreme Court during the Civil War Era* (Baton Rouge: Louisiana State Univ. Press, 2003), esp. chapter 8; Michael A. Ross, "Justice Miller's Reconstruction: The *Slaughter-House Cases,* Health

Codes, and Civil Rights in New Orleans, 1861–1873," *Journal of Southern History* 64, no. 4 (November 1998): 649–676; Joe Gray Taylor, *Louisiana Reconstructed, 1863–1877* (Baton Rouge: Louisiana State Univ. Press, 1974); Ted Tunnell, *Crucible of Reconstruction: War, Radicalism, and Race in Louisiana, 1862–1877* (Baton Rouge: Louisiana State Univ. Press, 1984).

2. For earlier concepts of New Orleans as disorderly, see Shannon Lee Dawdy, *Building the Devil's Empire: French Colonial New Orleans* (Chicago: Univ. of Chicago Press, 2008).

3. See Arnold Hirsch and Joseph Logsdon, preface to *Creole New Orleans: Race and Americanization,* ed. Arnold Hirsch and Joseph Logsdon (Baton Rouge: Louisiana State Univ. Press, 1992), ix–xiii.

4. Peirce F. Lewis, *New Orleans: The Making of an Urban Landscape,* 2nd ed. (Santa Fe, N.M.: Center for American Places, 2003), 50; Richard Campanella, *Geographies of New Orleans: Urban Fabrics Before the Storm* (Lafayette: Center for Louisiana Studies, University of Louisiana, Lafayette, 2006), 297–298 and passim.

5. For attempts to modernize New Orleans's infrastructure during Reconstruction, see Michael A. Ross, "Obstructing Reconstruction: John Archibald Campbell and the Legal Campaign Against Louisiana's Republican Government, 1868–1873," *Civil War History* 49, no. 3 (September 2003): 235–253, and Ross, "Justice Miller's Reconstruction."

6. The phrase "The Americanization of Black New Orleans" comes from Bell and Logsdon's essay of the same name in Hirsch and Logsdon, eds., *Creole New Orleans.* I have paraphrased to broaden the concept—whites in the city also "Americanized" their racial sensibilities as the nineteenth century gave way to the twentieth and racial identification took on a much greater significance.

7. Rebecca J. Scott, "Public Rights, Social Equality, and the Conceptual Roots of the *Plessy* Challenge," *Michigan Law Review* 106, no. 5 (March 2008): 777–804; Rebecca J. Scott, "The Atlantic World and the Road to *Plessy v. Ferguson," Journal of American History* 94, no. 3 (December 2007): 726–733.

8. Scott, "The Atlantic World and the Road to *Plessy v. Ferguson*"; Rebecca J. Scott, "Public Rights and Private Commerce: A Nineteenth-Century Atlantic Creole Itinerary," *Current Anthropology* 48, no. 2 (April 2007): 237–256.

9. Anthony J. Stanonis, *Creating the Big Easy: New Orleans and the Emergence of Modern Tourism, 1918–1945* (Athens: Univ. of Georgia Press, 2006); J. Mark Souther, *New Orleans on Parade: Tourism and the Transformation of the Crescent City* (Baton Rouge: Louisiana State Univ. Press, 2006).

10. Joseph Roach, *Cities of the Dead: Circum-Atlantic Performance* (New York: Columbia Univ. Press, 1996), 180.

11. Herbert A. Kellar, ed., "A Journey through the South in 1836: Diary of James D. Davidson," *Journal of Southern History* 1, no. 3 (August 1935): 345–377, 357.

12. Florence Roos Brink, "Literary Travellers in New Orleans between 1803 and 1860," *Louisiana Historical Quarterly* 31, no. 2 (April 1948): 394–422, 397. See also Frank De Caro, ed., *Louisiana Sojourns: Travelers' Tales and Literary Journeys* (Baton Rouge: Louisiana State Univ. Press, 1998).

13. Brink, "Literary Travellers," 398.

14. Edward Said, *Orientalism* (New York: Vintage Books, 1979), 177. See also David Spurr, *The Rhetoric of Empire: Colonial Discourse in Journalism, Travel Writing, and Imperial Administration* (Durham, N.C.: Duke Univ. Press, 1993).

15. George Wilson Pierson, *Tocqueville in America* (1938; Baltimore: Johns Hopkins Univ. Press, 1996), 620.

16. Kellar, ed., "Journey through the South," 357.

17. Loren Schweninger, "A Negro Sojourner in Antebellum New Orleans," *Louisiana History* 20 (Summer 1979): 305–314.

18. Matilda Charlotte (Jesse) Fraser Houstoun, *Texas and the Gulf of Mexico; or, Yachting in the New World* (1844; Austin, Tex.: W. Thomas Taylor, 1991), 49.

19. Ibid., 50.

20. Quote: Sir Charles Lyell, *A Second Visit to the United States of North America,* 2 vols. (New York: Harper and Brothers, 1850), 2:104; Albert Pickett, *Eight Days in New Orleans in February, 1847, by Albert J. Pickett, of Montgomery, Alabama,* 19–20, Beinecke Rare Book and Manuscript Library, Yale University, New Haven, Connecticut; A. Oakey Hall, *The Manhattaner in New Orleans; or, Phases of "Crescent City" Life* (New York: J. C. Morgan, 1851), Beinecke Rare Book and Manuscript Library, Yale University, New Haven, Connecticut. Hall was the mayor of New York from 1868 to 1872.

21. Karl Bernhard, Duke of Saxe-Weimar-Eisenach, *Travels through North America, during the Years 1825 and 1826,* 2 vols. (Philadelphia: Carey, Lea and Carey, 1828), 2:53–54, Beinecke Rare Book and Manuscript Library, Yale University, New Haven, Connecticut.

22. W. Bullock, *Sketch of a Journey through the Western States of North America, from New Orleans, by the Mississippi, Ohio, City of Cincinnati and Falls of Niagara, to New York, in 1827* (London: John Miller, 40, Pall Mall, 1827), 122, Beinecke Rare Book and Manuscript Library, Yale University, New Haven, Connecticut.

23. Ibid., 125.

24. Pickett, *Eight Days in New Orleans,* 19–20.

25. Joseph H. Ingraham, *The Sunny South; a Southerner at Home* (Philadelphia: G. G. Evans, 1860), 338.

26. Hall, *Manhattaner,* 23.

27. Albert Emile Fossier, *New Orleans: The Glamour Period, 1800–1840* (New Orleans: Pelican, 1957), 45. See also Harold Sinclair, *The Port of New Orleans* (Garden City, New York: Doubleday, Doran and Company, 1942).

28. Norman Walker, "Commercial and Mercantile Interests," in *Standard History of New Orleans, Louisiana,* ed. Henry Rightor (Chicago: Lewis Publishing Company, 1900), 538.

29. Justin Nystrom, *New Orleans after the Civil War: Race, Politics, and a New Birth of Freedom* (Baltimore: Johns Hopkins Univ. Press, 2010), 6–27.

30. Dennis Charles Rousey, *Policing the Southern City: New Orleans, 1805–1889* (Baton Rouge: Louisiana State Univ. Press, 1996); Campanella, *Geographies of New Orleans.*

31. Pickett, *Eight Days in New Orleans,* 18.

32. Bernhard, *Travels,* 84.

33. Bullock, *Sketch,* 124–125.

34. Hall, *Manhattaner,* 23–24.

35. Houstoun, *Texas and the Gulf of Mexico,* 51–52.

36. Reid Mitchell, *All on a Mardi Gras Day: Episodes in the History of New Orleans Carnival* (Cambridge, Mass.: Harvard Univ. Press, 1995), 17.

37. Bernhard, *Travels,* 84.

38. Kellar, ed., "Journey through the South," 358.

39. Bullock, *Sketch,* 124–125.

40. Sir Charles Lyell, quoted in Brink, "Literary Travellers," 409.

41. Lawrence N. Powell, *New Masters: Northern Planters during the Civil War and Reconstruction* (New Haven, Conn.: Yale Univ. Press, 1980).

42. Of course, the division is denominational as well: Catholic Creoles versus Protestant Anglos. The stereotypes there persist, too. See Max Weber, *The Protestant Ethic and the Spirit of Capitalism,* trans. Talcott Parsons (New York: Charles Scribner's Sons, 1958).

43. See Joseph G. Tregle Jr., "Creoles and Americans," in *Creole New Orleans: Race and Americanization,* ed. Arnold R. Hirsch and Joseph Logsdon (Baton Rouge: Louisiana State Univ. Press, 1992), 131–185; Mitchell, *All on a Mardi Gras Day,* 10–28, 51–81, and passim.

44. Pickett, *Eight Days in New Orleans,* 27.

45. Ibid., 19–20.

46. Ibid., 26–27.

47. Bullock, *Sketch,* 122.

48. Bernhard, *Travels,* 55.

49. Pickett, *Eight Days in New Orleans,* 27.

50. Kimberly S. Hanger, *Bounded Lives, Bounded Places: Free Black Society in Colonial New Orleans, 1769–1803* (Durham, N.C.: Duke Univ. Press, 1997), 53.

51. Quoted ibid., 53–54.

52. Ross, "Justice Miller's Reconstruction," 654. The quotation is from a doctor testifying in a postbellum case, but the situation of slaughtering animals had by then endured in the city for many decades. For more descriptive travel literature, see Shirley Elizabeth Thompson, "The Passing of a People: Creoles of Color in Mid-Nineteenth Century New Orleans" (Ph.D. diss., Harvard University, 2001), chapter 1.

53. Cf. Mark Twain, *Life on the Mississippi* (1883; New York: Penguin, 1984), 259. Audubon quoted in Ross, "Justice Miller's Reconstruction," 653.

54. Cf. Jean-Christophe Agnew, *Worlds Apart: The Market and the Theater in Anglo-American Thought, 1550–1750* (Cambridge, Eng.: Cambridge Univ. Press, 1986), and Saidiya Hartman, *Scenes of Subjection: Terror, Slavery, and Self-Making in Nineteenth-Century America* (New York: Oxford Univ. Press, 1997), chapter 1, "Innocent Amusements," 17–48 and passim.

55. Hall, *Manhattaner,* 6–7. My italics. Full stop added.

56. Cf. Walter Benjamin, *The Arcades Project,* trans. Howard Eiland and Kevin Mc-Claughlin (Cambridge, Mass.: Belknap Press, 1999). Also see Paul S. Landau, "An Amazing Distance: People and Pictures in Africa," introduction to *Images and Empires: Visuality in Colonial and Postcolonial Africa,* ed. Paul S. Landau and Deborah D. Kaspin (Berkeley: Univ. of California Press, 2002), 1–40, and Roach, *Cities of the Dead.* Ann Fabian writes similarly of the mythic west in her essay, "History for the Masses: Commercializing the Western Past,"

in *Under an Open Sky: Rethinking America's Western Past,* ed. William Cronon and George Miles (New York: Norton, 1993), 223–238.

57. Quoted in Brink, "Literary Travellers," 416. The "American Exchange" referred to the slave auction that took place in the hotel's rotunda.

58. Houstoun, *Texas and the Gulf,* 51, 157 (dome), 158 (first rate), 163 (rooms), and 164 (cuisine).

59. Lyell, *A Second Visit to the United States of North America,* 2:105.

60. Hall, *Manhattaner,* 15. Cf. Neil Harris, *Humbug: The Art of P. T. Barnum* (Chicago: Univ. of Chicago Press, 1973).

61. Hall, *Manhattaner,* 15.

62. Eliza Potter, *A Hairdresser's Experience in High Life* (1859; New York: Oxford Univ. Press, 1991), 179.

63. Ross, "Justice Miller's Reconstruction," 659.

64. Edward King, *The Great South: A Record of Journeys in Louisiana, Texas, the Indian Territory, Missouri, Arkansas, Mississippi . . .* (Hartford, Conn.: American Publishing Company, 1875), 17.

65. Henry Grady, "The New South," speech published in *Joel Chandler Harris' Life of Henry W. Grady, Including His Writings . . . ,* ed. Joel Chandler Harris (New York: Cassell Publishing Company, 1890), 83. See Paul M. Gaston, *The New South Creed: A Study in Southern Mythmaking* (Montgomery, Ala.: NewSouth Books, 2002).

66. Roach, *Cities of the Dead,* 180. This continues to be the trick—and the pattern—of New Orleans city boosters.

67. Hugh DeSantis, "The Democratization of Travel: The Travel Agent in American History," *Journal of American Culture* 1, no. 1 (Spring 1978): 9. See also Barbara Young Welke, *Recasting American Liberty: Gender, Race, Law, and the Railroad Revolution, 1865–1920* Cambridge, Eng.: Cambridge Univ. Press, 2001), who shows that with increased numbers of travelers, railroad travel remained hazardous.

68. Kevin Fox Gotham, *Authentic New Orleans: Tourism, Culture, and Race in the Big Easy* (New York: NYU Press, 2007), 73–74.

69. The City of New Orleans, *The Book of the Chamber of Commerce and Industry of Louisiana and Other Public Bodies of the "Crescent City"* (New Orleans: G. W. Engelhardt, 1894), 5.

70. *Guidebook for Strangers Visiting the Crescent City; Carnival, 1883* (New Orleans: F. F. Hansell, Stationer and Printer, 30 Camp St., 1883), 1.

71. Ibid.

72. See Alan Trachtenberg, *The Incorporation of America: Culture and Society in the Gilded Age* (New York: Hill and Wang, 1982), chapter 2, "Mechanization Takes Command," 38–69.

73. For the "unique panorama" New Orleans presented to tourists because of its Old World heritage, see Joy Jackson, *New Orleans in the Gilded Age: Politics and Urban Progress, 1880–1896* (Baton Rouge: Louisiana State Univ. Press, 1969), 9.

74. *"Eden." An Excursion from New Orleans to the Pacific by Rail through Texas and Mexico via the "Star & Crescent" and "Sunset" Route. Compliments of Passenger Department. T. W. Pierce, Jr. General Passenger Agent.* (T. W. Pierce, Jr., 1882), Beinecke Rare Book and Manuscript Library, Yale University, New Haven, Connecticut.

75. *The Picayune's Guide to New Orleans* (New Orleans: Picauyne, 1897), 3, 41, Louisiana and Special Collections, Howard-Tilton Library, Tulane University. This guide was revised and reprinted through the early 1900s.

76. Southern Railway Company, *New Orleans, City of Old Romance and New Opportunity* (New Orleans: Baurlein, 1927). Main Reading Room, Library of Congress, Washington, D.C.

77. *Winter in New Orleans* (Passenger Traffic Department, Southern Pacific-Sunset Route, New Orleans, Louisiana [1910]), 5, and next quote, 7, Beinecke Rare Book and Manuscript Library, Yale University, New Haven, Connecticut.

78. Ibid., 7.

79. Eric Arnesen, *Waterfront Workers in New Orleans: Race, Class, and Politics, 1863–1923* (Urbana: Univ. of Illinois Press, 1994), 75. For more on "the Ring," see George Reynolds, *Machine Politics in New Orleans, 1897–1926* (New York: AMS Press, 1936).

80. Jackson, *New Orleans in the Gilded Age,* chapters 6, 7, and 8 (pages 145–231).

81. John Smith Kendall, *History of New Orleans,* 3 vols. (Chicago: Lewis Publishing Company, 1922), 1:517, 520, and next paragraph, 525.

82. Raymond O. Nussbaum, "'The Ring is Smashed!': The New Orleans Municipal Election of 1896," *Louisiana History* 17, no. 3 (Summer 1976): 283–297. For profiles of the Citizens' League and the Old Regulars, their members and methods, see Edward F. Haas, *Political Leadership in a Southern City: New Orleans in the Progressive Era, 1896–1902* (Ruston, La.: McGinty Publications, 1988), and Reynolds, *Machine Politics in New Orleans.*

83. See the following chapter, in which I discuss the advertising strategies of the proprietors of Storyville's upper echelon bordellos and pleasure spots.

84. See also Alecia P. Long, *The Great Southern Babylon: Sex, Race, and Respectability in New Orleans, 1865–1920* (Baton Rouge: Louisiana State Univ. Press, 2004), chapter 3, "Where the Least Harm Can Result," 102–47.

85. *New Orleans Daily Picayune,* January 1, 1891.

86. Charles Bernheimer, *Figures of Ill Repute: Representing Prostitution in Nineteenth-Century France* (1989; Durham, N.C.: Duke Univ. Press, 1997), 31–32 and (second quote from Parent-Duchatelet) 16. See also Alain Corbin, *Women for Hire: Prostitution and Sexuality in France after 1850,* trans. Alan Sheridan (Cambridge, Mass.: Harvard Univ. Press, 1990).

87. Allan M. Brandt, *No Magic Bullet: A Social History of Venereal Disease in the United States since 1880* (New York: Oxford Univ. Press, 1987), 32; David J. Pivar, *The Purity Crusade: Sexual Morality and Social Control, 1868–1900* (Westport, Conn.: Greenwood Press, 1973); Neil Larry Shumsky, "Tacit Acceptance: Respectable Americans and Segregated Prostitution, 1870–1910," *Journal of Social History* 19, no. 4 (Summer 1986): 665–679. And see the introduction to the present work.

88. Tregle, "Creoles and Americans," 131–185; Powell, *New Masters*; Lawrence N. Powell, "The Battle of Canal Street: An Upper-Class Dream of Power and Preferment," unpublished paper in the possession of the author.

89. For Yankees who went South during the Civil War and Reconstruction hoping to make their fortunes as cotton planters, see Powell, *New Masters.*

90. Mary Douglas, *Purity and Danger: An Analysis of the Concepts of Pollution and Taboo* (1966; London: Routledge, 1996), quote from page 4.

91. *New Orleans Daily States,* June 25, 1890, page 4.

92. *New Orleans Daily Picayune,* June 19, 1890, page 4.

93. *New Orleans Daily States,* July 5, 1890, page 4.

94. Ibid.

95. *New Orleans Daily Picayune,* February 8, 1891.

96. Cf. Mikhail Bakhtin, *Rabelais and His World,* trans. Hélene Iswolsky (Bloomington: Indiana Univ. Press, 1984).

97. Scott, "Public Rights and Private Commerce"; Kirk Savage, *Standing Soldiers, Kneeling Slaves: Race, War, and Monument in Nineteenth-Century America* (Princeton, N.J.: Princeton Univ. Press, 1997). See also Warwick Anderson, "Excremental Colonialism: Public Health and the Poetics of Pollution," *Critical Inquiry* 21, no. 3 (Spring 1995): 640-669, 651-652.

98. Karen Leathem, "A Carnival According to Their Own Desires" (Ph.D. diss., University of North Carolina, Chapel Hill, 1995), 1-27. I note the ongoing debates about the constructed nature of tradition, premised on Terence Ranger and Eric Hobsbawm, *The Invention of Tradition* (London: Verso, 1985).

99. Mitchell, *All on a Mardi Gras Day,* especially chapters 4, 5, and 6 ("Rex," "Comus," "Northerners").

100. *New Orleans Daily Picayune,* February 8, 1891, and February 3, 1891.

101. Mitchell, *All on a Mardi Gras Day,* 96-101.

102. *New Orleans Daily Picayune,* February 8, 1891. My emphasis.

103. Arnesen, *Waterfront Workers in New Orleans,* 148-149, chapters 4 and 5; Dale Somers, "Black and White in New Orleans: A Study in Urban Race Relations, 1865-1900," *Journal of Southern History* 40, no. 1 (February 1974): 42; and William Ivy Hair, *Carnival of Fury: Robert Charles and the New Orleans Race Riot of 1900* (Baton Rouge: Louisiana State Univ. Press, 1976).

104. Letter to Mayor Capdeville re: Robert Charles, Capdeville Papers, City Archives, Louisiana Division, New Orleans Public Library. There is an alternative narrative that depicts Charles as a folk hero in song. See Jelly Roll Morton, *Jelly Roll Morton: The Complete Library of Congress Recordings by Alan Lomax* (Rounder Records, 2005), disc 2, track 3.

105. Peter Stallybrass and Allon White, *The Politics and Poetics of Transgression* (Ithaca, N.Y.: Cornell Univ. Press, 1986), especially chapter 3.

106. *New Orleans Daily Picayune,* January 1, 1898.

107. *New Orleans Daily States,* October 9, 1896, 6.

108. Long, *The Great Southern Babylon,* 83, 101, and passim.

109. Ibid., 65-66.

110. Arrest Books at the New Orleans Public Library for the years between 1890 and 1900 list "4434," the number of the ordinance creating the "new" limits of tacitly accepted prostitution, as the charge.

111. Rousey, *Policing the Southern City,* passim; New Orleans Federation of Clubs, Committee on Social Hygiene, "Segregation versus Morality" (New Orleans, [1900]), Acc. No. 78-890-RL, Williams Research Center, The Historic New Orleans Collection.

112. Isidore Dyer, Ph.B., M.D., "The Municipal Control of Prostitution in the United States" (Brussels: H. Lamertin, 1900), 18, Williams Research Center, The Historic New Or-

leans Collection, PAM HQ 121 N5, reprint of an article from the *New Orleans Medical and Surgical Journal* (December 1899), 18.

113. *New Orleans Item,* December 31, 1902.

114. *New Orleans Item,* December 30, 1902; *New Orleans Times-Democrat,* editorial reprinted in *New Orleans Item,* December 30, 1902, 2; and *New Orleans Item,* January 1, 1903.

115. *New Orleans Item,* January 12, 1903.

116. Ibid.

117. New Orleans Tax Assessment Records, 1895–1920, City Archives, Louisiana Division, New Orleans Public Library.

118. *New Orleans Item,* December 30, 1902, and December 31, 1902.

119. *L'Hote v. City of New Orleans,* 177 U.S. 587 (1900), 29.

120. Papers of Paul Capdeville, City Archives, Louisiana Division, New Orleans Public Library.

121. Letter, June 5, 1899, City Council Papers, City Archives, Louisiana Division, New Orleans Public Library.

122. City Council Papers, City Archives, Louisiana Division, New Orleans Public Library.

123. Letter, January 23, 1900, City Council Papers, City Archives, Louisiana Division, New Orleans Public Library.

124. Papers of Martin Behrman, City Archives, Louisiana Division, New Orleans Public Library.

125. Ibid.

126. *New Orleans Item,* December 30, 1902, and December 31, 1902.

127. *New Orleans Item,* January 14, 1903, and January 2, 1903.

128. *State of Louisiana vs. Mrs. D. Sanchez Relative to Operating a House of Assignation,* Criminal District Court, Docket No. 37,899, City Archives, Louisiana Collection, New Orleans Public Library.

129. Cf. Stallybrass and White, *The Politics and Poetics of Transgression*; Douglas, *Purity and Danger*; Anderson, "Excremental Colonialism." An 1857 article from the British medical journal *The Lancet* describes almost exactly this situation: "If he [the respectable Paterfamilias] look from his window he sees the pavement—his pavement—occupied by the flaunting daughters of sin, whose loud, ribald talk forces him to keep his casement closed." Quoted in Stallybrass and White, *The Politics and Poetics of Transgression,* 137.

130. *State of Louisiana vs. Mrs. D. Sanchez Relative to Operating a House of Assignation,* Criminal District Court, Docket No. 37,899, City Archives, Louisiana Collection, New Orleans Public Library.

131. See Anderson, "Excremental Colonialism."

132. *New Orleans Item,* January 14, 1903, and January 2, 1903.

4. WHERE THE LIGHT AND DARK FOLKS MEET

1. Joseph Roach, "Slave Spectacles and Tragic Octoroons: A Cultural Genealogy of Antebellum Performance," *Theatre Survey* 33, no. 2 (November 1992): 167–187, 173–174.

2. See, for example, Kristen L. Hoganson, *Fighting for American Manhood: How Gender Politics Provoked the Spanish-American and Philippine-American Wars* (New Haven, Conn.: Yale Univ. Press, 1998).

3. Victor Turner, *The Forest of Symbols: Aspects of Ndembu Ritual* (Ithaca, N.Y.: Cornell Univ. Press, 1967), chapter 4, "Betwixt and Between: The Liminal Period in *Rites de Passage*," 93–111 and passim.

4. Joseph Roach, *Cities of the Dead: Circum-Atlantic Performance* (New York: Columbia Univ. Press, 1996), 213.

5. Ibid.

6. Cf. Peggy Pascoe, *What Comes Naturally: Miscegenation Law and the Making of Race in America* (New York: Oxford Univ. Press, 2009). The history of miscegenation law shows that it was not only black male/white female relationships that troubled whites in turn-of-the-century America—and not only in the South.

7. The term miscegenation was coined during the Civil War. Anti-Lincoln propagandists claimed that Lincoln's desire to free the slaves was a plea for "social equality," meaning interracial marriage.

8. Acc. No. 1969.19.4, Williams Research Center, The Historic New Orleans Collection.

9. Pamela Arceneaux, "Storyville's Blue Books," *Historic New Orleans Collection Quarterly* 13, no. 1 (winter 1995): 8. See also Pamela Arceneaux, "Guidebooks to Sin: The Blue Books of Storyville," *Louisiana History* 28, no. 4 (Autumn 1987): 397–405. Union Station, on Rampart Street, built in 1892, and the Louisville & Nashville line station, at the foot of Canal Street, were supplemented in 1908 by the Southern Rail Terminal Station.

10. *The Lid,* Acc. No. 1969.19.1, n.p., n.d., Williams Research Center, The Historic New Orleans Collection.

11. *Hell-O,* Acc. No. 1969.19.2, n.p., n.d, Williams Research Center, The Historic New Orleans Collection.

12. Blue Book (1907), Acc. No. 1969.19.8, Williams Research Center, The Historic New Orleans Collection.

13. Blue Book (1915), Acc. No. 1969.19.12, Williams Research Center, The Historic New Orleans Collection. The 1910 edition may also be found at the Beinecke Rare Book and Manuscript Library, Yale University, New Haven, Connecticut. The 1915 edition may also be found at the City Archives, Louisiana Division, New Orleans Public Library, New Orleans, Louisiana.

14. Blue Book (1907), Acc. No. 1969.19.8, Williams Research Center, The Historic New Orleans Collection. A brace game is a gambling game designed to swindle the players.

15. Blue Book Acc. No. 1969.19.4. Williams Research Center, The Historic New Orleans Collection.

16. Blue Book (1907), Acc. No. 1969.19.8, Williams Research Center, The Historic New Orleans Collection.

17. Both ads from Blue Book, Acc. No. 1969.19.4, Williams Research Center, The Historic New Orleans Collection.

18. For an analysis of the commercial classes' attempts to penetrate high society at this time, see Lawrence W. Levine, *Highbrow, Lowbrow: The Emergence of Cultural Hierarchy in America* (Cambridge, Mass.: Harvard Univ. Press, 1988).

19. Blue Book, Acc. No. 1969.19.4, Williams Research Center, The Historic New Orleans Collection.

20. Ibid.

21. Ibid.

22. Blue Book, Acc. Nos. 1969.19.3, 1969.19.4, 1969.19.8, Williams Research Center, The Historic New Orleans Collection.

23. Blue Book (1898), Acc. No. 1969.19.4, Williams Research Center, The Historic New Orleans Collection.

24. This is not to say that segregation was enforced in the various dance halls; it is, rather, to point out precisely what Storyville promoted in its guidebooks.

25. See chapter 3.

26. Blue Book, Acc. No. 1969.19.8, Williams Research Center, The Historic New Orleans Collection.

27. Chad Heap, *Slumming: Sexual and Racial Encounters in American Nightlife, 1885–1940* (Chicago: Univ. of Chicago Press, 2009), introduction and passim; Kevin Mumford, *Interzones: Black/White Sex Districts in Chicago and New York in the Early Twentieth Century* (New York: Columbia Univ. Press, 1997), passim.

28. Compare Al Rose, *Storyville, New Orleans: Being an Authentic, Illustrated Account of the Notorious Red-Light District* (Tuscaloosa: Univ. of Alabama Press, 1974), 73. On sporting culture, see Elliott J. Gorn, *The Manly Art: Bare-Knuckle Prize Fighting in America* (Ithaca, N.Y.: Cornell Univ. Press, 1986). For the connection between aristocracy, status, and rituals of prowess, see Thorstein Veblen, *The Theory of the Leisure Class: An Economic Study of Institutions* (1899; New York: Modern Library, 2001).

29. Blue Book (1898), Acc. No. 1969.19.4, Williams Research Center, The Historic New Orleans Collection.

30. Nina Silber, *Romance of Reunion: Northerners and the South, 1865–1900* (Chapel Hill: Univ. of North Carolina Press, 1993), especially chapter 3, "Sick Yankees in Paradise," 66–92.

31. Levine, *Highbrow, Lowbrow*, 129–130.

32. Roach, *Cities of the Dead*, 199.

33. Albert J. Pickett, *Eight Days in New Orleans in February, 1847, by Albert J. Pickett, of Montgomery, Alabama*, 19–20, Beinecke Rare Book and Manuscript Library, Yale University, New Haven, Connecticut.

34. Blue Book (1898), Acc. No. 1969.19.4, Williams Research Center, The Historic New Orleans Collection.

35. Blue Books, Acc. Nos. 86-165-RL (Gipsy) and 1969.19.7 (Grace); Jean-Christophe Agnew, "The Consuming Vision of Henry James," in *The Culture of Consumption: Critical Essays in American History, 1880–1980*, ed. Richard Wightman Fox and T. J. Jackson Lears (New York: Pantheon, 1983), 65–100.

36. Walter Johnson, *Soul by Soul: Life inside the Antebellum Slave Market* (Cambridge, Mass.: Harvard Univ. Press, 1999), 17–18 and passim.

37. Roach, *Cities of the Dead*, chapter 5, "One Blood," 179–237, and passim.

38. Cf. Cynthia M. Blair, *I've Got to Make My Livin': Black Women's Sex Work in Turn-of-the-Century Chicago* (Chicago: Univ. of Chicago Press, 2010), introduction. The relation-

ships between slavery, wage labor, and prostitution are old and embattled; and, as the rhetoric of workers, abolitionists, purity crusaders, and others suggests, they exist more on a continuum than each in its own separate category. An apt example of these multiple, overlapping metaphors is the use of the term "white slavery" as a metaphor for wage labor and for prostitution at different times. Cf. Amy Dru Stanley, *From Bondage to Contract: Wage Labor, Marriage, and the Market in the Age of Slave Emancipation* (Cambridge, Eng.: Cambridge Univ. Press, 1998), and Laura Edwards, "The Politics of Marriage and Households in North Carolina during Reconstruction," in *Jumpin' Jim Crow: Southern Politics from Civil War to Civil Rights*, ed. Jane Dailey, Glenda Elizabeth Gilmore, and Bryant Simon (Princeton, N.J.: Princeton Univ. Press, 2000), 7–27.

39. Roach, *Cities of the Dead,* chapter 5, "One Blood," 179–237.

40. Blue Book (1898), Acc. No. 1969.19.4, Williams Research Center, The Historic New Orleans Collection. For "French" as a code for oral sex and other "unnatural practices," see Timothy J. Gilfoyle, *City of Eros: New York City, Prostitution, and the Commercialization of Sex, 1790–1920* (New York: Norton, 1992), chapter 8, "Bawdy Houses," 161–178.

41. Richard Symanski, *The Immoral Landscape: Female Prostitution in Western Societies* (Toronto: Butterworth, 1981), 142. Symanski writes that a cry of anti-Semitism ended the special "Jew" designation in the Blue Books. "No such sentiments," writes Symanski, "were expressed on behalf of the blacks."

42. Hereafter the quotation marks are assumed in the concept and dropped in the text.

43. Even the introductions to the Blue Books might be seen as mimicking the guides that accompanied world's fairs. See Cindy S. Aron, *Working at Play: A History of Vacations in the United States* (New York: Oxford Univ. Press, 1999), 152.

44. Aron, *Working at Play,* 152.

45. Blue Books, Acc. Nos. 1969.19.3-12, 77-370-RL, 77-2346-RL, 86-165-RL, and 94-092-RL, Williams Research Center, The Historic New Orleans Collection.

46. Blue Book, Acc. No. 1969.19.6, Williams Research Center, The Historic New Orleans Collection.

47. *The New Mahogany Hall,* Acc. No. 56-15, Williams Research Center, The Historic New Orleans Collection, and Beinecke Rare Book and Manuscript Library, Yale University, New Haven, Connecticut.

48. See Aron, *Working at Play*; John F. Kasson, *Amusing the Million: Coney Island at the Turn of the Century* (New York: Hill and Wang, 1978); David Nasaw, *Going Out: The Rise and Fall of Public Amusements* (Cambridge, Mass.: Harvard Univ. Press, 1993); Robert Rydell, *All the World's a Fair: Visions of Empire at American International Exhibitions, 1876–1916* (Chicago: Univ. of Chicago Press, 1984).

49. Blue Book, Acc. No. 1969.19.6, Williams Research Center, The Historic New Orleans Collection.

50. *New Orleans Sunday Sun,* "Carnival Edition," February 25, 1906.

51. Blue Book, Acc. No. 1969.19.10, Williams Research Center, The Historic New Orleans Collection.

52. Blue Book, Acc. No. 1969.19.7, Williams Research Center, The Historic New Orleans Collection.

53. Kim Townsend, *Manhood at Harvard: William James and Others* (Cambridge, Mass.: Harvard Univ. Press, 1998), 19.

54. Ibid. For some of the broad changes and transformations in America in these years, see also Herbert G. Gutman, *Work, Culture, and Society in Industrializing America* (New York: Vintage Books, 1977, especially the title essay; John F. Kasson, *Civilizing the Machine: Technology and Republican Values in America, 1877–1900* (New York: Penguin, 1977); James T. Kloppenberg, *Uncertain Victory: Social Democracy and Progressivism in European and American Thought, 1870–1920* (New York: Oxford Univ. Press, 1986); T. J. Jackson Lears, *No Place of Grace: Antimodernism and the Transformation of American Culture, 1880–1920* (Chicago: Univ. of Chicago Press, 1981); Nell Irvin Painter, *Standing at Armageddon, 1877–1917* (New York: Norton, 1987); Dorothy Ross, *The Origins of American Social Science* (Cambridge, Eng.: Cambridge Univ. Press, 1991); Kathryn Kish Sklar, *Florence Kelly and the Nation's Work: The Rise of Women's Political Culture, 1830–1900* (New Haven, Conn.: Yale Univ. Press, 1995); Robert H. Weibe, *The Search for Order, 1877–1920* (New York: Hill and Wang, 1967). See also Neil Parsons, *King Khama, Emperor Joe, and the Great White Queen: Great Britain through African Eyes* (Chicago: Univ. of Chicago Press, 1998).

55. For examples, see Philip S. Foner, *The Great Labor Uprising of 1877* (New York: Pathfinder, 1977); Elliott J. Gorn, *Mother Jones: The Most Dangerous Woman in America* (New York: Hill and Wang, 2001); Paul Krause, *The Battle for Homestead, 1880–1892: Politics, Culture, and Steel* (Pittsburgh: Univ. of Pittsburgh Press, 1992); David Montgomery, *Citizen Worker: The Experience of Workers in the United States with Democracy and the Free Market During the Nineteenth Century* (Cambridge, Eng.: Cambridge Univ. Press, 1993).

56. Rockefeller quoted in Alan Trachtenberg, *The Incorporation of America: Culture and Society in the Gilded Age* (New York: Hill and Wang, 1982), 84–85.

57. Richard Hofstadter, *Social Darwinism in American Thought* (1944; Boston, Mass.: Beacon Press, 1992), 57. See also, Robert C. Bannister, *Social Darwinism: Science and Myth in Anglo-American Social Thought* (Philadelphia: Temple Univ. Press, 1979); Carl N. Degler, *In Search of Human Nature: The Decline and Revival of Darwinism in American Social Thought* (New York: Oxford Univ. Press, 1991); Stanley, *From Bondage to Contract*.

58. Hofstadter, *Social Darwinism in American Thought*, 51–66 and passim; William Graham Sumner, *What Social Classes Owe to Each Other* (1883; New York: Harper and Brothers, 1920).

59. Cf. Bannister, *Social Darwinism*. Bannister argues that the battle *against* competition and material gain was more characteristic of dominant American attitudes than were Darwinian natural selection and Herbert Spenserian survival of the fittest.

60. Cynthia Russet, *Sexual Science: The Victorian Construction of Womanhood* (Cambridge, Mass.: Harvard Univ. Press, 1989), 14. Cf. Townsend, *Manhood at Harvard*, 195.

61. Ann Douglas, *The Feminization of American Culture* (New York: Knopf, 1977); George M. Fredrickson, *The Inner Civil War: Northern Intellectuals and the Crisis of the Union* (1965; Urbana: Univ. of Illinois Press, 1993); John Higham, "The Reorientation of American Culture," in *Writing American History* (Bloomington: Indiana Univ. Press, 1970); Hoganson, *Fighting for American Manhood;* Matthew Frye Jacobson, *Barbarian Virtues: The United States*

Encounters Foreign Peoples at Home and Abroad, 1876–1917 (New York: Hill and Wang, 2000); Russett, *Sexual Science*; Townsend, *Manhood at Harvard.*

62. Fredrickson, *The Inner Civil War,* especially chapter 12, "The Moral Equivalent of War," 217–237. The title comes from a 1906 essay by William James.

63. Townsend, *Manhood at Harvard,* 23.

64. See also Gorn, *The Manly Art.*

65. Higham, "Reorientation," passim.

66. Trachtenberg, *The Incorporation of America.*

67. Ibid., passim. See also Agnew, "The Consuming Vision of Henry James"; Ellen Gruber Garvey, *The Adman in the Parlor: Magazines and the Gendering of Consumer Culture, 1880s to 1910s* (New York: Oxford Univ. Press, 1996); William Leach, *Land of Desire: Merchants, Power, and the Rise of a New American Culture* (New York: Vintage Books, 1993); T. J. Jackson Lears, *Fables of Abundance: A Cultural History of Advertising in America* (New York: Basic Books, 1994); Lears, *No Place of Grace*; James Livingston, *Pragmatism and the Political Economy of Cultural Revolution, 1850–1940* (Chapel Hill: Univ. of North Carolina Press, 1994); Susan Strasser, *Satisfaction Guaranteed: The Making of the American Mass Market* (Washington, D.C.: Smithsonian Institution Press, 1989).

68. See Agnew, "The Consuming Vision of Henry James"; Jean-Christophe Agnew, *Worlds Apart: The Market and the Theater in Anglo-American Thought,1550–1750* (Cambridge, Eng.: Cambridge Univ. Press, 1986); Lears, *No Place of Grace.*

69. Trachtenberg, *The Incorporation of America,* 39.

70. Mark C. Carnes, *Secret Ritual and Manhood in Victorian America* (New Haven, Conn.: Yale Univ. Press, 1989), 1. Fifteen to forty percent of middle-class men belonged to such organizations.

71. Carnes, *Secret Ritual,* 14 and passim.

72. Susan Strasser, *Satisfaction Guaranteed*; Agnew, "Consuming Vision."

73. On changing patterns of work and leisure, see Daniel T. Rodgers, *The Work Ethic in Industrial America, 1850–1920* (Chicago: Univ. of Chicago Press, 1978).

74. Kathy Peiss, *Cheap Amusements: Working Women and Leisure in Turn-of-the-Century New York* (Philadelphia: Temple Univ. Press, 1986), 4.

75. Nasaw, *Going Out,* 4.

76. See Myra B. Young Armstead, *"Lord, Please Don't Take Me in August": African Americans in Newport and Saratoga Springs, 1870–1930* (Urbana: Univ. of Illinois Press, 1999); Aron, *Working at Play.*

77. See Turner, *The Forest of Symbols,* "Betwixt and Between."

78. Kasson, *Amusing the Million,* passim.

79. Rydell, *All the World's a Fair.* For the creation of hegemonic institutions and mystification, see also Trachtenberg, *The Incorporation of America,* especially chapter 7, "White City," 208–234. But also see James Gilbert, *Whose Fair: Experience, Memory, and the History of the Great St. Louis Exposition* (Chicago: Univ. of Chicago Press, 2009), for a nuanced counterargument about the distinctions between fair organizers' aims and fairgoer's experiences.

80. Cf. Pascoe, *What Comes Naturally*. Pascoe makes clear through her in-depth investigation into miscegenation law that it was not only black male-white female partnerships that troubled those concerned with white supremacy, but the very prospect of mixing itself, past, present, and future, that gave them pause and spurred legislation.

81. Nasaw, *Going Out*, 66, 67, 68.

82. Blue Book (1906), Acc. No. 1969.19.7, Williams Research Center, The Historic New Orleans Collection, and Beinecke Rare Book and Manuscript Library, Yale University, New Haven, Connecticut.

83. Nasaw is particularly illuminating on the meanings of the old plantation exhibitions. See *Going Out*, chapter 6, "The City as Playground: The World's Fair Midways," 62–79. See also Rydell, *All the World's a Fair*, chapter 3, "The New Orleans, Atlanta, and Nashville Expositions: New Markets, 'New Negroes,' and a New South," 72–104.

84. Rydell, *All the World's a Fair*, 73–75.

85. Nasaw, *Going Out*, 75–77, quote on page 75.

86. Ida B. Wells, *The Reason Why the Colored American Is Not in the World's Columbian Exposition: The Afro-American's Contribution to Colored Literature*, ed. Robert Rydell (1893; Urbana: Univ. of Illinois Press, 1999). See also Rydell, *All the World's a Fair*, and Nasaw, *Going Out*.

87. Trachtenberg, *The Incorporation of America*, 131.

88. That is, if they attended a world's fair before seeing the film *The Birth of the Nation*. I discuss the film in chapter 6, below.

89. See Donna Haraway, "Teddy Bear Patriarchy: Taxidermy in the Garden of Eden, New York City, 1908–1936," in *Cultures of United States Imperialism*, ed. Amy Kaplan and Donald E. Pease (Durham, N.C.: Duke Univ. Press, 1993), 237–291. See also Catherine Hodeir, "Decentering the Gaze at French Colonial Exhibitions," in *Images and Empires: Visuality in Colonial and Postcolonial Africa*, ed. Paul Landau and Deborah Kaspin (Berkeley: Univ. of California Press, 2002), 233–252.

90. Nasaw, *Going Out*, 74–75.

91. This is in stark contrast to the lyrics and rhythms of the music playing in the black dance halls of Storyville, where (a form of) black male sexual prowess was elaborated.

92. Eric Lott, *Love and Theft: Blackface Minstrelsy and the American Working Class* (New York: Oxford Univ. Press, 1993), 4. For the proliferation of "consumable" images of African Americans as subordinated symbols of white domesticity, see, for instance, M. M. Manring, *Slave in a Box: The Strange Career of Aunt Jemimah* (Charlottesville: Univ. Press of Virginia, 1998).

93. Sam Devincent Collection of Illustrated Sheet Music, Division of Cultural History, National Museum of American History, Smithsonian Institution, Washington, D.C.

94. Grace Elizabeth Hale, *Making Whiteness: The Culture of Segregation in the South, 1890–1940* (New York: Pantheon, 1998).

95. Ibid., 203.

96. Jacquelyn Dowd Hall, *Revolt Against Chivalry: Jesse Daniel Ames and the Women's Campaign Against Lynching*, rev. ed. (New York: Columbia Univ. Press, 1993). The more recent scholarship of Crystal Feimster, Amy Louise Wood, and Hannah Rosen, for example,

has further drawn out the links between the rhetoric of protection and how it differed for white and black women, the spectacular nature of lynching and its place in popular culture, and the sexual nature of racial violence. Crystal Nicole Feimster, *Southern Horrors: Women and the Politics of Rape and Lynching* (Cambridge, Mass.: Harvard Univ. Press, 2009); Hannah Rosen, *Terror in the Heart of Freedom: Citizenship, Sexual Violence, and the Meaning of Race in the Post-Emancipation South* (Chapel Hill: Univ. of North Carolina Press, 2009); Amy Louise Wood, *Lynching and Spectacle: Witnessing Racial Violence in America, 1890–1940* (Chapel Hill: Univ. of North Carolina Press, 2009).

97. Hannah Rosen, "'Not That Sort of Women': Race, Gender, and Sexual Violence during the Memphis Race Riot of 1866," in *Sex, Love, Race: Crossing Boundaries in North American History,* ed. Martha Hodes (New York: New York Univ. Press, 1999), 267–293. See also Glenda Gilmore, *Gender and Jim Crow: Women and the Politics of White Supremacy in North Carolina, 1896–1920* (Chapel Hill: Univ. of North Carolina Press, 1996), especially chapter 4, "Sex and Violence in Procrustes' Bed," on the 1898 Wilmington race riot, and William Ivy Hair, *Carnival of Fury: Robert Charles and the New Orleans Race Riot of 1900* (Baton Rouge: Louisiana State Univ. Press, 1976), on the Robert Charles riot in New Orleans.

98. For examples, see Gail Bederman, *Manliness and Civilization: A Cultural History of Gender and Race in the United States, 1880–1917* (Chicago: Univ. of Chicago Press, 1995); Gilmore, *Gender and Jim Crow*; Hoganson, *Fighting for American Manhood*; Amy Kaplan, *The Anarchy of Empire in the Making of U.S. Culture* (Cambridge, Mass.: Harvard Univ. Press, 2002); Silber, *The Romance of Reunion*; Laura Wexler, *Tender Violence: Domestic Visions in an Age of U.S. Imperialism* (Chapel Hill: Univ. of North Carolina Press, 2000).

99. See Richard Drinnon, *Facing West: The Metaphysics of Indian-Hating and Empire-Building* (1980; Norman: Univ. of Oklahoma Press, 1997), and Hoganson, *Fighting for American Manhood,* on the brutality of the war in the Philippines.

100. "Whiteness" was even used to articulate American superiority over Spain, which, for the purposes of propaganda, was portrayed as uncivilized and racially "other." See Michael Hunt, *Ideology and U.S. Foreign Policy* (New Haven, Conn.: Yale Univ. Press, 1987).

101. For a cultural historical analysis of the ways gender categories take on supposed racial attributes, and vice versa, see Bederman, *Manliness and Civilization.*

102. Rudyard Kipling, "The White Man's Burden," *McClure's* 12 (February 1899).

103. Amy Kaplan, "Black and Blue on San Juan Hill," in *Cultures of United States Imperialism,* ed. Amy Kaplan and Donald E. Pease (Durham, N.C.: Duke Univ. Press, 1993), 219–236. In *The Romance of Reunion,* Nina Silber also argues convincingly that the Spanish-American War helped to effect national reconciliation at least in part by restoring the southern white man's "manhood."

5. DIAMOND QUEEN

1. See chapters 3 and 4.

2. Julia Kristeva, *Powers of Horror: An Essay on Abjection,* trans. Leon S. Roudiez (New York: Columbia Univ. Press, 1982), 4.

3. For the uneven process of establishing Jim Crow generally in the South, see C. Vann Woodward, *The Strange Career of Jim Crow,* 3rd rev. ed. (New York: Oxford Univ. Press, 1974). For a different understanding of the effects of Jim Crow on black communities, especially in southern cities, see Howard N. Rabinowitz, *Race Relations in the Urban South, 1865–1890* (1978; Athens: Univ. of Georgia Press, 1996).

4. Warwick Anderson on Kristeva in "Excremental Colonialism: Public Health and the Poetics of Pollution," *Critical Inquiry* 21, no. 3 (Spring 1995): 640–669, 668 n. 89.

5. U.S. Bureau of the Census, *Ninth Census of the United States* (Washington, D.C., 1870). Lulu White is not mentioned in that census, but she was probably about two years old by then. Special thanks to Shelley Johnson Carey. Contrast to Al Rose, *Miss Lulu White de Basin Street, Nouvelle Orléans,* traduction par Henry Manicacci (Paris: Gaston Lachurie, 1991.) The translation is into *French*; there is no English version of this book.

6. The surviving fragments of the 1890 census do not include Louisiana.

7. U.S. Bureau of the Census, *Twelfth Census of the United States (Louisiana), Schedule 1 —Population* (Washington, D.C., 1900), Enumeration District 36, page 14.

8. Further lending credence to this birth date is her 1898 pamphlet *The New Mahogany Hall,* in which she claims to be thirty-one.

9. U.S. Bureau of the Census, *Thirteenth Census of the United States (Louisiana), Schedule 1 —Population* (Washington, D.C., 1910), Enumeration District 58, page 6.

10. U.S. Bureau of the Census, *Fourteenth Census of the United States (Louisiana), Schedule 1 —Population* (Washington, D.C., 1920), Enumeration District 36–62, page 33, and *Fifteenth Census of the United States (Louisiana), Schedule 1—Population* (Washington, D.C., 1930).

11. *Fourteenth and Fifteenth Censuses of the United States (Louisiana).*

12. See Martha Hodes, "Fractions and Fiction in the United States Census of 1890," in *Haunted by Empire: Geographies of Intimacy in North American History,* ed. Ann Laura Stoler (Durham, N.C.: Duke Univ. Press, 2006), 240–270.

13. Alecia P. Long, *The Great Southern Babylon: Sex, Race, and Respectability in New Orleans, 1865–1920* (Baton Rouge: Louisiana State Univ. Press, 2004), chapter 5, "As Rare as White Blackbirds," 191–224, on Willie Piazza's legacy. See also Succession of Mary A. Deubler [Josie Arlington], Docket No. 107,603, Civil District Court, Parish of Orleans, Division "C," and Docket No. 22,898 Supreme Court of Louisiana, Supreme Court of Louisiana Collection, Acc. No. 108, Department of Archives and Manuscripts, Earl K. Long Library, University of New Orleans. Soon after her death in 1914, Arlington's estate was the subject of a legal dispute between her long-time lover, who married Arlington's niece after her death, and thus inherited much of the property, and Arlington's brother, who claimed it rightfully belonged to him. For details of the dispute and of Arlington's life and legacy, see Long, *The Great Southern Babylon,* chapter 4, "Unusual Situations and Remarkable People," 148–190.

14. Affidavit, *State of Louisiana v. Lulu White,* Criminal District Court, Docket No. 58,107 (1931). On the affidavit, White's address is given as 312 North Franklin Street, with 1405 Bienville crossed out above it. Al Rose includes a photocopy of this affidavit in *Lulu White de Basin Street,* but the affidavit is missing from the Criminal District Court files. The case is listed in the Docket Books of the Criminal District Court, City Archives, Louisiana Division, New Orleans Public Library.

15. Death Certificate of Lulu White, shown to the author by Shelley Johnson Carey, who retains possession of it.

16. *Soards New Orleans City Directory* (New Orleans: L. Soards and Co., 1888) and Sanborn Fire Insurance Maps, City of New Orleans (Teaneck, N.J.: Chadwick-Healey, 1885–1893). In 1894 the city renumbered all the houses in New Orleans to ease delivery of mail, and White's first New Orleans address translates into 110 South Basin Street in the present system, just uptown of the Canal Street dividing line, between Canal and what was then Gasquet Street, and is now Tulane Avenue.

17. *Mascot,* May 21, 1892, excerpted in Al Rose, *Storyville, New Orleans: Being an Authentic, Illustrated Account of the Notorious Red-Light District* (Tuscaloosa: Univ. of Alabama Press, 1974), 30.

18. *Soard's New Orleans City Directory* (New Orleans: L. Soards and Co., 1890). The address in today's New Orleans in 930 Iberville, in the French Quarter between Burgundy and Dauphine streets.

19. Rose, *Storyville,* 100.

20. *Soard's New Orleans City Directory* (New Orleans: L. Soards and Co., 1891–1898). The directory listed White as "colored" throughout this period.

21. *Mascot,* January 20, 1894.

22. Helen Taylor, *Gender, Race, and Region in the Writings of Grace King, Ruth McEnery Stuart, and Kate Chopin* (Baton Rouge: Louisiana Univ. Press, 1989).

23. Robert Allen, *Horrible Prettiness: Burlesque and American Culture* (Chapel Hill: Univ. of North Carolina Press, 1991).

24. *Mascot,* January 20, 1894.

25. Ibid., December 15, 1894.

26. Virginia R. Dominguez, *White by Definition: Social Classification in Creole Louisiana* (1986; New Brunswick, N.J.: Rutgers Univ. Press, 1997). It was not until the 1880s and later that the term "creole," meaning native, was appropriated by white New Orleanians as a specific racial designation. See Charles Gayarré, "The Creoles of History and the Creoles of Romance: A Lecture Delivered in the Hall of the Tulane University, New Orleans, by the Hon. Charles Gayarré, on the 25th of April, 1885" (New Orleans, 1885), Rare Book Division, Library of Congress, and chapter 2 of the present work.

27. Stephan Palmié, *Wizards and Scientists: Explorations in Afro-Cuban Modernity and Tradition* (Durham, N.C.: Duke Univ. Press, 2002).

28. White was not the only woman of ambiguous race to have claimed the West Indies as her native land. See Walter Johnson, "The Slave Trader, the White Slave, and the Politics of Racial Determination in the 1850s," *Journal of American History* 87, no. 1 (June 2000): 13–38. Alexina Morrison's lawyers suggested that she might be from the West Indies as a way to indicate her "whiteness." See also Martha Hodes, "Fractions and Fictions in the United States Census of 1890"; John Robert Keeling III, "A Planter and the Courts in Antebellum Louisiana: The Cases of John F. Miller" (Ph.D. diss., University of Georgia, 2002), especially chapter 5, "Constructing Bridget Wilson," 192–249; Carol Wilson, "Sally Muller, the White Slave," *Louisiana History: The Journal of the Louisiana Historical Association* 40, no. 2 (Spring 1999): 133–153. Thanks to an anonymous reader at LSU Press for directing me to Bobby

Keeling's dissertation, and thanks to Bobby Keeling for helping to clear up a mystery regarding Sally Muller.

29. *Cambridge Dictionary of American English* (Cambridge, Eng.: Cambridge Univ. Press, 2000), for "hot regions."

30. The scope of literature on photography, erotica, pornography, gender inequity, exploitation, etc., is too great to include in this chapter, which is, after all, about an individual woman who had a personal relationship to all these things. But, some examples of the scholarship on Victorian erotics and/or photography include, Roland Barthes, *Image/Music/Text,* trans. Stephen Heath (New York: Hill and Wang, 1977); Peter Gay, *The Bourgeois Experience: Victoria to Freud,* 5 vols. (New York: Oxford Univ. Press, 1984–1998); Sander Gilman, *Difference and Pathology: Stereotypes of Sexuality, Race, and Madness* (Ithaca, N.Y.: Cornell Univ. Press, 1985); Thomas B. Hess and Linda Nochlin, eds., *Woman as Sex Object: Studies in Erotic Art* (London: Allen Lane, 1973); Lynn Hunt, ed., *The Invention of Pornography: Obscenity and the Origins of Modernity, 1500–1800* (New York: Zone Books, 1993); Thomas Walter Laqueur, *Making Sex: Body and Gender from the Greeks to Freud* (Cambridge, Mass.: Harvard Univ. Press, 1992); Steven Marcus, *The Other Victorians: A Study of Sexuality and Pornography in Mid-Nineteenth-Century England* (1966; New York: Basic Books, 1975); Gerald Needham, "Manet, Olympia, and Pornographic Photography," in *Woman as Sex Object: Studies in Erotic Art,* ed. Thomas B. Hess and Linda Nochlin (London: Allen Lane, 1973), 80–89; Paul Ryan, ed., *The Sins of Our Fathers: A Study in Victorian Pornography* (London: Erotic Print Society, 2000); Graham Ovenden and Peter Mendes, *Victorian Erotic Photography* (New York: St. Martin's Press, 1973); Erik Norgard, *With Love to You: A History of the Erotic Postcard* (New York: Crown Publishers, 1969); Carol Mavor, *Pleasures Taken: Performances of Sexuality and Loss in Victorian Photographs* (Durham, N.C.: Duke Univ. Press, 1995); Anne McClintock, *Imperial Leather: Race, Gender and Sexuality in the Colonial Contest* (London: Routledge, 1995); Linda Williams, *Hard Core: Power, Pleasure, and the "Frenzy of the Visible"* (Berkeley: Univ. of California Press, 1999); Deborah Willis, *The Black Female Body: A Photographic History* (Philadelphia: Temple Univ. Press, 2002).

31. This is, of course, controversial material. The degree of White's voluntariness is open to interpretation; there are degrees of coercion and one could argue that her life as a colored prostitute, model, and madam was determined by the conditions of the Jim Crow South. However, such an interpretation would obviate White's profound individuality, her strategic self-fashioning, and her wealth and influence in New Orleans. It would render her a one-dimensional character, where I am seeking to show her as a fully formed, unique, and complex individual. I am not suggesting that the pictures were not exploitative; certainly they were. I do suggest that White exploited herself—down to her "one drop" of "African blood"—for profit. I elaborate this interpretation throughout the chapter. Alecia Long, too, writes that Lulu White both created and controlled the eroticized image of the octoroon and made the pictures herself to profit from that image. She writes that White "eagerly and creatively marketed herself and her girls as sexual objects" (*The Great Southern Babylon,* 209).

32. Photographs of Lulu White, by anonymous photographer, 1892 (KI-DC: 2817, 70240, 70254, 70255, 70256, 70257, 70258, 70259, 70260, 70261, 70262, 70263), The Kinsey Institute

for Research in Sex, Gender, and Reproduction, Bloomington, Indiana. I am grateful to Catherine Johnson-Roehr at the Kinsey Institute for her help with these photographs.

33. Alain Corbin, *Women for Hire: Prostitution and Sexuality in France after 1850,* trans. Alan Sheridan (Cambridge, Mass.: Harvard Univ. Press, 1990), 124; Gay, *The Bourgeois Experience,* 2:353.

34. Johnson also continued these practices in Storyville. (Rose, *Storyville,* 50–52.)

35. Gay, *The Bourgeois Experience,* 2:353. See also Corbin, *Women for Hire,* 124.

36. See, for instance, Beth Bailey, *From Front Porch to Back Seat: Courtship in Twentieth-Century America* (Baltimore: Johns Hopkins Univ. Press, 1989); Elizabeth Alice Clement, *Love for Sale: Courting, Treating, and Prostitution in New York City, 1900–1945* (Chapel Hill: Univ. of North Carolina Press, 2006).

37. McClintock, *Imperial Leather,* 149.

38. These photographs are in the Josie Arlington Collection, Manuscripts and Rare Books Division, Louisiana Collections, Earl K. Long Library, University of New Orleans. I am grateful to John Kelly and Florence Jumonville at the Earl K. Long Library for their help with these photographs.

39. On the appropriation of "native" décor in bourgeois homes, see Nicolas Thomas, *Colonialism's Culture: Anthropology, Travel, and Government* (Princeton, N.J.: Princeton Univ. Press, 1994). See also Deborah Willis, *The Black Female Body,* 39.

40. Linda Williams, "'White Slavery' Versus the Ethnography of 'Sexworkers': Women in Stag Films at the Kinsey Archive," *Moving Image* 2, no. 2 (2005): 107–134.

41. George Chauncy, *Gay New York: Gender, Urban Culture, and the Making of the Gay Male World, 1890–1940* (New York: Basic Books, 1994), 78. Chauncy emphasizes that the sailor was an iconic figure in the "gay cultural imagination" as well as a major figure in the subculture. He also writes that "women and gay men alike" tried to seduce sailors, indicating that the sailor's iconic status was not limited to the gay subculture (figure 3.1, page 64).

42. Very few blacks participated, except as the service personnel or entertainment for the burgeoning white middle class. See Myra B. Young Armstead, *"Lord, Please Don't Take Me in August": African Americans in Newport and Saratoga Springs, 1870–1930* (Urbana: Univ. of Illinois Press, 1999).

43. Gay, *The Bourgeois Experience,* 2:329.

44. Michel Foucault, *The History of Sexuality,* vol. 1, *An Introduction,* trans. Robert Hurley (New York: Vintage Books, 1990), passim; Ann Laura Stoler, *Race and the Education of Desire: Foucault's* History of Sexuality *and the Colonial Order of Things* (Durham, N.C.: Duke Univ. Press, 1995), passim.

45. Foucault, *The History of Sexuality,* passim. See also Peter Stallybrass and Allon White, *The Politics and Poetics of Transgression* (Ithaca, N.Y.: Cornell Univ. Press, 1986), 137.

46. Lisa V. Sigel, "Filth in the Wrong People's Hands: Postcards and the Expansion of Pornography in Britain and the Atlantic World, 1880–1914," *Journal of Social History* 33, no. 4 (2000): 859–885, 859.

47. This was still months before the ordinance was to go into effect, and years before the injunction against opening the district, occasioned by L'Hote's lawsuit, was lifted. See chapter 1 of the present work.

48. The transaction took place on July 3, 1897, but the record shows that White began negotiating to buy the property as early as June 14. Act No. 17 under notary George W. Flynn, July 3, 1897, Research Center, New Orleans Notarial Archives, New Orleans (cited hereafter as NONA).

49. Plan #250, Survey by George De Armas, appended to Act of Sale from R. J. Moss to Third District Building Association under notary Fred Zenzel, July 28, 1893, NONA; Book 166, folio 752, Register of the Office of Conveyances, New Orleans (cited hereafter as Conveyance Office).

50. Notarial Act No. 17 under notary George W. Flynn, July 3, 1897, NONA.

51. Ibid.; Martin Behrman, *Martin Behrman of New Orleans: Memoirs of a City Boss,* ed. John R. Kemp (Baton Rouge: Louisiana State Univ. Press, 1977); Edward F. Haas, *Political Leadership in a Southern City: New Orleans in the Progressive Era, 1896–1902* (Ruston, La.: McGinty Publications, 1988), 20. Years later, at the height of her fame, she would hire Flynn as her attorney.

52. Conveyance Office Book 166, folio 752 (August 2, 1897), and Conveyance Office Book 169, folio 193 (December 14, 1897), Conveyance Office, and Notarial Act No. 9280 under notary J. D. Taylor, July 26, 1897, and Notarial Act no. 9437, December 13, 1897, Research Center, NONA. I owe a debt of gratitude to Sally Reeves, the head of the notarial archives. Her knowledge of New Orleans architecture and her special attention to my project helped me immeasurably.

53. *The New Mahogany Hall,* Acc. No. 56-15, Williams Research Center, The Historic New Orleans Collection, New Orleans, Louisiana, and also at the Beinecke Rare Book and Manuscript Library, Yale University, New Haven, Connecticut. For conditions of plumbing and poverty in much of the South in this period, see John Ettling, *The Germ of Laziness: Rockefeller Philanthropy and Public Health in the New South* (Cambridge, Mass.: Harvard Univ. Press, 1981).

54. *Lulu White vs. City of New Orleans, et al.,* Civil District Court for the Parish of Orleans, State of Louisiana, Division "E," Docket 5, no. 119,511, City Archives, Louisiana Division, New Orleans Public Library. This document describes Mahogany Hall as "a three-story stone and brick building," as opposed to the four stories she describes in her souvenir booklet.

55. *The New Mahogany Hall.*

56. Williams, *Hard Core.* Williams analyzes the "money shot" in early pornography, the clear purpose of the filmmaker's "exertions." See especially chapter 4, "Fetishism and Hard Core," 93–119.

57. ". . . blue eyes, which have justly gained for her the title of the 'Queen of the Demi-Monde,'" *The New Mahogany Hall.*

58. Joan Wallach Scott, "Gender: A Useful Category of Historical Analysis," *American Historical Review* 91, no. 5 (December 1986): 1053–1075, 1074.

59. See Joseph Roach, *Cities of the Dead: Circum-Atlantic Performance* (New York: Columbia Univ. Press, 1996); Joseph Roach, "Slave Spectacles and Tragic Octoroons: A Cultural Genealogy of Antebellum Performance," *Theatre Survey* 33, no. 2 (November 1992): 167–187; and chapter 2 of the present work.

60. *The New Mahogany Hall.*

61. *State of Louisiana v. Fred Miller and Felicia Carter,* Criminal District Court, Docket No. 36,996, City Archives, Louisiana Division, New Orleans Public Library, New Orleans, Louisiana (May 19, 1909).

62. *New Orleans Daily Picayune,* November 14–15, 1904; Russell Levy, "Of Bards and Bawds: New Orleans Sporting Life Before and During the Storyville Era, 1897–1917" (Master's thesis, Tulane University, 1967), 138–139.

63. *State of Louisiana ex rel. John Journee v. Board of Commissioners of the Police Department of the City of New Orleans,* Supreme Court of Louisiana, Docket No. 16,506, Supreme Court of Louisiana Collection, mss. 106, Department of Special Collections, Earl K. Long Library, University of New Orleans. Journée denied the charges brought against him for dereliction of duty and corruption, diagnosing the matter as a frame-up to put Whitaker in his job. He lost his case. See Levy, "Of Bards and Bawds," 121.

64. *Mascot,* May 21, 1892, printed in Rose, *Storyville,* 51.

65. Levy, "Of Bards and Bawds," 120, 121.

66. *State of Louisiana v. Edward Whitaker,* Criminal District Court, Docket nos. 38,837 (Eveline Navarre) (January 3, 1911); 38,228 (Mary Jacobs) (April 14, 1910); 38,829 (Lillian Miller—Carnal Knowledge) (November 23, 1910); 38,827 (Hazel Wagner) (March 13, 1911); 38,847 (Henrietta Hidden) (December 21, 1910).

67. *State of Louisiana v. Edward S. Whitaker,* Supreme Court of Louisiana, Docket No. 18,946, Supreme Court of Louisiana Collection, Department of Special Collections, Earl K. Long Library, University of New Orleans; *State v. Edward S. Whitaker,* Criminal District Court, Docket No. 38,813, City Archives, Louisiana Division, New Orleans Public Library, New Orleans, Louisiana.

68. These indictments are housed in the City Archives, Louisiana Division, New Orleans Public Library, New Orleans, Louisiana.

69. *State of Louisiana v. Lulu White,* Supreme Court of the State of Louisiana, Docket No. 15,896, Supreme Court of Louisiana Collection, Department of Special Collections, Earl K. Long Library, University of New Orleans.

70. *State of Louisiana v. Lulu White,* Supreme Court of the State of Louisiana, Docket No. 15,896, "Brief for the State," 2–3.

71. Blue Book, Acc. No. 1969.19.8, Williams Research Center, The Historic New Orleans Collection. Piazza certainly signaled the "mixed blood" of her octoroon with this statement, but it did signify that she sold beer rather than wine.

72. *State of Louisiana v. Lulu White,* Supreme Court of the State of Louisiana, Docket No. 15,896, page 32. In addition to White's testimony in this case, the jazz musicians who remembered Mahogany Hall remembered it as a place where champagne was served. See chapter 1 of the present work.

73. Louis Armstrong, *Satchmo: My Life in New Orleans* (1954; New York: Da Capo Press, 1968), 147.

74. *State of Louisiana v. Lulu White,* Supreme Court of the State of Louisiana, Docket No. 15,896, page 35.

75. Ibid., 35, 29.

76. Ibid., 29.

77. Ibid., p. 28.

78. Ibid., 35.

79. Ibid. In contrast, Luc Santé writes that 10 cents was steep for a bottle of beer at the same time in New York City's underworld. (Luc Santé, *Low Life: Lures and Snares of Old New York* (New York: Vintage Books, 1992).

80. *State of Louisiana v. Lulu White,* Supreme Court of the State of Louisiana, Docket No. 15,896, pages 47–49.

81. Ibid., 40–47.

82. Tax Assessment Records, City Archives, Louisiana Division, New Orleans Public Library.

83. *State of Louisiana v. Lulu White,* Supreme Court of the State of Louisiana, Docket No. 15,896, page 40. A recent *New York Times Magazine* article reminds us how expensive this was. In the article, the author remembers that in 1940, New York City's premier French restaurant, Le Pavillion, sold Chateaux Margeaux 1929 for $4.50 a bottle—a price then considered prohibitively expensive. (*New York Times Magazine,* Sunday, January 2, 2005.)

84. Clarence Williams, in *Hear Me Talkin' to Ya: The Story of Jazz by the Men Who Made It,* comp. Nat Shapiro and Nat Hentoff (1955; New York: Dover Publications, 1966), 11–13; Manuel Manetta, Oral History Collection, William Ranson Hogan Jazz Archive, Tulane University, New Orleans, Louisiana. See chapter 1 of the present work.

85. *State of Louisiana v. Lulu White,* Supreme Court of the State of Louisiana, Docket No. 15,896, page 38–40.

86. This was more than twice as much as in January, but still less than she spent on beer.

87. *State of Louisiana v. Lulu White,* Supreme Court of the State of Louisiana, Docket No. 15,896, page 38–40. Sales declined with Lent, and continued to fall as the weather grew warmer: White spent $223 on wine in March, $129 in April, and $64.50 in May. In June business rebounded—White paid Anderson $258 for eight cases of wine, all purchased on June 3, presumably to be stored at Anderson's until White ordered it and porters delivered it.

88. *State of Louisiana v. Lulu White,* Supreme Court of the State of Louisiana, Docket No. 15,896, page 28.

89. *New Orleans Item,* December 7, 1906.

90. On associations between prostitution, sex, and lower bodily functions generally, see Stallybrass and White, *The Politics and Poetics of Transgression,* passim. See also Warwick Anderson, "Excremental Colonialism," passim. See also Timothy J. Gilfoyle, *City of Eros: New York City, Prostitution, and the Commercialization of Sex, 1790–1920* (New York: Norton, 1992), especially chapter 4, "Brothel Riots and Broadway Pimps," 76–91.

91. *New Orleans Item,* November 30, 1906.

92. Ibid., December 7, 1906.

93. Ibid., December 24, 1906.

94. Ibid., December 22, 1906.

95. Ibid., December 22 and 24, 1906. It was said that Lulu White had herself been poisoned in an earlier round of "joking," but she denied this under oath.

96. *New Orleans Item,* December 22, 1906.

97. Ibid., December 22, 1906.

98. Ibid., December 22, 1906.

99. *New Orleans Times-Democrat,* January 18, 1913, 7. Thanks to Tad Jones for bringing this article to my attention.

100. *New Orleans Daily Picayune,* November 4, 1909.

101. Conveyance Office Book 249, folio 297, February 28, 1912, Conveyance Office. This saloon is the only extant Storyville structure. It is now a modest grocery store.

102. *New Orleans Daily Picayune,* November 14, 1904; *State of Louisiana v. Lulu White,* First City Criminal Court, Parish of Orleans, Docket No. 40,733, City Archives, Louisiana Division, New Orleans Public Library; *City of New Orleans (appellee) v. Lulu White (appellant),* Supreme Court of Louisiana, Docket No. 23,010, p. 18.

103. *New Orleans Daily Picayune,* November 14, 1904.

104. Ibid., November 15, 1904.

105. Levy, "Of Bards and Bawds," 138-139.

106. *New Orleans Daily Picayune,* September 10, 1911. According to Al Rose, White gave Killshaw $150,000 in 1907 to invest in Hollywood, thinking that she would like to try her hand at the movie business, and Killshaw disappeared with the money, double-crossing White and leaving her heartbroken. Rose's account is not to be believed—he provides neither evidence nor argument to support it. It is intriguing as part of the Lulu White myth in that it contains elements that are believable: White imagined herself a mogul of sorts and desired a much bigger stage on which to act out her own drama of life on the color line. There is some scant evidence that she may at one time have traveled to California.

107. *State of Louisiana vs. Lulu White,* First City Criminal Court, Docket No. 40,733.

108. Levy, "Of Bards and Bawds," 140.

109. *City of New Orleans (appellee) v. Lulu White (appellant),* Supreme Court of Louisiana, Docket No. 23,010.

110. In chapter 6, I will discuss the reform efforts that led to this ordinance. Also see Long, *The Great Southern Babylon,* chapter 5, "As Rare as White Blackbirds," 191-224.

111. Ordinance No. 4118, C.C.S., February 7, 1917.

112. Armstrong, *Satchmo.*

113. *Lulu White vs. City of New Orleans,* Civil District Court, Parish of Orleans, Docket 5, no. 119,511, Division "E," City Archives, Louisiana Division, New Orleans Public Library.

114. Civil Court Docket Books, City Archives, Louisiana Division, New Orleans Public Library.

115. *Agnes Morris* [or *Morrison?*] *v. City of New Orleans,* Civil District Court, Parish of Orleans, Docket 5, no. 120,693, Division "A," City Archives, Louisiana Division, New Orleans Public Library.

116. *Carrie Gross v. City of New Orleans,* Civil District Court, Parish of Orleans, Docket 5, no. 120,325, Division "D," Louisiana Division, New Orleans Public Library.

117. City Attorney Records (1917), City Archives, Louisiana Division, New Orleans Public Library.

118. In chapter 6, I will detail the arguments each side made.

119. *Lulu White v. City of New Orleans,* Civil District Court, Parish of Orleans, Docket 5, no. 119,511. The wording is awkward and ungrammatical, but the message is clear.

120. *Lulu White vs. City of New Orleans,* Civil District Court, Parish of Orleans, Docket 5, no. 119,511.

121. See Shirley Elizabeth Thompson, *Exiles at Home: The Struggle to Become American in Creole New Orleans* (Cambridge, Mass.: Harvard Univ. Press, 2009), for the interplay of claims of Native American and African ancestry among Creoles of color, especially chapter 1, "Seeking Shelter under White Skin," 24–66.

6. THE LAST STRONGHOLD OF THE OLD REGIME

1. Russell Levy, "Of Bards and Bawds: New Orleans Sporting Life Before and During the Storyville Era, 1897–1917" (Master's thesis, Tulane University, 1967), 46, Howard Tilton Memorial Library, Tulane University, New Orleans, Louisiana; Sanborn Fire Insurance Maps, City of New Orleans (Teaneck, N.J.: Chadwick-Healey, 1896), City Archives, Louisiana Division, New Orleans Public Library, New Orleans, Louisiana.

2. Recall that Journée's tenure as chief came to an end in 1905, when Whitaker was appointed.

3. *New Orleans Item,* quoted in Levy, "Of Bards and Bawds," 47; "Hush hush money," quoted in Levy, "Of Bards and Bawds," 48.

4. City Council Records (1899), City Archives, Louisiana Division, New Orleans Public Library.

5. Cf. Stephanie McCurry, "The Two Faces of Republicanism: Gender and Proslavery Politics in Antebellum South Carolina," *Journal of American History* 78, no. 4 (March 1992): 1245–1264; Stephanie McCurry, *Masters of Small Worlds: Yeoman Households, Gender Relations, and the Political Culture of the Antebellum South Carolina Low Country* (New York: Oxford Univ. Press, 1997). See also Pierre Nora, "Between History and Memory: Les Lieux de Mémoire," *Representations,* no. 26 (Spring 1989): 7–25.

6. *New Orleans Item,* June 15, 1902.

7. Ibid., November 23, 1902.

8. Ibid., November 16, 1902.

9. Ibid., June 15, 1902.

10. Ibid., November 23, 1902.

11. Ibid., November 16, 23, 1902.

12. Ibid., November 23, 1902.

13. Ibid., November 30, 1902, 1.

14. Ibid., November 1902, December 1902, January 1903.

15. Ibid., December 3, 1902. Dance halls in Storyville continued to operate until 1913, when a spectacular double murder spurred the city to close dance halls and institute new rules. (For details of this double murder, see Levy, "Of Bards and Bawds"; Alecia P. Long, *The Great Southern Babylon: Sex, Race, and Respectability in New Orleans, 1865–1920* [Baton Rouge: Louisiana State Univ. Press, 2004]; and Al Rose, *Storyville, New Orleans: Being an Authentic, Illustrated Account of the Notorious Red-Light District* [Tuscaloosa: Univ. of Alabama

Press, 1974].) After 1913, *contra* reform efforts, the dancing—and much prostitution—moved into the "Tango Belt," which was located along a string of blocks on Rampart Street, in the French Quarter.

16. See, for instance, Charles Hersch, *Subversive Sounds: Race and the Birth of Jazz in New Orleans* (Chicago: Univ. of Chicago Press, 2007); Bruce Boyd Raeburn, *New Orleans Style and the Writing of American Jazz History* (Ann Arbor: Univ. of Michigan Press, 2009); and J. Mark Souther, "Making the 'Birthplace of Jazz': Tourism and Musical Heritage Marketing in New Orleans," *Louisiana History* 44, no. 1 (winter 2003): 39–73.

17. Jelly Roll Morton, *Jelly Roll Morton: The Complete Library of Congress Recordings by Alan Lomax,* CD Set and Full Transcript (Rounder Records, 2005.) The published book, *Mr. Jelly Roll,* does not include the sexually explicit lyrics of many of the popular early jazz numbers. In fact, Lomax's editorial comment about one song, "Winding Boy Blues," is that "stanzas of this blues would burn the pages they were printed on," 48. The raunchy lyrics may serve to remind us that sexuality is capacious and multivalent. What people did for pleasure beyond the gaze of reformers—or anyone who might record their actions—cannot be neatly fit into categories; people acted out of a multiplicity of motives, desires, emotions, logics, etc., in ways that contested, and at times conformed to, cultural expectations. Those expectations were not on their minds when they sang and danced and drank and celebrated, and their thoughts and actions remain beyond the scope of our vision.

18. *New Orleans Daily Picayune,* December 21, 1907.

19. See the *New Orleans Item* and the *New Orleans Daily Picayune,* 1907–1908.

20. James B. Bennett, "Religion and the Rise of Jim Crow in New Orleans" (Ph.D. diss., Yale University, 1999); James B. Bennett, *Religion and the Rise of Jim Crow in New Orleans* (Princeton, N.J.: Princeton Univ. Press, 2005).

21. Act No. 176, House Bill No. 307, Substitute House Bill No. 95, by Mr. Shattuck.

22. These were like the so-called Raines Law hotels in New York City.

23. Karen Leathem, "Luring Young Girls to Their Ruin," unpublished paper prepared for the Louisiana Historical Association Meeting, March 14, 1997, in the possession of the author. See also Levy, "Of Bards and Bawds." Records of arrests are in the Docket Books and Arrest Index, City Archives, Louisiana Division, New Orleans Public Library.

24. Business Men's League Papers, Archives and Manuscripts, Earl K. Long Library, University of New Orleans.

25. Long, *The Great Southern Babylon,* 160.

26. The plans for the station began in 1903. This time line means that Burnham was working simultaneously on the New Orleans Terminal Station and Union Station, which was built from 1903–1908. Pamela Scott and Antoinette J. Lee, *Buildings of the District of Columbia* (New York: Oxford Univ. Press, 1993). See C. Vann Woodward, *Origins of the New South, 1877–1913* (1951; Baton Rouge: Louisiana State Univ. Press, 1997), especially chapter 11, "The Colonial Economy."

27. *New Orleans Daily Picayune,* May 31, 1908.

28. *New Orleans Times-Democrat,* June 1, 1908, quoted in Long, *The Great Southern Babylon,* 160.

29. Long, *The Great Southern Babylon,* 160.

30. New Orleans Travelers' Aid Society Papers, RG 365, Louisiana and Special Collections, Howard-Tilton Library, Tulane University, New Orleans, Louisiana.

31. Levy, "Of Bards and Bawds," 75.

32. *New Orleans Item,* February 14, 23, 1910, and March 22, 1910; Levy, "Of Bards and Bawds," 75.

33. *New Orleans Item,* August 12, 1908.

34. Levy, "Of Bards and Bawds," 75; *New Orleans Item,* February 14, 23, 1910, and March 22, 1910.

35. *New Orleans Item* February 2, 10, 15, 1910, quoted in Levy, "Of Bards and Bawds," 74; Long, *The Great Southern Babylon,* 211.

36. New Orleans Chamber of Commerce Records, MSS 66, Louisiana and Special Collections, Earl K. Long Library, University of New Orleans.

37. Docket Books, City Archives, Louisiana Division, New Orleans Public Library. For a compelling account of interracial mingling that did not include interracial sex, see Long, *The Great Southern Babylon,* 197. She describes the experience of an African American itinerant worker from Alabama who patronized Storyville's music clubs, particularly the "Pig Ankle."

38. *State of Louisiana v. Treadaway,* Louisiana Supreme Court, Docket No. 18,149 (April 1910), reported in 126 Louisiana Reports, 300–331, and 52 Southern Reporter, 500–512. All quotations below come from these reports.

39. See Judith Kelleher Schafer, *Slavery, the Civil Law, and the Supreme Court of Louisiana* (Baton Rouge: Louisiana State Univ. Press, 1994), chapter 7; Judith Kelleher Schafer, "Open and Notorious Concubinage: The Emancipation of Slave Mistresses by Will and the Supreme Court in Antebellum Louisiana," *Louisiana History* 28, no. 2 (Spring 1987): 165–182; see also chapter 1 of the present work.

40. *State of Louisiana v. Treadaway,* 126 Louisiana Reports, 300–331.

41. *State of Louisiana v. Treadaway,* 52 Southern Reporter, 510. My emphasis.

42. Virginia R. Dominguez, *White by Definition: Social Classification in Creole Louisiana* (1986; New Brunswick, N.J.: Rutgers Univ. Press, 1997), 33.

43. *New Orleans Item,* February 1, 1910, page 4.

44. Quoted in Rose, *Storyville,* 64.

45. Rose, *Storyville,* 64.

46. *New Orleans Item,* February 2, 10, 15, 1910, quoted in Levy, "Of Bards and Bawds," 74; Long, *The Great Southern Babylon,* 211. Emma Johnson was not "negro," or even "octoroon," but she did call herself "French." While there was at least one woman of color named Emma Johnson in Storyville, the Basin Street madam is consistently classified as "white" in the Blue Books. (Blue Books, Acc. Nos. 1969.19.1–1969.19.12, Williams Research Center, The Historic New Orleans Collection, New Orleans, Louisiana.)

47. Quoted in Rose, *Storyville,* 64.

48. See David Blight, *Race and Reunion: The Civil War in American Memory* (Cambridge, Mass.: Harvard Univ. Press, 2001); Gaines Foster, *Ghosts of the Confederacy: Defeat, the Lost Cause, and the Emergence of the New South* (New York: Oxford Univ. Press, 1987); Kirk Savage, *Standing Soldiers, Kneeling Slaves: Race, War, and Monument in Nineteenth-Century Amer-*

ica (Princeton, N.J.: Princeton Univ. Press, 1997); Kristin L. Hoganson, *Fighting for American Manhood: How Gender Politics Provoked the Spanish-American and Philippine-American Wars* (New Haven, Conn.: Yale Univ. Press, 1998); and Amy Kaplan, *The Anarchy of Empire in the Making of U.S. Culture* (Cambridge, Mass.: Harvard Univ. Press, 2002).

49. Glenda Gilmore, *Gender and Jim Crow: Women and the Politics of White Supremacy in North Carolina, 1896–1920* (Chapel Hill: Univ. of North Carolina Press, 1996), 71.

50. Michael Rogin is especially enlightening in his essay, "'The Sword Became a Flashing Vision': D. W. Griffith's *The Birth of a Nation,*" *Representations,* vol. 0, no. 9, Special issue: American Culture Between the Civil War and World War I (Winter 1985): 150–195; also reprinted in Robert Lang, ed., *The Birth of a Nation: D. W. Griffith, Director* (New Brunswick, N.J.: Rutgers Univ. Press, 1994), which contains other illuminating essays as well as contemporary reviews of the film. Also see John Hope Franklin, "*Birth of a Nation*—Propaganda as History," *Massachusetts Review* 20 (Autumn 1979): 417–434; Linda Williams, *Playing the Race Card: Melodramas of Black and White from Uncle Tom to O. J. Simpson* (Princeton, N.J.: Princeton Univ. Press, 2001), chapter 3 and passim; and Kaplan, *The Anarchy of Empire,* esp. chapter 5, "The Birth of an Empire." On Dixon's fear of miscegenation, see Cathy Boeckmann, *A Question of Character: Scientific Racism and the Genres of American Fiction, 1892–1912* (Tuscaloosa: Univ. of Alabama Press, 2000); Susan Gillman, *Blood Talk: American Race Melodrama and the Culture of the Occult* (Chicago: Univ. of Chicago Press, 2003); Gilmore, *Gender and Jim Crow,* 67–71; and Joel Williamson, *A Rage for Order: Black/White Relations in the American South since Emancipation* (New York: Oxford Univ. Press, 1986), 98–115. See also the essays in Michele K. Gillespie and Randal L. Hall, eds., *Thomas Dixon, Jr., and the Birth of Modern America* (Baton Rouge: Louisiana State Univ. Press, 2006).

51. Gillman, *Blood Talk;* Boeckmann, *A Question of Character;* Raymond Cook, *Fire from the Flint: The Amazing Careers of Thomas Dixon* (Winston-Salem, N.C.: John F. Blair, Publisher, 1968). For the intersection of *Birth of a Nation* with U.S. empire building and the Spanish-American War, see Kaplan, *The Anarchy of Empire.*

52. Friends of Stevens responded to these implications with plausible denials. See Charles I. Landis, *Thaddeus Stevens, a letter written to the* Daily New Era, *Lancaster, Pennsylvania, by the Honorable Charles I. Landis, President Judge of the Second Judicial District of Pennsylvania* (Lancaster, Pa.: Press of New Era Printing Company, 1916), Main Reading Room, Library of Congress, Washington, D.C.

53. *The Birth of a Nation,* shooting script, direction 133, reproduced in Lang, ed., *The Birth of a Nation,* 51.

54. Richard Schickel, *D. W. Griffith: An American Life* (New York: Limelight Editions, 1996), 268.

55. Rogin, "'The Sword Became a Flashing Vision,'" 152.

56. Franklin, "*Birth of a Nation*—Propaganda as History," 425; Schickel, *D. W. Griffith,* 269.

57. Wilson quoted in Franklin, "*Birth of a Nation*—Propaganda as History," 425; Schickel, *D. W. Griffith,* 270.

58. Joseph L. Morrison, *Josephus Daniels Says . . . : An Editor's Political Odyssey from Bryan to Wilson and FDR, 1894–1913* (Chapel Hill: Univ. of North Carolina Press, 1962); Woodward, *Origins of the New South,* 475.

59. Franklin, "*Birth of a Nation*—Propaganda as History," 425; Schickel, *D. W. Griffith,* 270.

60. Franklin, "*Birth of a Nation*—Propaganda as History," 425-426; Schickel, *D. W. Griffith,* 270-271.

61. *New Orleans Item,* March 24, 1916, page 15.

62. Ibid., March 25, 1916, page 15.

63. Ibid.

64. Woodward, *Origins of the New South,* 324.

65. Christopher Lasch, "The Anti-Imperialists, the Philippines, and the Inequality of Man," *Journal of Southern History* 25 (August 1958): 319-331. See also Hoganson, *Fighting for American Manhood,* especially chapters 6 and 7, on the links between race, gender, and empire-building, and Laura Wexler, *Tender Violence: Domestic Visions in an Age of U.S. Imperialism* (Chapel Hill: Univ. of North Carolina Press, 2000), chapter 7, "The Missing Link," 262-290, on the links between race, domesticity, and empire-building.

66. Woodward, *Origins of the New South,* chapter 12, "The Mississippi Plan as the American Way," 321-349. Matthew Jacobson elaborates the "racial" criteria for self-government and equal political participation in *Whiteness of a Different Color,* arguing that though whiteness was a necessary condition, it was not always deemed sufficient for American citizenship. Hence, "whiteness" was unified as defined against blacks, but fractured regarding the question of political rights and privileges. (*Whiteness of a Different Color: European Immigrants and the Alchemy of Race* [Cambridge, Mass.: Harvard Univ. Press, 1998]).

67. Morrison, *Josephus Daniels Says*; Woodward, *Origins of the New South,* chapter 17, "The Return of the South," 456-481. Woodward begins his discussion with Theodore Roosevelt's reaction to the "lily whites" of his party. Roosevelt made overtures to black leaders, including inviting Booker T. Washington to the White House. He was repudiated throughout the South as a traitor to his race. Then, when the next election cycle came, in 1904, Roosevelt's "wooing" of the South left southern blacks disillusioned.

68. Woodward, *Origins of the New South,* 478.

69. Quoted in Woodward, *Origins of the New South,* 480. It is worth noting the source Woodward quotes: Judson C. Welliver, "The Triumph of the South," *Munsey's Magazine* (New York), 49 (1913): 738, 740.

70. The NAACP did protest, but to no avail. See Franklin, "*Birth of a Nation*—Propaganda as History."

71. Carroll Smith-Rosenberg, *Disorderly Conduct: Visions of Gender in Victorian America* (New York: Oxford Univ. Press, 1985), "Bourgeois Discourse and the Progressive Era: An Introduction," 167-181.

72. Paul Boyer, *Urban Masses and Moral Order in America, 1820-1920* (Cambridge, Mass.: Harvard Univ. Press, 1978); George Frederickson, *The Inner Civil War: Northern Intellectuals and the Crisis of Union* (1965; Urbana: Univ. of Illinois Press, 1993). This is not to mention the economic "trust-busting" elements of progressivism, which also figured largely in the South. The movement is also to be distinguished from the political party which called itself Progressive.

73. Dewey Grantham, *Southern Progressivism: The Reconciliation of Progress and Tradition* (Knoxville: Univ. of Tennessee Press, 1983); Woodward, *Origins of the New South*, especially chapters 14 and 17.

74. For Gordon's involvement in the southern woman's suffrage movement, see Marjorie Spruill Wheeler, *New Women of the New South: The Leaders of the Woman Suffrage Movement in the Southern States* (New York: Oxford Univ. Press, 1993).

75. *Literary Digest*, March 24, 1917, 821.

76. Ibid.

77. Ibid. For more on the clean-up campaign, especially how it revolved around issues of race, see Long, *The Great Southern Babylon,* chapter 5, "As Rare as White Blackbirds," 190–224.

78. Long, *The Great Southern Babylon,* 191.

79. Roger L. Rice, "Residential Segregation by Law, 1910–1917," *Journal of Southern History* 34, no. 2 (May 1968): 179–199.

80. *City of New Orleans v. Piazza,* Supreme Court of Louisiana, Docket No. 22,624, Supreme Court of Louisiana Collection, Acc. No. 106, Department of Archives and Manuscripts, Earl K. Long Library, University of New Orleans. See also *City of New Orleans v. Sweetie Miller, et al.,* Supreme Court of Louisiana, Docket No. 22,625, Supreme Court of Louisiana Collections, Acc. No. 106, Department of Archives and Manuscripts, Earl K. Long Library, University of New Orleans.

81. *City of New Orleans v. Piazza,* Supreme Court of Louisiana, Docket No. 22,624.

82. Ibid.

83. In the next census, Willie Piazza's "race" was listed as "white." For an in-depth discussion of the case, see Long, *The Great Southern Babylon,* chapter 5, "As Rare as White Blackbirds."

84. *New Orleans Item,* July 10, 1917, clipping found in the War Department records, NARA, College Park.)

85. The phrase "internal domestic enemy" belongs to Ruth Rosen, *The Lost Sisterhood: Prostitution in America, 1900–1918* (Baltimore: Johns Hopkins Univ. Press, 1982), 1, 33.

86. Mary Spongberg, *Feminizing Venereal Disease: The Body of the Prostitute in Nineteenth-Century Medical Discourse* (New York: New York Univ. Press, 1997).

87. John D'Emilio and Estelle B. Freedman, *Intimate Matters: A History of Sexuality in America* (New York: Harper and Row, 1998), 173.

88. Nancy F. Cott, *The Grounding of Modern Feminism* (New Haven, Conn.: Yale Univ. Press, 1987); Cf. D'Emilio and Freedman, *Intimate Matters,* and William Leach, *True Love and Perfect Union: The Feminist Reform of Sex and Society* (Middletown, Conn.: Wesleyan Univ. Press, 1989).

89. Nancy F. Cott, *Public Vows: A History of Marriage and the Nation* (Cambridge, Mass.: Harvard Univ. Press, 2000), 160. See also Beth Bailey, *From Front Porch to Back Seat: Courtship in Twentieth-Century America* (Baltimore: Johns Hopkins Univ. Press, 1989), and Elizabeth Alice Clement, *Love for Sale: Courting, Treating, and Prostitution in New York City, 1900–1945* (Chapel Hill: Univ. of North Carolina Press, 2006).

90. For "passionlessness," see Nancy F. Cott, "Passionlessness: An Interpretation of Victorian Sexual Ideology, 1790–1850," *Signs* 4, no. 2 (Winter 1978): 219–236.

91. Cf. Michel Foucault, *The History of Sexuality,* vol. 1, *An Introduction,* trans. Robert Hurley (New York: Vintage Books, 1990).

92. Nancy Bristow, *Making Men Moral: Social Engineering During the Great War* (New York: New York Univ. Press, 1996).

93. For the activities of the CTCA, see Bristow, *Making Men Moral*; Allan M. Brandt, *No Magic Bullet: A Social History of Venereal Disease in the United States since 1880* (New York: Oxford Univ. Press, 1987), 52–95; and D'Emilio and Freedman, *Intimate Matters,* 211–214.

94. "Propaganda Posters for World War I," Division of Science and Technology, National Museum of American History, Smithsonian Institution, Washington, D.C.

95. *Keeping Fit to Fight* (New York: American Social Hygiene Association, 1918).

96. Kirk Savage, *Standing Soldiers, Kneeling Slaves.*

97. *Keeping Fit to Fight.*

98. Ibid. The tragic irony of this message might have become apparent in the 1918 influenza epidemic.

99. Gompers quoted in Brandt, *No Magic Bullet,* 67. Daniels delivered a lecture entitled "Men Must Live Straight if They Would Shoot Straight," in which he encouraged civilians to do their part to protect soldiers and sailors from "harpies of the underworld." Cited in Brandt, *No Magic Bullet,* 58–59. It is significant in this context that Gompers was an immigrant and labor leader and thus a step removed from the values of "civilized morality" represented by the middle class.

100. D'Emilio and Freedman, *Intimate Matters,* 211.

101. Quoted in Bristow, *Making Men Moral,* 135.

102. D'Emilio and Freedman, *Intimate Matters,* 212.

103. Bristow, *Making Men Moral,* 135. For no men being arrested, see D'Emilio and Freedman, *Intimate Matters,* 212.

104. *Keeping Fit to Fight,* emphasis in the original.

105. See Travelers' Aid Society Papers, RG 365, Louisiana and Special Collections, Howard-Tilton Library, Tulane University.

106. Brandt, *No Magic Bullet,* 67.

107. Daniels quoted ibid., 59.

108. Bristow, *Making Men Moral,* 137–178.

109. Quoted in Mark Thomas Connelly, *The Response to Prostitution in the Progressive Era* (Chapel Hill: Univ. of North Carolina Press, 1980), 147.

110. Thurman W. Reeves, *From the Scarlet Past of Fabulous New Orleans: Souvenir Edition of the World Famous Tenderloin Directory "The Blue Book" with a Brief Story of Storyville* (New Orleans: T. W. Reeves, 1951, n.p.), PAM HQ 146 .N4 .R4 1951, Williams Research Center, The Historic New Orleans Collection.

111. Ibid.

112. War Department records, NARA, College Park.

113. "Mayor Answers Tale of 'Troop Removal,'" *New Orleans Daily States,* July 11, 1917, page 1, clipping in War Department records, NARA, College Park.

114. War Department records, NARA, College Park.

115. Ibid.

116. Jean Gordon to Newton Baker, Secretary of War, New Orleans, La., August 22, 1917, NARA FILE doc 4659, War Department records, NARA, College Park.

117. National Municipal League, *National Municipal Review,* vol. 7 (Concord, N.H.: Rumford Press, 1918), 96.

118. Long, *The Great Southern Babylon,* 214–216.

119. Letter to Fosdick, in War Department records, NARA, College Park.

120. Rose, *Storyville,* 67–69 and Appendix H.

121. Letter to Fosdick, War Department records, NARA, College Park.

122. Ibid. It is worth noting that Shreveport had one of the South's largest red-light districts before World War I.

123. Letter to Margaret Ellis, forwarded to Fosdick, War Department records, NARA, College Park. Cf. Charles Van Onselen, *Studies in the Social and Economic History of the Witswatersrand, 1886–1914,* vol. 1, *New Babylon,* and vol. 2, *New Nineveh* (Johannesburg, South Africa: Ravan Press, 1982), especially chapters 2 and 3 of volume 1: "Randlords and Rotgut" and "On Prostitutes and Proletarians," on the interests of brewers in relation to prostitution and morality in Johannesburg at the same time.

124. Of course, tens of thousands perished from disease during the Civil War.

125. Quoted in Brandt, *No Magic Bullet,* 75.

126. Reports to the CTCA, War Department records, NARA, College Park.

127. Citizens' League report to Fosdick, October 27, 1917, War Department records, NARA, College Park.

128. Letter from Baker to Fosdick, War Department records, NARA, College Park.

129. Telegram from Railey to Fosdick, War Department records, NARA, College Park.

130. Telegram from Fosdick to Railey, War Department records, NARA, College Park.

131. Railey to Fosdick, War Department records, NARA, College Park.

132. Letter to Fosdick, War Department records, NARA, College Park.

133. *New Orleans Times-Picayune,* November 13, 1917. Dix hired the attorney Armand Romain to file an injunction against the closing of the district. Romain was a Creole of color who had been instrumental in the civil rights struggles of the 1890s in New Orleans. He also helped muster creole and black troops for the Spanish-American War and served as an officer in that conflict. Thanks to Rebecca J. Scott for pointing out this confluence.

134. Report, December 20, 1917, War Department records, NARA, College Park. This report was made after the district officially closed.

135. Report, December 20, 1917, War Department records, NARA, College Park.

136. Report, December 21, 1917, War Department records, NARA, College Park.

137. Ibid.

138. Newspaper ad for White's restaurant, December 1, 1917, clipping found in the War Department records, NARA, College Park, emphasis in original; testimony in *City of New Orleans (Appellee) v. Lulu White (Appellant),* Supreme Court of Louisiana, Docket No. 23,010, Supreme Court of Louisiana Collection, Acc. No. 106, Department of Archives and Manuscripts, Earl K. Long Library, University of New Orleans; *State of Louisiana v. Lulu White*

and Clyde Robinson, Criminal District Court, Docket No. 44,008, City Archives, Louisiana Division, New Orleans Public Library. In making the rounds of Storyville during the month after its closure, inspectors for the Citizens' League found that for $2 interested couples could engage a room at Lulu White's Hotel (formerly known as Mahogany Hall). "This place is patronized by women formerly living in the district," reads the report. (War Department records, NARA, College Park.)

139. White's testimony, *City of New Orleans v. Lulu White,* Docket No. 23,010, page 18. In this trial White gave her age as "going on 53." In 1918 that would make her birth date 1866 or possibly 1865, again confusing the record. See also 78 *Southern Reporter,* page 745, and 143 *Louisiana Reports,* page 487.

140. White's testimony, *City of New Orleans v. Lulu White,* Docket No. 23,010, page 18.

141. White's testimony, *City of New Orleans v. Lulu White,* Docket No. 23,010, page 21.

142. Special Agents' testimony from *City of New Orleans v. Lulu White,* Docket No. 23,010, page 7.

143. *City of New Orleans v. Lulu White,* Docket No. 23,010, page 7.

144. The charge was for a violation in May 1918.

145. *United States v. Lulu White, et al.,* U.S. District Court, Eastern Division of Louisiana, New Orleans District, Docket No. 4097, National Archives Records Administration, Fort Worth, Texas.

146. She was found guilty of running an immoral house within five miles of a government military post (*New Orleans States,* March 1, 1919). In some reports the distance was five miles, in others, ten. Sections 12 and 13 of the Draft Act provided that all brothels and saloons within five miles of military camps be declared illegal. The Act was later expanded to ten miles in some areas. To deal with Storyville specifically, the Act was expanded again to include naval training stations. See Brandt, *No Magic Bullet,* page 229 n 66, page 75.

147. *New Orleans States,* December 2, 1918. Thanks to Tad Jones for bringing to this article to my attention.

148. *United States v. Lulu White, et al.,* U.S. District Court, Eastern Division of Louisiana, New Orleans District, Docket No. 4097, National Archives Records Administration, Fort Worth, Texas, October 10, 1918.

149. *New Orleans States,* March 6, 1919. Thanks to Tad Jones for bringing to this article to my attention.

150. Application for Executive Clemency, Justice Department Records, Rec. 33, pages 616–1185, Record Group 204, Box 850, Series Title, "Pardon," National Archives Records Administration, College Park, Md. (hereafter cited as Justice Department Records, NARA, College Park).

151. There was a rule that sentences of one year did not allow for parole.

152. Application for Executive Clemency, Justice Department Records, NARA, College Park.

153. Ibid.

154. Ibid.

155. Ibid.

156. Ibid.; "Lulu White, Sentence Commutation 1919-08-23," Case File No. Record 33-616, Location RG 204, Box 850, "Pardon Case Files 1853–1946," microfiche at Law Division, Library of Congress, Washington, D.C.

157. Conveyance Office Book 315, folio 328, Conveyance Office Records.

158. *Soard's New Orleans City Directory* (New Orleans: L. Soards and Co., 1891–1898).

159. Letter, William Edler, Scientific Assistant, United States Public Health Service, September 4, 1920, in Application for Executive Clemency, Justice Department Records, NARA College Park.

160. Application for Executive Clemency, Justice Department Records, NARA College Park.

161. Ibid.

162. *State of Louisiana v. Lulu White and Clyde Robinson,* Criminal District Court, Docket No. 44,008, City Archives, Louisiana Division, New Orleans Public Library. There was no structure between Mahogany Hall, at 235 North Basin Street, and the corner saloon, at 1200 Bienville Street, and no building beyond the saloon on Basin, so this address is the corner saloon, which was later referred to as 241 Basin and 241 Saratoga.

163. *United States v. Lulu E. Hendley (Alias Lulu White) and Clyde Robinson,* U.S. District Court, Eastern Division of Louisiana, New Orleans Division, Docket No. 6011, filed October 25, 1922, National Archives Records Administration, Fort Worth, Texas.

164. *United States v. Lulu Hendley and Corrolanus Hopkins,* U.S. District Court, Eastern Division of Louisiana, New Orleans Division, Docket No. 7633, filed December 12, 1923, National Archives Records Administration, Fort Worth, Texas.

165. Robinson paid $100, and Hopkins $50. *United States v. Lulu E. Hendley and Corolanus Hopkins, and Clyde Robinson,* U.S. District Court, Eastern Division of Louisiana, New Orleans Division, Docket No. 8465, filed June 11, 1924, National Archives Records Administration, Fort Worth, Texas.

166. *United States vs. Lulu Hendley, alias Lulu White,* U.S. District Court, Eastern Division of Louisiana, New Orleans Division, Docket No. 13,432, May 7, 1929, National Archives Records Administration, Fort Worth, Texas. Witnesses called included three men residing at 241 North Basin Street and one woman at 1200 Bienville. Perhaps she did have lodgers.

167. Rose, *Storyville,* 98.

168. Conveyance Office Book 447, folio 368, April 8, 1929, and Conveyance Office Book 451, folio 446, July 15, 1929, Conveyance Office records.

169. This address for White also appears in the Conveyance Office records of White's sale of Mahogany Hall. See above.

170. Eleanor Early, *New Orleans Holiday* (New York: Rinehart, 1947), 242.

171. There was a small notice in the *Times-Picayune* that a "Lula White" had passed away in the early morning of August 20. And there is also a death certificate for a woman of that name from East Feliciana, a parish outside of the city, that matches the *Times-Picayune* notice. The East Feliciana woman was given as married to a Dr. White with children, and her race was listed as "white." Though a stunning coincidence, our Lulu White's death certificate clearly indicates that she died out of state. (*New Orleans Times-Picayune,* August 21,

1931; Lulu White's death certificate, shown to author by Shelley Johnson Carey, who has it in her possession.)

172. In truth, she had gone to be with relatives, but the notion of the tragic octoroon as always isolated and bereft of kin apparently persisted still.

173. Early, *New Orleans Holiday,* 242.

174. U.S. Bureau of the Census, *Fifteenth Census of the United States (Louisiana), Schedule 1 —Population* (Washington, D.C., 1930), Enumeration District 36–62, page 33.

175. For Piazza's legacy, see Long, *The Great Southern Babylon,* chapter 5, "As Rare as White Blackbirds."

176. Timothy J. Gilfoyle, *City of Eros: New York City, Prostitution, and the Commercialization of Sex, 1790–1920* (New York: Norton, 1992), 313–315.

CONCLUSION: FAREWELL TO STORYVILLE

1. Cf. David Oshinsky, *Worse than Slavery: Parchman Prison and the Ordeal of Jim Crow Justice* (New York: Free Press, 1997). Oshinsky, because he writes about the penal system, confronts and explicates the racial differential even among "dishonorable" or "dishonored" men and women and the cultural, legal, and linguistic elements that constructed that difference.

2. Cf. Cynthia M. Blair, *I've Got to Make My Livin': Black Women's Sex Work in Turn-of-the-Century Chicago* (Chicago: Univ. of Chicago Press, 2010); Alecia P. Long, *The Great Southern Babylon: Sex, Race, and Respectability in New Orleans, 1865–1920* (Baton Rouge: Louisiana State Univ. Press, 2004); and Victoria Widgeon Wolcott, *Remaking Respectability: African American Women in Interwar Detroit* (Chapel Hill: Univ. of North Carolina Press, 2001).

3. For the transformation of patriarchy, see the present work, and also see Pamela Haag, *Consent: Sexual Rights and the Transformation of American Liberalism* (Ithaca, N.Y.: Cornell Univ. Press, 1999); Carole Pateman, *The Sexual Contract* (Stanford, Calif.: Stanford Univ. Press, 1988); and Amy Dru Stanley, *From Bondage to Contract: Wage Labor, Marriage, and the Market in the Age of Slave Emancipation* (Cambridge, Eng.: Cambridge Univ. Press, 1998). For the construction of Civil War memory, see David Blight, *Race and Reunion: The Civil War in American Memory* (Cambridge, Mass.: Harvard Univ. Press, 2001); Gaines Foster, *Ghosts of the Confederacy: Defeat, the Lost Cause, and the Emergence of the New South* (New York: Oxford Univ. Press, 1987); and Kirk Savage, *Standing Soldiers, Kneeling Slaves: Race, War, and Monument in Nineteenth-Century America* (Princeton, N.J.: Princeton Univ. Press, 1997). For the image of the South in the northern construction of Civil War memory, see Nina Silber, *The Romance of Reunion: Northerners and the South, 1865–1900* (Chapel Hill: Univ. of North Carolina Press, 1993). For the reconstruction of patriarchy in the southern legal system after the Civil War, see Peter W. Bardaglio, *Reconstructing the Household: Families, Sex, and the Law in the Nineteenth-Century South* (Chapel Hill: Univ. of North Carolina Press, 1995). For the thoroughgoing cultural and economic transformation of the South after the war, see Edward Ayers, *The Promise of the New South: Life after Reconstruction* (New York: Oxford Univ. Press, 1992); C. Vann Woodward, *Origins of the New South, 1877–1913* (1951; Baton

Rouge: Louisiana State Univ. Press, 1997); Gavin Wright, *Old South, New South: Revolutions in the Southern Economy since the Civil War* (New York: Basic Books, 1986).

4. Joan M. Martin, "*Plaçage* and the Louisiana *Gens de Couleur Libre*: How Race and Sex Defined the Lifestyles of Free Women of Color," in *Creole: The History and Legacy of Louisiana's Free People of Color,* ed. Sybil Kein (Baton Rouge: Louisiana State Univ. Press, 2000), 57–70, 57.

5. "Visions of sexual desire" and "enslaved versions of mastery" are from Walter Johnson, "Masters and Slaves at the Market: Slavery and the New Orleans Trade, 1804–1864" (Ph.D. diss., Princeton University, 1995).

6. On category violations, see Mary Douglas, *Purity and Danger: An Analysis of the Concepts of Pollution and Taboo* (1966; London: Routledge, 1996), especially chapter 6, "Powers and Dangers," 95–114.

7. Alecia P. Long, "Poverty Is the New Prostitution: Race, Poverty, and Public Housing in Post-Katrina New Orleans," *Journal of American History* 94, no. 3 (December 2007): 795–803. As of April 2012, federal funds to redevelop the area had been approved. The plan is to create mixed-use housing and includes money to help current Iberville residents relocate. See: www.nola.com/politics/index.ssf/2012/04/iberville_housing_complex_rede.html.

8. J. Mark Souther, *New Orleans on Parade: Tourism and the Transformation of the Crescent City* (Baton Rouge: Louisiana State Univ. Press, 2006), 103.

9. Sherrie Tucker, "A Feminist Perspective on New Orleans Jazz Women" (New Orleans Jazz National Historic Park, National Park Service, New Orleans, Louisiana, 2004), unpublished study in the possession of the author.

10. Long, "Poverty Is the New Prostitution," 796.

BIBLIOGRAPHY

COURT CASES

United States Supreme Court

L'Hote v. City of New Orleans 177 U.S. 587 (1900).
Plessy v. Ferguson 163 U.S. 537 (1896).

Federal Court
(National Archives and Records Administration, Fort Worth, Texas)

United States v. Lulu E. Hendley (Alias Lulu White) and Clyde Robinson. U. S. District
  Court, Eastern Division of Louisiana, New Orleans Division, Docket No. 6011,
  October 25, 1922.
United States v. Lulu Hendley and Corrolanus Hopkins. U.S. District Court, Eastern Di-
  vision of Louisiana, New Orleans Division, Docket No. 7633, December 12, 1923.
United States v. Lulu E. Hendley and Corrolanus Hopkins, and Clyde Robinson. U.S.
  District Court, Eastern Division of Louisiana, New Orleans Division, Docket No.
  8465, June 11, 1924.
United States vs. Lulu Hendley, alias Lulu White, U.S. District Court, Eastern Division
  of Louisiana, New Orleans Division, Docket No. 13,432, May 7, 1929.
United States v. Lulu White. U.S. District Court, Eastern Division of Louisiana, New
  Orleans Division, Docket No. 4015, October 10, 1918.
United States v. Lulu White, et al. United States District Court, Eastern Division of
  Louisiana, New Orleans Division, Docket No. 4097.

Louisiana Supreme Court
(Department of Archives and Manuscripts, Earl K. Long Library,

University of New Orleans, New Orleans, Louisiana,
Supreme Court of Louisiana Collection [Acc. 106])

City of New Orleans (Appellee) v. Lulu White (Appellant), Docket No. 23,010.

City of New Orleans v. Piazza, Docket No. 22,624.

City of New Orleans v. Sweetie Miller et al, Docket No. 22,625.

Ex parte Homer A. Plessy, Docket No. 11,134 [Digested in 45 La. Ann. 80] (1892).

L'Hote v. City of New Orleans et al., Docket No. 12,753 [Digested in 51 La. Ann. 94] (1898).

State of Louisiana ex. rel. John Journee v. Board of Commissioners of the Police Department of the City of New Orleans. Supreme Court of Louisiana, Docket No. 16,506 (1907).

State of Louisiana v. Edward S. Whitaker, Docket No. 18,946.

State of Louisiana v. Lulu White, Docket No. 15,896.

State of Louisiana v. Treadaway, Docket No. 18,149 [Digested in 126 La. 300-331 and 52 So. 500-512] (April 1910).

Succession of Deubler, Mary A. [Josie Arlington], Docket No. 22,898 (1918).

New Orleans Civil District Court
(City Archives, Louisiana Division, New Orleans Public Library)

Agnes Morris [or *Morrison*?] *v. City of New Orleans,* Docket 5, no. 120,693 (1917).

Carrie Gross v. City of New Orleans, Docket 5, no. 120,325 (1917).

Freddie Crocket et al. v. City of New Orleans, Docket No. 18,051 [18,061] (1908).

George L'Hote v. City of New Orleans et al., Division B, Docket No. 54,533 (1897).

Lulu White v. City of New Orleans, Docket 5, no. 119,511.

Succession of Deubler, Mary A. [Josie Arlington], Division C, Docket No. 107,603 (1914).

New Orleans Criminal District Court
(City Archives, Louisiana Division, New Orleans Public Library)

City of New Orleans v. Freddie Crockett, Criminal District Court, Docket No. 33,816 (September 24, 1904).

City v. Freddie Crockett, Appeal, Criminal District Court, Docket No. 33,603.

City v. Freddie Crockett, et al., Criminal District Court, Docket No. 18,051 [18,061].

State of Louisiana v. Freddie Crockett, Criminal District Court, Docket No. 42,032 (October 16, 1913).

State of Louisiana v. Benjamin Connelly, Criminal District Court, Docket No. 23,708.

State of Louisiana v. Edward S. Whitaker, Criminal District Court, Docket No. 38,813.

State of Louisiana v. Edward Whitaker, Criminal District Court, Docket Nos. 38,837 (Eveline Navarre) (January 3, 1911); 38,228 (Mary Jacobs) (April 14, 1910); 38,829 (Lillian Miller—Carnal Knowledge) November 23, 1910; 38,827 (Hazel Wagner) (March 13, 1911); 38,847 (Henrietta Hidden) (December 21, 1910).

State of Louisiana v. Ernest Chapital, Criminal District Court, Docket No. 38,360.

State of Louisiana v. Fred Miller and Felicia Carter, Criminal District Court, Docket No. 36,996 (May 19, 1909).

State of Louisiana v. Hillary Waters, Criminal District Court, Docket No. 37,823.

State of Louisiana v. Leon Reed, Criminal District Court, Docket No. 38,460.

State of Louisiana v. Lulu White, Criminal District Court, Docket No. 40,733.

State of Louisiana v. Lulu White, Criminal District Court, Docket No. 58,107 (1931)

State of Louisiana v. Lulu White and Clyde Robinson, Criminal District Court, Docket No. 44,008.

State of Louisiana v. Mrs. D. Sanchez Relative to Operating a House of Assignation, Criminal District Court, Docket No. 37,899.

GOVERNMENT DOCUMENTS AND OFFICIAL RECORDS

Federal Records

Censuses

U.S. Bureau of the Census, *Ninth Census of the United States.* Washington, D.C., 1870.

U.S. Bureau of the Census. *Tenth Census of the United States (Alabama).* Washington, D.C., 1880.

U.S. Bureau of the Census. *Twelfth Census of the United States (Louisiana), Schedule 1— Population.* Washington, D.C., 1900.

U.S. Bureau of the Census. *Thirteenth Census of the United States (Louisiana), Schedule 1— Population.* Washington, D.C., 1910.

U.S. Bureau of the Census. *Fourteenth Census of the United States (Louisiana), Schedule 1— Population.* Washington, D.C., 1920.

U.S. Bureau of the Census. *Fifteenth Census of the United States (Alabama), Schedule 1—Population.* Washington, D.C., 1930.

Library of Congress, Washington, D.C.

"Lulu White, Sentence Commutation 191 9-08-23." Case File Record No. 33-616, Location RG 204, Box 850, "Pardon Case Files 1853–1946." Microfiche. In Law Division.

National Archives and Records Administration, College Park, Md.

Application for Executive Clemency. Rec. 33, p. 616–1185, Record Group 204, Box 850, Series Title, "Pardon." In Justice Department Records.

Records of the War Department General and Special Staffs, War College Division and War Plans Division, Subordinate Offices Education and Recreation Branch, Commission on Training Camp Activities, Entry 395, Reports Relating to Training Camp Activities, 1917, Record Group 165, Box 8, "Kentucky to Louisiana."

National Archives and Records Administration, Washington, D.C.

Letter, Record Group 85. Entry 9, Box 111, File 52484/7. In Immigration and Naturalization Services Records.

Municipal Records

New Orleans Records (at the New Orleans City Archives, Louisiana Division New Orleans Public Library)

Arrest Books.

Arrest Index.

Behrman, Martin. *Papers.*

Capdeville, Paul. *Papers.*

City Attorney Records.

Jewell, Edwin. *Jewell's Digest of the City Ordinances . . . of the City of New Orleans.* New Orleans, 1882, 1887.

Leovy, Henry J. and C. H. Luzenberg, [compilers], *The Laws and General Ordinances of the City of New Orleans, Together with the Acts of the Legislature, Decisions of the Supreme Court, and Constitutional Provisions, Relating to the City Government.* New Orleans, 1857.

New Orleans Board of Police Commissioners. *Annual Report of Board of Police Commissioners and the Superintendent of Police of the City of New Orleans, 1889–1915.*

New Orleans City Council Records.

Sanborn Fire Insurance Maps, City of New Orleans. Teaneck, N.J.: Chadwick-Healey, 1885–1893.

Soards New Orleans City Directory. New Orleans: L. Soards and Co., 1880–1931.

Tax Assessment Records (microfilm).

Orleans Parish Conveyance Records (at the Register of the Office of Conveyances, New Orleans, La.)

Book 166 folio 752

Book 169 folio 193

Book 249 folio 297

Book 447 folio 368

Book 451 folio 446

Notarial Acts (at the Research Center, New Orleans Notarial Archives, New Orleans, La.)

Notary Fred Zenzel, Plan no. 250, Survey by George De Armas, appended to Act of Sale from R. J. Moss to Third District Building Association, July 28, 1893.

Notary George W. Flynn, Act. no. 17, July 3, 1897.

Notary J. D. Taylor, Act. no. 9280, July 26, 1897, and Act. no. 9437, December 13, 1897.

MANUSCRIPTS AND SPECIAL COLLECTIONS

Beinecke Rare Book and Manuscript Library, Yale University,
New Haven, Conn.

Bernhard, Karl, Duke of Saxe-Weimar-Eisenach. *Travels through North America, during the Years 1825 and 1826,* 2 vols. Philadelphia: Carey, Lea and Carey, 1828.

Blue Books, 1906 and 1910.

Bullock, W. *Sketch of a Journey through the Western States of North America, from New Orleans, by the Mississippi, Ohio, City of Cincinnati and Falls of Niagara, to New York, in 1827.* London, 1827.

"Eden." An Excursion from New Orleans to the Pacific by Rail through Texas and Mexico via the "Star & Crescent" and "Sunset" Route. Compliments of Passenger Department. T.W. Pierce, Jr. General Passenger Agent. T. W. Pierce, Jr., 1882.

Hall, A. Oakey. *The Manhattaner in New Orleans; or, Phases of "Crescent City" Life.* New York, 1851.

Longfellow, Henry Wadsworth. "The Quadroon Girl." In Leed's Anti Slavery Series. *The New Mahogany Hall.*

Pickett, Albert. *Eight Days in New Orleans in February, 1847, by Albert J. Pickett, of Montgomery, Alabama.* Montgomery, Ala.: A. J. Pickett, 1847.

Winter in New Orleans. Passenger Traffic Department, Southern Pacific-Sunset Route, New Orleans, La. [1910].

Kinsey Institute for Research in Sex, Gender, and Reproduction,
Bloomington, Ind.

Anonymous photographer, Lulu White with dog, 1892, Acc. Nos. KI-DC 70240; 70254; 70255; 70256; 70257; 70258; 70259; 70260; 70261; 70262; and 70263. In Photograph Collection.

Earl K. Long Library, University of New Orleans,
New Orleans, La.

Josie Arlington Collection, MSS. 270. In Louisiana and Special Collections.

New Orleans Chamber of Commerce Records, MSS 66. In Louisiana and Special Collections.

National Museum of American History, Smithsonian Institution,
Washington, D.C.

Sam Devincent Collection of Illustrated Sheet Music. In Division of Cultural History.

Propaganda Posters. In Division of Science and Technology.

New Orleans City Archives, Louisiana Collection,
New Orleans Public Library, Rare Vertical File

Blue Book. 1915.

Tulane University, New Orleans, La.

Kroupa, B. *An Artist's Tour: Gleanings and Impressions of Travels in North and Central America and the Sandwich Islands.* London: Ward and Downey, 1890. Descriptions File, Vertical Files, Louisiana and Special Collections.

New Orleans Travelers' Aid Society Papers. RG 365. In Louisiana and Special Collections.

Recorded Oral History Interviews. In Hogan Jazz Archive.

Williams Research Center, Historic New Orleans Collection, New Orleans, La.

Blue Books. Acc. Nos. 1969.19.3–1969.19.12, 77-370-RL, 77-2346-RL, 85-517-RL, 86-165-RL, and 94-092-RL.

Dyer, Isidore, Ph.B., M.D. "The Municipal Control of Prostitution in the United States," (Brussels: H. Lamertin, 1900), 18. PAM HQ 121 N5. Reprint of an article from the *New Orleans Medical and Surgical Journal* (December 1899).

Hell-O. Acc. No. 1969.19.2.

The Lid. Acc. No. 1969.19.1.

The New Mahogany Hall. Acc. No. 56-15. This collection of Blue Books is now available on microfilm at the Williams Research Center and Yale University.

New Orleans Federation of Clubs, Committee on Social Hygiene. "Segregation versus Morality." Acc. no. 78-890-RL. [1900].

Reeves, Thurman W. *From the Scarlet Past of Fabulous New Orleans: Souvenir Edition of the World Famous Tenderloin Directory with a Brief Story of Storyville.* New Orleans: T.W. Reeves, 1951. PAM HQ 146 .N4 .R4 1951.

A Resident. "New Orleans As It Is: Its Manners and Customs—Morals—Fashionable Life—Profanation of the Sabbath—Prostitution—Licentiousness—Slave Markets and Slavery, &c. &c." Utica, N.Y.: Dewitt C. Grove, Printer, 1849.

NEWSPAPERS

New Orleans Daily Item (1900).
New Orleans Daily Picayune (1864–1908).
New Orleans Daily States (1891–1917).
New Orleans Mascot (1886–1892).
New Orleans Republican (1873).

New Orleans States (1920).
New Orleans Sunday States (1902).
New Orleans Sunday Sun (1889–1906).
New Orleans Times-Democrat (1890–1908).
New Orleans Times-Picayune (1917–2012).

PUBLISHED PRIMARY SOURCES

Armstrong, Louis. *Satchmo: My Life in New Orleans.* 1954. New York: Da Capo Press, 1968.

Behrman, Martin. *Martin Behrman of New Orleans: Memoirs of a City Boss.* Edited by John R. Kemp. Baton Rouge: Louisiana State Univ. Press, 1977.

Bell, Ernest A., ed. *Fighting the Traffic in Young Girls; or, War on the White Slave Trade.* G. S. Ball, 1910.

Boucicault, Dion. *The Octoroon; or, Life in Louisiana.* 1859. Miami, Fla.: Mnemosyne Publishing, 1969.

City of New Orleans. *The Book of the Chamber of Commerce and Industry of Louisiana and Other Public Bodies of the "Crescent City."* New Orleans: G. W. Engelhardt, 1894.

Early, Eleanor. *New Orleans Holiday.* New York: Rinehart, 1947.

Edholm, Charlton. *Traffic in Girls and Florence Crittenden Missions.* Chicago: Women's Temperance Publishing Association, 1893.

Fitzhugh, George. *Cannibals All! or, Slaves without Masters.* Edited by C. Vann Woodward. 1857. Cambridge, Mass.: Belknap Press of Harvard Univ. Press, 1960.

Gayarré, Charles Etienne. "The Creoles of History and the Creoles of Romance: A Lecture Delivered in the Hall of the Tulane University, New Orleans, by the Hon. Charles Gayarré, on the 25th of April, 1885." New Orleans, 1885.

———. *History of Louisiana.* 4 vols. New Orleans: Armand Hawkins, 1885.

Grady, Henry W. "The New South." Speech published in *Joel Chandler Harris' Life of Henry W. Grady, Including His Writings. . . .* Ed. Joel Chandler Harris. New York: Cassell Publishing Company, 1890.

Griffith, D. W. *Birth of a Nation.* 1915. (Film.)

Guidebook for Strangers Visiting the Crescent City; Carnival, 1883. New Orleans: F. F. Hansell, Stationer and Printer, 30 Camp St., 1883.

Houstoun, Matilda Charlotte (Jesse) Fraser. *Texas and the Gulf of Mexico; or, Yachting in the New World.* 1844. Austin, Tex.: W. Thomas Taylor, 1991.

Ingraham, Joseph H. *The Sunny South; a Southerner at Home.* Philadelphia: G. G. Evans, 1860.

Johnson, James Weldon. *The Autobiography of an Ex-Colored Man.* 1912. New York: Penguin, 1990.

Keeping Fit to Fight. New York: American Social Hygiene Association, 1918.

Kellar, Herbert A., ed. "A Journey through the South in 1836: Diary of James D. Davidson." *Journal of Southern History* 1, no. 3 (August 1935): 345–377.

King, Edward. *The Great South: A Record of Journeys in Louisiana, Texas, the Indian Territory, Missouri, Arkansas, Mississippi. . . .* Hartford, Conn.: American Publishing Company, 1875.

King, Grace. *New Orleans: The Place and the People.* New York: Macmillan, 1904.

Kipling, Rudyard. "The White Man's Burden." *McClure's Magazine* 12 (1899).

Landis, Charles I. *Thaddeus Stevens, a letter written to the* Daily New Era, *Lancaster, Pennsylvania, by the Honorable Charles I. Landis, President Judge of the Second Judicial District of Pennsylvania.* Lancaster, Pa.: Press of New Era Printing Company, 1916.

Law, E. Norine. *The Shame of a Great Nation: The Story of the "White Slave Trade."* Harrisburg, Pa.: United Evangelical Publishing House, 1909.

Lyell, Sir Charles. *A Second Visit to the United States of North America,* 2 vols. New York: Harper and Brothers, 1850.

Martineau, Harriet. *Society in America.* London: Saunders and Otley, Conduit Street, 1837. New York: Ams Press, 1966.

Mattison, H. *Louisa Picquet, the Octoroon; or, Views of Southern Domestic Life* (New York: H. Mattison, 1861). In *Collected Black Women's Narratives,* edited by Henry Louis Gates Jr. New York: Oxford Univ. Press, 1988.

Morton, Jelly Roll. *Jelly Roll Morton: The Complete Library of Congress Recordings by Alan Lomax.* Rounder Records, 2005.

National Municipal League. *National Municipal Review,* vol. 7. Concord, N.H.: Rumford Press, 1918.

New Orleans Chamber of Commerce. *Book of the Chamber of Commerce.* New Orleans, 1894.

Olmsted, Frederick Law. *The Cotton Kingdom, A Traveller's Observations on Cotton and Slavery in the American Slave States, 1853–1861.* Edited by Arthur M. Schlesinger. New York: Knopf, 1953. New York: Da Capo Press, 1996.

The Picayune's Guide to New Orleans. New Orleans: Picayune, 1897.

Pierson, G. W. "Alexis de Tocqueville in New Orleans, January 1–3, 1832." *Franco-American Review* 1, no. 1 (June 1936): 25–42.

Potter, Eliza. *A Hairdresser's Experience in High Life.* Cincinnati: Originally published for the author, 1859. New York: Oxford Univ. Press, 1991.

Ripley, Eliza. *Social Life in New Orleans, Being Recollections of My Girlhood.* New York: D. Appleton and Company, 1912.

Roe, Clifford A. *Panders and Their White Slaves.* Chicago: Fleming H. Revell, 1910.

Semper Idem (pseud.). *The "Blue Book," a Bibliographical Attempt to Describe the Guidebooks to the Houses of Ill-Fame as They Were Published There. Together with some pertinent and illuminating remarks pertaining to the establishments and courtesans as well as to harlotry in general in New Orleans.* Heartman's Historical Series, no. 50. [New Orleans?]: Privately printed, 1936.

Shapiro, Nat, and Nat Hentoff, comp. *Hear Me Talkin' to Ya: The Story of Jazz by the Men Who Made It.* New York: Rinehart, 1955. New York: Dover Publications, 1966.

Souchon, Edmund, "King Oliver: A Very Personal Memoir." *Jazz Review* 3, no. 4 (May 1960): 6–11.

Southern Railway Company. *New Orleans: City of Old Romance and New Opportunity.* New Orleans: Baurlein, 1927.

Stowe, Harriet Beecher. *Uncle Tom's Cabin; or, Life among the Lowly,* in *Harriet Beecher Stowe: Three Novels.* 1852. New York: Library of America, 1982.

Sumner, William Graham. *What Social Classes Owe to Each Other.* 1883. New York: Harper and Brothers, 1920.

Tinker, Edward Laroque. "Cable and the Creoles." *American Literature* 5, no. 4 (January 1934): 313–326.

Tourgée, Albion. *A Fool's Errand, by One of the Fools.* New York: Fords, Howard, and Hulbert, 1880.

Trollope, Frances Milton (Fanny). *Domestic Manners of the Americans.* Edited by Pamela Neville-Sington. 1832. London: Penguin, 1997.

Twain, Mark. *Life on the Mississippi.* 1883. New York: Penguin, 1984.

Warmoth, Henry Clay. *War, Politics, and Reconstruction: Stormy Days in Louisiana.* Edited by John Rodrigue. Columbia: Univ. of South Carolina Press, 2006.

Warner, Charles Dudley. *Studies in the South and West with Comments on Canada.* New York: Harper and Brothers, 1889.

Wells, Ida B. *The Reason Why the Colored American Is Not in the World's Columbian Exposition: The Afro-American's Contribution to Colored Literature.* Edited by Robert Rydell. 1893. Urbana: Univ. of Illinois Press, 1999.

Williams, Spencer. "Basin Street Blues." Edwin H. Morris and Co., 1926.

———. "Farewell to Storyville," featured in the film and on the soundtrack to *New Orleans.* Majestic Productions, 1947.

SECONDARY SOURCES

Books and Articles

Agnew, Jean-Christophe. "Capitalism, Culture and Catastrophe: Lawrence Levine and the Opening of Cultural History." *Journal of American History* (December 2006): 772–791.

———. "The Consuming Vision of Henry James." In *The Culture of Consumption,* edited by Richard Wightman Fox and T. J. Jackson Lears. New York: Pantheon, 1983.

———. *Worlds Apart: The Market and the Theater in Anglo-American Thought, 1550–1750.* Cambridge, Eng.: Cambridge Univ. Press, 1986.

Allain, Mathé. *Not Worth a Straw: French Colonial Policy and the Early Years of Louisiana.* Lafayette: Center for Louisiana Studies, University of Southwestern Louisiana, 1988.

Allen, Michael. *Western Rivermen, 1763–1861: Ohio and Mississippi Boatmen and the Myth of the Alligator Horse.* Baton Rouge: Louisiana State Univ. Press, 1990.

Allen, Robert C. *Horrible Prettiness: Burlesque and American Culture.* Chapel Hill: Univ. of North Carolina Press, 1991.

Allison, Anne. *Night Work: Sexuality, Pleasure, and Corporate Masculinity in a Tokyo Hostess Club.* Chicago: Univ. of Chicago Press, 1994.

Anderson, Warwick. "Excremental Colonialism: Public Health and the Poetics of Pollution." *Critical Inquiry* 21, no. 3 (Spring 1995): 640–699.

Applegate, Debby. *The Most Famous Man in America: The Biography of Henry Ward Beecher.* New York: Doubleday, 2006.

Arbery, Glenn Cannon. "Victims of Likeness: Quadroons and Octoroons in Southern Fiction." *Southern Review* 25, no. 1 (Winter 1989): 52–71.

Arceneaux, Pamela. "Guidebooks to Sin: The Blue Books of Storyville." *Louisiana History* 28, no. 4 (Autumn 1987): 397–405.

———. "Storyville's Blue Books." *Historic New Orleans Collection Quarterly* 13, no. 1 (Winter 1995): 8–9.

Armstead, Myra B. Young. *"Lord, Please Don't Take Me in August": African Americans in Newport and Saratoga Springs, 1870–1930.* Urbana: Univ. of Illinois Press, 1999.

Arnesan, Eric. *Waterfront Workers in New Orleans: Race, Class, and Politics, 1863–1923.* Urbana: Univ. of Illinois Press, 1994.

Aron, Cindy S. *Working at Play: A History of Vacations in the United States.* New York: Oxford Univ. Press, 1999.

Asbury, Herbert. *The French Quarter: An Informal History of the New Orleans Underworld.* New York: Garden City Publishing, 1936.

Aslakson, Kenneth. "The 'Quadroon-*Plaçage*' Myth of Antebellum New Orleans: Anglo-American (Mis)interpretations of a French-Caribbean Phenomenon." *Journal of Social History* 45, no. 3 (Spring 2012): 709–734.

Ayers, Edward. *The Promise of the New South: Life after Reconstruction.* New York: Oxford Univ. Press, 1992.

Bailey, Beth. *From Front Porch to Back Seat: Courtship in Twentieth-Century America.* Baltimore: Johns Hopkins Univ. Press, 1989.

Bakhtin, Mikhail. *Rabelais and His World.* Translated by Hélène Iswolsky. Bloomington: Indiana Univ. Press, 1984.

Bancroft, Frederic. *Slave Trading in the Old South.* Baltimore: J. H. Furst Company, 1931. Columbia: Univ. of South Carolina Press, 1996.

Bannister, Robert C. *Social Darwinism: Science and Myth in Anglo-American Social Thought*. Philadelphia: Temple Univ. Press, 1979.

Baptist, Edward. "'Cuffy,' 'Fancy Maids,' and 'One-Eyed Men': Rape, Commodification, and the Domestic Slave Trade in the United States." *American Historical Review* 106, no 5 (December 2001): 1619–1650.

Bardaglio, Peter W. "Rape and the Law in the Old South: 'Calculated to excite Indignation in every heart.'" *Journal of Southern History* 60, no. 4 (November 1994): 749–772.

———. *Reconstructing the Household: Families, Sex, and the Law in the Nineteenth-Century South*. Chapel Hill: Univ. of North Carolina Press, 1995.

———. "'Shameful Matches': The Regulation of Interracial Sex and Marriage in the South before 1900." In *Sex, Love, Race: Crossing Boundaries in North American History*, edited by Martha Hodes, 112–138. New York: New York Univ. Press, 1999.

Barthes, Roland. *Image/Music/Text*. Translated by Stephen Heath. New York: Hill and Wang, 1977.

Bederman, Gail. *Manliness and Civilization: A Cultural History of Gender and Race in the United States, 1880–1917*. Chicago: Univ. of Chicago Press, 1995.

Bell, Caryn Cossé. *Revolution, Romanticism, and the Afro-Creole Protest Tradition in Louisiana, 1718–1868*. Baton Rouge: Louisiana State Univ. Press, 1997.

Bell, Caryn Cossé, and Joseph Logsdon. "The Americanization of Black New Orleans." In *Creole New Orleans*, edited by Arnold R. Hirsch and Joseph Logsdon, 201–261. Baton Rouge: Louisiana State Univ. Press, 1992.

Benjamin, Walter. *The Arcades Project*. Translated by Howard Eiland and Kevin McClaughlin. Cambridge, Mass.: Belknap Press, 1999.

Bennett, James B. *Religion and the Rise of Jim Crow in New Orleans*. Princeton, N.J.: Princeton Univ. Press, 2005.

Berlin, Ira. *Slaves without Masters: The Free Negro in the Antebellum South*. New York: Pantheon, 1974.

Bernheimer, Charles. *Figures of Ill Repute: Representing Prostitution in Nineteenth-Century France*. 1989. Durham, N.C.: Duke Univ. Press, 1997.

Berry, Mary Frances. "Negro Troops in Blue and Gray: The Louisiana Native Guards, 1861–1863." *Louisiana History* 8, no. 2 (Spring 1967): 165–190.

Berzon, Judith. *Neither White nor Black: The Mulatto Character in American Fiction*. New York: New York Univ. Press, 1978.

Blair, Cynthia M. *I've Got to Make My Livin': Black Women's Sex Work in Turn-of-the-Century Chicago*. Chicago: Univ. of Chicago Press, 2010.

Blassingame, John. *Black New Orleans, 1860–1880*. Chicago: Univ. of Chicago Press, 1973.

Bleser, Carol, ed. *In Joy and in Sorrow: Women, the Family, and Marriage in the Victorian South*. New York: Oxford Univ. Press, 1991.

Blight, David. *Race and Reunion: The Civil War in American Memory.* Cambridge, Mass.: Harvard Univ. Press, 2001.

Blocker, Jack S., Jr. *American Temperance Movements: Cycles of Reform.* Boston: Twayne Publishers, 1989.

Boeckmann, Cathy. *A Question of Character: Scientific Racism and the Genres of American Fiction, 1892–1912.* Tuscaloosa: Univ. of Alabama Press, 2000.

Bordin, Ruth. *Woman and Temperance: The Quest for Power and Liberty, 1873–1900.* New Brunswick, N.J.: Rutgers Univ. Press, 1990.

Boyer, M. Christine. *City of Collective Memory: Its Historical Imagery and Architectural Entertainments.* Cambridge, Mass.: MIT Press, 1996.

Boyer, Paul. *Urban Masses and Moral Order in America, 1820–1920.* Cambridge, Mass.: Harvard Univ. Press, 1978.

Brandt, Allan M. *No Magic Bullet: A Social History of Venereal Disease in the United States since 1880.* New York: Oxford Univ. Press, 1987.

Brink, Florence Roos. "Literary Travellers in New Orleans between 1803 and 1860." *Louisiana Historical Quarterly* 31, no. 2 (April 1948): 394–422.

Bristow, Nancy. *Making Men Moral: Social Engineering during the Great War.* New York: New York Univ. Press, 1996.

Brooks-Higginbothom, Evelyn. *Righteous Discontent: The Women's Movement in the Black Baptist Church, 1880–1920.* Cambridge, Mass.: Harvard Univ. Press, 1993.

Bryan, Violet Harrington. *The Myth of New Orleans in Literature: Dialogues of Race and Gender.* Knoxville: Univ. of Tennessee Press, 1993.

Burnham, John C. "Medical Inspection of Prostitutes in America in the Nineteenth Century: The St. Louis Experiment and Its Sequel." *Bulletin of the History of Medicine* 45, no. 3. (May–June 1971): 203–218.

Bynum, Victoria. *Unruly Women: The Politics of Social and Sexual Control in the Old South.* Chapel Hill: Univ. of North Carolina Press, 1992.

Campanella, Richard. *Geographies of New Orleans: Urban Fabrics before the Storm.* Lafayette: Center for Louisiana Studies, University of Louisiana, Lafayette, 2006.

Carby, Hazel V. "Policing the Black Woman's Body in an Urban Context." *Critical Inquiry* (Summer 1992): 738–755.

———. *Reconstructing Womanood: The Emergence of the Afro-American Woman Novelist.* New York: Oxford Univ. Press, 1987.

Carew, Roy. "The New Orleans Legend." *Jazz Music: The International Jazz Magazine* 5, no. 6 (July–August 1954): 3–10, 23–24.

Carnes, Mark C. *Secret Ritual and Manhood in Victorian America.* New Haven, Conn.: Yale Univ. Press, 1989.

Carney, Court. *Cuttin' Up: How Early Jazz Got America's Ear.* Lawrence: Univ. of Kansas Press, 2009.

Carter, Hodding et al., eds. *The Past as Prelude: New Orleans, 1718–1968.* New Orleans: Tulane University, 1968.

Charters, Samuel Barclay. *Jazz: New Orleans, 1865–1963: An Index to the Negro Musicians of New Orleans*, rev. ed. New York: Oak Publications, 1963.

———. *A Trumpet around the Corner: The Story of New Orleans Jazz*. Jackson: Univ. Press of Mississippi, 2008.

Chase, John Churchill. *Frenchmen, Desire, Good Children, and Other Streets of New Orleans: A Delightful History of America's Most Romantic City*, 3rd ed. 1949. New York: Simon and Schuster, 1997.

Chauncy, George. *Gay New York: Gender, Urban Culture, and the Making of the Gay Male World, 1890–1940*. New York: Basic Books, 1994.

Cheung, Floyd D. "*Les Cenelles* and Quadroon Balls: 'Hidden Transcripts' of Resistance and Domination in New Orleans, 1803–1845." *Southern Literary Journal* 29, no. 2 (Spring 1997): 5–16.

Clark, Emily. "By All the Conduct of Their Lives: A Laywoman's Confraternity in New Orleans, 1730–1744." *William and Mary Quarterly*, 3rd ser., vol. 54, no. 4. (October, 1997): 769–794.

———. *Masterless Mistresses: New Orleans Ursulines and the Development of a New World Society, 1727–1834*. Chapel Hill: Univ. of North Carolina Press, 2007.

Clark, Emily, and Virginia Meacham Gould. "The Feminine Face of Afro-Catholicism in New Orleans, 1727–1852." *William and Mary Quarterly* 59, no. 2 (April 2002): 409–445.

Clement, Elizabeth Alice. *Love for Sale: Courting, Treating, and Prostitution in New York City, 1900–1945*. Chapel Hill: Univ. of North Carolina Press, 2006.

Clinton, Catherine. "'Public Women' and Sexual Politics during the American Civil War." In *Battle Scars: Gender and Sexuality in the American Civil War*, edited by Catherine Clinton and Nina Silber, 61–77. New York: Oxford Univ. Press, 2006.

———. "Southern Dishonor: Flesh, Blood, Race, and Bondage." In *In Joy and in Sorrow: Women, the Family, and Marriage in the Victorian South*, edited by Carol Bleser, 52–68. New York: Oxford Univ. Press, 1991.

Connelly, Mark Thomas. *The Response to Prostitution in the Progressive Era*. Chapel Hill: Univ. of North Carolina Press, 1980.

Cook, Raymond. *Fire from the Flint: The Amazing Careers of Thomas Dixon*. Winston-Salem, N.C.: John F. Blair, Publisher, 1968.

Cooper, Frederick, and Ann Laura Stoler, eds. *Tensions of Empire: Colonial Cultures in a Bourgeois World*. Berkeley: Univ. of California Press, 1997.

Corbin, Alain. *Women for Hire: Prostitution and Sexuality in France after 1850*. Translated by Alan Sheridan. Cambridge, Mass.: Harvard Univ. Press, 1990.

Cott, Nancy F. *The Bonds of Womanhood: "Woman's Sphere" in New England, 1780–1835*, 2nd ed. 1977. New Haven, Conn.: Yale Univ. Press, 1997.

———. *The Grounding of Modern Feminism*. New Haven, Conn.: Yale Univ. Press, 1987.

———. "Passionlessness: An Interpretation of Victorian Sexual Ideology, 1790–1850." *Signs* 4, no. 2 (Winter 1978): 219–236.

———. *Public Vows: A History of Marriage and the Nation.* Cambridge, Mass.: Harvard Univ. Press, 2000.

Davis, F. James. *Who Is Black: One Nation's Definition.* University Park, Pa.: Pennsylvania State Univ. Press, 1991.

Dawdy, Shannon Lee. *Building the Devil's Empire: French Colonial New Orleans.* Chicago: Univ. of Chicago Press, 2008.

De Caro, Frank, ed. *Louisiana Sojourns: Travelers' Tales and Literary Journeys.* Baton Rouge: Louisiana State Univ. Press, 1998.

Degler, Carl N. *In Search of Human Nature: The Decline and Revival of Darwinism in American Social Thought.* New York: Oxford Univ. Press, 1991.

D'Emilio, John, and Estelle B. Freedman. *Intimate Matters: A History of Sexuality in America.* New York: Harper and Row, 1998.

DeSantis, Hugh. "The Democratization of Travel: The Travel Agent in American History." *Journal of American Culture* 1, no. 1 (Spring 1978): 1–17.

Desdunes, Rodolphe. *Our People and Our History.* Baton Rouge: Louisiana State Univ. Press, 1973.

Dominguez, Virginia R. *White by Definition: Social Classification in Creole Louisiana.* 1986. New Brunswick, N.J.: Rutgers Univ. Press, 1997.

Douglas, Ann. *The Feminization of American Culture.* New York: Knopf, 1977.

Douglas, Mary. *Purity and Danger: An Analysis of the Concepts of Pollution and Taboo.* 1966. London: Routledge, 1996.

Drinnon, Richard. *Facing West: The Metaphysics of Indian-Hating and Empire-Building.* 1980. Norman: Univ. of Oklahoma Press, 1997.

Eder, Donald Gray. "Time under the Southern Cross: The Tannenbaum Thesis Reappraised." *Agricultural History* 50, no. 4 (October 1976): 600–614.

Edwards, Elizabeth, ed. *Anthropology and Photography.* New Haven, Conn.: Yale Univ. Press, 1992.

Edwards, Laura F. *Gendered Strife and Confusion: The Political Culture of Reconstruction.* Urbana: Univ. of Illinois Press, 1997.

———. "The Politics of Marriage and Households in North Carolina during Reconstruction." In *Jumpin' Jim Crow: Southern Politics from Civil War to Civil Rights,* edited by Jane Dailey, Glenda Elizabeth Gilmore, and Bryant Simon, 7–27. Princeton, N.J.: Princeton Univ. Press, 2000.

Elfenbein, Anna. *Women on the Color Line: Evolving Stereotypes and the Writings of George Washington Cable, Grace King, Kate Chopin.* Charlottesville: Univ. Press of Virginia, 1989.

Elliott, Mark. *Color-Blind Justice: Albion Tourgée and the Quest for Racial Equality from the Civil War to Plessy v. Ferguson.* New York: Oxford Univ. Press, 2006.

———. "Race, Color Blindness, and the Democratic Public: Albion Tourgée's Radical Principles in *Plessy v. Ferguson.*" *Journal of Southern History* 67, no. 2 (May 2001): 287–330.

Ettling, John. *The Germ of Laziness: Rockefeller Philanthropy and Public Health in the New South.* Cambridge, Mass.: Harvard Univ. Press, 1981.

Everett, Donald E. "Emigrés and Militiamen: Free Persons of Color in New Orleans." *Journal of Negro History* 38, no. 4 (October 1953): 377–402.

———. "Free Persons of Color in Colonial Louisiana." *Louisiana History* 7, no. 1 (Winter 1966): 21–50.

Fabian, Ann. "History for the Masses: Commercializing the Western Past." In *Under an Open Sky: Rethinking America's Western Past,* edited by William Cronon and George Miles, 223–238. New York: Norton, 1993.

Fabre, Genevieve, and Robert O'Meally, eds. *History and Memory in African-American Culture.* New York: Oxford Univ. Press, 1994.

Faust, Drew Gilpin. *James Henry Hammond and the Old South: A Design for Mastery.* Baton Rouge: Louisiana State Univ. Press, 1982.

———. *Mothers of Invention: Women of the Slaveholding South in the American Civil War.* New York: Vintage Books, 1997.

Feimster, Crystal Nicole. *Southern Horrors: Women and the Politics of Rape and Lynching.* Cambridge, Mass.: Harvard Univ. Press, 2009.

Fiehrer, Thomas. "Saint Domingue/Haiti: Louisiana's Caribbean Connection." *Louisiana History* 30, no. 4 (Autumn 1989): 419–437.

Fischer, Roger. "Racial Segregation in Antebellum New Orleans." *American Historical Review* 74, no. 3 (February 1969): 926–937.

———. *The Segregation Struggle in Louisiana, 1862–77.* Urbana: Univ. of Illinois Press, 1974.

Foner, Eric. *A Short History of Reconstruction.* New York: Harper and Row, 1990.

———. *The Story of American Freedom.* New York: Norton, 1998.

Foner, Laura. "The Free People of Color in Louisiana and St. Domingue: A Comparative Portrait of Two Three-Caste Societies." *Journal of Social History* 3, no. 4 (Summer 1970): 406–430.

Foner, Philip S. *The Great Labor Uprising of 1877.* New York: Pathfinder, 1977.

Fossier, Albert Emile. *New Orleans: The Glamour Period, 1800–1840.* New Orleans: Pelican, 1957.

Foster, Gaines. *Ghosts of the Confederacy: Defeat, the Lost Cause, and the Emergence of the New South.* New York: Oxford Univ. Press, 1987.

———. *Moral Reconstruction: Christian Lobbyists and the Federal Legislation of Morality, 1865–1920.* Chapel Hill: Univ. of North Carolina Press, 2002.

Foucault, Michel. *Discipline and Punish: The Birth of the Prison.* Translated by Alan Sheridan. New York: Vintage Books, 1979.

———. *The History of Sexuality,* vol. 1, *An Introduction.* Translated by Robert Hurley. New York: Vintage Books, 1990.

Fox, Richard Wightman, and T. J. Jackson Lears, eds. *The Culture of Consumption.* New York: Pantheon, 1983.

Fox-Genovese, Elizabeth. *Within the Plantation Household: Black and White Women of the Old South.* Chapel Hill: Univ. of North Carolina Press, 1988.

Franklin, John Hope. "*Birth of a Nation*—Propaganda as History." *Massachusetts Review* 20 (Autumn 1979): 417–434.

Fredrickson, George M. *The Black Image in the White Mind: The Debate on Afro-American Character and Destiny, 1817–1914.* Middletown, Conn.: Wesleyan Univ. Press, 1971.

———. *The Inner Civil War: Northern Intellectuals and the Crisis of the Union.* 1965. Urbana: Univ. of Illinois Press, 1993.

Friends of the Cabildo. *New Orleans Architecture,* vol. 6, *Faubourg Tremé and the Bayou Road.* Gretna, La.: Pelican, 1971.

Fussell, Elizabeth. "Constructing New Orleans, Constructing Race: A Population History of New Orleans." *Journal of American History* 94, no. 3 (December 2007): 846–855.

Gaines, Kevin K. *Uplifting the Race: Black Leadership, Politics, and Culture in the Twentieth Century.* Chapel Hill: Univ. of North Carolina Press, 1996.

Garvey, Ellen Gruber. *The Adman in the Parlor: Magazines and the Gendering of Consumer Culture, 1880s to 1910s.* New York: Oxford Univ. Press, 1996.

Gaston, Paul M. *The New South Creed: A Study in Southern Mythmaking.* Montgomery, Ala.: NewSouth Books, 2002.

Gatewood, Willard. *Black Americans and the White Man's Burden, 1898–1903.* Chicago: Univ. of Illinois Press, 1987.

———. "*Smoked Yankees" and the Quest for Empire: Letters from Negro Soldiers, 1898–1902.* Fayetteville: Univ. of Arkansas Press, 1987.

Gay, Peter. *The Bourgeois Experience: Victoria to Freud.* 5 vols. New York: Oxford Univ. Press, 1984–1998.

Gayarré, Charles Etienne. *History of Louisiana.* 4 vols. New Orleans: Armand Hawkins, 1885.

Geary, Christraud M., and Virginia-Lee Webb, eds. *Delivering Views: Distant Cultures in Early Postcards.* Washington, D.C.: Smithsonian Institution Press, 1998.

Gehman, Mary. "Visible Means of Support: Businesses, Professions, and Trades of Free People of Color." In *Creole: The History and Legacy of Louisiana's Free People of Color,* edited by Sybil Kein, 208–222. Baton Rouge: Louisiana State Univ. Press, 2000.

Gerstle, Gary. *American Crucible: Race and Nation in the Twentieth Century.* Princeton, N.J.: Princeton Univ. Press, 2001.

Gilbert, James. *Whose Fair: Experience, Memory, and the History of the Great St. Louis Exposition.* Chicago: Univ. of Chicago Press, 2009.

Gilfoyle, Timothy J. *City of Eros: New York City, Prostitution, and the Commercialization of Sex, 1790–1920.* New York: Norton, 1992.

Gillespie, Michele K., and Randal L. Hall, eds. *Thomas Dixon, Jr., and the Birth of Modern America.* Baton Rouge: Louisiana State Univ. Press, 2006.

Gillman, Susan. *Blood Talk: American Race Melodrama and the Culture of the Occult.* Chicago: Univ. of Chicago Press, 2003.

———. "The Mulatto, Tragic or Triumphant? The Nineteenth-Century American Race Melodrama." In *The Culture of Sentiment: Race, Gender and Sentimentality in Nineteenth-Century America,* edited by Shirley Samuels, 221–243. New York: Oxford Univ. Press, 1992.

Gilman, Sander. *Difference and Pathology: Stereotypes of Sexuality, Race, and Madness.* Ithaca, N.Y.: Cornell Univ. Press, 1985.

Gilmore, Glenda. *Gender and Jim Crow: Women and the Politics of White Supremacy in North Carolina, 1896–1920.* Chapel Hill: Univ. of North Carolina Press, 1996.

Gorn, Elliott J. *The Manly Art: Bare-Knuckle Prize Fighting in America.* Ithaca, N.Y.: Cornell Univ. Press, 1986.

———. *Mother Jones: The Most Dangerous Woman in America.* New York: Hill and Wang, 2001.

Gotham, Kevin Fox. *Authentic New Orleans: Tourism, Culture, and Race in the Big Easy.* New York: NYU Press, 2007.

Gould, Virginia. "A Chaos of Discord and Iniquity." In *The Devil's Lane: Sex and Race in the Early South,* edited by Catherine Clinton and Michele Gillespie, 232–246. New York: Oxford Univ. Press, 1999.

Grantham, Dewey. *Southern Progressivism: The Reconciliation of Progress and Tradition.* Knoxville: Univ. of Tennessee Press, 1983.

Greenberg, Kenneth. *Honor and Slavery.* Princeton, N.J.: Princeton Univ. Press, 1996.

Grittner, Frederick K. *White Slavery: Myth, Ideology, and American Law.* New York: Garland Press, 1990.

Guillory, Monique. "Under One Roof: The Sins and Sanctity of the New Orleans Quadroon Balls." In *Race Consciousness: African-American Studies for the New Century,* edited by Judith Jackson Fossett and Jeffrey Tucker, 67–92. New York: New York Univ. Press, 1997.

Gutman, Herbert G. *Work, Culture, and Society in Industrializing America.* New York: Vintage Books, 1977.

Guy, Donna J. *Sex and Danger in Buenos Aires: Prostitution, Family, and Nation in Argentina.* Lincoln: Univ. of Nebraska Press, 1990.

Haag, Pamela. *Consent: Sexual Rights and the Transformation of American Liberalism.* Ithaca, N.Y.: Cornell Univ. Press, 1999.

Haas, Edward F. *Political Leadership in a Southern City: New Orleans in the Progressive Era, 1896–1902.* Ruston, La.: McGinty Publications, 1988.

Hair, William Ivy. *Bourbonism and Agrarian Protest: Louisiana Politics, 1877–1900.* Baton Rouge: Louisiana State Univ. Press, 1969.

——. *Carnival of Fury: Robert Charles and the New Orleans Race Riot of 1900.* Baton Rouge: Louisiana State Univ. Press, 1976.

Hale, Grace Elizabeth. *Making Whiteness: The Culture of Segregation in the South, 1890–1940.* New York: Pantheon, 1998.

Hall, Gwendolyn Midlo. "The Formation of Afro-Creole Culture." In *Creole New Orleans: Race and Americanization,* edited by Arnold Hirsch and Joseph Logsdon, 58–87. Baton Rouge: Louisiana State Univ. Press, 1992.

Hall, Jacquelyn Dowd. "The Mind That Burns in Each Body." In *Powers of Desire: The Politics of Sexuality,* edited by Ann Snitow, Christine Stansell, and Sharon Thompson, 329–349. New York: Monthly Review Press, 1983.

——. *Revolt Against Chivalry: Jesse Daniel Ames and the Women's Campaign Against Lynching,* rev. ed. New York: Columbia Univ. Press, 1993.

Hanger, Kimberly S. *Bounded Lives, Bounded Places: Free Black Society in Colonial New Orleans, 1769–1803.* Durham, N.C.: Duke Univ. Press, 1997.

Hapke, Laura. "Conventions of Denial: Prostitution in Late Nineteenth-Century American Anti-Vice Narrative." *Michigan Occasional Paper* 24 (Winter 1982).

——. *Girls Who Went Wrong: Prostitutes in American Fiction, 1885–1917.* Bowling Green, Ohio: Bowling Green State Univ. Popular Press, 1989.

Haraway, Donna. "Teddy Bear Patriarchy: Taxidermy in the Garden of Eden, New York City, 1908–1936." In *Cultures of United States Imperialism,* edited by Amy Kaplan and Donald E. Pease, 237–291. Durham, N.C.: Duke Univ. Press, 1993.

Harris, Neil. *Humbug: The Art of P. T. Barnum.* Chicago: Univ. of Chicago Press, 1973.

Hartman, Saidiya. *Scenes of Subjection: Terror, Slavery, and Self-Making in Nineteenth-Century America.* New York: Oxford Univ. Press, 1997.

Heap, Chad. *Slumming: Sexual and Racial Encounters in American Nightlife, 1885–1940.* Chicago: Univ. of Chicago Press, 2009.

Hearn, Chester G. *When the Devil Came Down to Dixie: Ben Butler in New Orleans.* Baton Rouge: Louisiana State Univ. Press, 1997.

Hersch, Charles. *Subversive Sounds: Race and the Birth of Jazz in New Orleans.* Chicago: Univ. of Chicago Press, 2007.

Hershatter, Gail. *Dangerous Pleasures: Prostitution and Modernity in Twentieth-Century Shanghai.* Berkeley: Univ. of California Press, 1997.

Hess, Thomas B., and Linda Nochlin, eds. *Woman as Sex Object: Studies in Erotic Art.* London: Allen Lane, 1973.

Hickey, Georgina. *Hope and Danger in the New South City: Working-Class Women and Urban Development in Atlanta, 1890–1940.* Athens: Univ. of Georgia Press, 2003.

Higham, John. "The Reorientation of American Culture." In *Writing American History.* Bloomington: Indiana Univ. Press, 1970.

Hirsch, Arnold R. "Simply a Matter of Black and White: The Transformation of Race and Politics in Twentieth-Century New Orleans." In *Creole New Orleans: Race and Americanization,* edited by Arnold Hirsch and Joseph Logsdon, 262–320. Baton Rouge: Louisiana State Univ. Press, 1992.

Hirsch, Arnold R., and Joseph Logsdon. *Creole New Orleans: Race and Americanization.* Baton Rouge: Louisiana State Univ. Press, 1992.

Hobson, Barbara Meil. *Uneasy Virtue: The Politics of Prostitution and the American Reform Tradition.* Chicago: Univ. of Chicago Press, 1987.

Hodes, Martha. "Fractions and Fictions in the United States Census of 1890." In *Haunted by Empire: Geographies of Intimacy in North American History,* edited by Ann Laura Stoler, 240–270. Durham, N.C.: Duke Univ. Press, 2006.

———, ed. *Sex, Love, Race: Crossing Boundaries in North American History.* New York: New York Univ. Press, 1999.

———. "The Sexualization of Reconstruction Politics: White Women and Black Men in the South after the Civil War."*Journal of the History of Sexuality* 3 (January 1993): 402–417.

———. *White Women, Black Men: Illicit Sex in the 19th-Century South.* New Haven, Conn.: Yale Univ. Press, 1997.

Hodeir, Catherine. "Decentering the Gaze at French Colonial Exhibitions." In *Images and Empires: Visuality in Colonial and Postcolonial Africa,* edited by Paul Landau and Deborah Kaspin, 233–252. Berkeley: Univ. of California Press, 2002.

Hofstadter, Richard. *Social Darwinism in American Thought.* 1944. Boston: Beacon Press, 1992.

Hoganson, Kristen L. *Fighting for American Manhood: How Gender Politics Provoked the Spanish-American and Philippine-American Wars.* New Haven, Conn.: Yale Univ. Press, 1998.

Hollandsworth, James G., Jr. *An Absolute Massacre: The New Orleans Race Riot of July 30, 1866.* Baton Rouge: Louisiana State Univ. Press, 2001.

Horsman, Reginald. *Race and Manifest Destiny: The Origins of American Racial Anglo-Saxonism.* Cambridge, Mass.: Harvard Univ. Press, 1981.

Hunt, Lynn, ed. *The Invention of Pornography: Obscenity and the Origins of Modernity, 1500–1800.* New York: Zone Books, 1993.

Hunt, Michael. *Ideology and U.S. Foreign Policy.* New Haven, Conn.: Yale Univ. Press, 1987.

Hunter, Tera W. *To 'Joy My Freedom: Southern Black Women's Lives and Labors after the Civil War.* Cambridge, Mass.: Harvard Univ. Press, 1997.

Ingersoll, Thomas. *Mammon and Manon in Early New Orleans: The First Slave Society in the Deep South, 1718–1819.* Knoxville: Univ. of Tennessee Press, 1999.

Jackson, Joy. *New Orleans in the Gilded Age: Politics and Urban Progress, 1880–1896.* Baton Rouge: Louisiana State Univ. Press, 1969.

Jacobs, Harriet A. *Incidents in the Life of a Slave Girl, Written by Herself.* Edited by L. Maria Child. Enlarged ed., edited by Jean Fagan Yellin. Cambridge, Mass.: Harvard Univ. Press, 2000.

Jacobson, Matthew Frye. *Barbarian Virtues: The United States Encounters Foreign Peoples at Home and Abroad, 1876–1917*. New York: Hill and Wang, 2000.

———. *Whiteness of a Different Color: European Immigrants and the Alchemy of Race.* Cambridge Mass.: Harvard Univ. Press, 1998.

Johnson, Jerah. "Colonial New Orleans: A Fragment of the Eighteenth-Century French Ethos." In *Creole New Orleans: Race and Americanization,* edited by Arnold Hirsch and Joseph Logsdon, 12–57. Baton Rouge: Louisiana State Univ. Press, 1992.

Johnson, Walter. "The Slave Trader, the White Slave, and the Politics of Racial Determination in the 1850s." *Journal of American History* 87, no. 1 (June 2000): 13–38.

———. *Soul by Soul: Life inside the Antebellum Slave Market.* Cambridge, Mass.: Harvard Univ. Press, 1999.

Jones, Jacqueline. *Labor of Love, Labor of Sorrow: Black Women, Work, and the Family from Slavery to the Present.* 1985. New York: Vintage Books, 1995.

Kane, Thomas Harnett. *Queen New Orleans, City by the River.* New York: W. Morrow, 1949.

Kaplan, Amy. *The Anarchy of Empire in the Making of U.S. Culture.* Cambridge, Mass.: Harvard Univ. Press, 2002.

———. "Black and Blue on San Juan Hill." In *Cultures of United States Imperialism,* edited by Amy Kaplan and Donald E. Pease, 219–236. Durham, N.C.: Duke Univ. Press, 1993.

Kaplan, Amy, and Donald E. Pease, eds. *Cultures of United States Imperialism.* Durham, N.C.: Duke Univ. Press, 1993.

Kasson, John F. *Amusing the Million: Coney Island at the Turn of the Century.* New York: Hill and Wang, 1978.

———. *Civilizing the Machine: Technology and Republican Values in America, 1877–1900.* New York: Penguin, 1977.

Kein, Sybil, ed. *Creole: The History and Legacy of Louisiana's Free People of Color.* Baton Rouge: Louisiana State Univ. Press, 2000.

Kendall, John Smith, *History of New Orleans.* 3 vols. Chicago: Lewis Publishing Company, 1922.

Kinney, James. *Amalgamation! Race, Sex, and Rhetoric in the Nineteenth-Century American Novel.* Westport, Conn.: Greenwood Press, 1985.

Kloppenberg, James T. *Uncertain Victory: Social Democracy and Progressivism in European and American Thought, 1870–1920.* New York: Oxford Univ. Press, 1986.

Krause, Paul. *The Battle for Homestead, 1880–1892: Politics, Culture, and Steel.* Pittsburgh: Univ. of Pittsburgh Press, 1992.

Kristeva, Julia. *Powers of Horror: An Essay on Abjection.* Translated by Leon S. Roudiez. New York: Columbia Univ. Press, 1982.

Kunzel, Regina G. *Fallen Women, Problem Girls: Unmarried Mothers and the Professionalization of Social Work, 1890–1945.* New Haven, Conn.: Yale Univ. Press, 1993.

Kutzinski, Vera M. *Sugar's Secrets: Race and the Erotics of Cuban Nationalism.* Charlottesville: Univ. Press of Virginia, 1993.

Lachance, Paul F. "The 1809 Immigration of Saint-Domingue Refugees to New Orleans: Reception, Integration, and Impact." *Louisiana History* 29, no. 2 (Spring 1988): 109–141.

Landau, Paul S. "An Amazing Distance: People and Pictures in Africa." Introduction to *Images and Empires: Visuality in Colonial and Postcolonial Africa,* edited by Paul S. Landau and Deborah D. Kaspin, 1–40. Berkeley: Univ. of California Press, 2002.

———. "Empires of the Visual: Photography and Colonial Administration in Africa." In *Images and Empires: Visuality in Colonial and Postcolonial Africa,* edited by Paul S. Landau and Deborah D. Kaspin, 141–171. Berkeley: Univ. of California Press, 2002.

Lang, Robert, ed. *The Birth of a Nation: D. W. Griffith, director.* New Brunswick, N.J.: Rutgers Univ. Press, 1994.

Langum, David J. *Crossing over the Line: Legislating Morality and the Mann Act.* Chicago: Univ. of Chicago Press, 1994.

Laqueur, Thomas Walter. *Making Sex: Body and Gender from the Greeks to Freud.* Cambridge, Mass.: Harvard Univ. Press, 1992.

Lasch, Christopher. "The Anti-Imperialists, the Philippines, and the Inequality of Man." *Journal of Southern History* 25 (August 1958): 319–331.

Lasch-Quinn, Elizabeth. *Black Neighbors: Race and the Limits of Reform in the American Settlement House Movement, 1890–1945.* Chapel Hill: Univ. of North Carolina Press, 1993.

Leach, William. *Land of Desire: Merchants, Power, and the Rise of a New American Culture.* New York: Vintage Books, 1993.

———. *True Love and Perfect Union: The Feminist Reform of Sex and Society.* Middletown, Conn.: Wesleyan Univ. Press, 1989.

Lears, T. J. Jackson. *Fables of Abundance: A Cultural History of Advertising in America.* New York: Basic Books, 1994.

———. *No Place of Grace: Antimodernism and the Transformation of American Culture, 1880–1920.* Chicago: Univ. of Chicago Press, 1981.

Levine, Lawrence W. *Highbrow, Lowbrow: The Emergence of Cultural Hierarchy in America.* Cambridge, Mass.: Harvard Univ. Press, 1988.

Levine, Philippa. *Prostitution, Race and Politics: Policing Venereal Disease in the British Empire.* New York: Routledge, 2003.

Lewis, Pierce F. *New Orleans: The Making of an Urban Landscape,* 2nd ed. Santa Fe, N. Mex.: Center for American Places, 2003.

Livingston, James. *Pragmatism and the Political Economy of Cultural Revolution, 1850–1940.* Chapel Hill: Univ. of North Carolina Press, 1994.

Lofgren, Charles A. *The Plessy Case: A Legal-Historical Interpretation.* New York: Oxford Univ. Press, 1987.

Lomax, Alan. *Mister Jelly Roll: The Fortunes of Jelly Roll Morton.* 1950. New York: Grove Press, 1956.

Long, Alecia P. *The Great Southern Babylon: Sex, Race, and Respectability in New Orleans, 1865–1920.* Baton Rouge: Louisiana State Univ. Press, 2004.

———. "(Mis)Remembering General Order No. 28: Benjamin Butler, The Woman Order, and Historical Memory." In *Occupied Women: Gender, Military Occupation, and the American Civil War,* edited by LeeAnn Whites and Alecia P. Long, 17–32. Baton Rouge: Louisiana State Univ. Press, 2009.

———. "Poverty Is the New Prostitution: Race, Poverty, and Public Housing in Post-Katrina New Orleans." *Journal of American History* 94, no. 3 (December 2007): 795–803.

Lott, Eric. *Love and Theft: Blackface Minstrelsy and the American Working Class.* New York: Oxford Univ. Press, 1993.

Lui, Mary Ting Yi. *The Chinatown Trunk Mystery: Murder, Miscegenation, and Other Dangerous Encounters in Turn-of-the-Century New York City.* Princeton, N.J.: Princeton Univ. Press, 2005.

Maclean, Nancy. "The Leo Frank Case Reconsidered: Gender and Sexual Politics in the Making of Reactionary Populism." In *Jumpin' Jim Crow: Southern Politics from Civil War to Civil Rights,* edited by Jane Dailey, Glenda Elizabeth Gilmore, and Bryant Simon, 183–218. Princeton, N.J.: Princeton Univ. Press, 2000.

Manring, M. M. *Slave in a Box: The Strange Career of Aunt Jemimah.* Charlottesville: Univ. Press of Virginia, 1998.

Marcus, Steven. *The Other Victorians: A Study of Sexuality and Pornography in Mid-Nineteenth-Century England.* 1966. New York: Basic Books, 1975.

Martin, Joan M. "*Plaçage* and the Louisiana *Gens de Couleur Libre*: How Race and Sex Defined the Lifestyles of Free Women of Color." In *Creole: The History and Legacy of Louisiana's Free People of Color,* edited by Sybil Kein, 57–70. Baton Rouge: Louisiana State Univ. Press, 2000.

Mavor, Carol. *Pleasures Taken: Performances of Sexuality and Loss in Victorian Photographs.* Durham, N.C.: Duke Univ. Press, 1995.

McClintock, Anne. *Imperial Leather: Race, Gender and Sexuality in the Colonial Contest.* London: Routledge, 1995.

McCulloch, Jock. *Black Peril, White Virtue: Sexual Crime in Southern Rhodesia, 1902–1935.* Bloomington and Indianapolis: Indiana Univ. Press, 2000.

McCurry, Stephanie. *Masters of Small Worlds: Yeoman Households, Gender Relations, and the Political Culture of the Antebellum South Carolina Low Country.* New York: Oxford Univ. Press, 1997.

———. "The Two Faces of Republicanism: Gender and Proslavery Politics in Antebellum South Carolina." *Journal of American History* 78, no. 4 (March 1992): 1245–1264.

McLaurin, Melton A. *Celia, a Slave: A True Story.* New York: Avon Books, 1991.

Medley, Keith Weldon. *We as Freemen:* Plessy v. Ferguson. Gretna, La: Pelican, 2003.

Meyerowitz, Joanne J. *Women Adrift: Independent Wage Earners in Chicago, 1880–1930.* Chicago: Univ. of Chicago Press, 1988.

Miller, Paul Eduard, ed. *Esquire's 1945 Jazz Book.* New York: A. S. Barnes and Company, 1945.

Mitchell, Mary Niall. "'Rosebloom and Pure White,' or So It Seemed." *American Quarterly* 54, no. 3 (September 2002): 369–410.

Mitchell, Reid. *All on a Mardi Gras Day: Episodes in the History of New Orleans Carnival.* Cambridge, Mass.: Harvard Univ. Press, 1995.

Montgomery, David. *Citizen Worker: The Experience of Workers in the United States with Democracy and the Free Market during the Nineteenth Century.* Cambridge, Eng.: Cambridge Univ. Press, 1993.

Morrison, Joseph L. *Josephus Daniels Says . . . : An Editor's Political Odyssey from Bryan to Wilson and FDR, 1894–1913.* Chapel Hill: Univ. of North Carolina Press, 1962.

Mumford, Kevin. *Interzones: Black/White Sex Districts in Chicago and New York in the Early Twentieth Century.* New York: Columbia Univ. Press, 1997.

Nasaw, David. *Going Out: The Rise and Fall of Public Amusements.* Cambridge, Mass.: Harvard Univ. Press, 1993.

Needham, Gerald. "Manet, Olympia, and Pornographic Photography." In *Woman as Sex Object: Studies in Erotic Art,* edited by Thomas B. Hess and Linda Nochlin, 80–89. London: Allen Lane, 1973.

Nora, Pierre. "Between History and Memory: Les Lieux de Mémoire." *Representations,* no. 26 (Spring 1989): 7–25.

Norgard, Erik. *With Love to You: A History of the Erotic Postcard.* New York: Crown Publishers, 1969.

Nussbaum, Raymond O. "'The Ring is Smashed!': The New Orleans Municipal Election of 1896." *Louisiana History* 17, no. 3 (Summer 1976): 283–297.

Nystrom, Justin. *New Orleans after the Civil War: Race, Politics, and a New Birth of Freedom.* Baltimore: Johns Hopkins Univ. Press, 2010.

Odem, Mary E. *Delinquent Daughters: Protecting and Policing Adolescent Female Sexuality in the United States, 1885–1920.* Chapel Hill: Univ. of North Carolina Press, 1995.

Oshinsky, David. *Worse than Slavery: Parchman Prison and the Ordeal of Jim Crow Justice.* New York: Free Press, 1997.

Ovenden, Graham, and Peter Mendes. *Victorian Erotic Photography.* New York: St. Martin's Press, 1973.

Painter, Nell Irvin. "Soul Murder and Slavery: Toward a Fully Loaded Cost Accounting." In *U.S. History as Women's History: New Feminist Essays,* edited by Linda K. Kerber, Alice Kessler Harris, and Kathryn Kish Sklar, 125–146. Chapel Hill: Univ. of North Carolina Press, 1995.

———. *Standing at Armageddon, 1877–1917.* New York: Norton, 1987.

Palmié, Stephan. *Wizards and Scientists: Explorations in Afro-Cuban Modernity and Tradition.* Durham, N.C.: Duke Univ. Press, 2002.

Parsons, Neil. *King Khama, Emperor Joe, and the Great White Queen: Great Britain through African Eyes.* Chicago: Univ. of Chicago Press, 1998.

Pascoe, Peggy. *Relations of Rescue: The Search for Female Moral Authority in the American West, 1874–1939.* New York: Oxford Univ. Press, 1990.

———. *What Comes Naturally: Miscegenation Law and the Making of Race in America.* New York: Oxford Univ. Press, 2009.

Pateman, Carole. *The Sexual Contract.* Stanford, Calif.: Stanford Univ. Press, 1988.

Peiss, Kathy. *Cheap Amusements: Working Women and Leisure in Turn-of-the-Century New York.* Philadelphia: Temple Univ. Press, 1986.

Pierson, George Wilson. *Tocqueville in America.* New York: Oxford Univ. Press, 1938. Baltimore: Johns Hopkins Univ. Press, 1996.

Pivar, David J. *Purity and Hygiene: Women, Prostitution, and the "American Plan."* Westport, Conn.: Greenwood Press, 2001.

———. *The Purity Crusade: Sexual Morality and Social Control, 1860–1900.* Westport, Conn.: Greenwood Press, 1973.

Powell, Lawrence N. *The Accidental City: Improvising New Orleans.* Cambridge, Mass.: Harvard Univ. Press, 2012.

———. *New Masters: Northern Planters during the Civil War and Reconstruction.* New Haven, Conn.: Yale Univ. Press, 1980.

Pratt, Mary Louise. *Imperial Eyes: Travel Writing and Transculturation.* New York: Routledge, 1992.

Rabinowitz, Howard N. *Race Relations in the Urban South, 1865–1890.* 1978. Athens: Univ. of Georgia Press, 1996.

Raeburn, Bruce Boyd. *New Orleans Style and the Writing of American Jazz History.* Ann Arbor: Univ. of Michigan Press, 2009.

Rafael, Vicente L. *White Love and Other Events in Filipino History.* Durham, N.C.: Duke Univ. Press, 1993.

Ranger, Terence, and Eric Hobsbawm. *The Invention of Tradition.* London: Verso, 1985.

Rankin, David. "The Tannenbaum Thesis Reconsidered: Slavery and Race Relations in Antebellum Louisiana." *Southern Studies* 18, no. 1 (1979): 5–31.

Reed, Germaine A. "Race Legislation in Louisiana, 1864–1920." *Louisiana History* 6 (Fall 1965): 379–392.

Reynolds, Donald E. "The New Orleans Riot of 1866, Reconsidered." *Louisiana History* 5 (1964): 5–27.

Reynolds, George. *Machine Politics in New Orleans, 1897–1926.* New York: AMS Press, 1936.

Rice, Roger L. "Residential Segregation by Law, 1910–1917." *Journal of Southern History* 34, no. 2 (May 1968): 179–199.

Rightor, Edward. *Standard History of New Orleans, Louisiana.* Chicago: Lewis Publishing Company, 1900.

Roach, Joseph. *Cities of the Dead: Circum-Atlantic Performance.* New York: Columbia Univ. Press, 1996.

———. "Slave Spectacles and Tragic Octoroons: A Cultural Genealogy of Antebellum Performance." *Theatre Survey* 33, no. 2 (November 1992): 167–187.

Robinson, Lura. *It's an Old New Orleans Custom.* New York: Vanguard Press, 1948.

Rodgers, Daniel T. *The Work Ethic in Industrial America, 1850–1920.* 1974. Chicago: Univ. of Chicago Press, 1978.

Rodrigue, John. Introduction to Henry Clay Warmoth, *War, Politics, and Reconstruction: Stormy Days in Louisiana,* edited by John Rodrigue, ix–xlvi. Columbia: Univ. of South Carolina Press, 2006.

Roediger, David R. *The Wages of Whiteness: Race and the Making of the American Working Class.* London: Verso, 1991.

Rogin, Michael. "'The Sword Became a Flashing Vision': D. W. Griffith's *The Birth of a Nation.*" *Representations,* no. 9, Special issue: American Culture Between the Civil War and World War I (Winter 1985): 150–195.

Rose, Al. *Miss Lulu White de Basin Street, Nouvelle Orléans.* Traduction par Raymond Manicacci. Paris: Gaston Lachurie, 1991.

———. *Storyville, New Orleans: Being an Authentic, Illustrated Account of the Notorious Red-Light District.* Tuscaloosa: Univ. of Alabama Press, 1974.

Rosen, Hannah. "'Not That Sort of Women': Race, Gender, and Sexual Violence during the Memphis Race Riot of 1866." In *Sex, Love, Race: Crossing Boundaries in North American History,* edited by Martha Hodes, 267–293. New York: New York Univ. Press. 1999.

———. *Terror in the Heart of Freedom: Citizenship, Sexual Violence, and the Meaning of Race in the Post-Emancipation South.* Chapel Hill: Univ. of North Carolina Press, 2009.

Rosen, Ruth. *The Lost Sisterhood: Prostitution in America, 1900–1918.* Baltimore: Johns Hopkins Univ. Press, 1982.

Ross, Dorothy. *The Origins of American Social Science.* Cambridge, Eng.: Cambridge Univ. Press, 1991.

Ross, Michael A. "Justice Miller's Reconstruction: The *Slaughter-House Cases,* Health Codes, and Civil Rights in New Orleans, 1861–1873." *Journal of Southern History* 64 no. 4 (November 1998): 649–676.

———. *Justice of Shattered Dreams: Samuel Freeman Miller and the Supreme Court during the Civil War Era.* Baton Rouge: Louisiana State Univ. Press, 2003.

———. "Obstructing Reconstruction: John Archibald Campbell and the Legal Campaign Against Louisiana's Republican Government, 1868–1873." *Civil War History* 49, no. 3 (September 2003): 235–253.

Rothman, Joshua D. *Notorious in the Neighborhood: Sex and Families across the Color Line in Virginia.* Chapel Hill: Univ. of North Carolina Press, 2003.

Rousey, Dennis Charles. *Policing the Southern City: New Orleans, 1805–1889.* Baton Rouge: Louisiana State Univ. Press, 1996.

Russet, Cynthia. *Sexual Science: The Victorian Construction of Womanhood.* Cambridge, Mass.: Harvard Univ. Press, 1989.

Ryan, Mary P. *Civic Wars: Democracy and Public Life in the American City during the Nineteenth Century.* Berkeley: Univ. of California Press, 1997.

———. *Women in Public: Between Banners and Ballots, 1825–1880.* Baltimore: Johns Hopkins Univ. Press, 1990.

Ryan, Paul, ed. *The Sins of Our Fathers: A Study in Victorian Pornography.* London: Erotic Print Society, 2000.

Rydell, Robert. *All the World's a Fair: Visions of Empire at American International Exhibitions, 1876–1916.* Chicago: Univ. of Chicago Press, 1984.

Said, Edward. *Orientalism.* New York: Vintage Books, 1979.

Saks, Eva. "Representing Miscegenation Law." *Raritan* 8, no. 2 (Fall 1988): 39–69.

Sanchez-Eppler, Karen. *Touching Liberty: Abolition, Feminism, and the Politics of the Body.* Berkeley: Univ. of California Press, 1997.

Santé, Luc. *Low Life: Lures and Snares of Old New York.* New York: Vintage Books, 1992.

Savage, Kirk. *Standing Soldiers, Kneeling Slaves: Race, War, and Monument in Nineteenth-Century America.* Princeton, N.J.: Princeton Univ. Press, 1997.

Schafer, Judith Kelleher. *Becoming Free, Remaining Free: Manumission and Enslavement in New Orleans, 1846–1862.* Baton Rouge: Louisiana State Univ. Press, 2003.

———. *Brothels, Depravity, and Abandoned Women: Illegal Sex in Antebellum New Orleans.* Baton Rouge: Louisiana State Univ. Press, 2009.

———. "Open and Notorious Concubinage: The Emancipation of Slave Mistresses by Will and the Supreme Court in Antebellum Louisiana." *Louisiana History* 28, no. 2 (Spring 1987): 165–182.

———. *Slavery, the Civil Law, and the Supreme Court of Louisiana.* Baton Rouge: Louisiana State Univ. Press, 1994.

Schickel, Richard. *D. W. Griffith: An American Life.* New York: Limelight Editions, 1996.

Schweninger, Loren. "A Negro Sojourner in Antebellum New Orleans." *Louisiana History* 20 (Summer 1979): 305–314.

Scott, James C. *Domination and the Arts of Resistance: Hidden Transcripts.* New Haven, Conn.: Yale Univ. Press, 1992.

Scott, Joan Wallach. "Gender: A Useful Category of Historical Analysis." *American Historical Review* 91, no. 5 (December 1986): 1053–1075.

Scott, Pamela, and Antoinette J. Lee. *Buildings of the District of Columbia.* New York: Oxford Univ. Press, 1993.

Scott, Rebecca J. "The Atlantic World and the Road to *Plessy v. Ferguson.*" *Journal of American History* 94, no. 3 (December 2007): 726–733.

———. *Degrees of Freedom: Louisiana and Cuba after Slavery.* Cambridge, Mass.: Harvard Univ. Press, 2008.

———. "Public Rights and Private Commerce: A Nineteenth-Century Atlantic Creole Itinerary." *Current Anthropology* 48, no. 2 (April 2007): 237–256.

———. "Public Rights, Social Equality, and the Conceptual Roots of the *Plessy* Challenge." *Michigan Law Review* 106, no. 5 (March 2008): 777–804.

———. "Reinventing Slavery, Securing Freedom: From Saint-Domingue to Santiago to New Orleans, 1803–1809." Paper given at the Southern Historical Association, New Orleans, October 2008.

———. "'She . . . Refuses to Deliver Herself Up as the Slave of Your Petitioner': Émigrés, Enslavement, and the 1808 Louisiana Digest of the Civil Laws." *Tulane European and Civil Law Forum* 24 (2009): 116–136.

Scott, Rebecca J., and Jean M. Hébrard. *Freedom Papers: An Atlantic Odyssey in the Age of Emancipation.* Cambridge, Mass.: Harvard Univ. Press, 2012.

Shumsky, Neil Larry. "Tacit Acceptance: Respectable Americans and Segregated Prostitution, 1870–1910." *Journal of Social History* 19, no. 4 (Summer 1986): 665–679.

Sigel, Lisa V. "Filth in the Wrong People's Hands: Postcards and the Expansion of Pornography in Britain and the Atlantic World, 1880–1914." *Journal of Social History* 33, no. 4 (2000): 859–885.

Silber, Nina. *The Romance of Reunion: Northerners and the South, 1865–1900.* Chapel Hill: Univ. of North Carolina Press, 1993.

Sinclair, Harold. *The Port of New Orleans.* Garden City, N.Y.: Doubleday, Doran and Company, 1942.

Sklar, Kathryn Kish. *Florence Kelly and the Nation's Work: The Rise of Women's Political Culture, 1830–1900.* New Haven, Conn.: Yale Univ. Press, 1995.

Slotkin, Richard. *Gunfighter Nation: The Myth of the Frontier in Twentieth-Century America.* 1992. Norman: Univ. of Oklahoma Press, 1998.

Smith-Rosenberg, Carroll. *Disorderly Conduct: Visions of Gender in Victorian America.* New York: Oxford Univ. Press, 1985.

Sollors, Werner. *Neither Black nor White yet Both: Thematic Explorations in Interracial Literature.* Cambridge, Mass.: Harvard Univ. Press, 1997.

Somers, Dale. "Black and White in New Orleans: A Study in Urban Race Relations, 1865–1900." *Journal of Southern History* 40, no. 1 (February 1974): 19–42.

Somerville, Diane. "The Rape Myth in the Old South Reconsidered." *Journal of Southern History* 61, no. 3 (August 1995): 481–518.

Souther, J. Mark. "Making the 'Birthplace of Jazz': Tourism and Musical Heritage Marketing in New Orleans." *Louisiana History* 44, no. 1 (Winter 2003): 39–73.

———. *New Orleans on Parade: Tourism and the Transformation of the Crescent City.* Baton Rouge: Louisiana State Univ. Press, 2006.

Spear, Jennifer M. "Colonial Intimacies: Legislating Sex in French Louisiana." *William and Mary Quarterly* 60, no. 1 (January 2003): 75–98.

———. *Race, Sex, and Social Order in Early New Orleans.* Baltimore: Johns Hopkins Univ. Press, 2008.

———. "'They Need Wives': Metissage and the Regulation of Sexuality in French Louisiana, 1699–1730." In *Sex, Love, Race: Crossing Boundaries in North American History,* edited by Martha Hodes, 35–59. New York: New York Univ. Press, 1999.

Spongberg, Mary. *Feminizing Venereal Disease: The Body of the Prostitute in Nineteenth-Century Medical Discourse.* New York: New York Univ. Press, 1997.

Spurr, David. *The Rhetoric of Empire: Colonial Discourse in Journalism, Travel Writing, and Imperial Administration.* Durham, N.C.: Duke Univ. Press, 1993.

Stallybrass, Peter, and Allon White. *The Politics and Poetics of Transgression.* Ithaca, N.Y.: Cornell Univ. Press, 1986.

Stanley, Amy Dru. *From Bondage to Contract: Wage Labor, Marriage, and the Market in the Age of Slave Emancipation.* Cambridge, Eng.: Cambridge Univ. Press, 1998.

Stanonis, Anthony J. *Creating the Big Easy: New Orleans and the Emergence of Modern Tourism, 1918–1945.* Athens: Univ. of Georgia Press, 2006.

Stephenson, Anders. *Manifest Destiny: American Expansion and the Empire of Right.* New York: Hill and Wang, 1995.

Sterkx, H. E. *The Free Negro in Ante-Bellum Louisiana.* Rutherford, N.J.: Fairleigh Dickinson Univ. Press, 1972.

Stoler, Ann Laura. *Carnal Knowledge and Imperial Power: Race and the Intimate in Colonial Rule.* Berkeley: Univ. of California Press, 2002.

———, ed. *Haunted by Empire: Geographies of Intimacy in North American History.* Durham, N.C.: Duke Univ. Press, 2006.

———. *Race and the Education of Desire: Foucault's* History of Sexuality *and the Colonial Order of Things.* Durham, N.C.: Duke Univ. Press, 1995.

Strasser, Susan. *Satisfaction Guaranteed: The Making of the American Mass Market.* Washington, D.C.: Smithsonian Institution Press, 1989.

Sublette, Ned. *The World That Made New Orleans: From Spanish Silver to Congo Square.* Chicago: Lawrence Hill Books, 2008.

Symanski, Richard. *The Immoral Landscape: Female Prostitution in Western Societies.* Toronto: Butterworth, 1981.

Tadman, Michael. *Speculators and Slaves: Masters, Traders, and Slaves in the Old South.* 1989. Madison: Univ. of Wisconsin Press, 1996.

Tansey, Richard. "Prostitution and Politics in Antebellum New Orleans." *Southern Studies* 19, no. 4 (Winter 1980): 449–479.

Taylor, Helen. *Gender, Race, and Region in the Writings of Grace King, Ruth McEnery Stuart, and Kate Chopin.* Baton Rouge: Louisiana State Univ. Press, 1989.

Taylor, Joe Gray. *Louisiana Reconstructed, 1863–1877.* Baton Rouge: Louisiana State Univ. Press, 1974.

Thomas, Brook. *Plessy v. Ferguson: A Brief History with Documents.* Boston: Bedford Books, 1997.

Thomas, Nicolas. *Colonialism's Culture: Anthropology, Travel, and Government*. Princeton, N.J.: Princeton Univ. Press, 1994.

Thompson, Shirley Elizabeth. "'Ah, Toucoutou, Ye Conin Vous': History and Memory in Creole New Orleans." *American Quarterly* 53, no. 2 (June 2001): 232–266.

———. *Exiles at Home: The Struggle to Become American in Creole New Orleans*. Cambridge, Mass.: Harvard Univ. Press, 2009.

Townsend, Kim. *Manhood at Harvard: William James and Others*. Cambridge, Mass.: Harvard Univ. Press. 1998.

Trachtenberg, Alan. *The Incorporation of America: Culture and Society in the Gilded Age*. New York: Hill and Wang. 1982.

Tregle, Joseph G., Jr. "Creoles and Americans." In *Creole New Orleans: Race and Americanization*, edited by Arnold R. Hirsch and Joseph Logsdon, 131–185. Baton Rouge: Louisiana State Univ. Press, 1992.

Trillin, Calvin. "American Chronicles: Black or White." *New Yorker Magazine*. April 14, 1986. 62–78.

Tunnell, Ted. *Crucible of Reconstruction: War, Radicalism, and Race in Louisiana, 1862–1877*. Baton Rouge: Louisiana State Univ. Press, 1984.

Turner, Victor. *The Forest of Symbols: Aspects of Ndembu Ritual*. Ithaca, N.Y.: Cornell Univ. Press, 1967.

Usner, Daniel H., Jr. *Indians, Settlers, and Slaves in a Frontier Exchange Economy: The Lower Mississippi Valley Before 1783*. Chapel Hill: Univ. of North Carolina Press, 1992.

Van Onselen, Charles. *The Fox and the Flies: The Secret Life of a Grotesque Master Criminal*. New York: Walker, 2007.

———. *Studies in the Social and Economic History of the Witwatersrand, 1886–1914*, vol. 1, *New Babylon*. Johannesburg, South Africa: Ravan Press, 1982.

———. *Studies in the Social and Economic History of the Witwatersrand, 1886–1914*, vol. 2, *New Ninevah*. Johannesburg, South Africa: Ravan Press, 1982.

Veblen, Thorstein. *The Theory of the Leisure Class: An Economic Study of Institutions*. New York: Macmillan, 1899. New York: Modern Library, 2001.

Wade, Richard C. *Slavery in the Cities: The South, 1820–1860*. New York: Oxford Univ. Press, 1964.

Walker, Norman. "Commercial and Mercantile Interests." In *Standard History of New Orleans, Louisiana*, edited by Edward Rightor, 538–577. Chicago: Lewis Publishing Company, 1900.

Walkowitz, Judith R. *City of Dreadful Delight: Narratives of Sexual Danger in Late-Victorian London*. Chicago: Univ. of Chicago Press, 1992.

———. *Prostitution and Victorian Society: Women, Class, and the State*. Cambridge, Eng.: Cambridge Univ. Press, 1982.

Walters, Ronald G. "The Erotic South: Civilization and Sexuality in American Abolitionism." *American Quarterly* 25 no. 2 (May 1973): 177–201.

Weber, Max. *The Protestant Ethic and the Spirit of Capitalism*. Translated by Talcott Parsons. New York: Charles Scribner's Sons, 1958.

Weibe, Robert H. *The Search for Order, 1877–1920*. New York: Hill and Wang, 1967.

Welke, Barbara Young. *Recasting American Liberty: Gender, Race, Law, and the Railroad Revolution, 1865–1920*. Cambridge, Eng.: Cambridge Univ. Press, 2001.

Welter, Barbara. "The Cult of True Womanhood." In *The Dimity Convictions: The American Woman in the Nineteenth Century*. Athens: Ohio Univ. Press, 1976.

Wexler, Laura. *Tender Violence: Domestic Visions in an Age of U.S. Imperialism*. Chapel Hill: Univ. of North Carolina Press, 2000.

Wheeler, Marjorie Spruill. *New Women of the New South: The Leaders of the Woman Suffrage Movement in the Southern States*. New York: Oxford Univ. Press, 1993.

White, Deborah Gray. *Ar'n't I a Woman? Female Slaves in the Plantation South*, rev. ed. New York: Norton, 1999.

Whites, LeeAnn. "Rebecca Latimer Felton and the Problem of 'Protection' in the New South." In *Visible Women: New Essays on American Activism*, edited by Nancy A. Hewitt and Suzanne Lebsock, 41–61. Urbana: Univ. of Illinois Press, 1993.

Whites, LeeAnn, and Alecia P. Long, eds. *Occupied Women: Gender, Military Occupation, and the American Civil War*. Baton Rouge: Louisiana State Univ. Press, 2009.

Wiegman, Robyn. *American Anatomies: Theorizing Race and Gender*. Durham, N.C.: Duke Univ. Press, 1995.

Williams, Linda. *Hard Core: Power, Pleasure, and the "Frenzy of the Visible,"* expanded paperback ed. Berkeley: Univ. of California Press, 1999.

———. *Playing the Race Card: Melodramas of Black and White from Uncle Tom to O. J. Simpson*. Princeton, N.J.: Princeton Univ. Press, 2001.

———. "'White Slavery' Versus the Ethnography of 'Sexworkers': Women in Stag Films at the Kinsey Archive." *Moving Image* 2, no. 2 (2005): 107–134.

Williamson, Joel. *A Rage for Order: Black/White Race Relations in the American South since Emancipation*. New York: Oxford Univ. Press, 1986.

Willis, Deborah. *The Black Female Body: A Photographic History*. Philadelphia: Temple Univ. Press, 2002.

Wilson, Carol. "Sally Muller, the White Slave." *Louisiana History: The Journal of the Louisiana Historical Association* 40, no. 2 (Spring 1999): 133–153.

Wolcott, Victoria Widgeon. *Remaking Respectability: African American Women in Interwar Detroit*. Chapel Hill: Univ. of North Carolina Press, 2001.

Wood, Amy Louise. *Lynching and Spectacle: Witnessing Racial Violence in America, 1890–1940*. Chapel Hill: Univ. of North Carolina Press, 2009.

Woodward, C. Vann. *Origins of the New South, 1877–1913*. Baton Rouge: Louisiana State Univ. Press, 1951, 1971, 1997.

———. *The Strange Career of Jim Crow*, 3rd rev. ed. New York: Oxford Univ. Press, 1974.

Woolston, Howard Brown. *Prostitution in the United States* [vol. 1] *Prior to the Entrance of the United States into the World War*. 1921. Montclair, N.J.: Patterson Smith, 1969.

Wright, Gavin. *Old South, New South: Revolutions in the Southern Economy since the Civil War*. New York: Basic Books, 1986.

Wyatt-Brown, Bertram. *Southern Honor: Ethics and Behavior in the Old South*. New York: Oxford Univ. Press, 1982.

Yellin, Jean Fagin. *Women and Sisters: The Antislavery Feminists in American Culture*. New Haven, Conn.: Yale Univ. Press, 1989.

Zanger, Jules. "The 'Tragic Octoroon' in Pre-Civil War Fiction." *American Quarterly* 18, no. 1 (Spring 1966): 63–70.

Dissertations, Theses, and Unpublished Papers

Bennett, James B. "Religion and the Rise of Jim Crow in New Orleans." Ph.D. diss., Yale University, 1999.

Blair, Cynthia Marie. "Vicious Commerce: African American Women's Sex Work and the Transformation of Urban Space in Chicago, 1850–1915." Ph.D. diss., Harvard University, 1999.

Everett, Donald Edward. "Free Persons of Color in New Orleans, 1803–1865." Ph.D. diss., Tulane University, 1952.

Gould, Lois Virginia Meacham. "In Full Enjoyment of Their Liberty: The Free Women of Color of the Gulf Ports of New Orleans, Mobile, and Pensacola, 1769–1860." Ph.D. diss., Emory University, 1991.

Guillory, Monique. "Some Enchanted Evening on the Auction Block." Ph.D. diss., New York University, 1999.

Hickey, Georgina Susan. "Visibility, Politics, and Urban Development: Working-Class Women in Early Twentieth-Century Atlanta." Ph.D. diss., University of Michigan, 1995.

Johnson, Walter. "Masters and Slaves at the Market: Slavery and the New Orleans Trade, 1804–1864." Ph.D. diss., Princeton University, 1995.

Keeling, John Robert, III. "A Planter and the Courts in Antebellum Louisiana: The Cases of John F. Miller." Ph.D. diss., University of Georgia, 2002.

Kellow, Margaret. "The Fair Circassion: The Concubine in Feminist Antislavery Discourse." Unpublished paper in the possession of the author.

———. "The Oriental Imaginary: Constructions of Female Bondage in Women's Antislavery Discourse." Unpublished paper in the possession of the author.

Lagler, Amy R. "'For God's Sake Do Something': White-Slavery Narratives and Moral Panic in Turn-of-the-Century American Cities." Ph.D. diss., Michigan State University, 2000.

Leathem, Karen. "A Carnival According to Their Own Desires." Ph.D. diss., University of North Carolina, Chapel Hill, 1995.

———. "Luring Young Girls to Their Ruin." Unpublished paper prepared for the Louisiana Historical Association Meeting, March 14, 1997, in the possession of the author.

Levy, Russell. "Of Bards and Bawds: New Orleans Sporting Life before and during the Storyville Era, 1897–1917." Master's thesis, Tulane University, 1967.

Logsdon, Joseph. "The Great Pandely Case: Race, Politics, and Family in Antebellum New Orleans." Unpublished paper in the possession of the author.

Long, Alecia P. "'The Great Southern Babylon': Sexuality, Race, and Reform in New Orleans, 1865–1920." Ph.D. diss., University of Delaware, 2001.

Mackey, Thomas. "Red Lights Out: A Legal History of Prostitution, Disorderly Houses, and Vice Districts, 1870–1971." Ph.D. diss., Rice University, 1984.

Powell, Lawrence N. "The Battle of Canal Street: An Upper-Class Dream of Power and Preferment." Unpublished paper in the possession of the author.

Ross, Michael A. "Creole Icarus." Paper delivered at the meeting of the Historical Society, Washington, D.C., Spring 2010.

———. "Letting the Past Dictate the Future: Commercial Crisis and Decline in New Orleans, 1865–1885." Paper presented at the Southern Historical Association Meeting, New Orleans, Louisiana, November 2001.

Thompson, Shirley Elizabeth. "The Passing of a People: Creoles of Color in Mid-Nineteenth Century New Orleans." Ph.D. diss., Harvard University, 2001.

Tucker, Sherrie. "A Feminist Perspective on New Orleans Jazz Women." New Orleans Jazz National Historic Park, National Park Service, New Orleans, Louisiana, 2004.

Williams, Robert Webb, Jr. "Martin Behrman: Mayor and Political Boss of New Orleans, 1904–1926." Master's thesis, Tulane University, 1952.

Wolcott, Victoria Widgeon. "Remaking Respectability: African American Women and the Politics of Identity in Inter-War Detroit." Ph.D. diss., University of Michigan, 1995.

INDEX

abject, 133, 134, 137, 147–48
abolitionism, 12, 50–56, 60, 142
Adams, Abigail, 206
Adams, St. Clair, 150
Adams, St. Clair, Jr., 196
advertisements. *See* guidebooks and
 advertisements
African Americans: and dance halls, 105,
 161–64; disenfranchisement and suppression of rights of, 49, 74–75, 79,
 91, 93, 97, 98, 129, 133, 176; divisions
 between Creoles of color and American
 blacks, 73–74; education of, 49, 204;
 interracial sex between black men and
 white women, 214n111; lynching and
 other violence against, 14, 74, 129–30,
 202, 214n11; manhood of, 128, 162,
 164; in middle class, 201; respectability
 and racial uplift for, 8, 201; sexuality
 of, 6, 8, 62, 128, 164; stereotypes of,
 14, 126–28; veterans group of, 161–62;
 voting rights for, 72, 73, 97; working
 conditions of, 125. *See also* Creoles of
 color; octoroons; race; segregation;
 slavery
alcohol. *See* liquor
Allen, Michael, 34
Allen, Robert, 9
Amacker, Frank, 25–26

American Citizens' Equal Rights Association, 47–49
American Revolution, 45, 69, 79
American Sector of New Orleans, 13–14,
 84, 92, 214n107
American Social Hygiene Association, 181,
 185
amusements. *See* entertainment; Storyville
Anderson, Thomas C. (Tom): liquor sales
 by, 151, 248n87; and Mardi Gras Ball,
 114–15; property named after, 112; saloons owned by, 18, 29, 111, 114–15, 151,
 186; as state legislator, 108, 111; wife of,
 190
Anderson, Warwick, 134
Anglo-Americans in antebellum New
 Orleans, 84, 85, 86, 95–96, 118
antebellum New Orleans: Anglo-Americans
 in, 84, 85, 86, 95–96, 118; Creoles of
 color in, 12, 36, 70–75, 84, 138; diseases
 in, 36, 87; international population of,
 83–86; manumission in, 69; prostitution
 in, 12, 35–37; travel accounts of, 81–89,
 119; unsanitary conditions of, 86–87;
 white Creoles in, 84–85. *See also* "fancy
 girl" auctions; Old South; quadroon
 balls; slave auctions; "tragic octoroon"
anti-Semitism. *See* Jews and anti-Semitism
anticoncubinage law, 169–71, 177